THE POLITICS OF ECONOMIC RESTRUCTURING

State-Society Relations and Regime Change in Mexico

U.S.-MEXICO CONTEMPORARY PERSPECTIVES SERIES, 7
CENTER FOR U.S.-MEXICAN STUDIES
UNIVERSITY OF CALIFORNIA, SAN DIEGO

Contributors

Jorge Alcocer V.
Marcelo Cavarozzi
Maria Lorena Cook
Wayne A. Cornelius
Enrique de la Garza Toledo
Denise Dresser
Jonathan Fox
Paul Lawrence Haber
Joseph L. Klesner
Julio Labastida Martín del Campo
Soledad Loaeza
Kevin J. Middlebrook
Juan Molinar Horcasitas
Jaime Ros
Víctor L. Urquidi
Francisco Valdés Ugalde
Laurence Whitehead

The Politics of Economic Restructuring

State-Society Relations and Regime Change in Mexico

MARIA LORENA COOK
KEVIN J. MIDDLEBROOK
JUAN MOLINAR HORCASITAS

Editors

Center for U.S.-Mexican Studies
University of California, San Diego

The Center for U.S.-Mexican Studies wishes to acknowledge the assistance of the William and Flora Hewlett Foundation in the publication of this book.

PRINTED IN THE UNITED STATES OF AMERICA BY
THE CENTER FOR U.S.-MEXICAN STUDIES,
UNIVERSITY OF CALIFORNIA, SAN DIEGO

1994

Cover design by Richard P. Burritt, Burritt Design.

ISBN 1-878367-18-8

Contents

Tables and Figures

Figures

Acknowledgments

The essays in this volume were originally prepared for an international research workshop held in Mexico City in June 1992. The workshop was cosponsored by the Center for U.S.-Mexican Studies at the University of California, San Diego and the Coordinación de Humanidades at the Universidad Nacional Autónoma de México. Most authors revised their essays in late 1992 and early 1993, taking into account both the comments that panel discussants and other participants made at the workshop in Mexico City and additional suggestions from the editors.

We are especially grateful to Wayne A. Cornelius (Director of the Center for U.S.-Mexican Studies) and Julio Labastida Martín del Campo (then Coordinador de Humanidades at the Universidad Nacional Autónoma de México) for their enthusiastic support for this project. Among their many important contributions, they generously agreed to write forewords to this book.

Debate at the June 1992 workshop was enriched by the participation of a number of people. We wish to thank Dr. José Sarukhán, Rector of the Universidad Nacional Autónoma de México, for his kind welcome. We are particularly grateful to Luis Aguilar, Carlos Bazdresch, Graciela Bensusán, Rolando Cordera, Luis Hernández, Rogelio Hernández, Matilde Luna, Jacqueline Peschard, José Luis Reyna, Peter H. Smith, and Sergio Zermeño for their insightful comments as panel discussants. We also wish to thank Juan Pablo Arroyo, Juan Felipe Leal, and Benito Rey for their contributions to our discussions in their role as panel moderators.

Organizing the workshop that gave rise to this book required the time and energy of many talented people. We particularly wish to recognize the assistance of Antonio Azuela, Selva Daville, and Silvia Laphan, all at the Coordinación de Humanidades. Their tireless efforts helped make our plans a reality.

Aníbal Yáñez Chávez ably translated those essays originally written in Spanish. Sandra del Castillo supervised the editing and production processes with her customary skill, efficiency, and patience.

A Spanish-language edition of this book will be published in Mexico City by Cal y Arena.

Maria Lorena Cook
Kevin J. Middlebrook
Juan Molinar Horcasitas
August 1994

Foreword

Wayne A. Cornelius

With the virtual completion of the great wave of economic adjustment and restructuring that swept through Mexico and many other Third World countries during the 1980s and early 1990s, scholars have begun to ask increasingly tough questions about the social and political concomitants of this phenomenon. Will the so-called neoliberal economic revolution provide a basis for consolidation of still fragile democratic regimes? Will it prove to be a powerful stimulus for political liberalization (if not genuine democratization) in countries where authoritarian regimes cling to power, or will the new development model only reinforce elements of authoritarian rule (such as tight government control over organized labor or a "closed," technocratic decision-making style)? How can ruling coalitions and their social bases be reshaped to support a market-driven, internationalist development strategy? Will the reformed economies have the capacity to generate enough jobs, in countries where the potential labor force is still growing by 3 percent or more each year? Can new compensatory policies be devised (consistent with the fiscal constraints of the new macroeconomic model) to cushion the social costs of economic restructuring and prevent mass explosions of discontent?[1]

The international research workshop from which this volume evolved was conceived as both a retrospective examination of the experience of Mexico with economic adjustment and restructuring programs, and as an attempt to define an agenda for future research that would illuminate the longer-term social consequences and political requirements of this fundamental economic transformation. The papers

---

[1] Volumes that seek to grapple with the same kinds of questions through broader, cross-national and cross-regional comparisons include Nelson et al. 1989; Nelson 1990; Williamson 1990, 1994; Grindle and Thomas 1991. See also Haggard and Webb 1993.

assembled here will undoubtedly raise more questions in the reader's mind than they answer with certitude. This lack of closure is appropriate, however, since in Mexico, as in most other countries that have undergone similar economic restructuring, it is still too early to assess either the sustainability or the potential benefits of this policy mix.

THREATS TO SUSTAINABILITY

This is an especially appropriate moment to examine the politics and broader public policy implications of economic restructuring in a country like Mexico. Further deepening of economic liberalization, even though the process may still be far from complete in some sectors, no longer seems socially tolerable nor politically prudent in the short-to-medium term. As Mexican economist Rogelio Ramírez de la O observed, the peasant insurrection in Chiapas "has buried the long-held notion that in Mexico you can operate without anesthesia" (quoted in Darling 1994).

Not just to win future elections convincingly, but to maintain social peace, the government must now move more aggressively to ease the pain that economic liberalization and internationalization have inflicted on millions of Mexicans, by stepping up spending on social programs and on productive projects that will create jobs more quickly in the most impoverished parts of the country, even if it necessitates a return to deficit spending.[2] Reflecting this need to shift priorities, the ruling PRI's 1994 presidential candidate, Ernesto Zedillo, one of the principal architects of neoliberal economic reforms during the Salinas *sexenio*, pledged that his government would give top priority to such goals as increasing rates of economic growth and job creation, boosting workforce productivity (which will require major new investments in public education and vocational training), improving health services, and increasing the flow of credit to small and medium-sized businesses (Zedillo 1994).

Since January 1, 1994, there have been clear danger signals indicating that the economic reforms of the 1985–1993 period remain vulnerable to mounting social problems that, if unchecked, could cause an unraveling of the broad coalition that has thus far supported radical economic restructuring in Mexico. As Víctor Urquidi points out in his contribution to this volume, the new development model has yet to demonstrate that it is capable of generating rates of economic growth that even begin to approximate the average of 6 percent per annum achieved during earlier periods of Mexican development. The high point of economic growth during the Salinas *sexenio* occurred in 1990, when GDP grew by 4.5

---

[2]After five consecutive years of nearly balanced budgets or budget surpluses, deficit spending during the last year of the Salinas *sexenio* was expected to equal 2 percent or more of GDP. Spending on social services was increased by 14.5 percent during the first quarter of 1994 alone.

percent; since then, the growth rate has plummeted, to 0.4 and 0.6 percent in 1993 and 1994, respectively—far below the rate of population growth (officially, 1.9 per cent per annum).[3]

High inflation has a disproportionately severe impact on low-income wage earners, especially in an economy where most people's incomes are not indexed. Thus it could be argued that during the Salinas *sexenio*, inflation reduction was the government's most successful policy for cushioning the impacts of economic restructuring on the average Mexican. Since 1988, inflation has declined steadily, reaching single-digit levels in 1993–1994 for the first time in more than two decades.[4]

In the absence of a rate of employment creation that keeps pace with labor force growth, however, the sharp drop in inflation has been inadequate to reduce poverty and inequality during a period of massive economic restructuring and opening of the Mexican economy to foreign competition. Only about 1.5 million new jobs were created, and some 500,000 jobs were lost due to business closures and downsizing from 1988 to 1993—a period when 800,000–900,000 new job seekers were entering the labor force each year. Since the economic crisis of the 1980s hit with full force, the majority of new job seekers, as well as workers laid off by formal-sector employers, have been absorbed into the informal economy (mostly in street vending and services), which according to some estimates now accounts for about one-quarter to one-third of the jobs held by economically active Mexicans.[5]

Net job creation continues to be anemic, despite a heavy influx of foreign capital, partly because well over half of the foreign funds are being invested in stocks and other financial instruments, rather than in job-creating direct investment projects. And the industrial reconversion process must continue if Mexican businesses are to withstand the greatly intensified competition from foreign imports that NAFTA and unilateral trade liberalization measures have brought, raising the prospect of additional significant job losses in the remainder of the 1990s.

---

[3]In per capita terms, GDP actually declined by 0.9 percent in 1993. The 1994 projection of 0.6 percent aggregate growth was made by the Centro de Estudios Económicos del Sector Privado (CEESP), a leading private-sector think tank (*Latin American Weekly Report*, June 2, 1994). Other private forecasts for growth in 1994 were more optimistic, but none exceeded 2.7 percent.

[4]The government's inflation target for 1994 was 5 percent, although many private analysts forecast a rate of 7–8 percent.

[5]Recent estimates range from 23.5 percent (Consejo Nacional de Población/INEGI) to 45 percent of the country's labor force (Universidad Autónoma Metropolitana), depending on different definitions and methodological assumptions. In a study of seven Mexican cities surveyed in 1989, the informally employed (small-scale entrepreneurs, self-employed workers, workers in microenterprises, and unpaid workers) represented about 32 percent of the labor force (Roberts 1993: note 4). As economist Nora Lustig has pointed out, in a country offering no unemployment insurance benefits, wage earners forced out of formal-sector employment by economic restructuring have had little alternative but to accept much lower paying work in the informal sector. "To be unemployed is a luxury that most Mexicans cannot afford" (Lustig 1991: 14).

Not surprisingly, there has been no progress in reducing the degree of income inequality in Mexico during the era of economic restructuring. On the contrary, large new concentrations of wealth emerged, partly as a result of the sale of the country's banks and other large public enterprises to consortia of private investors. A 1994 study by the Instituto de Investigaciones Económicas of the Universidad Nacional Autónoma de México found that the sweeping privatization policy pursued by the de la Madrid and Salinas governments had resulted in 50 percent of the country's assets being held by just five conglomerates (*El Financiero International*, May 2–8, 1994). The internationalization of the economy has created other types of inequalities. For example, workers employed in foreign-linked companies have seen their real wages rise in recent years as much as 30 percent, while the wages of workers in domestically oriented firms (such as textile and apparel plants) have dropped as much as 15 percent.

At the family level, national surveys conducted by INEGI, the government's statistical research agency, revealed that the degree of income inequality increased by 10 percent between 1984 and 1989, before leveling off during the 1989–1992 period.[6] In the 1994 presidential campaign, the growing concentration of wealth in a "reformed" economy became an object of criticism not only by the Cardenista left but by the conservative National Action Party (PAN). In an effort to curb abuses by large private enterprises that have benefited from its free market economic policies, the government in 1994 began to levy substantial fines on such companies for monopolistic practices of various sorts.[7]

There has been sharp dispute over the magnitude and direction of changes in mass poverty levels during Mexico's most intense period of economic liberalization (1989–1993). A controversial national survey conducted jointly by the United Nations Economic Commission on Latin America (CEPAL) and the Mexican government's statistical agency (INEGI) found that the number of Mexicans living in "extreme poverty" (as measured by their capacity to purchase a minimum "market basket" of basic foodstuffs) fell from 14.9 million people (18.8 percent of the national population) in 1989 to 13.6 million (16.1 percent of the population) in 1992. Altogether, the CEPAL-INEGI survey found 37.2 million Mexicans (43.8 percent of the population) living at or below the official poverty line (ONU-CEPAL and INEGI 1993). The apparent reduction in extreme poverty, which was viewed with skepticism by independent Mexican researchers, was touted by Salinas's former chief-of-staff as evidence that "the social safety net provided by the government offered

---

[6] As measured by the Gini coefficient. See Cortés and Rubalcava 1992: 11; Córdoba 1994: 272.

[7] The Federal Economic Competition Act, passed in 1992, allows the government to impose fines of up to U.S.$1.6 million per company, and/or 10 percent of the company's annual sales or assets. Penalties imposed in 1994 averaged $300,000 per firm.

some shelter to poor households" from the ravages of economic crisis and restructuring, and that "a gradual improvement has already taken place with the economic recovery and the advent of the Solidarity program in the early 1990s" (Córdoba 1994: 271).

However, the absolute number of Mexicans living in extreme poverty, according to the CEPAL-INEGI survey results, was still higher in 1992 than in 1984, when the figure was 11.0 million (15.4 percent of the population at that time). Moreover, the 1989–1992 drop in extreme poverty at the national level masks a trend in the opposite direction in the country's rural areas, where more than two-thirds of "extremely poor" Mexicans reside. While the number of "extremely poor" urban dwellers fell from 6.5 million in 1989 to 4.8 million in 1992, according to the CEPAL-INEGI study, the number of "extremely poor" rural dwellers *increased* from 8.4 to 8.8 million.[8] A 1984 survey by INEGI had found 6.7 million rural dwellers living in extreme poverty. Noting this disturbing trend, Jonathan Fox cautions that "while national economic growth is likely to have significant spillover effects within urban areas, reaching at least some of those near the poverty line, there is no reason at all to assume that [aggregate] economic growth will reduce extreme poverty in rural areas . . . unless the Mexican government pursues an anti-poverty strategy that is much more targeted to employment creation and basic service provision in rural areas" (personal correspondence, December 1993).

SOCIAL POLICY IN THE ERA OF ECONOMIC RESTRUCTURING

After falling sharply in the austerity budgets of the de la Madrid government (from 7.6 percent of GDP in 1981–1982 to 5.6 percent in 1987–1988) (see Cordera Campos and González Tiburcio 1991), aggregate spending on social programs rebounded under Salinas. From 1988 to 1993, social spending increased by more than 85 percent in real terms. By 1994, such expenditures represented 10 percent of GDP (higher than at any point in Mexican history) and 54 percent of the programmable federal government budget, as compared with 32 percent in 1988.[9] After the Chiapas rebellion erupted on January 1, 1994, a further boost in social spending was authorized, including a U.S.$900 million package of social service and infrastructure investments for the state of Chiapas alone.

As has been characteristic of Mexican social policy during most of the postrevolutionary period, social spending in the era of intensified

---

[8]The cutting point between urban and rural areas used in this study was 15,000 inhabitants.

[9]Even so, Mexico's level of public investment in social welfare does not compare favorably with that of other middle-developed countries in Latin America. In Brazil, for example, the share of GDP allocated to social expenditures has fluctuated around 15 percent in recent years.

economic restructuring has been selectively targeted.[10] Across-the-board subsidies to consumers and guaranteed support prices for all agricultural producers gave way to more focused programs like National Solidarity (PRONASOL), the Salinas administration's principal anti-poverty initiative, and PROCAMPO, a transitional, direct-subsidy program for very small scale agricultural producers, including those who do not produce enough to commercialize (and thus had never benefited from government *precios de garantía*).

During its first five years of operation, the government invested about U.S.$12 billion in PRONASOL, which quickly became the Salinas administration's most important signature program and one of the factors most responsible for the ruling party's impressive recovery at the polls in the 1991 midterm elections (Córdoba 1994: 269). While government reports showed Solidarity projects being undertaken in more than 95 percent of the country's 2,378 municipalities by 1993, field studies found little uniformity in the program's impacts (see Cornelius, Craig, and Fox 1994: 20 and passim). Moreover, opposition party leaders frequently complained that PRONASOL funding levels (per state, locality, and so on) were being determined by partisan political criteria— that is, in such a way that the program's resources were targeted to areas of demonstrated opposition strength.

Whatever their underlying political rationales or consequences, it is clear that PRONASOL and PROCAMPO were government programs explicitly intended to ease the transition from heavy-handed state interventionism to an economy driven primarily by market forces. They represented a recognition by the technocrats in power that some compensatory measures would be needed to maintain social peace and permit the consolidation of neoliberal economic reforms as well as potentially disruptive changes such as the privatization of ejido land, made possible by amendments to Article 27 of the Constitution.

But did such programs effectively address the root causes of poverty and inequality, or were they mere palliatives, capable perhaps of improving living conditions but not of helping the poor to generate wealth? A summary index of well-being constructed from such indicators as quality of housing construction materials, the number of persons per room, access to basic services such as water, electricity, and sewerage, and children's school enrollment shows significant progress on these social indicators during the 1989–1992 period (Córdoba 1994: 270–71), an outcome explicable only by the National Solidarity Program's success in delivering government resources to low-income urban neighborhoods and rural communities.

Such improvements in household standards of living should not be dismissed too quickly by critics seeking more fundamental reductions

---

[10]For evidence of the historical pattern, see Nord 1994; Ward 1986.

in poverty. But neither are they likely to be accepted, even by the immediate beneficiaries, as long-term substitutes for the kinds of public programs and investments that would have a greater, more direct impact on poverty and income inequality. Foremost among those types of interventions would be sectoral and region-focused programs designed to create new, permanent employment opportunities, to upgrade public education (especially preschool, elementary, and secondary education),[11] to make job training more accessible to both the urban and rural poor, and to establish new financing and technology-transfer mechanisms for small and medium-sized businesses.[12] In sum, Mexico's macroeconomically oriented policy makers cannot afford to overlook the opportunities for socially beneficial microeconomic intervention by the state in a liberalized economy.

The gradual shift of emphasis within the National Solidarity Program, beginning in 1993, to supporting more production projects that directly raise incomes and multiply employment opportunities is one indication that the government recognizes the limitations of the program's earlier focus on urban services and infrastructure improvements (see Cornelius, Craig, and Fox 1994: 24–25). Similarly, PRI presidential candidate Zedillo's proposals to create job banks and to promote completion of primary schooling in rural areas through the award of 1.5 million scholarships through the year 2000—as key elements of a new poverty-alleviation strategy—suggest awareness of the need for a social policy that more directly attacks the structural bases of poverty in Mexico.

POLITICAL CONSTRAINTS ON GOVERNMENT RESPONSIVENESS

Laurence Whitehead and other contributors to this volume illustrate the ways in which the PRI's alliances with its traditional constituencies (to say nothing of still unorganized groups like workers in the informal economy) have been weakened by economic restructuring and internationalization. The state-shrinking pursued so vigorously by Presidents de la Madrid and Salinas, together with the creation of new federal government programs like Solidarity that intentionally bypassed the

---

[11] While 78 percent of school-age children were enrolled in primary school in 1990, only 54 percent of those who start elementary school in Mexico finish it, according to Ministry of Education statistics analyzed by the Mexican Center for Child Resources (CEMDIN). Moreover, a large proportion of elementary school graduates lack easy access to a secondary school—a major disincentive to continuing their education—and only 2.9 percent of Mexican children aged four and five had access to preschool education in 1994.

[12] While averaging only seven employees per firm, small businesses in Mexico provide 60 percent of all employment opportunities (research by Clemente Ruiz Durán, Facultad de Economía, Universidad Nacional Autónoma de México). While many larger enterprises continue to shed labor in order to become more competitive exporters, small businesses continue to absorb most of the new entrants to the labor force. Nevertheless, Mexico's rapid trade liberalization since 1989 has severely reduced the sales and profitability of small businesses, especially in traditional manufacturing industries like textiles, apparel, and shoes.

entrenched PRIísta machines in the states and *municipios*, have deprived the old corporatist structures of much of the patronage and other resources that for decades were channeled through them. It could be argued that, at this juncture in history, the PRI's nearly sixty-year-old labor and campesino organizations are too ossified and discredited, its leadership too divided on issues ranging from labor law reform to democratization, and the party too dependent on local caciques and other agents of exploitation and repression to be of much help to the government in containing the social tensions that threaten to overwhelm the newly established macroeconomic model.

The social explosion that shook Chiapas and the nation as a whole in 1994 provided ample proof that even generously funded federal social programs like Solidarity—which had invested U.S.$192 million in Chiapas in 1993 alone—can be sabotaged by state and local elements of the PRI-government apparatus, in ways that not only fail to buy time for the consolidation of neoliberal economic reforms but create new popular grievances against the state. In the case of Chiapas, there was a pattern of gross misuse of Solidarity program funds by state and local officials, to serve their own political ends (see, for example, Harvey et al. 1994). Between 1990 and 1992, the state governor dismissed regional Solidarity program representatives who had attempted to support projects proposed by campesino organizations that were independent of his control, and he had several of them jailed. He also manipulated a Solidarity program designed to support subsistence farmers in ways that strengthened the power of municipal presidents and local caciques who were political allies of the governor. He and other "elected" officials in Chiapas, where vote fraud by the PRI was more blatant and more deeply institutionalized than in any other state, never had to show any responsiveness to general constituent needs or preferences in order to remain in power.[13]

Thus the case of Chiapas illustrates dramatically the importance of functioning, truly representative political institutions—in a word, democracy—to an effective social policy in Mexico. Distributive and redistributive programs, however carefully designed and well funded, can work only where state and local political and economic interests do not prevent them from reaching their target populations. In sum, a broader political opening, including a willingness by federal authorities to break long-standing symbiotic alliances with subnational power brokers, is likely to be necessary. Otherwise, the state will be hobbled in

---

[13] Among all Mexican states, Chiapas could be counted upon to deliver the highest percentage of its votes to the PRI, despite abysmal social and economic conditions that would suggest the potential for a very large opposition party vote. In Ocosingo, the largest of the four *municipios* where the 1994 rebellion was centered, official statistics show that 105 percent of the total population eligible to vote in the most recent elections had actually done so. Apparently even the dead voted.

its attempts to implement the kinds of "softening" measures that could make Mexico's market-driven economic policies socially tolerable and politically sustainable in the long term.

REFERENCES

Cordera Campos, Rolando, and Enrique González Tiburcio. 1991. "Crisis and Transition in the Mexican Economy." In *Social Responses to Mexico's Economic Crisis of the 1980s*, edited by Mercedes González de la Rocha and Agustín Escobar Latapí. U.S.-Mexico Contemporary Perspectives Series, no. 1. La Jolla: Center for U.S.-Mexican Studies, University of California, San Diego.

Córdoba, José. 1994. "Mexico." In *The Political Economy of Policy Reform*, edited by John Williamson. Washington, D.C.: Institute for International Economics.

Cornelius, Wayne A., Ann L. Craig, and Jonathan Fox, eds. 1994. *Transforming State-Society Relations in Mexico: The National Solidarity Strategy*. U.S.-Mexico Contemporary Perspectives Series, no. 6. La Jolla: Center for U.S.-Mexican Studies, University of California, San Diego.

Cortés, Fernando, and Rosa María Rubalcava. 1992. "Cambio estructural y concentración: un análisis de la distribución del ingreso familiar en México, 1984–1989." Paper presented at the conference "Socio-Demographic Effects of the 1980s Economic Crisis in Mexico," University of Texas at Austin, April 23–25.

Darling, Juanita. 1994. "Chiapas Revolt Puts Mexico's Economic Future on Hold," *Los Angeles Times*, January 25.

Grindle, Merilee S., and John W. Thomas. 1991. *Public Choices and Policy Change: The Political Economy of Reform in Developing Countries*. Baltimore, Md.: Johns Hopkins University Press.

Haggard, Stephan, and Steven Webb. 1993. "What Do We Know about the Political Economy of Economic Policy Reform?" *The World Bank Research Observer* 8:1 (July): 143–68.

Harvey, Neil, et al. 1994. *Rebellion in Chiapas*. Transformation of Rural Mexico Series, no. 5. La Jolla: Center for U.S.-Mexican Studies, University of California, San Diego.

Lustig, Nora. 1991. "Mexico: The Social Impact of Adjustment, 1983–89." Washington, D.C.: The Brookings Institution, October. Manuscript.

Nelson, Joan M., ed. 1990. *Economic Crisis and Policy Choice: The Politics of Adjustment in the Third World*. Princeton, N.J.: Princeton University Press.

Nelson, Joan M., et al. 1989. *Fragile Coalitions: The Politics of Economic Adjustment*. New Brunswick, N.J.: Transaction Books/Overseas Development Council.

Nord, Bruce. 1994. *Mexican Social Policy: Affordability, Conflict, and Progress*. Lanham, Md.: University Press of America.

ONU-CEPAL and INEGI. 1993. "Informe sobre la magnitud y evolución de la pobreza en México, 1884–1992." Unpublished summary report presented in Mexico City, October 24.

Roberts, Bryan R. 1993. "The Dynamics of Informal Employment in Mexico." In *Work without Protections: Case Studies of the Informal Sector in Developing Countries*. Washington, D.C.: Bureau of International Affairs, U.S. Dept. of Labor.

Ward, Peter. 1986. *Welfare Politics in Mexico: Papering over the Cracks*. Boston: Allen & Unwin.

Williamson, John, ed. 1990. *Latin American Adjustment: How Much Has Happened?* Washington, D.C.: Institute for International Economics.

―――. 1994. *The Political Economy of Policy Reform.* Washington, D.C.: Institute for International Economics.

Zedillo, Ernesto. 1994. "La propuesta económica de Ernesto Zedillo." Address to the conference "Crecimiento Económico para el Bienestar Familiar," Mexico City, June 6.

Foreword

Julio Labastida Martín del Campo

Since the mid-1980s the economic restructuring program applied in Mexico has replaced the old postwar development model with another based on the systematic liberalization of the market and the growing privatization and internationalization of the Mexican economy. In this process the role of the state has been steadily redefined, both as a regulator of the economic sphere and in its relationship with important social actors. Although the fact that these processes have been under way is widely accepted in political and academic circles in Mexico, there remain more questions than answers, more conjectures than certainties, and more arenas for further discussion than clearly defined analytical spaces. This is especially the case when discussing how the *political* dimensions of this restructuring process relate to the conditions and impact of economic adjustment.

An essential premise of any analysis should be to abandon deterministic formulations in order to think through the relationship between economic and political processes. To speak of the relationship between economic adjustment and political change poses the complex task of linking two macro-processes that do not permit either linear interpretations or globalizing approaches. Accordingly, it is no longer possible to think about recent changes from a perspective that assumes "necessary relationships" between structural adjustment and the political regime, or between economic restructuring and levels of equity, as is evident from the comparative study of dissimilar Latin American experiences over the last decade.

With these concerns in mind, a group of distinguished specialists from Mexico and the United States came together in a research workshop titled "The Political Dimensions of Economic Restructuring in

Translated by Aníbal Yáñez.

Mexico." The event took place June 15–16 in Mexico City, and was organized by the Coordinación de Humanidades of the Universidad Nacional Autónoma de México and the Center for U.S.-Mexican Studies of the University of California, San Diego.

At the risk of offering a simplified vision of that rich and at times arduous discussion, the debate at the workshop revolved around the response of political and social actors to the economic crisis of the 1980s. Two papers were devoted to an examination of the changes in the Mexican economy (crisis, adjustment, and restructuring) that have taken place over the last decade. A second group of papers analyzed the difficult link between economic change and the behavior of political actors: the state, the "official" party, and opposition parties. Finally, several papers focused on the responses provided by some fundamental social actors: the business sector, trade unions, peasants, and urban popular movements.

These essays range across topics as important and diverse as the problem of modernization; the so-called transition to democracy; the old corporatist structure and emerging neocorporatist practices; the transition from a stable political party system based on the predominance of a single party to an incipient, but still precarious, competitive party system; and the shift from a society penetrated by an omnipresent state to the more recent vision of a civil society that is more active, informed, and demanding. Together, the chapters in this volume reflect the most recent academic thinking on Mexico's economic, social, and political prospects at the end of the twentieth century.

CRISIS, ADJUSTMENT, AND ECONOMIC RESTRUCTURING

Two workshop papers established the general framework that guided the discussion with regard to the issue of economic change throughout the 1980s. In the first, Jaime Ros ("Mexico in the 1990s: A New Economic Miracle? Some Notes on the Economic and Policy Legacy of the 1980s") emphasizes that it is necessary to distinguish between the features of the adjustment model as such and the national conditions, particularly the economic conditions, where it was applied. From this perspective, the author develops three main arguments or hypotheses. First, Ros notes that the comparative success of the Mexican adjustment experience should be attributed to the special features of the Mexican economy rather than to the worthiness of an abstract model. Ros's analysis suggests that, in fact, these features are not to be found in Mexico's economic policy, political structure, or geopolitical advantages, but rather they are firmly rooted in the country's macroeconomic structure. Thus the success of Mexican structural adjustment was due not so much to the validity of orthodox neoliberal prescriptions, but rather to the specific characteristics that the model took on in the context of the Mexican economy.

Second, Ros's paper invites us to view structural reforms as a set of nontraditional instruments used to overcome the increasing costs of the decade-long process of macroeconomic adjustment. These costs explain why the reforms were accelerated in the second half of the 1980s. The special nature of macroeconomic policy trade-offs, and not the intrinsic merits of market reforms, explains the sustainability of the package of measures implemented up to now. Finally, the author warns us that the Mexican economy is entering the 1990s severely weakened by the process of adjustment over the last decade. It would be appropriate to surmise, therefore, that it is unlikely that we will witness a new Mexican economic miracle, despite some heartening signals in the early 1990s. Ros also reminds us that there is perhaps less to be copied from the neoliberal model than what was generally believed.

The paper by Víctor Urquidi ("The Outlook for Mexican Economic Development in the 1990s") offers a concise overview of the evolution of the Mexican economic crisis from the end of the 1960s through the mid-1980s and its subsequent "resolution" under the terms of the macroeconomic adjustment model begun in 1982–1983. Urquidi also provides a detailed analysis of the current economic model, pointing out its achievements but also highlighting its mistakes and potential dangers. In particular, he decries the lack of a development policy in contemporary Mexico. For Urquidi, a development policy is one that "would strategically encompass employment, strengthening the domestic market, reducing income inequality, improving social indicators, and, especially, setting priorities over the next five to ten years. . . . The least that could be desired is that major sector goals be mutually consistent, especially in light of the uncertainties generated in the domestic market by the excessive trade opening and NAFTA." According to Urquidi, this situation could result in a less favorable scenario for the Mexican economy, which economic projections seem to ignore all too frequently.

POLITICAL ACTORS AND ECONOMIC REFORM

A second line of inquiry at the workshop examined the complex linkages between economic change and the behavior of political actors. In this vein, Marcelo Cavarozzi, in his paper "Mexico's Political Formula, Past and Present," notes that many political analyses of the 1980s have not yet overcome a fascination with the politics that produced the democratic transition.[1] Analysts tend to conceive of the 1982–1992 period as one in which the transition from an economic model based on state interven-

---

[1] Here the author refers to, and quotes from, a preliminary version of Cavarozzi's paper presented at the June 1992 workshop. —*Editors' note.*

tionism to another centered more fully on the market was juxtaposed with another transition—the replacement of military authoritarianism by democratic political regimes. According to this view, regime change was inextricably linked to the change in the economic model.

In Cavarozzi's opinion, the problem with this perspective is that it overlooks political changes that are of the same magnitude as the economic transformations. In other words, this approach has not recognized that the processes of "destructuring" and restructuring currently under way include political and economic dimensions of similar significance articulated around what Cavarozzi calls the "state-centered matrix." In this sense, the most significant challenge faced by a number of Latin American countries in the 1980s was not exclusively "that of the democratization of their political regimes . . . but that of the success or failure of reorganization around an alternative political-economic matrix.

The incidence of cases in which democratic political institutions coincided with economic restructuring is relatively limited. Accordingly, "during the crucial conjuncture that extended from 1982 to 1990, the surviving authoritarian regimes (Chile and Mexico) had a more satisfactory performance in terms of their ability to discipline the various social sectors and to administer 'bitter pills,' while the democracies (Argentina, Brazil, Peru) did not have this ability." Nevertheless, Cavarozzi understands that it is worthwhile to explore an alternative explanation for what may otherwise appear as a simplistic equation (authoritarian governments = economic success; democratic governments = failure). We must keep in mind that in those cases where a transition from authoritarian to democratic regimes preceded the process of economic restructuring, the dynamics generated by the political transition imposed an extremely heavy burden on a situation that was already nearly ungovernable. Cavarozzi suggests that in comparing Latin American cases of "successful" adjustments with the less successful ones, we should pay less attention to the question of regime type and more to the process of institutional continuity.

Soledad Loaeza, in her essay "Political Liberalization and Uncertainty in Mexico," reminds us that despite some predictions in the 1980s that anticipated the collapse of the Mexican political system, "by the early 1990s, the most serious problems threatening the survival of postrevolutionary authoritarianism in Mexico appeared to have been favorably resolved." She nonetheless warns, "Mexico's experiences during the past ten years include many contrasting developments (even contradictions) that qualify the impression that the regime has returned to the status quo ante." The author argues that the combination of economic crisis and anti-authoritarian mobilizations, in the context of the democratizing climate that Latin America experienced in the 1980s, led many analysts to believe that Mexico, too, was experiencing a process of democratization. However, and with the benefit of hindsight, it would be more accurate to refer to this as a process of liberalization.

Liberalization—understood as the dissolution of mechanisms of control over participation and a resulting pluralism—is seen here as an alternative to democratization. Following O'Donnell and Schmitter's now classic analysis (see O'Donnell, Schmitter, and Whitehead 1986), Loaeza explains that "liberalization can be an option for authoritarian elites who want to remain in power and who respond to the demands for political liberalization by broadening spaces for the free action of individuals and groups. Hence, liberalization enlarges the social bases of the regime. For those in power, this type of limited change is attractive for at least two reasons. First, the elite does not abdicate its power to direct change and it retains the possibility of reversing the process—which is a powerful negotiating card vis-à-vis mobilized groups or individuals. Second, to the extent that liberalization is seen as a transitional formula, it offers a wide margin for pragmatic and ad hoc solutions."

The paper by Jorge Alcocer, "Party System and Political Transition in Mexico: A Pragmatic Approach," provides a concise description of the evolution of the party system in Mexico during the so-called democratic transition. Alcocer recognizes that, strictly speaking, the country has lacked a party system. For decades, he tells us, "Mexico's politico-electoral life consisted of the dominant party (PRI), a tolerated token opposition (PAN), and the occasional appearance of groups that adopted party form in order to compete in a specific election and then disappeared almost without a trace." However, this situation began to change in the 1970s and turned around significantly in the 1980s. Alcocer reminds us that the nationalization of the banks in 1982, the denouement of the economic crisis, the economic demise of the middle class, and the worsening of conditions for the popular classes, combined with traumatic experiences such as the 1985 earthquakes, all contributed to the increase in electoral protests that Mexico experienced in the 1980s.

The 1988 elections, in particular, substantially modified "Mexico's party system and opened up a (still incomplete) process that has been called the 'Mexican transition to democracy.'" In addition to reviewing the most significant changes that have taken place within the opposition parties that contested that election, Alcocer also outlines several possible scenarios for the period leading up to the 1994 presidential election. The first scenario is a three-way competition between the Institutional Revolutionary Party (PRI), the Party of the Democratic Revolution (PRD), and the National Action Party (PAN) in which each of the competitors would try to present a clearly differentiated alternative to the voters. In principle, this scenario would favor the formation of a pluralist party system, but it would also be beneficial for the PRI because the ruling party would benefit from a divided opposition vote.

The other scenario, in contrast, is the most problematic for the PRI, but also the least plausible: that of "a PAN-PRD alliance, which would lead toward total confrontation, a battle at close quarters in which the PRI would stand alone." There is also a third scenario which Alcocer does not consider: a two-party arrangement in which only the PAN and the PRI would have a strong presence at the national level, independently of whether or not the PRD or some other political grouping was strong in some regions. In any case, according to Alcocer there is one essential condition if evolution in the party system is to take place under conditions of social peace and relative economic stability: clean elections and their resulting credibility, which the author identifies as the keystone of Mexico's political future. One might ask, therefore, to what extent the elections that took place during 1993 aided or undermined the credibility of the electoral process for the crucial contest in 1994.

In "Realignment or Dealignment? Consequences of Economic Crisis and Restructuring for the Mexican Party System," Joseph L. Klesner examines the complex links between the long process of modernization and the electoral base of the governing party. The deep economic transformations carried forward by the governments of Miguel de la Madrid (1982–1988) and Carlos Salinas de Gortari (1988–1994) have especially weakened the PRI's traditional electoral base (organized labor, *ejidatarios*, workers in public enterprises, technocrats and the nationalist political class). In this sense, following Ruth Berins Collier and David Collier (1991: 27–29), Klesner asks whether Mexico has reached a "critical juncture"—that is, a period during which fundamental political alliances are rearranged to form new political coalitions.

The questions Klesner raises are whether there will be a dealignment of the PRI's electoral bases and whether it will be possible to realign part of those old bases of support in new political coalitions capable of generating an alternative electoral majority. After examining the electoral results of recent years (1988–1991), Klesner argues that we can already speak of a process of electoral dealignment to the degree that "the electorate has become more and more free to vote as it wishes." This process has its origins in the changes in social structure associated with modernization: "as Mexico continues to urbanize and as its population becomes more educated, the PRI may see a substantial number of children of its past supporters voting for the opposition." Whether a new majority opposition realignment will take shape remains a question for future research.

Denise Dresser, in her essay "Embellishment, Empowerment, or Euthanasia of the PRI? Neoliberalism and Party Reform in Mexico," analyzes the long-term impact of economic liberalization and adjustment policy on the governing party. She argues that the severity of the economic crisis has generated serious tensions between the state leadership and the party apparatus. According to Dresser, the crisis did away with the previous high levels of communication and continuity between the government and the party. Thus, while state elites concentrated on designing policies to meet the economic crisis, the party acted as a "blotter," absorbing the costs of unpopular decisions while in the midst of a leadership crisis and while assigned the task of winning elections in a context of economic adjustment.

This crisis of the party raises important questions about the future of the PRI. The technocrats who have gained key positions of power have no experience with corporatist politics, but they are in favor of ending corruption and clientelism—thereby eliminating the very features that long sustained the PRI's hegemony. They are also in favor of transforming the old PRI into a modern party based on individual affiliation and membership. Even if this were possible, Dresser believes that the problem of generating consensus for state actions would remain because dismantling the PRI would imply the "destructuring" of those crucial elements of the country's institutional life that are based upon a corporatist form of organization.

In the context of an ambitious economic transformation, Mexican political elites have opted for an unusual strategy of political survival: the transformation of the "official" party while it is in power, the refoundation of the PRI within the very structures of the PRI. Thus the old PRI is being simultaneously "embellished," "empowered," and subjected to partial "euthanasia." This strategy consists of maintaining the party's sectoral organization and the old styles of political rule while the party is being redefined as a competitive electoral entity.

ECONOMIC CHANGE AND SOCIAL ACTORS

It is also important to consider the behavior of those actors which have had a direct impact on the processes of economic adjustment and political change. As Francisco Valdés Ugalde notes in his paper, "From Bank Nationalization to State Reform: Business and the New Mexican Order," the behavior of social actors in situations of crisis follows a pattern in which they "sharpen their senses and the instruments through which they both guide their own actions and influence those of other actors and institutions. The result is an intense struggle to (re)arrange society's material resources and patterns of authority." Valdés analyzes the behavior of the private sector in the context of the transformation of Mexico's economic and political order, in which "state hegemony once rested on the public enterprise system, economic protectionism, and corporatist arrangements that included broad segments of the working population, [while] today regime legitimation depends on a state that privileges regulatory mechanisms, opens Mexico to international competition, and selectively distributes 'solidarity' resources." Valdés notes that, through its actions in the sociopolitical arena, the private sector has come to occupy a privileged position among social actors. The private sector has become "the social actor with the greatest capacity to mobilize available economic resources and command authority." We therefore should ask, together with Valdés, what role other social actors will play in the context of these changes.

Mexico's "corporatist" political system, whose traditional features have been showing signs of exhaustion, is moving toward a new configuration whose final outlines are as yet difficult to foresee. In this context, we are faced with the question of whether and how it is possible for an old type of trade union structure to coexist with a newer style of social concertation. There is no doubt that corporatism no longer occupies the central place that it did during preceding decades. As a result, the corporatist phenomenon is undergoing a transformation of the well-known "articulations" that the welfare state demanded of it.

The essay by Enrique de la Garza Toledo, "The Restructuring of State-Labor Relations in Mexico," seeks to explain the behavior of trade unions when confronted by the change from a development model that he calls "social authoritarian" toward a "neoliberal authoritarian" model. De la Garza sees a transformation taking place, but without the disappearance of essential features of the old corporatist structure. In his view, traditional corporatism is experiencing contradictions that in turn can open up new spaces for action. For example, the economic decentralization imposed by the need to increase productivity under the new production model clashes with the authoritarian features of state-labor relations. Similarly, the multipolarity of trade union restructuring enters into contradiction with union federations that are organized along different lines. And the centralization of power within the labor movement bureaucracy is counterposed to the need for greater worker initiative and involvement in production.

The demands of economic restructuring in Mexico have led to significant changes in the links between the state, political parties, and important actors in civil society. In "The Art and Implications of Political Restructuring in Mexico: The Case of Urban Popular Movements," Paul Lawrence Haber argues that the old system of alliances upon which authoritarian stability was based has been seriously affected by the crisis of economic and political hegemony that occurred during the 1982–1988 period. In contrast to the de la Madrid administration, the Salinas government recognized the need to rebuild relations with potentially destabilizing social actors. Drawing upon his study of urban popular movements, Haber maintains that political elites saw themselves forced to establish a dialogue with emerging actors which could not easily be contained within traditional institutional channels and which demanded a place in the political system. The Salinas administration's new strategy was aimed at incorporating these new movements (many of which had been excluded from previous government programs) via mechanisms such as "concertation" agreements and programs such as PRONASOL, the Salinas government's strategy for combating poverty and social marginality. In Haber's opinion, the Salinas government worked to establish new types of relationships outside traditional corporatist arrangements. These new relationships, in turn, have helped generate new support for the regime, or at least resources that can be used in order to minimize conflict.

Finally, Jonathan Fox's paper, "Political Change in Mexico's New Peasant Economy," analyzes the changes that the economic crisis of the 1980s wrought in the rural sector and in the behavior of peasant actors. After showing that there has been a mass exodus of peasants that has eroded the traditional structure of rural life, Fox asks how these changes affect the political behavior of peasants, who constitute a key traditional base of PRI support.

According to Fox, changes in rural-sector policies may produce two different scenarios. In one, the exodus toward the cities may increase (the "exit" strategy, in Hirschman's terms); in the other, independent organizations' ability to articulate demands may grow so that their voices are heard, increasing their capacity for self-management (the "voice" option). Both exodus and migration, as well as the strengthening of peasant organizations, represent challenges to the regime's traditional social and political support base. However, while exodus affects the regime's base of support in the medium term, this support may eventually be renewed by programs like PRONASOL. Moreover, if peasants migrate to the cities and become urban marginals, they can be controlled more easily through such social programs than can independent peasant organizations. Fox raises the issue of whether the stability of the regime may depend more on the success of the former than on the increased and organized participation of the independent peasant movement.

Perhaps the principal conclusion that can drawn from these essays is that Mexico's future is open to different possible paths of change. While these essays may not present clear patterns of causation or draw unambiguous conclusions, they uniformly combine solid empirical analysis and theoretical reflection in a critical and suggestive manner. Although it may seem, upon reading these chapters, that the path toward the political, social, and economic transformation of Mexico in the 1990s is a difficult one, it also becomes clear that this is a path along which we can discern new opportunities for building a more democratic and equitable society.

REFERENCES

Collier, Ruth Berins, and David Collier. 1991. *Shaping the Political Arena: Critical Junctures, the Labor Movement, and Regime Dynamics in Latin America*. Princeton: Princeton University Press.

O'Donnell, Guillermo A., Philippe C. Schmitter, and Laurence Whitehead, eds.
  1986. *Transitions from Authoritarian Rule in Latin America and Southern Europe.*
  Baltimore, Md.: Johns Hopkins University Press.

PART I

INTRODUCTION

1

The Politics of Economic Restructuring in Mexico: Actors, Sequencing, and Coalition Change

Maria Lorena Cook, Kevin J. Middlebrook,
and Juan Molinar Horcasitas

The parallel movements toward political democratization and economic liberalization that have swept many countries in Latin America, Central and Eastern Europe, and Africa since the early 1980s are a challenging subject of scholarly inquiry. Different analysts have examined the origins and timing of these developments, the combinations of international and domestic factors that produced such historically significant changes, and the interaction between political opening and market reforms (including trade and exchange rate liberalization, deregulation of commercial and investment opportunities, and privatization of state-owned enterprises) in different national contexts. It is certainly the coincidence of shifts toward political democratization and economic liberalization that makes these developments a particularly compelling subject for students of comparative political economy. Yet in many instances, one of these processes clearly antedated the other, often by a substantial period of time.

In recognition of this fact, some analysts underscore the potential importance that the sequencing of political and economic opening may have for the timing of regime change and the political profile of newly inaugurated democracies.[1] For example, if economic liberalization leads to more rapid growth, an authoritarian regime may bolster its perfor-

---

[1] See, for example, Haggard and Kaufman 1992: 332–41. This was also one of the central themes examined by the "Southern California Workshop on Political and Economic Liberalization," organized in 1992–1993 by the Center for International Studies, School of International Relations, University of Southern California.

mance-based legitimacy sufficiently to prolong its hold on power. Extensive market reform under authoritarian rule may strengthen the private sector's control over important economic activities and increase the political leverage of international and domestic business groups tied to the export sector. At the same time, reductions in public-sector employment and changes in industrial relations can undercut the mobilizational capacity and negotiating strength of labor unions. Other aspects of economic restructuring may have similarly negative consequences for the bargaining leverage of other mass organizations. Over the longer term, market reforms may gradually promote the development of a more densely textured civil society in which autonomously organized interest groups mobilize to demand increased opportunities for political representation and greater accountability on the part of state authorities. But in the short run, economic liberalization under authoritarian rule may lead to shifts in the relative power exercised by different social actors that substantially reduce popular groups' ability to redress accumulated socioeconomic needs or influence national policy debates.

Conversely, democratization before economic opening may significantly delay or limit the extent of market reforms. The transition from authoritarian rule can lead to increased mobilization by popular-sector organizations. It may also heighten their influence over policy making by permitting mass-based parties to gain control over key decision-making agencies or by strengthening their capacity to block policy initiatives that reduce the size of the public sector, eliminate consumption subsidies, and so forth. For these reasons, the prior consolidation of more democratic governance can limit the extent of privatization, market deregulation, and trade liberalization. Democratic governments may well lack the ability to implement unpopular but necessary economic reforms. Over time, their failure to resolve pressing economic problems may weaken their own ability to govern.[2]

Whether the sequencing of political opening and market reform has lasting consequences is a particularly compelling question in Mexico, where since the mid-1980s the scope and speed of economic transformation have considerably exceeded the extent and pace of political liberalization.[3] In economic matters, the administrations of Miguel de la Madrid Hurtado (1982–1988) and Carlos Salinas de Gortari (1988–1994) implemented stabilization and structural adjustment policies designed to control inflation by limiting wage increases and reducing government

---

[2]For a careful consideration of the relationship between economic crisis and electoral instability in Latin America in the 1980s, see Remmer 1991.

[3]Haggard and Kaufman (1992: 336–38) view Mexico as a case of simultaneous economic and political liberalization, although they note the difficulty of maintaining "the intended balance between political and economic reforms" (p. 337). For other views on the relationship between political liberalization and economic opening in Mexico, see Smith 1992; Roett 1993: 7, 11–12.

budgetary deficits. They also closed or privatized many state-owned enterprises, liberalized terms for foreign private investment, and sharply reduced tariff and nontariff barriers to imports. Export promotion replaced import substitution as the country's principal economic development strategy. Disciplined economic management and the rescheduling of Mexico's large foreign debt produced modest rates of growth after 1989, a considerable achievement given the severity of Mexico's post-1982 economic crisis. These macroeconomic gains came, however, at a very high social cost: per capita real disposable income fell throughout much of the 1980s, and although productivity increased, most workers' real wages were substantially lower in 1992 than a decade earlier.[4] Yet over time, political parties representing ideological positions across the political spectrum and a substantial proportion of the general public came to support economic reform. The inauguration in January 1994 of the North American Free Trade Agreement (NAFTA) among Canada, Mexico, and the United States marked the high point of this process.

Despite significant political changes, the liberalization of Mexico's authoritarian regime proceeded much more slowly than economic restructuring. Legislation enacted between 1977 and 1993 permitted opposition parties to play a more prominent role in national politics, and elections (particularly at the state and local levels) became much more competitive. The growing importance of human rights groups, community-based popular movements, and pro-democracy organizations also created a new dynamism in civil society. Even more notable, the unprecedented support mobilized by a leftist opposition coalition in the 1988 presidential election demonstrated that victory by the ruling Institutional Revolutionary Party (PRI) was no longer inevitable.[5] This important shift in political perceptions was reinforced when the center-right National Action Party (PAN) broke the ruling party's long-standing monopoly on state governorships by winning the 1989 gubernatorial election in Baja California. The PAN later won control over the state governments in Chihuahua and Guanajuato as well.

Yet overall, Mexico's governing political elite retained tight control over the pace and scope of political liberalization during the 1980s and early 1990s.[6] The institutionalized power of the presidency, the effectiveness of state controls over such mass actors as workers and peasants, and

---

[4]For data on real wage and consumption trends during the 1980s and early 1990s, see Lustig 1992: tables 3.2, 3.4; Ros, this volume: table 3.1.

[5]The coalition's candidate, Cuauhtémoc Cárdenas, officially won 31.1 percent of the valid votes cast in the presidential election. The PRI's share fell to a new low of 50.7 percent.

[6]President Salinas explicitly agreed that economic liberalization should precede democratization. He maintained that simultaneous political and economic opening (as in the former Soviet Union) risked undermining market reforms (*New Perspectives Quarterly* 8:1 [Winter 1991]: 8).

the continued organizational weakness of the political opposition were key factors in this regard. In addition, the combination of Salinas's forceful leadership, improved economic prospects (especially the effective control of inflation), and the popularity of the National Solidarity Program (PRONASOL)[7] permitted the PRI to win major victories in the 1991 midterm elections. The PRI's renewed electoral strength and the political momentum gained from final approval of the NAFTA permitted Salinas to impose his self-designated successor (Luis Donaldo Colosio Murrieta, minister of social development at the time of his nomination in late November 1993) as the PRI's 1994 presidential candidate.[8] Indeed, some observers concluded that Salinas's capacity to select his successor in a closed process that is the linchpin of Mexican authoritarianism indicated that significant democratization had once again been postponed, perhaps until the next presidential succession in the year 2000.

However, the January 1994 revolt by the Zapatista Army of National Liberation (EZLN) in the southern state of Chiapas and the assassination of Colosio in March 1994 sharply altered political expectations. The Chiapas uprising dramatically called attention to the negative social consequences of neoliberal economic reform (especially for indigenous peoples) and squarely focused national and international attention on the question of democracy in Mexico.[9] The Colosio assassination threw the PRI onto the defensive as a remarkably open struggle raged between Salinas's allies and party traditionalists over the selection of a successor candidate. Together these events created a greater degree of uncertainty within the governing political elite than at any time since Mexico's "official" party was founded in 1929.

Whether these startling events and the 1994 general elections mark the beginning of regime transition in Mexico remains to be seen. Yet if piecemeal liberalization of Mexico's party system and electoral rules finally gives way to a more open-ended process of democratization, it will be due in considerable measure to the growing disunity of Mexico's

---

[7]PRONASOL was a large-scale poverty alleviation program founded by President Salinas in December 1988 with proceeds from the sale of state-owned firms. For a careful evaluation of the program and its political and socioeconomic impact, see Cornelius, Craig, and Fox 1994a.

[8]In late 1993 Salinas judged the PRI's position sufficiently strong to permit him to implement a new round of political reform in order to increase the legitimacy of electoral outcomes. This legislation increased the size of the federal Senate and guaranteed that opposition parties would control at least one-quarter of its seats; eliminated the "governability clause" enacted in 1986 (which ensured the PRI majority representation in the federal Chamber of Deputies even if it failed to win a similar share of the national vote); placed overall limits on campaign spending and loosely regulated private campaign financing; reduced somewhat the government's control over electoral authorities; and permitted independent verification of voter registration procedures and national election observers. For details, see Zaldívar Lelo de Larrea 1993; *New York Times*, September 14, 1993, p. A4; September 19, 1993, p. 11.

[9]The electoral reforms adopted in the wake of the Chiapas rebellion are summarized in the second part of this chapter.

postrevolutionary governing coalition and significant shifts in the balance of state-society relations—changes that in many (though not all) instances occurred as either the direct or indirect consequence of economic crisis and restructuring during the 1980s and early 1990s. These developments also potentially have important consequences for the kind of new regime that might eventually take shape in Mexico.

This book analyzes the relationship between political and economic liberalization and the prospects for regime change in Mexico, focusing particularly on the period from the mid-1980s through the early 1990s. Evaluating the extent and character of political change under continued authoritarian rule is never easy. This challenge is particularly acute in the case of Mexico, whose durable authoritarian regime differs in major ways from the highly repressive, exclusionary, military-dominated regimes that came to power in a number of Latin American countries in the 1960s and 1970s. Such elements as the formal guarantee of liberal political rights in a civilian-ruled system, regular elections and the presence of legally recognized opposition parties, the heterogeneity of Mexico's governing political elite, a reliable system of office rotation (including a constitutional prohibition against presidential reelection), and a comparatively low level of repression all contribute to the relative openness of the Mexican regime. Even in the wake of the Chiapas uprising and the Colosio assassination, these features—and the Mexican regime's renowned resilience in the face of pressures for political change—make it difficult to determine whether a particular set of electoral reforms marks the beginning of democratization or simply another round of limited concessions to opposition forces, modifications that reduce strain within the regime but leave the governing elite's authority essentially intact.

The most promising analytical approach to this problem—and the perspective that informs many of the contributions to this volume—is to focus on the shifts in state-society relations that have occurred in the context of economic restructuring and the redefinition of Mexico's long-term development strategy. The post-1982 economic crisis and the ongoing process of economic restructuring eroded the regime's traditional bases of support and threatened the interests of key social actors. The Salinas administration in particular marked an important transition in that it both implemented major economic changes and oversaw the initial transformation of the political coalition that had long supported postrevolutionary authoritarian rule. The principal objective of this book is to examine both the pressures that gave rise to these coalitional changes and their political implications. Several of the essays commissioned for this volume do so by evaluating developments affecting political parties and major social actors (organized labor, the private sector, rural organizations, and urban popular movements).

The principal advantage of an actor-centered approach to the study of political change in an established authoritarian regime is that it permits a disaggregated examination of the intersection between economic and political opening, without assuming that democratization is necessarily the outcome. It is especially important not to make such an assumption in the case of contemporary Mexico because the implications of recent shifts in state-society relations do not all point in the same direction for all sectors. For example, during the Salinas administration a generally more open relationship between state elites and urban popular movements contrasted with the more closed political environment for labor unions; the government tolerated a greater degree of electoral competitiveness while at the same time resorting more frequently to repression against leftist opponents; state officials established ties with a broader range of politically independent social actors but had limited tolerance for militant political activity.

What emerges from the analyses in this volume, then, is not a predictive account of the direction of political change in Mexico. Rather, contributors portray a conflictive, often quite contradictory, process in which the complex factors that link economic and political liberalization begin to emerge. Although most of these chapters were written before the Zapatista uprising, the Colosio assassination, and the intense speculation that these events produced concerning the immediate prospects for democratization in Mexico, their assessment of the ways in which economic restructuring reconfigured the national political environment during the 1980s and early 1990s establishes a basis for evaluating future political developments in Mexico.

This introductory chapter addresses three topics. The first section examines the historical origins of Mexico's postrevolutionary authoritarian regime, focusing on the principal institutional and coalitional legacies of regime formation in the aftermath of the 1910–1920 Mexican Revolution. It also addresses briefly the relationship between authoritarian rule and import-substituting industrialization from the 1940s through the 1970s, as well as the challenges posed by economic crisis in the 1980s. The second part of this chapter analyzes in greater detail the impact of economic crisis and restructuring on the stability of Mexico's governing coalition and the growing importance of opposition parties and electoral competition in the 1980s and early 1990s. The third section examines the ways in which economic restructuring and key political developments altered established patterns of state-society relations. This chapter concludes by considering the implications of these developments for democratization. The conclusion also asks whether the remaining obstacles to regime change can be solved incrementally, or whether the transition to democracy in Mexico will necessarily involve a sharp break from past political practices.

POSTREVOLUTIONARY POLITICS AND THE CHALLENGE OF ECONOMIC TRANSFORMATION

Despite the passage of time and significant transformations, major aspects of Mexican politics in the 1980s and early 1990s still reflected the regime's revolutionary origins. By examining the institutional characteristics and coalitional bases of authoritarian rule, this section establishes a historical baseline for evaluating contemporary political change. It also discusses briefly the post-1982 economic crisis, the consequences of neoliberal economic reforms for Mexico's future growth prospects, and the implications of these economic developments for regime legitimacy.

FORGING MEXICO'S POSTREVOLUTIONARY AUTHORITARIAN REGIME

Mexico's 1910–1920 social revolution redrew the political landscape. The overthrow of Porfirio Díaz's personalistic authoritarian regime (the Porfiriato, 1876–1911) initiated a protracted, violent struggle for political power among rival factions with different capabilities and disparate, often conflicting goals. Some elements sought only a limited political reform of the old order, while others pursued a broad transformation of social structures and class relations. Military confrontation and serious factional rivalry persisted until the late 1920s. However, the last successful military revolt occurred in 1920 and brought to the fore a "northwestern coalition" led by Alvaro Obregón, a principal military leader of the "Constitutionalist" forces after 1913 and the dominant figure in national politics between his election as president in 1920 and his assassination in 1928. The new postrevolutionary elite was bent on the expansion and centralization of political power, both to effect socioeconomic change and to defend the revolution against domestic and foreign threats.

Peasants' and workers' entry into national politics during the revolution was a major departure in Mexican history. The rapid expansion of political consciousness among mass actors and their mobilization behind a program of far-reaching socioeconomic and political reform helped bring about significant change. For example, revolutionary mobilization undercut the political power of the landowning class and eroded foreign control over natural resource industries. Explicit recognition of unions as legitimate bargaining agents in the workplace, constitutional protection of the right to strike, and creation of state administrative agencies to mediate conflicts also reshaped worker-employer relations. More generally, by creating new opportunities for the competitive mobilization of support, the presence of peasants and workers in the political arena redefined the character of elite-mass interactions.

Mass mobilization also influenced the content of the distinctive body of political beliefs that was associated with the revolutionary experience.

These beliefs combined liberal conceptions of individual rights and
constitutional rule, nationalism, and a broad programmatic commitment to economic redistribution and social justice. Liberal ideas of
constitutionalism, federalism and municipal autonomy (*municipio libre*),
and private property particularly informed debate about political and
socioeconomic change during the early phases of the revolutionary
struggle (Córdova 1973: 16, 18, 21, 27). However, the armed peasantry's
demand for large-scale land distribution and the growing political and
economic importance of organized labor in urban areas made commitment to extensive social reform an essential element in revolutionary
political discourse. The 1917 federal Constitution, for example, included
separate articles providing for land reform (Article 27) and workers' legal
and social protection (Article 123). These articles were especially significant because they emphasized the *collective* character of new social and
political rights for peasants and workers, not just opportunities for
individual advancement. The fusion of nationalism and a commitment
to social reform in "revolutionary nationalism" provided a particularly
compelling focus for popular identification with the postrevolutionary
order.

Two pillars supported the postrevolutionary authoritarian regime
that took shape during the 1920s and 1930s: a strong, increasingly
centralized, and interventionist state, and a hegemonic "party of the
revolution" closely linked to the state apparatus.[10] Elite commitment to
maintaining political control and promoting socioeconomic change
made state structures centrally important in postrevolutionary Mexico.
Such measures as land reform and the regulation or nationalization of
foreign-owned properties required a strong state. Similarly, the governing party provided an institutional framework for mediating elite competition, limiting conflict, and mobilizing mass support during elections.

Centralized political power and active state intervention in socioeconomic affairs became hallmarks of the new, postrevolutionary order.
The 1917 federal Constitution divided decision-making responsibility
among executive, legislative, and judicial branches, and it created a
federal system in which states' rights and municipal autonomy were
explicitly recognized. Both the formal structure of government and the
guarantee of individual rights reflected the influence of liberal political
ideas. Nevertheless, in the belief that strong executive leadership was
necessary to guarantee the implementation of social reforms won during
the revolution and to ensure the political stability required for national
economic development, delegates to the 1916–1917 Constitutional Con-

---

[10]For an analysis of the distinctive characteristics of postrevolutionary authoritarian
rule and an examination of the Mexican case, see Middlebrook n.d.: chap. 1. Parts of this
section are drawn from Middlebrook.

vention placed preeminent authority in the presidency and limited the powers of the legislative and judicial branches.

The 1917 Constitution thus laid the legal foundation for postrevolutionary governments' relative decision-making autonomy. Presidents Alvaro Obregón (1920–1924) and Plutarco Elías Calles (1924–1928) acted forcefully to subordinate the armed forces to civilian authority and to establish political control over regional bosses (caciques) whose power had grown significantly during a decade of armed conflict. At the same time, Obregón and Calles created the administrative bases for active state economic intervention. The northwesterners who came to power under Obregón's leadership envisioned a political economy in which a vigorous domestic private sector would contribute actively to the development of national industry, thus reducing the influence of foreign (especially U.S.) capital. However, because of the manifest weakness of the national private sector, the absence of domestic financial institutions or a capital market, and the lack of adequate infrastructure, they understood that the state would necessarily play a leading role in economic development. By the late 1920s, the Obregón and Calles administrations had created a network of financial and regulatory institutions[11] and initiated a series of major infrastructure projects (especially roads, dams, and irrigation systems) that underpinned subsequent agricultural modernization and industrial development.

The formation of an "official" party in 1929 accelerated the trend toward the centralization of national political power. A number of small, often regionally based political parties formed during and after the revolution. Competition among parties with narrow social bases contributed to factional rivalries which culminated in Obregón's assassination in July 1928, shortly after he won reelection to the presidency. The death of the early postrevolutionary period's most important political figure threatened to throw the country into chaos over the question of presidential succession. Calles addressed this problem by renouncing any intention to seek a second presidential term, and in March 1929 he organized the Revolutionary National Party (PNR) to contain factional rivalries. He perceived the creation of a national "party of the revolution" to be an essential basis for ensuring the political stability necessary for economic development.[12]

The creation of the PNR was a significant step in the institutionalization of postrevolutionary Mexican politics. The PNR and its successors, the Party of the Mexican Revolution (PRM, 1938) and the PRI (1946), offered an organizational framework for the reconciliation of competing

---

[11] These included a central bank (the Banco de México) and national highway, irrigation, electrical power generation, agricultural credit, and banking commissions.

[12] The definitive study of political parties during and after the revolution and the circumstances surrounding the formation of the PNR is Garrido 1982, especially chaps. 1, 2.

political interests. For much of the period between 1929 and the 1980s, the "party of the revolution" grouped a heterogeneous collection of sociopolitical actors which, despite considerable internal competition and frequent conflict over policy goals, was linked by an overarching consensus on broad norms of political action and the general goals of economic development.[13] The very heterogeneity of this governing "revolutionary coalition" symbolized the established regime's commitment to the political representation of diverse interests.

Equally important, the governing party served as a major vehicle for regime legitimation through its dominance of the electoral process. The postrevolutionary elite's control over the state apparatus gradually permitted the "official" party to establish its electoral hegemony, though resistance from regional and local political bosses made this a slow, uneven process. Where ample access to government personnel and financial resources proved insufficient to secure victory for the party, fraudulent electoral practices were authorized or tolerated by government officials to secure the desired result. Indeed, from 1929 until 1988 the "official" party's candidates never lost an election for the presidency, the federal Senate, or state governorships. The party's close ties to the federal executive after the mid-1930s and its dominance in national electoral politics during subsequent decades substantially strengthened presidential control over the federal legislature and state governments. Moreover, the party's control over elected government positions contributed significantly to the emergence of a cohesive *clase política* drawn predominantly from the urban middle class, socialized by shared educational experiences, frequently linked by kinship ties, and distinct in background and experience from the national bourgeoisie.[14]

The party was able to fulfill such diverse functions because, at least until the late 1980s, it was closely identified with revolutionary nationalism—the political goals and social program of the Mexican Revolution. (Its colors are those of the Mexican flag: red, white, and green.) Opposition parties existed on both the left and right. The "party of the revolution," however, occupied the broad center of national political life, defining the essential dichotomy of postrevolutionary politics: its supporters were those committed to the realization of the revolution's diverse goals, while those who opposed it were necessarily "counterrevolutionary."[15]

---

[13]Among these were such crucial issues as the public sector's role in economic development, the need to provide competing political factions with regularized access to administrative and elective office, and the importance of opening channels of social and economic advancement to lower-class groups.

[14]The best analyses of Mexico's political elite are Smith 1979 and Camp 1980. For an examination of changes in elite composition and behavior, see Middlebrook 1988: 122–34.

[15]Calles made this distinction explicit in December 1928 when organizing support for the party. See Dulles 1961: 410.

A strong, interventionist state and a hegemonic party were crucial to forging (and preserving) a durable alliance between the ruling political elite and mass social forces. On the one hand, reliable control over the principal instruments of coercion allowed governing elites to repress challenges from popular forces, and the construction of a state administrative apparatus with the institutional capacity to mediate mass participation permitted successive presidential administrations to establish the de jure and de facto parameters of sociopolitical organization and mobilization. Yet at the same time, the Mexican state's far-reaching intervention in socioeconomic affairs provided government decision makers with the means to formulate development policies that responded to key peasant and labor demands. An extensive program of land distribution in the 1930s and the creation of elaborate credit and marketing arrangements to subsidize small-scale agricultural production transformed peasant communities into a reliable source of electoral support for the "official" party. Urban and industrial workers benefited from such measures as enterprise profit-sharing and a broad range of publicly financed social welfare programs, including subsidized access to basic commodities, health care, housing, and consumer credit. In general, these were socioeconomic benefits that peasant and worker organizations would have been hard pressed to win on their own. Securing them depended fundamentally on mass organizations' political alliance with state elites.

Similarly, the political dominance exercised by the governing party helped cement mass actors' loyalty to the regime. The "party of the revolution" was the principal channel of political mobility for the leaders of lower-class organizations.[16] Peasant and labor leaders' presence in important elective positions gave mass organizations a share (however modest) of political power, opening up opportunities to use their numerical importance in national politics both to influence government policy decisions and to defend past gains. More generally, peasant and labor organizations' affiliation with the governing party symbolized their inclusion in the postrevolutionary governing coalition. This is why the organized labor movement in particular vigorously resisted attempts by different presidential administrations to reduce the formal role of mass organizations in party affairs.

The governing elite's effective control over mass demands established the political foundations for rapid economic growth. Beginning in the early 1940s, Mexican decision makers embraced import-substituting industrialization as their principal development strategy. Pursuit of this approach, whose goal was to supply national demand with domestically manufactured consumer durable goods and intermediate products

---

[16]Beginning in 1938 the "official" party was organized on the basis of labor, agrarian, military, and "popular" sectors. The military sector was formally eliminated in 1943.

rather than with foreign imports, led successive presidential administrations to enact new policies to promote domestic industry. These included higher tariff barriers, direct import controls, and tighter government restrictions on foreign direct investment. Unlike their counterparts in Argentina and Brazil, Mexican policy makers had by the late 1950s realized their double goals of producing steady economic expansion and rising per capita income while at the same time controlling inflation (a period that was, therefore, often referred to as "stabilizing development").

Economic success both strengthened postrevolutionary governments' performance-based claim to the legitimate exercise of authority and reinforced the elite-mass alliances that underpinned authoritarian rule. Many analysts subsequently noted that, over the longer term, the import-substitution policies adopted in the early 1940s created a number of problems which contributed to serious economic difficulties in the 1970s and 1980s (Thorp 1992; Hirschman 1968).[17] Moreover, the period of growth often characterized as the "Mexican miracle" contributed to greater economic and social inequality.[18] Yet from the 1940s through the 1970s, the strategy of import-substituting industrialization enjoyed broad support within Mexico's governing coalition. Economic growth produced new sources of employment, and especially after the mid-1950s, rising real wages and expanding social welfare benefits significantly improved many workers' standard of living. The ability of labor and peasant leaders to deliver substantial resources to their members strengthened their position within government-allied mass organizations, thereby reinforcing the elite-mass alliances so crucial to regime stability.

ECONOMIC CRISIS IN THE 1980s: STRUCTURAL ADJUSTMENT AND NEOLIBERAL REFORM

Mexico's post-1982 economic crisis posed serious potential risks to the established political and social order, and it forced government decision makers to undertake a process of economic restructuring that had lasting political consequences. The proximate source of financial difficulty lay in heavy borrowing from international creditors during the 1970s and early 1980s. Foreign borrowing contributed to rapid growth during Mexico's petroleum-led economic boom in 1978–1981,[19] but the

---

[17]These problems included excessive dependence on imports of intermediate and capital goods, overvalued exchange rates and chronic balance-of-payments difficulties, inefficient domestic industries producing high-cost consumer products for a heavily protected domestic market, and a very limited capacity to export manufactured goods.

[18]Mexico's gross domestic product rose by an annual average of 6.5 percent in real terms between 1941 and 1981. Calculated from data presented in INEGI 1985: vol. 1, table 9.1.

[19]Gross domestic product grew by an average of 8.4 percent per year in real terms in these years. Calculated from data presented in INEGI 1985: vol. 1, table 9.1.

level of public- and private-sector indebtedness was not sustainable. As Víctor L. Urquidi notes (this volume), excessive debt payment obligations coupled with declining petroleum prices in 1981–1982 produced growing economic instability. Escalating short-term debt service obligations, increasing capital flight, large-scale devaluations, and worsening balance-of-payments problems finally led to a liquidity crisis in August 1982 which detonated the Latin American debt crisis.

In response, the newly inaugurated de la Madrid administration adopted an orthodox economic stabilization plan that sharply limited wage increases, cut government social spending, and reduced or eliminated a broad range of government consumption subsidies. The government also attempted in 1983 and 1984 to reschedule the country's foreign debt. But as Urquidi indicates, debt service payments remained very high. Economic recovery was further constrained by unstable prices for Mexico's petroleum exports, low levels of domestic and foreign investment, and insufficient access to foreign credit. Despite high interest rates, the inflation rate averaged 88 percent per year between 1982 and 1988 (and reached an annual rate of 177 percent in January 1988).

Economic policy makers managed to bring inflation under control only by negotiating the Economic Solidarity Pact (PSE) with business, labor, and peasant representatives in December 1987. Jaime Ros (this volume) concludes that several singular advantages—economic policy makers' relative decision-making autonomy in a strongly presidentialist system, Mexico's geostrategic importance for the United States (which led the U.S. government to view the country as an essential "test case" for its debt restructuring initiatives in the mid- and late 1980s), the historically low degree of indexation in the wage/price system, and the remarkable flexibility that Mexico's system of state-labor relations gave economic policy makers in setting wages—permitted structural adjustment to proceed much more rapidly and smoothly in Mexico than in a number of other Latin American countries. Nevertheless, the economy grew by less than 0.1 percent per year in real terms between 1982 and 1988.[20]

The depth and length of the economic crisis compelled government officials to reexamine the role of the public sector and the country's overall strategy for economic development. Beginning in 1985–1987, economic policy makers radically liberalized Mexico's trade and industrial policy regime, rapidly privatized state-owned enterprises, and aggressively deregulated foreign investment flows and domestic economic activities. To explain why this occurred, Ros presents a "political economy model" of market reforms that emphasizes the interaction among the willingness of policy makers to adopt market reforms, foreign lenders' willingness to support these measures by increasing the

[20]Calculated from data presented in Lustig 1992: table 2.4.

flow of capital to the reforming country, the cost of not obtaining external finance, the policy trade-offs between stabilization and structural reform, and the extent of domestic opposition to market reforms.

Because attracting foreign capital was vitally important, Mexican decision makers had strong incentives to adopt market reforms. Indeed, the U.S. government's Baker (1985) and Brady (1989) plans conditioned additional foreign lending on debtor countries' willingness to adopt such measures. The result was a sharp shift toward export-oriented economic development, greater scope for market forces, and a more prominent role for the private sector in promoting economic growth. These policies were accompanied by other measures (including the elimination of government budget deficits, more effective tax collection, and greater institutional autonomy for the Banco de México) designed to maintain business confidence and place the Mexican economy on the path toward sustained long-term growth.

The political implications of economic restructuring are examined in detail in the following two sections. It is important to note, however, that these neoliberal reforms may constitute an ambiguous economic legacy for Mexico. Both Urquidi and Ros (this volume) observe that, despite important gains in the late 1980s and early 1990s, a number of unresolved problems may constrain future economic growth. These include decidedly mixed productivity growth in the manufacturing sector; a low private savings rate; inadequate levels of public investment; the pressing need to use additional public resources to resolve serious, accumulated social needs; and the economy's limited ability to generate sufficient levels of employment, especially unskilled jobs.[21] Moreover, the Mexican economy remains heavily dependent on the continued massive inflow of foreign capital, which may not continue at the levels reached during the period before the approval of the North American Free Trade Agreement.

ECONOMIC RESTRUCTURING AND POLITICAL CHANGE

The economic crisis of the 1980s and the shift in national development strategy had important political consequences for Mexico's postrevolutionary authoritarian regime. Prolonged economic stagnation seriously eroded the regime's performance-based claims to political legitimacy. Conflicts arising over the direction of economic policy aggravated tensions within the governing political elite, leading to factional splits that strengthened the position of opposition parties. Moreover, public concerns regarding management of the economy, corruption in government, and electoral fraud badly tarnished the prestige of the presidency.

---

[21] In his contribution to this volume, Francisco Valdés Ugalde also asks whether the private sector's greatly increased influence in Mexican politics is compatible with an efficient allocation of resources among national priorities.

Accumulated socioeconomic discontent and growing demands for democracy produced in 1988 an unprecedented challenge to the Institutional Revolutionary Party's electoral hegemony. This section examines the factors that have contributed to the heightened importance of opposition parties in Mexican politics and increased electoral competitiveness since the early 1980s.

PRESIDENTIALISM, ECONOMIC RESTRUCTURING, AND COALITION CHANGE

Many analysts would argue that a broad program of economic restructuring could be implemented more easily in Mexico's highly centralized authoritarian regime than under a democratic government or in an authoritarian regime with a weaker executive. From this perspective, the combination of a strong presidency and a hegemonic party was especially well suited to pushing through controversial market reforms because in Mexico the federal executive commands overwhelming political power. This interpretation of Mexican politics stresses that the strength of the PRI and the weakness of the political opposition are both products of a strong presidency (Hansen 1971; Purcell 1975; Carpizo 1985; Garrido 1987; Cornelius and Craig 1988; Aguilar Camín and Meyer 1993).

A less orthodox interpretation of Mexican *presidencialismo* holds that the federal executive's power depends on unified partisan control of both chambers of Congress, the president's ability to discipline the "official" party, and continued PRI dominance over the political opposition. Yet there are significant tensions among these different conditions. For example, the president's capacity to lead and control the PRI depends upon his ability to satisfy the party's diverse constituencies. Thus, if the coalition of interests grouped in the ruling party is too large, the president may face contradictory, ultimately irreconcilable demands. The president may find it especially difficult during bad economic times to maintain a broad governing coalition. From this perspective, the president might under such conditions seek to reduce the PRI coalition to a more manageable size and reorganize it consistent with his own policy preferences. At the same time, however, the president also faces strong pressures to enlarge and diversify the PRI coalition in order to deprive opposition parties of mass support. The tension between policy incentives to reduce the heterogeneity of the PRI coalition and political pressures to enlarge it is particularly intense during difficult economic times (Scott 1959; Vernon 1963; Story 1986; Philip 1992; Molinar Horcasitas 1994).

These alternative interpretations illuminate both the sources of policy instability in Mexico during much of the 1970s and early 1980s and the reasons why accelerated economic restructuring after the mid-1980s exacerbated factional division within the governing coalition. Political struggles over national economic policy began in the early 1970s when problems associated with import-substituting industrialization began to mount. Rising inflation, faltering economic growth, and growing balance-of-payments problems sparked an enduring "dispute for the nation" (Cordera and Tello 1981) that pitted "nationalists" against "neoliberals." The former advocated policies that would "deepen" the process of import-substituting industrialization, including increased public investment and measures that would stimulate domestic demand. In contrast, the neoliberals proposed policies to control inflation, dismantle protectionism, and increase Mexico's long-term economic competitiveness and export potential (Solís 1985; Villarreal 1976; Ortiz Mena 1980). Both policy agendas included several initiatives that promised to be politically costly, and the Echeverría (1970–1976) and López Portillo (1976–1982) governments' efforts to avoid splintering the PRI coalition explain in large part the policy zigzags associated with their administrations. Indeed, the Echeverría and López Portillo presidencies ended in economic and political crises that contrasted sharply with the much more orderly presidential successions that occurred in 1958, 1964, and 1970 during the period of stabilizing development.

Under the pressures of prolonged economic crisis and the urgent need to secure long-term access to capital, the de la Madrid and Salinas administrations broke this policy deadlock in favor of neoliberal economic restructuring. This shift had important political implications. Among other things, adoption of an export-oriented development model increased the political significance and policy leverage of the private sector.

Salinas signaled this departure in a campaign speech that he delivered in Garza García, Nuevo León (a suburb of Monterrey, the home of Mexico's most important industrialists), in May 1988: "The engines of sustained economic growth in future years will be private investment, nonpetroleum exports, public investment in infrastructure, and the expansion of the domestic market" (La Jornada, May 20, 1988). Salinas made it clear that this ordering was not coincidental; domestic and foreign private investment would take clear precedence over public investment, which would be restricted to infrastructure projects. Moreover, nonpetroleum exports would receive priority over the expansion of domestic consumer demand. This position stood in sharp contrast to postrevolutionary governments' traditional nationalist commitments to economic protectionism and tight regulation of foreign investment, a "mixed" economy in which the state played a key role in the production of goods and services, and an inward-oriented development strategy in which the capacity for economic expansion depended heavily on increased domestic demand.

Nevertheless, as Francisco Valdés Ugalde observes (this volume), the recovery of business confidence and the consolidation of an alliance between neoliberal reformers and the private sector required considerable time. Memory of the 1982 bank nationalization was the principal obstacle. Even though the de la Madrid administration took several steps to heal this rift (including constitutional reforms enacted in 1982 to clarify the state's role in economic affairs and limit state ownership to specified, strategic areas), many entrepreneurs feared a resurgence of "populism." In the course of their struggle to win a durable government commitment to a more favorable state–private-sector relationship, business organizations gained new confidence concerning their involvement in partisan politics.[22] What finally convinced them that neoliberal policy makers were serious about ceding significant space to the private sector was the de la Madrid and Salinas administrations' aggressive privatization program (the symbolic high point of which was the reprivatization of banks and other financial institutions in 1990–1992), the decision to abrogate peasants' constitutional right (Article 27) to the redistribution of land and permit the private sale of collectively owned ejido lands, and the negotiation of the North American Free Trade Agreement.

As Echeverría and López Portillo had feared, the government's decisive turn toward neoliberal economic policies and the private sector's more prominent political role split the PRI coalition. Two factors were particularly important in this regard. First, the groups most adversely affected by cuts in government subsidies and the privatization of state-owned enterprises were organized workers and peasants, the PRI's most important base of mass support. The consistent pursuit of economic policies that produced declining real wages and lower per capita incomes during the 1980s threatened the PRI's long-standing claim to represent a multiclass coalition forged in the aftermath of the Mexican Revolution. In particular, resource constraints severely undermined the patron-client ties and distributional alliances that were traditionally at the heart of the PRI (Dresser, this volume).

Second, de la Madrid and Salinas named to prominent policy-making positions political technocrats whose mentalities and ideological preferences differed sharply from those of traditional PRI politicians.[23] Individuals rising to high national office in the 1980s and early 1990s on the basis of their educational achievements and technical expertise were members of a generation far removed from the violent political and social upheaval that produced the Mexican regime. (The contrast was particularly marked in the case of the labor movement, which was still led in the early 1990s by individuals personally linked to

---

[22]Dresser (this volume) notes that in the 1991 midterm elections 17 percent of the PRI's candidates came from the business sector.

[23]The term political technocrat is used by Camp (1985).

the 1910–1920 revolutionary experience.) Control over key posts by young, often foreign-educated technocrats increased discontent within the political elite because traditional politicians (sometimes referred to as *dinosaurios*) believed that their opportunities for mobility and policy influence were blocked.

The ascent of this neoliberal faction faced stubborn resistance from nationalist sectors of the governing coalition. In 1986 some of these dissident elements formed the Democratic Current (CD) within the PRI, a movement calling for the democratization of the governing party's method of selecting presidential candidates and a more equitable model of economic development. Its most prominent supporters were Cuauhtémoc Cárdenas (son of former president Lázaro Cárdenas and governor of Michoacán from 1980 to 1986) and Porfirio Muñoz Ledo (a former PRI president who had held major cabinet positions during the Echeverría and López Portillo administrations and who had also served as Mexico's representative to the United Nations in the late 1970s and early 1980s).

Although members of the Democratic Current repeatedly espoused their loyalty to the PRI and described their initiative as an example of disciplined criticism designed to promote internal party reform, the PRI hierarchy considered the group's activities a veiled attack on the de la Madrid administration and attempted to limit the movement's impact by threatening to expel its supporters from the party. When the PRI leadership prevented Cárdenas from competing for the party's presidential nomination and de la Madrid selected Salinas as his successor (thereby signaling the continuation of de la Madrid's neoliberal program and the new dominance of a political faction centered in key economic policy-making centers, particularly the Banco de México and the Ministry of Finance), Cárdenas, Muñoz Ledo, and other advocates of traditionally nationalist policy positions broke with the governing party. Their exit produced the most serious division within the Mexican political elite since the early 1950s.[24]

The alienation of many traditional PRI supporters and the split in the governing elite contributed directly to the Institutional Revolutionary Party's electoral debacle in 1988. Opposition political parties— particularly the center-right National Action Party (PAN), but also leftist parties—had made major gains in municipal elections in 1983, and the PAN had strongly challenged the ruling party in several state elections in 1986.[25] But in 1988 the principal challenge came from the left. Cuauhtémoc Cárdenas, leading a heterogeneous opposition coalition called the National Democratic Front (FDN), officially received 31.1

---

[24]In the 1952 elections, General Miguel Henríquez Guzmán's Federation of People's Parties won 16 percent of the vote. This was the most serious challenge to the PRI's presidential candidate since the governing party's formation in 1929.

[25]Indeed, the government was forced to resort to massive fraud to deny the PAN victory in the gubernatorial race in Chihuahua in 1986.

percent of the valid votes cast in the presidential election.[26] Cárdenas's very strong showing reflected his close personal identification with revolutionary nationalist policy positions,[27] widespread discontent with government austerity measures and the de la Madrid administration's inadequate response to the housing and relocation problems caused by the 1985 Mexico City earthquakes, and growing public demands for democracy. Under the weight of these diverse pressures, the PRI's share of the presidential vote fell to a new low. Whether Salinas actually won a majority in a hotly contested election marred by extensive fraud remains a matter of considerable dispute. What is certain is that this outcome ended an era in which victory by the "party of the revolution" was accepted as a matter of course by actors across the political spectrum.

POLITICAL PARTIES AND ELECTIONS IN CONTEMPORARY MEXICO

The 1988 elections thus marked an important turning point in Mexican politics. The fact that popular discontent with government austerity measures and declining standards of living was expressed through electoral channels largely reflected the increased opportunities for political contestation made possible by López Portillo's 1977 political reform and subsequent changes in party registration requirements and electoral procedures.[28] Some analysts argue that the principal effect of these liberalizing measures was to preclude more complete democratization by directing pressures for political change into a seemingly endless series of party and electoral reforms that failed to modify the core elements of Mexican authoritarianism (Loaeza, this volume). Yet enhanced opportunities to constitute opposition parties, contest elections, and win a (still quite limited) share of power had important consequences. The combination of intra-elite conflict over economic policy and access to decision-making positions, popular dissatisfaction with some of the consequences of market reforms, and regularly scheduled electoral contests produced over time a much more competitive political environment, particularly at state and local levels. As a result, in the late 1980s and early 1990s, elections and party politics assumed unprecedented importance in Mexico.

---

[26]The National Action Party officially received 16.8 percent of the presidential vote.

[27]As president between 1934 and 1940, Cárdenas's father implemented an extensive agrarian reform program and nationalized foreign-owned petroleum companies.

[28]The López Portillo administration implemented an important political reform measure in order to integrate recently formed opposition parties into the officially recognized party system, reinvigorate the PRI by increasing the effectiveness of party competition, and restore public confidence in the regime in the aftermath of such events as the 1968 "Tlatelolco massacre," in which police and army troops killed or wounded hundreds of protesting students. For a discussion of the 1977 reform's origins and its consequences, see Middlebrook 1986.

The increased competitiveness of elections reflected important changes on both the left and right. On the left, Cárdenas formed the Party of the Democratic Revolution (PRD) in 1989 to institutionalize the opposition coalition he led in the 1988 elections. The PRD suffered from considerable factionalism as a result of both personal and ideological disputes among its principal leaders and Salinas administration officials' concerted efforts to co-opt and divide what they perceived to be their most serious political opponent. Because of conflicts over political strategy and because PRD organizers were frequently the targets of political violence, the party was only partially successful at forging ties with worker, peasant, and urban popular organizations. At the same time, the PRD's organizational weakness and government officials' resort to electoral fraud prevented the party from winning many important electoral contests, even in such core areas of Cardenista support as the state of Michoacán. These problems led the PRD in the early 1990s to adopt increasingly radical, antisystem positions on some issues, making collaboration with the National Action Party more difficult (Alcocer, this volume). Nevertheless, the PRD did make inroads into some of the PRI's traditional constituencies, and despite the many obstacles it faced, the PRD emerged as the most important opposition force positioned to the left of Mexico's ruling party.

The National Action Party remained the most important force on the right. In 1989 the PAN broke the PRI's monopoly on state governorships by winning the gubernatorial election in Baja California. As noted above, PAN candidates later won control over the state governments of Chihuahua and Guanajuato as well. Such victories gave the party both significant practical experience in governing at the state and municipal levels and an important base for political organization.[29] Somewhat paradoxically, the PAN also experienced considerable internal divisions as the Salinas administration adopted many of its traditional policy positions (including constitutional reforms limiting the extent of state economic intervention, permitting the sale and private ownership of ejido lands, and lifting the bans against the Roman Catholic Church's ownership of property and involvement in political affairs) and sought to form a loose political coalition with the PAN. Some PANistas viewed the Salinas government's offer of programmatic collaboration as little more than a sophisticated form of co-optation that undermined the party's capacity to push for democratization. Indeed, in 1992 conflict over this issue led several prominent PAN leaders to secede from the party.[30] Overall, however, the PAN benefited substantially from deepening

---

[29]See Rodríguez and Ward 1994 for a careful examination of PAN government in Baja California.

[30]The secessionists included Pablo Emilio Madero, grandson of Francisco Madero, who in 1910–1911 led the successful liberal challenge to Porfirio Díaz that initiated the Mexican Revolution.

public support for several of its principal policy positions, the financial assistance of some business organizations and the willingness of prominent entrepreneurs to stand as PAN candidates, and the fact that the Salinas administration was much more willing to accept electoral victories by the PAN than by the PRD.

Underlying these developments were important shifts in the partisan alignment of Mexican voters. Joseph L. Klesner (this volume) convincingly demonstrates how structural social change and the economic crisis of the 1980s undermined the PRI's electoral position. For many decades, the PRI exercised unchallenged electoral hegemony in the Mexican countryside (a product of both peasant loyalty to the regime that introduced an extensive land reform in the 1930s and the political control exercised by PRI-allied caciques) and drew considerable support from unionized urban and industrial workers, public employees, and portions of the urban middle class. Over time, however, rural-to-urban migration eroded the PRI's most reliable base of electoral support, and the party's capacity to attract urban middle-class voters declined sharply after the early 1970s. Competition from the opposition parties that were officially registered following the 1977 political reform also reduced the PRI's traditionally overwhelming electoral majorities.

Yet it was accumulated popular discontent with the government's post-1982 austerity and economic restructuring policies that produced unprecedented support for opposition parties in 1988. Klesner's analysis shows that leftist parties, for example, performed much better than in previous years among peasants and the urban poor. These parties increased their vote totals at the direct expense of the PRI. Klesner argues that these changes do not yet indicate electoral realignment—that is, the relatively stable reorganization within the electorate of the group basis of support for major political parties. However, partisan *dealignment* is an established fact in contemporary Mexican politics. Klesner concludes that "the Mexican electorate is less securely under the PRI's control than it has ever been."

The Salinas administration responded to these changing political realities in three principal ways. First, Salinas vigorously sought to restore the power and prestige of the presidency and build a new social coalition in support of his neoliberal program (see the following section). Second, he forged a de facto alliance with the National Action Party in order to split the political opposition and create a working congressional majority in support of key legislative initiatives. This alliance held considerable strategic value for the regime. In 1988, opposition parties had cooperated in an antisystem coalition formed around demands for democratization. Faced with government officials' continued resort to electoral fraud and other abuses of power, the principal opposition parties on the left and right set aside their ideological differences in order to cooperate against their common adversaries—the government and the Institutional Revolutionary Party. However, interparty dynamics changed when the Salinas administration adopted ideological positions closer to those advocated by the PAN. The opposition front against the PRI began to break up when the PAN was courted by the PRI and when the PRD and the PAN took divergent positions concerning various political liberalization proposals, an issue that had united them in 1988 (Alcocer, this volume).

Third, Salinas sought to reform and revitalize the Institutional Revolutionary Party. Reform of the PRI—characterized by some observers as a "mission impossible" (Meyer 1989)—has long been the goal of those regime loyalists seeking both to preserve power and to increase the competitiveness and legitimacy of the party and electoral systems. Like its recent predecessors, the Salinas administration attempted to open up internal party decision-making procedures and improve the quality of PRI candidates (Dresser, this volume). More important, PRI reformers sought to restrict the role of sectoral organizations within the party and to adopt a territorial structure for an envisioned "party of citizens." They believed that, given the declining capacity of "official" labor and peasant organizations to mobilize their members in support of PRI candidates, a territorial structure would allow the party to respond more effectively to the concerns of an increasingly diverse, urban electorate. However, many of the Salinas administration's most important party reform initiatives met strong opposition from PRI traditionalists. Aggressive lobbying by the Confederation of Mexican Workers (CTM) successfully blocked key organizational reforms. As a result, the PRI remained organized around a combination of sectoral and territorial bodies.[31]

Despite such setbacks, Salinas's various political initiatives won him widespread personal popularity, restored the political power of the presidency, and improved the PRI's electoral fortunes.[32] With the PRI's electoral recovery and the approval of the North American Free Trade Agreement, Salinas entered the last year of his presidency with considerable political capital. The presidential succession is the most important—and potentially most vulnerable—moment in Mexico's six-year political calendar, offering rival factions an institutionalized opportunity to compete for power. The potential for conflict is always great (the previous three presidential successions had been particularly fraught with political tension), and a slowdown in economic growth in late 1993

[31] As of late 1993, the PRI was organized around a National Front of Citizens' Organizations, an Urban Popular Territorial Movement, a Worker-Peasant Pact, and other organizations. The Worker-Peasant Pact, signed in June 1992 between the CTM and the National Peasants' Confederation (CNC), was designed to promote productivity and increase consumer access to commodities. For details, see Rodríguez Guillén and Mora Heredia 1993: 27.

[32] One important measure of Salinas's success was that the PRI won 61.4 percent of the vote in the 1991 midterm congressional elections.

was additional cause for concern. Yet the existence of substantial international financial reserves, a government budgetary surplus, and the prospect that the approval of the NAFTA would attract significant additional amounts of foreign investment all suggested that the government would be able to stimulate the economy prior to the 1994 elections and simultaneously guard against currency speculation. With the imposition of Luis Donaldo Colosio as the PRI's 1994 presidential candidate, Salinas seemed on the verge of completing his *sexenio* in a stronger political position than any Mexican president in the preceding three decades. More generally, Salinas's effective control of the succession process indicated to many observers that he had achieved his goal of implementing extensive market reforms before undertaking serious political liberalization.

However, two events dramatically brought the question of democracy to the center of national political debate. First, on January 1, 1994, some two thousand guerrilla fighters temporarily occupied San Cristóbal de las Casas and three other towns in Chiapas.[33] In a masterstroke of timing, the Zapatista Army of National Liberation took up arms on the very day that the North American Free Trade Agreement formally went into effect. The Zapatistas explicitly and forcefully challenged the negative social consequences of neoliberal economic reforms, especially for indigenous peoples.[34] They demanded broad political autonomy for regions populated predominantly by indigenous peoples, the reversal of Salinas's 1991 modifications to Article 27 of the 1917 federal Constitution, the reorientation of government economic policies, and political democracy in Mexico. Although many Mexicans disavowed violence as a means of redressing grievances, the groundswell of support the Zapatista movement received from across the social spectrum was compelling evidence of popular dissatisfaction with both key elements

[33] Among the immediate casualties of the Zapatista rebellion was the view that the Salinas administration had successfully engineered a far-reaching program of economic restructuring without provoking major political or social upheavals. For one statement of this view, see Lustig 1992: 12.

Whether President Salinas and his top national security and military advisers fully appreciated the scope of guerrilla activity in Chiapas, but failed to act against the Zapatistas for fear of endangering U.S. congressional approval of the NAFTA, remains a subject of debate. The Mexican army had clashed briefly with guerrillas in Chiapas in May 1993, and in August 1993 the Mexican press carried reports of a guerrilla movement in the state. See Castañeda 1994a: 21; *Economist*, January 8, 1994, p. 41.

This summary of the Chiapas uprising draws on the following sources: *New York Times*, January 3, 1994, p. A11, January 7, 1994, p. A4, January 9, 1994, p. 1, January 30, 1994, p. 9, February 2, 1994, p. A10, February 9, 1994, pp. A1, 7, February 20, 1994, p. 3, February 26, 1994, p. 6, March 4, 1994, p. A2, March 18, 1994, p. A3, March 23, 1994, p. A6; *Economist*, January 8, 1994, pp. 41–42; January 15, 1994, p. 39, February 19, 1994, p. 43; Academia Mexicana de Derechos Humanos 1994d.

[34] The EZLN's military leader and most prominent public spokesperson, who identified himself only as "Sub-Comandante Marcos," stated that "The free-trade agreement is a death certificate for the Indian peoples of Mexico" (quoted in *New York Times*, January 3, 1994, p. A11).

of Salinas's economic program and his attempt to postpone democratization.[35]

The Salinas administration initially blamed the uprising on liberation theology activists and Central American leftist subversives, and it responded to the Zapatista challenge with military force. In heavy fighting that left at least 145 dead, army troops supported by tanks and aircraft forced the Zapatistas to withdraw from occupied towns to more secure bases in the heavily forested highlands of Chiapas. Yet the scale of the government's military offensive and evidence of serious human rights abuses by government troops provoked intense domestic and international protests. Growing domestic opposition to the use of military force (including large demonstrations in Mexico City and other major Mexican cities in early January), indications that the EZLN enjoyed widespread political support in indigenous communities throughout central Chiapas, concern that prolonged conflict might spark armed opposition movements elsewhere in Mexico, and fear that foreign investors would lose confidence in his administration soon forced President Salinas to suspend military activities.

On January 12, 1994, President Salinas declared a unilateral ceasefire and proposed a negotiated settlement of the Chiapas conflict. He appointed Manuel Camacho Solís (the former mayor of Mexico City and Colosio's chief rival for the 1994 presidential nomination) as "commissioner for peace and reconciliation in Chiapas." By early March, Camacho had reached a tentative peace agreement with the Zapatistas. The "Accords for a Dignified Peace in Chiapas" pledged a significant increase in government social welfare (education, health care, housing) and infrastructure (improved roads and communications infrastructure) spending in Chiapas, resolution of long-standing peasant demands for land, explicit legal sanctions for discrimination against indigenous peoples, and a degree of local administrative autonomy for indigenous communities.

Just as the shock waves produced by the Zapatista uprising began to subside and the Salinas administration appeared to recover the political initiative,[36] Luis Donaldo Colosio was assassinated at a campaign rally in Tijuana on March 23, 1994. Government spokesmen initially claimed that the gunman, a *maquiladora* worker named Mario Aburto Martínez, had acted alone. However, in early April the special prosecutor in charge

---

[35]The Zapatista challenge was an all-the-more-telling indictment of the Salinas administration's economic and social policies because more PRONASOL funds had been expended in Chiapas than in any other state.

[36]Between January and mid-March 1994 there was intense speculation in Mexican political circles that Camacho would capitalize on the public attention generated by his role as government representative in the Chiapas peace negotiations by declaring his candidacy for the presidency. At times, the prospect of a Camacho candidacy overshadowed Colosio's presidential campaign. Only on March 22 did Camacho publicly announce that he would not run for the presidency (*New York Times*, March 23, 1994, p. A6).

of the case announced four additional arrests and indicated that as many as seven individuals (several of whom had close ties to the Baja California state police) had collaborated to kill Colosio.[37] Widespread public speculation about who might have masterminded the apparent conspiracy significantly complicated President Salinas's effort to impose a second PRI candidate. Indeed, the struggle that raged between Salinas's political and economic allies and PRI traditionalists over the selection of Colosio's successor was remarkably public.[38] In the end, however, Salinas retained sufficient political strength to control the nomination process. A week after the Colosio assassination, he designated Ernesto Zedillo Ponce de León (an economist with a Ph.D. from Yale University, who had served as both minister of planning and budget and minister of education in the Salinas cabinet before resigning his government position to manage Colosio's presidential campaign) as the PRI's presidential candidate.[39]

In the wake of these political shocks, the Salinas administration came under still greater domestic and international pressure to speed the pace of political liberalization. The result was a still more extensive electoral reform.[40] Legislation adopted in May 1994 further limited direct government and PRI influence over the Federal Electoral Institute (IFE),[41] provided for independent examination of voter registration lists, lowered the ceiling on campaign spending, permitted foreign observers to witness elections, banned the use of public funds and government personnel to benefit the PRI, and established a special prosecutor to

---

[37] *New York Times*, April 5, 1994, p. A1. The special prosecutor in the case subsequently issued a report stating that Aburto had in fact acted alone. This finding was greeted by widespread public skepticism, prompting President Salinas to order a sweeping reexamination of the case. For details, see *New York Times*, July 14, 1994, p. A1, July 15, 1994, p. A6.

[38] *New York Times*, March 28, 1994, p. A2, March 30, 1994, p. A1; *Economist*, April 2, 1994, p. 40.

Concerns regarding Mexico's economic and political stability appear to have shaped the succession struggle. Zedillo, who had played a prominent role in refinancing large Mexican private firms' foreign debt in the wake of Mexico's 1982 financial crisis, was evidently the candidate preferred by the domestic and foreign business communities. Moreover, a constitutional provision requiring that a presidential candidate resign government office at least six months prior to his election effectively barred some potentially strong rivals.

[39] The EZLN reacted to the political uncertainty created by the Colosio assassination by suspending negotiations with the government. It subsequently rejected the settlement proposed by the Salinas administration, arguing that the matters under discussion did not satisfy its demand for democratic change at the national level. For details, see *New York Times*, April 23, 1994, p. A4, June 13, 1994, pp. A1, 4, July 30, 1994, p. A3.

[40] This legislation originated in a "Pact for Peace, Democracy, and Justice" which the government and opposition parties negotiated in the immediate aftermath of the Chiapas revolt. See Whitehead, this volume.

[41] For example, the reform initiative increased the independence of the Federal Electoral Institute by creating an eleven-member governing board, six of whose members were distinguished "citizen magistrates" without ties to the government or political parties.

pursue those accused of electoral fraud.[42] Taken together, the four electoral reform laws enacted in 1990, 1993 (two different sets of changes), and 1994 formally established much more equal terms of interparty competition.

SHIFTING PATTERNS OF STATE-SOCIETY RELATIONS

The heightened prominence of opposition parties and increased electoral competitiveness in Mexico in the 1980s and early 1990s paralleled, and in part reflected the consequences of, significant changes in state-society relations. The successful transition from an import-substitution model of economic development to one focused on export promotion would seemingly imply a reordering or a reaccommodation of the coalition of social actors supporting the Mexican regime. One key issue is the extent to which important changes in relations between social actors and the state are the product of economic restructuring, or whether they derive from political developments that follow a logic distinct from transformations in the economic sphere. Another concern is the extent to which changes *within* different social actors themselves and in their relations with the state somehow facilitate the adoption or consolidation of neoliberal economic reforms.

The Salinas administration actively sought to redefine important aspects of state-society relations. This section examines the ways in which these relations were altered, whether the Salinas government succeeded in creating and consolidating new bases of social support for market reforms and the regime, and what implications these changes might have for future regime change in Mexico.

CHANGES IN STATE-SOCIETY RELATIONS

The Salinas government attempted more actively than any presidential administration since the 1930s and 1940s to transform state-society relations. Prior to this, however, and throughout most of the 1980s, it was the economic crisis more than any overt government effort to redefine the state's role and its relations with different groups that shaped the actions of various elements of Mexican society. In some instances, the inability of state officials to respond adequately to popular needs left a vacuum that, particularly in urban areas, was filled by autonomously organized social movements. Paul Lawrence Haber (this volume) argues that it was the de la Madrid administration's neglect of housing needs, especially in the aftermath of the 1985 Mexico City earthquakes, that spurred the formation of some of Mexico's strongest urban popular movements. In other cases, the combination of economic constraints and

---

[42]For evidence that the May 1994 reforms were only partially implemented before the August 1994 general elections, see *New York Times*, August 19, 1994, pp. A1, 4.

state officials' unwillingness or inability to entertain certain types of demands compelled social actors to alter their bargaining strategies. For example, the de la Madrid government's refusal to accede to organized labor's wage demands caused the labor movement to alter its negotiating strategy during the early years of the economic crisis. Rather than focusing on wage increases, the "official" labor movement led by the Confederation of Mexican Workers concentrated its efforts on gaining greater protection for the individual worker as consumer. In the country-side, too, state officials discouraged demands for land distribution, a policy that forced many rural organizations to focus on agricultural production issues and which generated divisions among them.

By the late 1980s and early 1990s, however, state officials initiated more directed efforts to alter the state's economic and social role. In a number of areas, the Salinas administration sought to reduce the extent of state regulation. For example, the government shifted from sector-wide price supports for rural producers to more focused initiatives such as PROCAMPO, a program that provided direct subsidies to small-scale agricultural producers. The National Solidarity Program also repre-sented an effort to redirect government social policy away from broadly inclusive public welfare programs toward programs that directed state resources to specific constituencies in poor communities.

A reduction in state regulation was consistent with the administra-tion's neoliberal orientation. Nevertheless, some policy changes and some aspects of state reform were driven mainly by partisan electoral considerations—especially the government's efforts to neutralize the electoral threat posed by the Cardenista opposition—rather than by the requirements of neoliberal economic restructuring. From the perspec-tive of government officials, more precisely targeted public programs would ease the social costs of economic adjustment, which were widely believed to have contributed heavily to the opposition vote in the 1988 elections. These programs also promised to create identifiable constitu-encies for the government's policy initiatives and build new bases of support for the regime.

President Salinas was compelled to innovate in this area because the most immediate challenge he faced was to dilute the powerful political threat that the 1988 electoral results posed to the legitimacy of his administration. The 1988 elections had demonstrated the extent of the public's dissatisfaction with the PRI and pointed to the real possibility that a center-left party, headed by Cárdenas, could consolidate durable support and pose a continuing threat to the ruling party. Moreover, the Cardenista campaign had successfully tapped into some of the PRI's traditional bases of support among workers and the urban poor, thereby underscoring the need for significant reform of the party. One of Salinas's first tasks, then, was to bring these sectors back into a relationship with the state (if not yet the PRI) and to isolate them from the new party that Cárdenas and his supporters were forming.

Among the most important strategies that the new government adopted in pursuit of this goal was the policy of *concertación social* (social concertation). *Concertación* was to represent a new form of state-society relations, one in which the state established problem-solving partnerships with social organizations. By advocating *concertación*, the Salinas administration simultaneously sought to isolate those groups that still opposed it, convey a sense that the new government was willing to open a dialogue with those groups that had previously been excluded from policy circles, and indicate the proper channel through which societal interests should present their demands.

The Salinas administration proceeded to extend offers of "dialogue" to targeted organizations, and it drew up agreements (*convenios de concertación*) between the government and independent social movement organizations. Some of the first agreements signed were with urban popular movements. The 1989 *convenio* with the Popular Defense Committee (CDP) in Durango bore immediate political fruit by helping to drive a wedge between the Cardenista camp and some of the autonomous popular movements that had supported Cárdenas during the 1988 elections (see Haber, this volume). Similarly, in the labor sector the government's focus on social concertation was interpreted as a gesture of support for the leader of the Mexican Telephone Workers' Union (STRM) and his efforts to form a new labor federation that might compete with the long-dominant CTM. For many groups, concertation represented a shift in the state's relationship with society, toward an arrangement in which state officials sought to forge targeted, problem-solving relationships with social organizations that demonstrated some degree of autonomy and the technical capacity to undertake specific projects.[43]

The best-known and perhaps most distinctive social policy implemented by the Salinas administration was the National Solidarity Program. Funds from the government's sale of state enterprises were channeled into community projects that were ostensibly developed in conjunction with local Solidarity committees. Official pronouncements touted PRONASOL as an efficient poverty-alleviation program that sought to transform state-society relations by encouraging citizens to design and implement community development and public works projects. Some evaluative studies, however, indicate other—even contrary—results. For instance, contrary to official claims, PRONASOL funds were often directed to organized groups—that is, to those organizations with "superior technical capacity" and bargaining power, not to the weakest and poorest groups. One consequence was that the program strength-

---

[43]It is important to note, however, that this policy did not mean an end to state repression. Labor unions, urban protest groups, rural organizations, and opposition party activists often encountered violent state responses to their demands.

ened existing organizations and deepened the gap between the organized and the unorganized (Haber, Fox, this volume).

Moreover, the government often channeled PRONASOL funds to areas where voters had supported Cárdenas in 1988, lending some credibility to critics' claims that the Salinas administration used the program to undermine the opposition's electoral base (Molinar Horcasitas and Weldon 1994). Program administrators also placed political conditions on the distribution of PRONASOL funding in some areas. Resources often went to those organizations that would prove "cooperative"—in other words, those that would refrain from open opposition to the PRI or the government (Haber, this volume). Most important, PRONASOL provided incentives for autonomous organizations to focus on local community development projects, rather than on national political demands or the construction of independent political alliances.

PRONASOL embodied key elements of the administration's proposed "new" relationship with society. This relationship was to consist of a state that was pluralistic in its relations with social groups, one that established ties to groups outside of the ruling party's traditional sector organizations—even at the expense of the latter and of political parties in general. For example, the CTM and the National Peasants' Confederation (CNC), which long enjoyed a privileged political position as official sectors of the PRI, were forced to compete for resources with more autonomous social organizations. In many cases, membership in the PRI was no longer a requirement for access to state resources. Policies such as these further weakened the regime's traditional social bases and the governing party's electoral coalition at a time when alternative sources of political support were not yet consolidated.

Although the Salinas administration established relationships with some organizations that could be considered democratic, the government's more pluralistic relations with societal interests did not necessarily indicate greater official support for more democratic forms of representation within these organizations. Nor did this approach signal state encouragement of independent forms of political expression. Rather, state officials' relations with a greater variety of social organizations reflected pragmatic concerns more than a new commitment to democracy. For instance, not only did Salinas administration officials maintain strong control over labor strikes, but several important labor conflicts involving workers' struggles for democratic union representation were repressed. In other cases, state officials and employers collaborated to impose more flexible industrial relations policies in the workplace, actions that sometimes undermined union democracy.[44]

---

[44] Among the most important of these conflicts were those that occurred at the Ford Motor Company's Cuautitlán plant, the Tornel Rubber Company, Modelo Brewery, Volkswagen, and the Cananea (Sonora) copper mines. For a discussion of these cases, see Cook n.d.; La Botz 1992.

Even as state officials developed ties with a broader range of societal interests during the Salinas years, they narrowed the scope of issues open to negotiation. Democratically governed social organizations had access to government resources if they were willing to concert with the state on local-level, "technical" problems directly affecting them. In the labor sector, for example, the Salinas government pursued somewhat contradictory agendas: support for more politically independent (and, at least in the past, more militant) unions, while conducting its overall relations with the labor movement in such a way that there was "less real negotiation than before" (de la Garza, this volume).

Furthermore, the state's relations with social actors were strongly influenced by both Salinas's personalistic style of governing and the institutional power of the presidency. Salinas, adopting a leadership style reminiscent of that practiced by former president Luis Echeverría, attempted to step "outside the system" in order to change it in the wake of the 1988 elections. In so doing, Salinas transferred popular perceptions of illegitimacy from his government to the PRI and successfully portrayed himself as a reformer struggling against hard-line interests within the party (see Dresser, this volume). Salinas's ability to manipulate this distinction between the party and his government depended on his effective use of the considerable powers afforded to the federal executive under the Mexican system. His attacks on "official" labor leaders, for example, were among a series of actions taken near the beginning of his term that marked Salinas as a strong president willing to employ his executive authority to change the system by punishing political enemies and hard-line opponents of reform. Moreover, Salinas's close personal identification with the National Solidarity Program (including weekly trips to different states to inspect PRONASOL projects and distribute funds) both bolstered his personal popularity and reinforced presidentialism (Bailey 1994: 117–19; Cornelius, Craig, and Fox 1994b: 14; Dresser 1991).

The strongly presidentialist character of the Salinas administration (a phenomenon noted by several authors in this volume) was in part a product of Salinas's efforts to build a political defense against the negative consequences of his administration's economic policies, some of which harmed the entrenched interests of key sectors of the president's own party. Dresser (this volume), for example, argues that a reinvigorated presidentialism reflected Salinas's quest for increased state autonomy during a period of rapid economic restructuring. In this sense, developments in Mexico in the late 1980s and early 1990s roughly paralleled those in some other Latin American countries (especially Argentina and Peru) where incumbent presidents sought to enhance their executive authority in order to implement neoliberal economic reforms. Yet strengthened executive authority poses difficult questions where democratization is concerned, an issue that has elicited a range of different opinions. For some analysts, a strong president is necessary to promote democratic reform against the resistance of state and local political bosses and other hard-line elements within the ruling party (Cornelius 1994). For others, presidentialism is one of the key obstacles to democratization (Garrido 1989; Meyer 1989).

In the shorter term, Salinas's personalist style of governing had important implications for the character of state-society relations. For example, his use of executive powers to reshape relations with different social actors encouraged the leaders of mass organizations to develop ties directly with him rather than with the PRI. This was especially true of some union leaders who, in a political environment that was generally hostile to labor, negotiated directly with the president for official recognition and political protection (Cook 1994). Leaders of urban popular organizations such as the CDP in Durango pursued similar tactics (Haber, this volume). Although this kind of direct relationship with the president is certainly not without precedent in Mexico, the relative decline of other sources of leverage or mediation (such as political representation in the PRI) makes stronger dependence on the executive a more significant political phenomenon.

In an important sense, social actors' heightened dependence on personalized relations with the president for organizational gains and survival indicated a serious weakening of key political institutions— especially the ruling party—that have long supported and legitimated the regime. Rather than reflecting a broad commitment to political beliefs such as those embodied in revolutionary nationalism or a pragmatic set of calculations regarding long-term political inclusion (such as state-subsidized organizations' claims of a "right" to political representation in the PRI), such ties to the federal executive reflected momentary, highly pragmatic, inherently unstable "alliances" based on specific bargaining relationships. In this context, one must ask whether personalistic ties forged between independent social actors and Salinas could represent the first step toward the creation of new bases of social support for market reforms and the regime.

CHANGES AMONG SOCIAL ACTORS

One way to answer this question is to examine the effects of the Salinas administration's policies on key social actors and to evaluate their responses to state officials' attempts to redefine state-society relations. There are two reasons why it is important to focus on changing relations between the state and mass actors. First, mass actors such as labor unions and peasant organizations have long comprised the Mexican regime's principal bases of social support. Second, a number of independent organizations have emerged within these sectors in the last two decades. Many of their members threw their support behind Cárdenas in the 1988 elections, giving their actions and their relationship to the regime an added political significance.

A wide variety of social organizations exists within different sectors, ranging from independent popular groups that emerged in the 1970s and 1980s to "official" sectoral organizations such as the CTM and the CNC which are more closely identified with the regime. It is, therefore, difficult to generalize by sector about the character of state-society relations. Indeed, even those organizations that could be labeled politically "independent" vary greatly in terms of their strategies and political orientation. Furthermore, many of these groups—both autonomous social movements and "official" organizations closely allied with state elites—have been undergoing a significant process of reorganization. Yet in spite of differences such as these, many independent social organizations were forced to respond to a similar set of circumstances in the late 1980s and early 1990s. Changes in the state's approach to these organizations had a significant impact on their strategies and, in some cases, their internal organization.

In the first instance, most popular organizations had to determine what position to take vis-à-vis Cárdenas's 1988 presidential campaign and the political aftermath of the elections. In the weeks and months after the elections, Cárdenas called for his supporters to reject the new government's overtures, while the Salinas administration demonstrated a willingness to channel resources to many organizations that had previously been politically marginalized. In practice, popular organizations adopted a range of strategic responses to this conjuncture. For example, Haber (this volume) discusses how the Assembly of Neighborhoods in Mexico City chose to remain loyal to the PRD, even when offered an opportunity to form its own political party and even when the price for loyalty to the political opposition was a decline in its own membership. In contrast, the Popular Defense Committee (CDP) in Durango was among the first groups to negotiate a *convenio de concertación* with the Salinas government. The CDP also left the PRD coalition and, along with other organizations and with the backing of the Salinas administration, formed a new political party (the Labor Party, PT) in order to compete in local and national elections. Other organizations, including the National Union of Autonomous Regional Peasant Organizations (UNORCA), refused to adopt a partisan position during the elections and continued their established practice of negotiating with state officials (Fox, this volume).

Those popular organizations that eventually decided to participate in state-sponsored programs shifted both their overall strategies and specific tactics in response to the Salinas administration's willingness to establish a dialogue and enter into specific agreements defined around community-based projects. For example, Fox (this volume) refers to the "new political pragmatism" evident among many rural organizations during this period as they moved to take advantage of state resources while simultaneously struggling to retain their autonomy and manage internal dissent. One challenge such organizations faced was to propose projects and alternative policies that stood a chance of being adopted (*ser propositivo*), rather than simply to contest government proposals or adopt confrontational strategies based on principle—a more common approach during the 1970s and early 1980s. This meant that many organizations occupied a large "gray area," not only in terms of strategy and tactics but also in terms of their degree of representativeness and their political affiliation. Fox points out that older distinctions between "official" and "independent" social organizations (the former category referring to state-subsidized and PRI-affiliated organizations and the latter to those groups not affiliated with the ruling party) are no longer very useful in differentiating among rural groups. Indeed, to the extent to which PRI affiliation is no longer a condition for access to state resources and ties to political parties do not accurately depict the specific policy positions taken by different organizations, these categories may have become less relevant in other sectors as well.

Direct negotiations between the government and popular organizations over local projects decentralized in practice the terrain on which dialogue (and conflict) took place. The opportunity to qualify for PRONASOL funds, for example, encouraged urban popular movements "to relegate national considerations to a lower priority in favor of concentrating on their own organizational development" (Haber, this volume). In the labor sector, issues related to productivity in the workplace (including the right to information, problems associated with the introduction of new technologies, worker training, workplace participation, and so forth) became the key point of negotiation for many unions (de la Garza, this volume). Popular organization politics, more so than party politics, is concerned with local issues and the immediate satisfaction of concrete demands. The Salinas administration's willingness to discuss such demands with previously marginalized groups soon after the 1988 electoral challenge helped to prevent the consolidation of broader opposition political alliances.

The shift in state officials' approach to dealing with popular organizations, and the change in strategy that some organizations adopted in turn, generated tensions between these organizations and the PRD, between popular organizations and the state, and both among and within these organizations. In the first case, strains between the PRD and many popular organizations that had supported Cárdenas's 1988 presidential campaign stemmed in part from the different priorities held by party leaders and social movements (Bruhn n.d.). In particular, the new opposition party's need to consolidate an identity distinct from the PRI conflicted with many organizations' need to negotiate with the state to secure benefits for their membership. According to Haber (this volume), the PRD's unwillingness to acknowledge the imperative of popular organizations to meet their members' needs by accepting public resources quickly led to conflict. The fact that some organizations had both struck deals with the government and, in the process, distanced themselves from the PRD further undermined the likelihood of future electoral alliances with Mexico's most important leftist party.

Popular organizations also found that their new relationship with the state raised a number of other thorny—and classic—problems. One of these concerned the degree to which their organizational autonomy was compromised by accepting state support. Although popular groups needed government resources (housing, potable water, paved roads, financial credit, and so forth) in order to sustain themselves organizationally and maintain membership support, reliance on the state for such resources often threatened their ability to make decisions autonomously, especially with regard to their strategy and political alliances.[45] As Fox points out in his chapter in this volume, defining a clear political or civic identity could endanger a popular organization's access to political elites and to the discretionary resources they controlled.[46]

Moreover, the Salinas administration's strategy of *concertación* and many popular groups' willingness to strike deals with the government generated significant divisions both among and within these organizations. Government representatives singled out those that participated in state programs as more "modern," pragmatic, and reasonable organizations, able to recognize the "change in terrain" and shift their strategies accordingly. Those that did not participate were labeled "confrontational," stuck in an earlier period when politics was more polarized. Within popular organizations, participation in government programs often generated tensions between leaders and rank-and-file members. Indeed, the more democratic or representative these organizations were, the greater the likelihood of such problems. Rural organizations' support for modifications of Article 27 of the Constitution was a case in point; opposition to the Salinas administration's plans meant loss of access to government resources, yet leaders who supported the reform risked alienating their membership (Fox, this volume).

Whether the practice of concertation between the state and popular organizations during the Salinas years merely constituted a form of co-optation, or whether participation of this kind reflects a more pragmatic yet still independent vision among popular organization leaders, are

---

[45]The alternative was perhaps best exemplified by the Assembly of Neighborhoods, a member of the urban popular movement. As noted above, its loyalty to the PRD and its commitment to a national political strategy cost it access to state resources and ultimately led to a decline in its membership (Haber, this volume).

[46]It is important to acknowledge, however, that tensions between popular organizations and the PRD were also the product of struggles over organizational autonomy, especially over the terms under which these organizations would participate in a political movement and the threat that such participation posed to their operational autonomy.

questions that are not easily answered. Leaders of the CDP, for example, claimed that they were practicing "situational politics" and that they could simply "take back" their autonomy whenever they chose (Haber, this volume). Moguel (1994: 176) points out that for some sectors of the left that participated in PRONASOL, the program represented more than a matter of pragmatism and a temporary coincidence of particular interests. Rather, it allowed them to "struggle against corporate and cacique interests" and "change the relationship between society and the state," long-time political goals for much of the social left.

In this context, conventional conceptions of co-optation may obscure more than they illuminate about new patterns of state-society relations. Participation in state programs under Salinas may well reflect organization leaders' beliefs that they were simply furthering their own social and political agenda, and that at least in the short term some of their goals coincided with those of reformist elements within the state bureaucracy. Participation of this kind (with its inevitable compromises and trade-offs) may also reflect the conflicting imperatives that movement leaders must face in both satisfying member demands and avoiding co-optation, as well as the limited number of choices (political and strategic) that popular organizations have traditionally had in Mexico. From this perspective, the absence thus far of a viable political party alternative in Mexico, the worldwide erosion of socialism as an economic and political project, and the still powerful role of the Mexican state in controlling key political and economic resources greatly limit the options of popular organizations that wish to survive.

Even if social concertation as practiced during the Salinas administration succeeded in undermining social actors' ability to form alliances with the political opposition, it remains to be seen whether the new, tentative alliances forged between heretofore independent popular organizations and the state will translate into medium- or long-term support for the regime. Although some groups may have gained materially and politically from their closer relationship with the state, evidence concerning the larger significance of these ties is mixed. On the one hand, Salinas administration spokespersons for PRONASOL claimed that the program "empowered" average citizens by encouraging them to design and help implement community-based projects. Academic analysts have also found evidence for the program's empowering potential among both organizations and unorganized individuals (Cornelius, Craig, and Fox 1994a; Haber 1994). A key issue, however, is how citizen empowerment in everyday activities will be reflected at the polls. Are the new clients created by PRONASOL likely to replace the regime's traditional allies as its principal bases of social and electoral support?

Many observers attributed the PRI's electoral comeback in 1991 in part to the popularity of PRONASOL. It is, however, difficult to separate the effect that PRONASOL might have had on voters' attitudes from the impact of other important developments, including a sharp decline in the rate of inflation (Cornelius, Craig, and Fox 1994b: 13–14). Moreover, several considerations raise unresolved questions about the long-term success of the Salinas administration's efforts to secure the political loyalty of PRONASOL beneficiaries and of those groups engaged in concertation with the government. The fact that PRONASOL was initially portrayed as a government—not a PRI—program (indeed, a program closely identified with Salinas, and later with Colosio,[47] personally); that beneficiaries of PRONASOL-sponsored public works did not always identify these projects with the program (Contreras and Bennett 1994: 286); and that many of the program's beneficiaries were autonomous social organizations that may in fact have used access to its resources to strengthen their independence and regional political influence all make it unlikely that PRONASOL successfully consolidated durable support for the ruling party. The personalist politics behind the program, the death of Colosio, and the way in which the Chiapas uprising at least partially discredited the program raise further questions concerning PRONASOL's future.

At the same time, there is also increasing uncertainty concerning the political loyalty of the regime's older social allies. In spite of the Salinas administration's early efforts to disassociate the government from traditional sectors of the ruling party, state elites were obliged to rely on these sectors for political support in a context of rapid, dramatic economic change and unstable political coalitions. The appearance of widespread public support for the administration's inflation-fighting economic package (the PECE), the North American Free Trade Agreement, and ejido reform was particularly important for the Salinas administration. However, the support of old allies has become increasingly contingent upon receiving significant economic or political concessions from the state. The "official" labor movement, for example, became an important (if reluctant) supporter of Salinas's economic program and his choice of successor—but at the price of the administration's retreat on key aspects of PRI reorganization and labor law reform. Concessions such as these may strengthen the political position of major sociopolitical organizations, perhaps leading to future conflicts as issues that were postponed for political reasons are revisited in a future administration.

However, continued reliance on the political support of traditional sector organizations raises difficult questions. How long can the Mexican regime retain the old-style corporatist features that have defined it for so long? Are such corporatist arrangements ultimately compatible with the country's new model of economic development and a more democratic regime? There is considerable debate on these points. Some

---

[47] As minister of social development, Colosio was the cabinet member directly responsible for the program.

observers argue that central features of Mexican corporatism—especially state intervention and tutelage over certain sectors of society, such as the labor movement, and the top-down controls that state-subsidized organizations exercise over their members—are strongly incompatible with a modern economy that must rely on the increased participation, initiative, and productivity of its workforce in order to thrive. Other analysts speak of a "reformed corporatism" or "neocorporatism" that differs from the previous form in that social organizations' relations with the PRI are more flexible or formally disappear, even though their central link with the government is maintained through the presidency (de la Garza, this volume).

One important question in this debate is whether some elements of the old corporatist system survive because hard-line elements (particularly leaders of the "official" labor movement and traditional PRI politicians with sectoral ties—the "dinosaurs") have successfully resisted change. Or have established corporatist arrangements remained in place because they contribute to economic and political elites' attempts to maintain political control and limit instability during a period of significant economic change? The distinction is an important one. The former interpretation suggests that older patterns of state-society relations in Mexico are gradually being replaced in a transition toward a different kind of regime. However, the latter interpretation implies that those features of Mexico's authoritarian regime that enabled elites to maintain control over workers and other mass actors will remain important elements of a more electorally competitive political regime because those groups that substantially strengthened their position in the 1980s and early 1990s—the private sector and technocrats—favor them.[48]

If, however, one accepts that the Salinas administration's concertation with popular organizations led to the greater empowerment of at least some of these groups, changes in state-society relations during the late 1980s and early 1990s may have helped instead to generate multiple empowered groups with significant local or regional political influence, organized elements that are capable of challenging the PRI machine in local and state elections. Indeed, there is evidence that this has already begun to happen in places like Durango, where a CDP candidate won the mayoralty of the capital city in 1992 (Haber, this volume). The material benefits and increased prestige and influence that popular organizations derive from access to public resources, and their consequent ability to meet membership demands, make it quite possible that these groups will exercise their local or regional power to influence future electoral contests. As a result, the Salinas administration may

---

[48]Future political change along these lines would be consistent with the "modernization of authoritarianism" scenario outlined by Cornelius, Gentleman, and Smith (1989: 40–41), in which Mexico's political elites would engage in an "energetic revival and remodeling of the existing corporatist system."

have helped to undermine PRI control in some regions, thus creating a political environment in which the PRI dominates at the national level but in which state and municipal elections are increasingly won by opposition parties in alliance with regional social movements. This is a model of political liberalization that may prove acceptable to factions of the national political elite that are willing to make such concessions at the expense of local PRI bosses.[49]

In sum, economic and political reforms undertaken in the 1980s and early 1990s alienated some of the regime's old allies, without yet securing the proven loyalty of new clients. In an environment in which established links between the electorate and political parties have weakened (the dealignment that Klesner describes), the Salinas administration's efforts to de-link the regime's traditional social bases from the PRI could render their future electoral support increasingly unstable, especially as political alternatives present themselves. During the Salinas years, state elites forged new ties with social actors outside the ruling party, but it remains to be seen whether these relationships can be institutionalized in the form of durable support for the PRI. In a context of decreased citizen tolerance of authoritarianism and increased pressures for full electoral democracy, the presence of dealigned social actors can be crucially important, contributing centrally to the emergence of a more competitive regime.

CONCLUSION

Whether authoritarian regimes are necessarily more capable than democratic governments of implementing economic stabilization measures and market reforms is a subject of continuing debate.[50] There is little doubt, however, that Mexico's experience with economic liberalization in the 1980s and early 1990s was strongly shaped by the survival of authoritarian political controls. Such key features of the postrevolutionary regime as the incumbent president's capacity to name his successor, the federal executive's dominance of the legislature, "official" party and state control over the electoral process, and state administrative restrictions on nonelectoral forms of mass participation persisted during much of this period despite a significant increase in electoral competitiveness and heightened activity by relatively autonomous societal groups.

The fact that the scope and speed of economic liberalization considerably exceeded the extent and pace of political opening in Mexico had important consequences both for the process of economic restructuring

---

[49]It is also a model of political liberalization whose expected outcome has been likened to India's political system, in which the Congress Party dominates national politics but other political movements enjoy considerable autonomy at the state and local levels (Cornelius, Gentleman, and Smith 1989: 41–43).

[50]For contrasting views, see Skidmore 1977 and Remmer 1990, 1993.

and for democratization. The sequencing of economic and political liberalization altered the balance of forces within the coalition that has traditionally supported the regime. In particular, privatization, deregulation, and the shift toward an export-oriented development model increased the influence of the private sector (especially large manufacturers and financial interests) within Mexico's governing coalition and privileged those businesses most closely linked to the international market. At the same time, the preservation of tight political controls on organized labor limited unions' capacity to redress the negative effects of market reforms. State administrative restrictions on labor participation also eased employers' implementation of changes in the production process that further undermined the bargaining power of workers. It is, moreover, doubtful that the Mexican government's economic stabilization measures and market reforms—policies that produced very high social costs in the form of a dramatic decline in real wage levels, increased unemployment in major industries, and a more unequal pattern of income distribution—could have been pursued as consistently in a democratic political context.

In some ways, economic reform strengthened the position of Mexico's ruling political elite. Generally improved economic prospects, effective control of inflation, and consumers' access to a much broader range of imported goods won considerable public support for market reforms and the Salinas administration. Renewed growth (even at a rate that was low by historical Mexican standards) and the sale of state-owned enterprises increased the financial resources available to government officials in their efforts to address social problems that were exacerbated by economic crisis and restructuring. The popularity of government social programs such as PRONASOL and PROCAMPO most likely contributed to the PRI's electoral recovery in the early 1990s. Broader public support for neoliberal policies also narrowed the programmatic options for opposition parties, making it more difficult for the PRD to convince voters that it represented a distinctive alternative. Of course, political factors (the strength of institutions such as the presidency, the continued loyalty of such traditional allies as the "official" organized labor movement, the regime's capacity for renewal from within through regular rotation in office) also contributed significantly to the governing elite's capacity to maintain control while limiting the scope and regulating the pace of political liberalization. But under less favorable economic conditions, the Mexican regime would probably have been much more vulnerable to uncontrolled pressures for political change.

Market reforms did not, however, succeed in delaying pressures for democratization, despite President Salinas's reliance on economic performance rather than political reform to legitimate his government. Certainly by the late 1980s the social dislocations caused by rapid economic restructuring contributed directly to challenges to authoritarian political controls. Popular dissatisfaction with austerity policies and the negative consequences of economic liberalization reinvigorated opposition parties, accelerated the partisan dealignment of Mexican voters, and contributed to the increased competitiveness of electoral contests. The Mexican government's implementation of market reforms also began to erode the regime's traditional bases of mass support and created new lines of division within the political elite. Moreover, the passage of the North American Free Trade Agreement substantially increased international scrutiny of domestic political practices. One consequence is that elements of future economic success (especially investor confidence and continued access to foreign capital) may become increasingly contingent upon the credibility of electoral outcomes.

The future prospect of improved economic performance may well restore public confidence in the governing political elite's ability to guide economic policy. However, in the absence of democracy it is unlikely that the Mexican regime can ever fully recoup the legitimacy that postrevolutionary governments once enjoyed. This challenge looms even larger now that neoliberal reformers have broken decisively with statist economic policies, thereby sharply curtailing their capacity to employ revolutionary nationalism to bind together ideologically a heterogeneous governing coalition. The philosophy of "social liberalism" espoused by the Salinas administration has yet to gel as an inclusive ideology capable of legitimating the Mexican regime in the way that revolutionary nationalism once did.[51]

Can one conclude, then, that the direct and indirect political consequences of economic restructuring have significantly increased the odds that Mexico will eventually make a successful transition to democracy? The evidence is mixed. The erosion of the regime's traditional social bases, greater disunity within Mexico's governing political elite, and more vigorous party competition all increase the likelihood of regime change. Opposition parties on both the left and right have developed a stronger organizational presence in many regions, and since the mid-1980s they have had significant practical experience in governing at state and municipal levels. At the same time, changes in state-society relations under the Salinas administration—including a greater degree of pluralism in the state's relations with social actors, the reduced relevance of ties to the "official" party for access to state-sponsored programs, and efforts to redefine the role of traditional sectoral organizations within the PRI— potentially increase the autonomy of major social actors vis-à-vis the state and the ruling party. These developments may hold important implications for national politics.

The 1994 election campaign clearly exemplified the political importance of a more vigorous civil society. Much more active involvement by

---

[51]A transcript of President Salinas's March 4, 1992, address to the PRI outlining the philosophy of social liberalism appears in *Examen* 35 (April 1992): 19–22.

nongovernmental organizations, together with new electoral rules and heightened international attention to political developments in Mexico, created a more open electoral environment, even though irregularities continued to be a significant problem in some areas.[52] Citizen organizations such as the Civic Alliance (AC), a coalition of some four hundred nongovernmental organizations committed to promoting clean elections, played an especially important role in monitoring the election process.[53] Similarly, the Democratic National Convention convened by the Zapatista Army of National Liberation in early August 1994—an event attended by some five thousand representatives from a wide range of urban, rural, and indigenous organizations, as well as by prominent intellectuals—demonstrated the commitment of broad sectors of the social and political left to free elections and a peaceful democratic transition.[54] Perhaps more than anything else, it was increased citizen interest and involvement in the electoral process (reflected in a record voter turnout of 77.7 percent) that set 1994 apart from any previous election in Mexican history.

Other developments during the late 1980s and early 1990s were, however, less conducive to the construction of democracy. The exercise of strong presidential authority that was a persistent feature of the Salinas administration undermined public credibility of the electoral process by, for example, substituting deals negotiated between the executive and opposition parties for the outcomes produced by legal procedures. Strong state controls over labor protest and other forms of nonelectoral participation greatly restricted mass organizations' room for maneuver and undercut efforts by some of their members to democratize their organizations. Social programs such as PRONASOL encouraged popular organizations formally aligned with the opposition to focus predominantly on local agendas, thus helping to diffuse and (at least until the Chiapas rebellion) postpone national debate over democracy during much of the Salinas period. Similarly, Salinas's success at fostering personalistic ties with some independent labor unions, urban popular movements, and other social organizations increased their dependence on the government and reduced the likelihood that they would forge alliances with opposition parties.

---

[52] For more on this aspect of the elections, see *El Financiero International*, August 29–September 4, 1994, p. 13, September 5–11, 1994, p. 15; *New York Times*, August 25, 1994, p. A3, September 27, 1994, p. A7; *Perfil de la Jornada*, September 20, 1994, pp. 1–4.

[53] Members of the Civic Alliance scrutinized voter registration lists, commissioned opinion polls concerning citizens' familiarity with the electoral process, published analyses showing that campaign coverage by electronic media was heavily biased in favor of the ruling PRI, and coordinated the activities of thousands of domestic and foreign election observers. In addition, the Alliance conducted a "fast count" of electoral results on the basis of a stratified national survey of polling places.

[54] For details, see *Los Angeles Times*, August 6, 1994, p. A10; Hernández Navarro 1994.

Such developments weakened the link between increased societal pluralism and pressures for electoral democracy.

Even more important, the concentrated power of the federal executive and the persistence of close links between the state apparatus and the PRI continued to limit political competition. Most national and international observers agreed that the 1994 elections were generally free of the extensive fraud and intimidation that had characterized many past elections. However, most observers also concurred that the outcome was heavily influenced by the PRI's tremendous advantages in resources, media coverage, and organizational capacity—advantages the ruling party derived from its privileged relationship with the state. Not only did PRI candidates benefit greatly from some communities' reliance on government social programs such as PRONASOL and PROCAMPO, but the party also continued to draw on government personnel and state resources to support its campaign despite laws expressly prohibiting such practices.[55] The ruling party also dominated mass media coverage, a situation produced both by the PRI's disproportionate access to financial resources for media advertising and by the close relationship between state officials and privately owned media companies.[56]

Moreover, the PRI enjoyed tremendous mobilizational advantages because of entrenched clientelist relations. In many poor neighborhoods and rural areas, local party leaders conditioned citizens' access to social services, government subsidies, and other benefits on their expressed commitment to vote for the ruling party.[57] Government-allied labor unions also demonstrated in 1994 that they retained the capacity to mobilize an important proportion of their members in support of the "official" party (*San Francisco Chronicle*, August 17, 1994, p. 1A). Indeed, because Ernesto Zedillo won the PRI's presidential nomination under difficult circumstances and had a comparatively short time in which to organize a national campaign, his victory owed much to the continued mobilizational capacity of the PRI's traditional social allies. These deeply rooted relationships, a product of the PRI's long incumbency, remained largely unaffected by electoral reforms.

---

[55]The advantages accruing to the PRI are discussed in *El Financiero*, July 6, 1994, p. 3; *Porqué*, July 6, 1994, pp. 13–15; *Reforma*, July 15, 1994, p. 4.

[56]See the detailed analyses of media coverage in Academia Mexicana de Derechos Humanos 1994a, 1994b, 1994c.

[57]For examples, see *El Financiero International*, August 29–September 4, 1994, p. 13, and *New York Times*, August 28, 1994, section 4, p. 4. Some of the electoral reforms adopted in 1993 and 1994 (especially measures designed to protect the secrecy of the vote and prohibitions against campaigning near polling stations) made it more difficult for government officials and PRI organizers to enforce compliance. Nonetheless, one should not underestimate the impact that this kind of voter coercion may have on citizens who are not fully aware of their political rights.

Given these considerations, what would be required for a successful transition to democracy in Mexico? Although specific organizational arrangements and political practices vary significantly from one country to another, there is considerable consensus on the minimum criteria for democracy. The elemental requirements are the guarantee of (often constitutionally defined) individual rights, including freedoms of expression and association and especially protection against arbitrary state action; frequently scheduled, fairly conducted elections in which all citizens are fully free to participate (universal suffrage) in the selection of representatives who will exercise public authority; and institutionalized procedures to ensure that citizens can through the rule of law hold rulers accountable for their public actions.[58] These requirements are mutually reinforcing.

Unlike many instances of regime change, the transition to democracy in Mexico does not involve a shift from a military junta or some other regime of exception to an elected civilian government. Indeed, one of the principal challenges in the Mexican case is to make effective the rights and procedures already formally guaranteed by the 1917 Constitution and by law. More specifically, changes in three areas would be necessary to bring about a successful transition from authoritarian to democratic rule: the effective guarantee of citizenship rights; reforms that ensure equality of opportunity in electoral competition; and the elimination of political controls on association and nonelectoral forms of mass participation. The common challenge in each of these areas is to limit the power of the Mexican state in its relations with individual citizens and the organizations of civil society.

Despite a long tradition of constitutional rule and formal guarantees of individual liberties, the exercise of citizenship rights remains a highly contested political arena in Mexico. There are no significant legal restrictions on the rights to vote or campaign for public office. But political activists are victims of physical violence or forced disappearance sufficiently frequently to cause many individuals to view the public expression of political views as risky.[59] Nor does the legal system adequately guarantee citizens equal treatment under the law.[60] In these and other contexts, the goal must be to make individuals secure against arbitrary government actions and increase the

---

[58]This definition draws on discussions in Dahl 1971: 2–9, 1982: 10–11; O'Donnell and Schmitter 1986: 7–11; Schmitter and Karl 1991; Rueschemeyer, Stephens, and Stephens 1992: 10, 43–44. Schmitter and Karl (p. 81) emphasize that democracy also requires that popularly elected officials be able to exercise their constitutional authority without overriding pressure from unelected officials, especially the military.

[59]For specific accounts, see among others Amnistía Internacional 1986; Americas Watch 1990; Centro de Derechos Humanos Miguel Agustín Pro Juárez 1992.

[60]For a careful analysis of Mexico's legal system, see Rubio, Magaloni, and Jaime 1994.

effectiveness of institutionalized procedures through which citizens can hold agents of the state (including the police) accountable for their public actions.

Additional legal modifications and procedural changes are also required to equalize the terms of electoral competition in Mexico. In particular, much more needs to be done to reduce disparities between the PRI and opposition parties in terms of access to mass media (especially radio and television) and financial resources. At the same time, further steps are necessary to increase the autonomy of electoral authorities, especially at state and local levels. The most significant issue in this area is the continued close relationship between the Institutional Revolutionary Party and the state apparatus. Only when the PRI has begun to compete for power without undue advantages from incumbency will electoral contests become meaningful tests of parties' programmatic positions and candidates' personal appeal. Civil service reforms that limit the extent of partisan control over middle- and lower-level positions in the state bureaucracy would facilitate such a change by making it more difficult for the ruling party to mobilize public employees on its behalf. Whether meaningful change can occur in this area while PRIístas control the federal executive remains an open question.

Equally important, the liberalization of electoral procedures in Mexico has not yet been accompanied by a significant reduction in political restrictions on the right of association and nonelectoral forms of mass participation. Establishing the political independence of social organizations is a decisive step in the transition from authoritarian to democratic rule. Respect for associational rights is crucial to democratization because what is at stake is the capacity of citizens to organize in defense of their interests without fear of state intervention or sanction (Fox 1994: 152). Increased associational autonomy vis-à-vis the state is also vitally important for holding government officials accountable for their public actions.[61] Yet in Mexico, state officials continue to exercise strong controls over association (especially by workers and peasants) and nonelectoral forms of mass participation such as strikes.

A core question concerning democratization in Mexico is whether these multiple challenges can be resolved incrementally, or whether the transition to democracy will necessarily involve a sharp break with past political practices. The trajectory followed by Mexican

---

[61]Schmitter (1992: 430, 437) correctly emphasizes that undemocratic patterns of state-society relations may persist long after electoral rules change. He notes that interest associations created under authoritarian rule may themselves seek to maintain their privileged relationship with the state. As a result, the transition to more democratic patterns of state-society relations may be quite slow, especially where regime change does not involve a dramatic political rupture.

governments thus far has clearly been one of incremental liberalization, a process that has contributed to greater political openness but which has not yet produced democracy. The outcome of the 1994 elections (a larger margin of victory for the PRI than had been expected in a context of high voter turnout and extensive national and international election observation[62]), as well as the virtual certainty that the Institutional Revolutionary Party will dominate the federal government until the end of the century, necessarily raise questions concerning whether Mexico's governing political elite will continue to follow this gradualist path in lieu of democratization (Loaeza, this volume). Indeed, much public debate in the aftermath of the 1994 elections focused on whether Zedillo, the PRI's victorious presidential candidate, would be inclined or able to push forward the process of political reform (see, for example, Castañeda 1994b; Cornelius and Bailey 1994).

The extent to which future political reforms will move Mexico closer to democracy will depend heavily on the vigilance and continued pressure of organized groups in civil society. Major opposition parties and pro-democracy civic organizations will play an especially significant role in this regard. The presence of a greater number of autonomous popular organizations can also help erode clientelist practices and exact greater accountability from political parties and state officials. Moreover, the actions of such groups may well determine whether the government will seek peaceful, negotiated outcomes or resort to repression in response to crises (such as the Chiapas uprising) that erupt if the pace of incremental reform proves too slow.

There are many analysts, however, who question whether a democratic regime can emerge in Mexico as the result of a gradual process of political reform. In particular, they doubt the outcome of a piecemeal liberalization process overseen, ultimately, by state officials linked to the PRI. For these critics, the credibility of elections may remain in doubt so long as the PRI continues to win. As Whitehead (this volume) cogently argues, a successful democratic transition would require convincing evidence that the regime's "basic operating principles" had changed. The minimal conditions for satisfying this criterion would be clear separation

---

[62]The PRI won 50.2 percent of the valid votes cast in the presidential election, while the PAN won 26.7 percent and the PRD won 17.1 percent. If one includes annulled ballots and those cast for unregistered candidates, the PRI's share was 48.8 percent of the total presidential vote. Using these same criteria, Salinas's proportion of the total vote in 1988 was 48.7 percent.

The other officially registered parties competing in the 1994 federal elections were the Socialist Popular Party (PPS), the Party of the Cardenista Front for National Reconstruction (PFCRN), the Authentic Party of the Mexican Revolution (PARM), the Mexican Democratic Party (PDM), the Mexican Green Party (PVEM), and the Labor Party (PT). Of these six parties, only the Labor Party surpassed the 1.5 percent minimum threshold established by law to retain its official registration; it received 2.8 percent of the valid votes cast in the presidential election. For vote totals by party, see IFE 1994.

of the PRI from the state bureaucracy, stronger limits on presidential authority, and unambiguous signs that the Institutional Revolutionary Party—a party born in power—was at last prepared to lose.

Even so, for many observers democracy in Mexico will only be possible—and made manifest—when the presidency finally passes from PRI to opposition party control. This is, however, a problematic test of democratic transition because other, intermediate scenarios may also signal that significant advances toward the effective guarantee of citizenship rights, equality of opportunity in electoral competition, freedom of association, and increased openness in nonelectoral participation have taken place. These scenarios include coalition government at the national level (with one or more opposition parties controlling key cabinet positions) and an opposition majority in the Congress, which could put an end to presidential dominance of the legislature.

Democratization, of course, may not proceed evenly at all levels and in all arenas. Even opposition control of the federal executive need not substantially (nor automatically) affect established state controls over nonelectoral forms of mass participation or extend full citizenship rights to traditionally marginalized sectors of the population. For these reasons, attention to changing relations between key social actors and the state may remain an important basis for assessing the contradictory and highly contingent process of political transition in Mexico.

REFERENCES

Academia Mexicana de Derechos Humanos. 1994a. "El gasto de campaña en la televisión mexicana," July 26.
———. 1994b. "Las elecciones federales en México según los noticieros *24 Horas* de Televisa y *Hechos* de Televisión Azteca, 30 de mayo a 30 de junio de 1994."
———. 1994c. "The Media and the 1994 Federal Elections in Mexico," May 19.
———. 1994d. *Special Bulletin: Conflict in Chiapas*, various issues.
Aguilar Camín, Héctor, and Lorenzo Meyer. 1993. *In the Shadow of the Mexican Revolution*. Austin: University of Texas Press.
Americas Watch. 1990. *Human Rights in Mexico: A Policy of Impunity*. Washington, D.C.
Amnistía Internacional. 1986. *México: los derechos humanos en zonas rurales*. London.
Bailey, John. 1994. "Centralism and Political Change in Mexico: The Case of National Solidarity." In *Transforming State-Society Relations in Mexico: The National Solidarity Strategy*, edited by Wayne A. Cornelius, Ann L. Craig, and Jonathan Fox. U.S.-Mexico Contemporary Perspectives Series, no. 6. La Jolla: Center for U.S.-Mexican Studies, University of California, San Diego.
Bruhn, Kathleen. n.d. "The Seventh-Month Itch? Neoliberal Politics, Popular Movements, and the Left in Mexico." In *Rethinking Participation in Latin America*, edited by Carlos Vilas, Katherine Roberts-Hite, and Monique Segarra. Forthcoming 1995.

Camp, Roderic A. 1980. *Mexico's Leaders: Their Education and Recruitment*. Tucson: University of Arizona Press.

————. 1985. "The Political Technocrat in Mexico and the Survival of the Political System," *Latin American Research Review* 20:1:97–118.

Carpizo, Jorge. 1985. *El presidencialismo mexicano*. Mexico City: Siglo Veintiuno.

Castañeda, Jorge G. 1994a. "The Other Mexico Reveals Itself in Chiapas," *Los Angeles Times*, January 6.

————. 1994b. "¿Qué pasó?" *Proceso* 930 (August 29): 44–46.

Centro de Derechos Humanos Miguel Agustín Pro Juárez. 1992. *Informe anual 1991: los derechos humanos en México*. Mexico City.

Contreras, Oscar, and Vivienne Bennett. 1994. "National Solidarity in the Northern Borderlands: Social Participation and Community Leadership." In *Transforming State-Society Relations in Mexico: The National Solidarity Strategy*, edited by Wayne A. Cornelius, Ann L. Craig, and Jonathan Fox. U.S.-Mexico Contemporary Perspectives Series, no. 6. La Jolla: Center for U.S.-Mexican Studies, University of California, San Diego.

Cook, Maria Lorena. 1994. "State-Labor Relations in Mexico: Old Tendencies and New Trends." In *Mexico Faces the 21st Century: Change and Challenge*, edited by Donald E. Schulz and Edward J. Williams. New York: Praeger.

————. n.d. "Mexican State-Labor Relations and the Political Implications of Free Trade," *Latin American Perspectives*. Forthcoming, winter 1995.

Cordera, Rolando, and Carlos Tello. 1981. *La disputa por la nación*. Mexico City: Siglo Veintiuno.

Córdova, Arnaldo. 1973. *La ideología de la revolución mexicana: la formación del nuevo régimen*. Mexico City: Era.

Cornelius, Wayne A. 1994. "Mexico's Delayed Democratization," *Foreign Policy* 95 (Summer): 53–71.

Cornelius, Wayne A., and John Bailey. 1994. "Perspective on Mexico: Six More Years on a Tightrope?" *Los Angeles Times*, August 23.

Cornelius, Wayne A., and Ann L. Craig. 1988. *Politics in Mexico: An Introduction and Overview*. Reprint Series, no. 1. Rev. ed. La Jolla: Center for U.S.-Mexican Studies, University of California, San Diego.

Cornelius, Wayne A., Ann L. Craig, and Jonathan Fox, eds. 1994a. *Transforming State-Society Relations in Mexico: The National Solidarity Strategy*. U.S.-Mexico Contemporary Perspectives Series, no. 6. La Jolla: Center for U.S.-Mexican Studies, University of California, San Diego.

————. 1994b. "Mexico's National Solidarity Program: An Overview." In *Transforming State-Society Relations in Mexico: The National Solidarity Strategy*, edited by Wayne A. Cornelius, Ann L. Craig, and Jonathan Fox. U.S.-Mexico Contemporary Perspectives Series, no. 6. La Jolla: Center for U.S.-Mexican Studies, University of California, San Diego.

Cornelius, Wayne A., Judith Gentleman, and Peter H. Smith. 1989. "Overview: The Dynamics of Political Change in Mexico." In *Mexico's Alternative Political Futures*, edited by Wayne A. Cornelius, Judith Gentleman, and Peter H. Smith. Monograph Series, no. 30. La Jolla: Center for U.S.-Mexican Studies, University of California, San Diego.

Dahl, Robert A. 1971. *Polyarchy: Participation and Opposition*. New Haven, Conn.: Yale University Press.

————. 1982. *Dilemmas of Pluralist Democracy: Autonomy vs. Control.* New Haven, Conn.: Yale University Press.

Dresser, Denise. 1991. *Neopopulist Solutions to Neoliberal Problems: Mexico's National Solidarity Program.* Current Issue Brief Series, no. 3. La Jolla: Center for U.S.-Mexican Studies, University of California, San Diego.

Dulles, John W.F. 1961. *Yesterday in Mexico: A Chronicle of the Revolution, 1919–1936.* Austin: University of Texas Press.

Fox, Jonathan. 1994. "The Difficult Transition from Clientelism to Citizenship: Lessons from Mexico," *World Politics* 46:2 (January): 151–84.

Garrido, Luis Javier. 1982. *El partido de la revolución institucionalizada: la formación del nuevo estado en México, 1928–1945.* Mexico City: Siglo Veintiuno.

————. 1987. "El partido del Estado ante la sucesión presidencial en México, 1929–1987," *Revista Mexicana de Sociología* 49:3 (July–September): 59–82.

————. 1989. "The Crisis of *Presidencialismo.*" In *Mexico's Alternative Political Futures,* edited by Wayne A. Cornelius, Judith Gentleman, and Peter H. Smith. Monograph Series, no. 30. La Jolla: Center for U.S.-Mexican Studies, University of California, San Diego.

Haber, Paul. 1994. "Political Change in Durango: The Role of National Solidarity." In *Transforming State-Society Relations in Mexico: The National Solidarity Strategy,* edited by Wayne A. Cornelius, Ann L. Craig, and Jonathan Fox. U.S.-Mexico Contemporary Perspectives Series, no. 6. La Jolla: Center for U.S.-Mexican Studies, University of California, San Diego.

Haggard, Stephen, and Robert R. Kaufman, eds. 1992. *The Politics of Economic Adjustment: International Constraints, Distributive Conflicts, and the State.* Princeton, N.J.: Princeton University Press.

Hansen, Roger D. 1971. *The Politics of Mexican Development.* Baltimore, Md.: Johns Hopkins University Press.

Hernández Navarro, Luis. 1994. "Aguascalientes: el túnel del tiempo," *La Jornada,* August 11.

Hirschman, Albert O. 1968. "The Political Economy of Import-Substituting Industrialization in Latin America," *Quarterly Journal of Economics* 82:1:1–32.

IFE (Instituto Federal Electoral). 1994. "Resultados definitivos de los cómputos distritales, elección de Presidente de los Estados Unidos Mexicanos." Mexico City: IFE, August 28.

INEGI (Instituto Nacional de Estadística, Geografía e Informática). 1985. *Estadísticas históricas de México.* 2 vols. Mexico City: Secretaría de Programación y Presupuesto.

La Botz, Dan. 1992. *Mask of Democracy: Labor Suppression in Mexico Today.* Boston, Mass.: South End Press.

Lustig, Nora. 1992. *Mexico: The Remaking of an Economy.* Washington, D.C.: Brookings Institution.

Meyer, Lorenzo. 1989. "Democratization of the PRI: Mission Impossible?" In *Mexico's Alternative Political Futures,* edited by Wayne A. Cornelius, Judith Gentleman, and Peter H. Smith. Monograph Series, no. 30. La Jolla: Center for U.S.-Mexican Studies, University of California, San Diego.

Middlebrook, Kevin J. 1986. "Political Liberalization in an Authoritarian Regime: The Case of Mexico." In *Latin America.* Vol. 2 of *Transitions from Authoritarian Rule: Prospects for Democracy,* edited by Guillermo O'Donnell, Philippe C.

Schmitter, and Laurence Whitehead. Baltimore, Md.: Johns Hopkins University Press.

———. 1988. "Dilemmas of Change in Mexican Politics," *World Politics* 41:1 (October): 120–41.

———. n.d. *The Paradox of Revolution: Labor, the State, and Authoritarianism in Mexico*. Baltimore, Md.: Johns Hopkins University Press. Forthcoming 1995.

Moguel, Julio. 1994. "The Mexican Left and the Social Program of Salinismo." In *Transforming State-Society Relations in Mexico: The National Solidarity Strategy*, edited by Wayne A. Cornelius, Ann L. Craig, and Jonathan Fox. U.S.-Mexico Contemporary Perspectives Series, no. 6. La Jolla: Center for U.S.-Mexican Studies, University of California, San Diego.

Molinar Horcasitas, Juan. 1994. "Changing the Balance of Power in a Hegemonic Party System." In *Institutional Design and Democratization*, edited by Arend Lijphart and Carlos Waisman. Boulder, Colo.: Westview.

Molinar Horcasitas, Juan, and Jeffrey A. Weldon. 1994. "Electoral Determinants and Consequences of National Solidarity." In *Transforming State-Society Relations in Mexico: The National Solidarity Strategy*, edited by Wayne A. Cornelius, Ann L. Craig, and Jonathan Fox. U.S.-Mexico Contemporary Perspectives Series, no. 6. La Jolla: Center for U.S.-Mexican Studies, University of California, San Diego.

O'Donnell, Guillermo, and Philippe C. Schmitter. 1986. *Tentative Conclusions about Uncertain Democracies*. Vol. 4 of *Transitions from Authoritarian Rule: Prospects for Democracy*, edited by Guillermo O'Donnell, Philippe C. Schmitter, and Laurence Whitehead. Baltimore, Md.: Johns Hopkins University Press.

Ortiz Mena, Antonio. 1980. "Acción sindical, salarios e inflación," *Trimestre Económico* 180:2.

Philip, George. 1992. *The Presidency in Mexican Politics*. New York: St. Martin's Press.

Purcell, Susan Kaufman. 1975. *The Mexican Profit-sharing Decision: Politics in an Authoritarian Regime*. Berkeley: University of California Press.

Remmer, Karen L. 1990. "Democracy and Economic Crisis: The Latin American Experience," *World Politics* 42:3 (April): 315–35.

———. 1991. "The Political Impact of Economic Crisis in Latin America in the 1980s," *American Political Science Review* 85:3 (September): 777–800.

———. 1993. "The Political Economy of Elections in Latin America, 1980–1991," *American Political Science Review* 87:2 (June): 393–407.

Rodríguez, Victoria E., and Peter M. Ward. 1994. *Political Change in Baja California: Democracy in the Making?* Monograph Series, no. 40. La Jolla: Center for U.S.-Mexican Studies, University of California, San Diego.

Rodríguez Guillén, Raúl, and Juan Mora Heredia. 1993. "El agotamiento del autoritarismo con legitimidad y la sucesión presidencial," *El Cotidiano* 58 (October–November): 22–28.

Roett, Riordan. 1993. "At the Crossroads: Liberalization in Mexico." In *Political and Economic Liberalization in Mexico: At a Critical Juncture?* edited by Riordan Roett. Boulder, Colo.: Lynne Rienner.

Rubio, Luis, Beatriz Magaloni, and Edna Jaime, eds. 1994. *A la puerta de la ley*. Mexico City: Cal y Arena.

Rueschemeyer, Dietrich, Evelyne Huber Stephens, and John D. Stephens. 1992. *Capitalist Development and Democracy*. Chicago: University of Chicago Press.

Schmitter, Philippe C. 1992. "The Consolidation of Democracy and Representation of Social Groups," *American Behavioral Scientist* 35:4–5 (March–June): 422–49.

Schmitter, Philippe C., and Terry Lynn Karl. 1991. "What Democracy Is . . . and Is Not," *Journal of Democracy* 2:3 (Summer): 75–88.

Scott, Robert E. 1959. *Mexican Government in Transition*. Urbana: University of Illinois Press.

Skidmore, Thomas E. 1977. "The Politics of Economic Stabilization in Postwar Latin America." In *Authoritarianism and Corporatism in Latin America*, edited by James M. Malloy. Pittsburgh, Penn.: University of Pittsburgh Press.

Smith, Peter H. 1979. *Labyrinths of Power: Political Recruitment in Twentieth-Century Mexico*. Princeton, N.J.: Princeton University Press.

———. 1992. "The Political Impact of Free Trade on Mexico," *Journal of Interamerican Studies and World Affairs* 34:1 (Spring): 1–25.

Solís, Leopoldo. 1985 [1970]. *La economía mexicana: retrospección y perspectivas*. Mexico City: Siglo Veintiuno.

Story, Dale. 1986. *Industry, the State, and Public Policy in Mexico*. Austin: University of Texas Press.

Thorp, Rosemary. 1992. "A Reappraisal of the Origins of Import-Substituting Industrialization, 1930–1950," *Journal of Latin American Studies* 24 (Quincentenary Supplement): 181–95.

Vernon, Raymond. 1963. *The Dilemma of Mexican Development*. Cambridge, Mass.: Harvard University Press.

Villarreal, René. 1976. *El desequilibrio externo en la industrialización de México, 1929–1975: un enfoque estructuralista*. Mexico City: Fondo de Cultura Económica.

Zaldívar Lelo de Larrea, Arturo F. 1993. "La propuesta priísta de reforma política," *Examen* 51 (August): 8–10.

PART II

Economic Restructuring and Political Change in Mexico

2

The Outlook for Mexican Economic Development in the 1990s

Víctor L. Urquidi

THE EXPERIENCE OF THE 1980S

During the 1980s, in order to avoid hyperinflation and financial, economic, and social chaos, Mexico had to carry out a severe macroeconomic adjustment program. The origins of this experience are to be found largely in the public sector's excessive domestic and external indebtedness in the 1970s and 1980s. However, elements of basic macroeconomic disequilibrium, among them the unprecedented expansion of productive but inefficient public enterprises over at least two decades, were also involved. Contributing factors were an increase in state subsidies for investment, production, and consumption without fiscal coverage, and the maintenance of an overvalued currency in the face of domestic inflation rates that were well above international ones.

In the 1970s a climate of mistrust had developed on the part of business interests, and private domestic investment had shrunk significantly. The boom that followed in the state-owned oil sector, with all its dynamic consequences, did not alter that climate. When in late 1981 it became clear that a change was imminent in the external conditions facing the Mexican economy—a lower price for crude oil exports and difficulty in obtaining further foreign credits—the business sector drew back further. Capital flight followed, and an entirely unmanageable financial and balance-of-payments crisis was at hand by early 1982. The situation worsened visibly by midyear.

This text, revised in early 1994, takes account of recent data, particularly figures for 1992 and 1993.

There was a clear lack of consistency in macroeconomic policy during the 1970s, with the economy being pushed to an unsustainable rate of expansion. The potential benefits of a high rate of growth quickly evaporated, and the 1980s witnessed increasing income inequality as the domestic market contracted and unemployment rose. All this occurred because, despite an international economic environment in which output and trade expanded, political factors—both domestic and external—were not highly favorable to the Mexican economy. The internal political dimension—the absence of real representative and participatory democracy—contributed to instability in economic and financial policy and, above all, to uncertainty.

The macroeconomic adjustment begun in 1982—initially labeled a "structural" adjustment, without actually being one—took a long time to implement due to the change in administration in December. After a promising start, it was sidetracked by the appearance of a trade surplus. This surplus arose not from an increase in exports sufficient to meet the very high costs of servicing the external debt, but rather from a marked decline in imports when domestic investment collapsed. Real wages also declined sharply, and the precipitous drop in the dollar value of the Mexican peso helped to halt imports of consumer goods. The price of crude oil held fairly stable in international markets; had it not, Mexico's crisis would have been much deeper, perhaps forcing the country to default on its foreign debt. Mexico rescheduled its debt in 1983 and again in 1984, but service payments on outstanding balances did not decline. Throughout this period Mexico held to a political decision not to default. Moreover, the Mexican government did not ally openly with an emerging group of Latin American debtors.

In 1985, equilibrium had begun to more or less reassert itself as exports of manufactures increased. After a devaluation of the peso in July and a cut in public expenditures, Mexican policy makers felt secure enough to engage in a vast trade opening in the second half of the year. They applied to join GATT, and they anticipated further growth of manufactured exports. However, the steady drop in oil prices toward the end of 1985, and their collapse in the first few weeks of 1986, had not been foreseen. Nor had much progress been made toward reducing the excessive public-sector deficit. An expanding domestic debt had been largely monetized through primary expansion of the money supply. Because Mexico still depended heavily on oil exports, the early 1986 price shock was devastating: one-third of foreign exchange receipts and one-fourth of projected tax revenues were lost almost instantly. Lacking any solid backing, the Mexican peso suffered another significant depreciation, which fueled an unprecedented rate of inflation (105 percent in 1986 alone). No new external credit support became available until late in the year, after the resignation of Finance Minister Silva Herzog, whose credibility had been seriously eroded. Fortunately, the Mexican economy finally got a breathing spell in early 1987.[1]

It is not yet clear why speculation broke out in the Mexican stock and financial markets that year, generating a fourfold increase in the nominal value of assets within a few months. A partial explanation might be that the real rate of interest (and of equivalent returns) had been allowed to rise very considerably in order to attract foreign funds. Also, the U.S. Department of the Treasury had launched the Baker Plan, which was intended to help some developing countries restructure their foreign debt. This initiative was to start with Mexico. But in October 1987 the weakest link in the chain gave way: the domestic purchasing power of Mexico's money and wages had declined heavily, and confidence had again almost vanished. As world stock market prices fell, Mexico suffered a similar decline coupled with a strong capital outflow driven by fear of yet another devaluation, which did in fact materialize. Inflation ended at 159 percent for the year, almost 50 percent above the annual rate in 1986. In December 1987 alone, prices rose by 15 percent. If this monthly rate had persisted, inflation could have exceeded 435 percent for the following twelve-month period. By December 1987, the external debt had risen to U.S.$107 billion, or 33 percent more than the outstanding balance at the end of 1981.

Given the proximity of the 1988 presidential and congressional election campaigns, the Mexican government decided in December 1987 to draw up and implement a "pact" between government, labor unions, and business, aimed at putting a brake on inflation and inducing a stabilization process. The supporting pillars of the Economic Solidarity Pact for 1988 were two: (1) the foreign exchange reserves recently accumulated through new external loans under the Baker Plan (about U.S.$13 billion gross), and (2) the rigorous contraction of public-sector spending to the point where an actual *primary fiscal surplus* would be generated equal to about 8 percent of gross domestic product (GDP).

These two strategic elements were reinforced with a policy of wage lags which further depressed domestic demand. Agreement was reached to regulate the prices of basic consumer goods, to raise major public-sector rates and reduce subsidies, and to keep the exchange rate stable. This is what in contemporary economics is called an intensive incomes policy; some described it as "shock therapy." Few countries have been fully successful with it, especially those that applied "unorthodox plans" without a sharp decline in the fiscal deficit. For instance, neither Argentina under the Austral Plan nor Brazil with the Cruzado Plan attained any measure of price stability.

In Mexico, the rate of inflation decreased fairly quickly. By mid-1988 the monthly rate was down to about 2.5 percent (equivalent to an annualized

[1] There are many detailed accounts of the 1981–1986 period; see, for example, Lustig 1992 and annual reports from the Banco de México. CIEMEX-WEFA regularly makes available basic data and analyses of Mexico's current economic situation and prospects.

rate of 30 percent). The stabilization policy adopted under the pact (which focused on maintaining a primary budget surplus) was instrumental in achieving the final and successful renegotiation of the external debt in 1989 within the terms of the Brady Initiative. The terms of the debt agreement permitted savings of some U.S.$1.5 billion annually in interest payments, a reduction of some U.S.$7 billion in outstanding capital, and conversion of much of the public debt owed to banks in the United States, Canada, Western Europe, and Japan into thirty-year bonds secured by a purchase of U.S. treasury bonds. These arrangements prompted new loans to Mexico and, especially, larger amounts of direct foreign private investment. The subsequent strengthening of public finances, combined with the privatization of large industrial enterprises and commercial banks, also contributed to the building up of a substantial budgetary reserve. High real interest rates prevailed, and these in turn attracted financial investments from other countries (and some repatriation of Mexican capital). Thus foreign exchange reserves began to rise significantly.

THE EARLY 1990S

The Mexican government's attack on inflation was fairly successful, though by mid-1992 the single-digit rate sought by monetary authorities had not been reached. The estimated rate of 10–15 percent forecast for the following twelve-month period, however, ensured manageability of the short-term situation provided that other macroeconomic elements held constant. End-of-year inflation (consumer price index) in 1992 came in at 11.9 percent; the GDP deflator for 1992 was 16.3 percent. Inflation for 1993 was officially projected at 7 percent, but it was probably closer to 9 percent (nominally, at least, a one-digit inflation rate).

Trade expansion continued in 1990–1991, particularly exports of manufactures. By mid-1992 the latter accounted for close to 60 percent of aggregate commodity exports.[2] Crude oil exports, on which Mexico had depended earlier for 60 percent of its export proceeds, were now about

---

[2]The Banco de México subsequently adjusted aggregate trade statistics by adding to "normal" merchandise imports the gross value of imported inputs of *maquiladora* operations at the border and elsewhere, and by treating the gross value of *maquila* exports as similar in kind to "normal" merchandise exports. This enabled "manufactured exports" to soar statistically (see Banco de México 1993: footnote 2 and table 48). Although the Banco de México argues that this is no more than bringing the Mexican balance-of-payments presentation "into line with" the definitions of the IMF Balance of Payments Manual, this procedure exaggerates the aggregate amount of Mexico's foreign trade, especially exports of manufactures and total imports. The Banco de México no doubt took this step in anticipation of the North American Free Trade Agreement (NAFTA), given that *maquiladora* operations are subject to special U.S. customs treatment and should not be directly compared with regular exports and imports. Nevertheless, the net value of *maquila* transactions—as estimated by the value added by Mexican labor to inputs entering in-bond for processing and reexport, which was previously reported as part of "non-factor services"—has also risen rapidly in recent years, thus bringing in much needed foreign exchange.

U.S.$6.5 to $7 billion per year, closer to 30 percent of aggregate merchandise exports. The expansion in manufactured exports consisted mainly of motor vehicles, engines and autoparts, machinery in general, chemical products, iron and steel, building materials, electronic appliances, and a long list of products exported in relatively small amounts, mostly to the United States. Value added in *maquiladoras* was on the order of U.S.$4.8 billion in 1992. Migrant workers' remittances have also contributed to Mexico's improved financial situation.

Since 1989, these readjustments have been accompanied by an unprecedented, rapid increase in merchandise imports (other than *maquiladora* inputs). The ordinary merchandise trade deficit rose from U.S.$2.6 billion in 1989 to U.S.$11.3 billion in 1991. This deficit was not offset by the value added in the *maquiladora* sector plus net tourist receipts and other net current account revenues. By 1992 the current account balance of payments showed a deficit of almost 7 percent of GDP. The official explanation minimized the problem by arguing that the deficit was more than covered by the influx of direct investment capital and financial flows, which in turn contributed to an unprecedented increase in gross foreign exchange reserves—to U.S.$19 billion by mid-1992 and U.S.$23 billion by mid-1993. It was even argued, somewhat simplistically, that it was precisely the inflow of capital that produced the trade deficit (see Banco de México 1993: 14–15). This, however, amounted to turning trade theory on its head, for it left out the impact of domestic demand for imports and the effect of an increasingly overvalued currency. The "buying rate" in Mexican pesos for U.S. dollars had been kept practically fixed since November 1991.

Thus the overall macroeconomic readjustment resulted in an apparently "sound" situation. It was essentially dependent upon a rapidly expanding net inflow of external private capital in the form of both financial investments and direct foreign investments, mostly the former. To attract this inflow, monetary policy in Mexico strove to maintain both a high real rate of return and a fixed basic rate of exchange. Such a policy, however, militates against both domestic investment and a broader-based increase in exports of manufactured goods. It is likely that expectations regarding the approval of NAFTA influenced the rate of capital inflow.

At mid-1992, Mexican GDP growth for the year was still projected to be about 3.5 percent, and the trade deficit was expected to reach U.S.$17 billion. But even taking into account the net foreign exchange revenues derived from *maquiladora* operations and tourism, capital inflow of some U.S.$19 billion could only mean "breaking even" on the trade and services current deficit. Thus additional foreign exchange would be needed to meet interest payments of some U.S.$7 billion on outstanding external debt. In fact, 1992 GDP growth turned out to be only 2.6 percent, and the trade deficit rose to U.S.$20.7 billion.

The official outlook for 1993 again somewhat optimistically assumed 3.5 percent GDP growth, with 7 percent inflation. However, later updates by forecasters downsized GDP growth to barely 1.5 percent, and Minister of Finance Pedro Aspe told the Mexican Congress in mid-November that GDP growth might be as low as 1.1 percent. Inflation for the year was generally expected to be 9.5 percent (again, nominally a one-digit rate). The trade deficit rose less than originally forecast, partly as a result of slower growth in GDP. It was estimated at U.S.$21 billion, which still required a more or less equivalent capital inflow. Final data for 1993 showed 0.4 GDP growth and 8.0 percent inflation—stagnation had set in.

THE REMAINDER OF THE 1990S

With the severe slowdown in 1993, some doubts began to crop up about 1994 and the general outlook for the rest of the decade. Many have asked, what precisely is the Mexican government's strategy for this upcoming period? Apparently it is to consolidate what has been achieved in terms of a lower rate of inflation, balanced public finances, a trimmed-back public sector, an incomes policy (especially wage restrictions and containment of the expansion of the domestic market), and the quasi-stabilization of the Mexican peso in relation to the U.S. dollar.

If this is the strategy, a number of important concerns arise. First, despite the many positive aspects and some actual results of this economic-financial strategy, it has not yet generated a significant rate of expansion in the Mexican economy as a whole. In the 1989–1991 period, average GDP growth was 3.8 percent, with GDP growth per capita at about 1.8 percent. But in 1992 GDP per capita rose barely 0.6 percent, and in 1993 it actually declined by 1.0 percent. In earlier periods, GDP growth was on the order of 6 percent annually (twice the rate of population growth), and GDP per capita rose about 3 percent per year for almost two decades.

The real challenge is not merely to compare GDP growth with population expansion and draw a positive conclusion from this ratio. The basic challenge is to achieve a growth rate in upcoming years that can absorb a larger proportion of the annual increase in the labor force, estimated to be above 3 percent per year. In addition, a significant level of open unemployment and underemployment (which appeared during the adjustment of the 1980s) has carried over into 1993–1994. This must be reduced. A reasonable estimate of open unemployment in Mexico is closer to 10 percent than to the official figure of around 3 percent, which refers only to urban unemployment in some thirty cities and is based on a questionable definition of nonemployment.[3] In any event, the slow recovery of the economy during 1989–1993 has yet to generate sufficient formal employment.

Second, the minimal expansion in employment is partly a consequence of closing down both public- and private-sector enterprises, as well as the decreasing demand for unskilled labor that results as industry reorganizes and modernizes to achieve a sound international competitive position. A further factor has been the considerable difference in investment rates between the large national and transnational enterprises, on the one hand, and the vast number of small and medium-sized businesses, on the other. The latter include factories and workshops that are largely obsolete, particularly in the textile, footwear, leather, and food processing industries, and other enterprises that have not gained sufficient access to bank loans or modern technology to become competitive suppliers to the large enterprises engaged in exporting manufactured goods. Another element has been the collapse of a large part of the iron and steel industry, as well as firms producing steel products, tools, machinery, and so forth. The trade liberalization that began in 1985 has seriously affected output in many manufacturing activities, as has growing currency overvaluation. To top it all, the prevalence of inordinately high real rates of interest—15–20 percent annually—has particularly hurt medium-sized and small industrial and service enterprises and discouraged new investment in plant and technology. Manufacturing output in many branches of industry has declined or attained only modest rates of increase. The rate of expansion was low, and declining, in 1992 and 1993.

---

[3]There is already considerable controversy about these figures, which derives in part from the officially announced population census returns of 1990: 81.3 million inhabitants as of mid-March. Since earlier census data—whatever the merits of the actual census returns—were always given for July, at least 500,000 people must be added to the 1990 total.

However, further adjustments are also required. Population census data in most developing countries, particularly in those covering vast territories, are subject to revision. United Nations statisticians frequently adjust the raw data, for instance, to allow for the undercounting of infants. Demographers at El Colegio de México have determined that such underreporting may be on the order of 2 million in Mexico. Moreover, the 1990 Mexican census may have resulted in higher levels of underreporting due to the period in which it was carried out, uncertainty as to whether family heads absent from the household (temporarily elsewhere in Mexico or in the United States as migrant workers) were to be reported, and so forth. All told, about 3.5 to 4 million inhabitants should be added to the 81.3 total reported for 1990. This would result in a higher estimate of the labor force than the one derived from the lower aggregate figure. Thus the rate of labor force growth would also be higher, as would the open unemployment rate. According to reliable estimates, growth in formal-sector employment has been negligible in the last few years. In sum, the 1990 population census must be thoroughly revised, since the actual Mexican population in mid-1990 was closer to 85.8 million. Assuming close to 2 million additional inhabitants per year, we can project a population of 89.8 million by mid-1992 and 91.8 million by mid-1993. There is as yet insufficient evidence that the fertility rate, which had dropped by 40 percent between 1975 and 1990, has continued to fall at that rate over the last three years.

Third, observation of many other aspects of aggregate export data leads to the conclusion that what is lacking in Mexico is a clear boost to industrial and agricultural output that could effectively be directed to external markets. The United States represents about 70 percent of Mexican exports (excluding *maquiladora* production, which is subject to a special regime). Farm products, such as coffee and sugar, are subject to weak external demand and falling prices (exceptions to this pattern include certain fruits and fresh vegetables). Mineral exports, a minor component of the total, are stagnant. Only a few branches of manufacturing industry have succeeded in making a strong contribution to exports. Others are hampered by serious financial, management, and marketing problems, as well as by a systematic lack of information about export markets. Minor manufactures together represent a significant share of aggregate exports, though individual categories rarely exceed a U.S.$20 million threshold. NAFTA is expected to stimulate many of these exports.

Fourth, a strategy that presupposes that the trade deficit may increase indefinitely so long as enough capital inflow can be secured carries serious risks. These risks could be avoided if exports of manufactured goods were about to take off across the board under NAFTA—that is, to expand at unprecedented rates, as occurred in Southeast Asia. Such export success could be achieved if Mexico were about to enter new, high-technology export areas, or if support programs for medium-sized and small businesses lead in the short run to vast amounts of exports of intermediate and consumer goods to the United States and Canada. If this were to happen, it would have important consequences for employment in Mexico.

It might also be posited that the international price of crude oil could rise considerably in the next few years. This is not likely, given the potential for an oversupply of petroleum from the Middle East at any given moment. Some analysts believe that net returns to Mexico from tourism are about to become a major source of foreign exchange. However, this view neglects the complexities of the tourist industry in Mexico, which in any case has not had steady government support. Current net foreign exchange revenues from tourism are barely above U.S.$1.7 billion per year, and they are offset by "border transactions" (that is, short-term border-crossing expenditures), yielding a negative balance for Mexico. In another sphere, one might suppose that exports of farm products could rise from the current U.S.$2 billion annually to U.S.$5–6 billion, since Mexico still has ample farmland available, some of which is particularly suited to quality seasonal products that could be shipped to the nearby U.S. market. This, however, is doubtful for a number of reasons, among which are the institutional obstacles to Mexican farm output expansion, the high costs of marketing, and so forth.

Relative price stability and the quasi-stabilization of the (still somewhat overvalued) Mexican peso vis-à-vis the U.S. dollar may be seen as favoring increased investment. The balancing of public finances and the accumulation of budgetary reserves through privatization of public-sector enterprises may also be seen as favorable to investment, although real public investment has been declining. There may be potentially dynamic elements in industry, farming, and services, and some improvement may take place in social and economic infrastructure, where a market approach simply cannot do the job. Some manufacturing industries have also been able to raise their total factor productivity, although it most likely remains below that of Canada and the United States, or even Brazil. Productivity per manhour has also risen in many instances.

There are many signs of progress. Nevertheless, what is lacking is an overall view that—using terminology that has fallen into disuse— might be described as a "development policy." Such a policy would strategically encompass employment, strengthening the domestic market, reducing income inequality, improving social indicators, and, especially, setting priorities over the next five to ten years—what used to be called "planning." The least that could be desired is that major sectoral goals be mutually consistent, especially in light of the uncertainties generated in the domestic market by the excessive trade opening and NAFTA. Export promotion should be among the objectives of sectoral policies, but room should also be made for efficient import substitution. Competitiveness should be promoted not only in external markets, but in the domestic market as well. This does not mean adopting an ultraprotectionist stance; bringing technological modernization to the domestic market should be a goal no less important than competing in the world market. Efficient domestic production would also slow the avalanche of imports that swells the trade deficit.

Any set of global and sectoral economic objectives must be consistent with population and labor force trends, as well as with programs to raise the quality of labor, especially through education, training, health improvement, housing, and public transportation. The Mexican population continues to expand at about 2 percent annually; it is not likely to increase by less than 1.6 percent per year before the end of the century, at which time the population will total at least 107 million. The open unemployment rate may rise to 12–15 percent, due in part to the demographic momentum of recent periods. The labor force will probably continue to expand at around 3 percent per year for some time, which means that between 800,000 and 900,000 additional young people will seek formal employment each year, as opposed to the informal employment and insecurity of the underground market.

Should progress be slower than anticipated or along less consistent paths, the scenario would be less favorable. The following is an outline of what may be expected in Mexico around the year 2000.

• Mexico's incorporation into the world economy will continue through a growing volume of exports of certain manufactured goods (and perhaps farm products as well) to major markets such as the United States and the European Community, and on a smaller scale to other areas. This trend will also involve a larger flow of foreign investment into Mexico than in past decades, although it may not equal the pace set in 1991–1992. However, insertion into the world economy is likely to be selective, largely deriving from the investments and operations of transnational enterprises. The Mexican business sector is less likely to carry out large investments or assume heavy and complex risks; it also expects much higher returns and is less prepared for global competition. Small and medium-sized enterprises are less likely to participate in developing manufactured exports and, in fact, will barely be able to supply an open domestic market. It is unlikely, therefore, that they will generate much additional employment.

• Mexico's farm sector will not absorb labor. As in other countries, surplus rural labor will continue to shift to urban centers, to formal and informal services, and to the underground economy. There it will join the redundant urban manufacturing labor force, and some portion of this combined group will emigrate further, to larger Mexican cities, to employment in the *maquiladora* sector, or to the United States. In general, more of these unskilled workers will find employment in services than in manufacturing.

• The *maquiladora* sector will continue to expand beyond the border areas to other regions of Mexico as the differences between *maquiladora*-type industries and traditional manufacturing are gradually erased. Mexico will enter a "post-*maquiladora*" phase characterized by induced and managed domestic and international subcontracting, like that which takes place in all major industrial centers of the world (see Carrillo Huerta and Urquidi 1989). Moreover, many new non-*maquiladora* industrial developments in Mexico will be based on duty-free imports of intermediate goods and components, to be reexported as finished products such as motor vehicles, televisions, personal computers, and so forth. In these industries the local value added to the imported components is much larger than in the "formal" *maquiladora* along the U.S.-Mexican border.

• Crude oil exports will continue to be marginal at best and may even contract. However, Mexico can be expected to increase its imports of petroleum products, such as high-octane unleaded gasoline and other fuels, lubricants, additives, and so forth.

- Mexico's excessively open trade policy will continue to attract an invasion of foreign consumer goods and intermediate products which will displace domestic manufactured goods.

- Mexico is unlikely to escape its structural balance-of-payments problems and reach a point where deficits are manageable. Its continuing current account deficits will require a substantial net inflow of capital. However, the high yields that attract this capital also operate to dissuade domestic investment.

- In the long term, the stability of the Mexican peso (as well as the Canadian dollar) is not assured, at least not in the sense in which the European Community (EC) currencies are likely to remain fairly stable. NAFTA is not a common market and does not establish commitments such as those accruing to EC member countries.

- It is likely that the Mexican economy will continue to feel the inflationary pressures resulting from the development process and from long-standing productivity problems in manufacturing industries and in agriculture. A moderate rate of inflation is manageable if budget deficits and other conditions are kept under control.

- The demand for education, health care, and welfare services will exceed the state's basic capacity to supply them. The demand for urban services will far outpace the capacity of municipal and state government authorities to meet it. This economic and financial problem has social and political dimensions as well.

CONCLUSION

Scenarios that are less than optimum are not necessarily forecasts or predictions. However, in the years leading up to 2000 the drastic changes needed to loosen up the inertias and long-standing resistances in the Mexican economy and in Mexican society are not likely to occur. A considerable share of what is likely to happen is already contained in recent trends—for instance, in population and labor force growth—so that changes may not come about easily. Certain changes may be induced progressively with positive results. However, what is still lacking in Mexico is a global, long-term approach, one that could avoid inconsistencies and factor in the time spans of various types of investments.

In Mexico it is often said that serious consideration of the long term will begin *mañana*. But when is *mañana*? How many tomorrows will come before Mexican society is shown a project that offers some assurance of development, with steady and substantial gains in well-being?

REFERENCES

Banco de México. 1993. *The Mexican Economy 1993*. Mexico City: Banco de México.

Carrillo Huerta, Mario, and Víctor L. Urquidi. 1989. "Trade Deriving from the International Division of Production: *Maquila* and Post*maquila* in Mexico," *Journal of the Flagstaff Institute* 13:1 (April): 14–46.

Lustig, Nora. 1992. *Mexico: The Remaking of an Economy*. Washington D.C.: Brookings Institution.

3

Mexico in the 1990s:
A New Economic Miracle?
Some Notes on the Economic and Policy
Legacy of the 1980s

Jaime Ros

Mexico, like many other developing countries in Latin America and elsewhere (though perhaps faster and farther than most), has moved in recent years toward a more outward-oriented development strategy that gives greater scope to market forces and a larger economic role to the private sector. Since 1983, and even more so after 1985, the market reforms package urged by the "Washington Consensus" has been applied fully: radical liberalization of the trade and industrial policy regime, large-scale privatization of state-owned enterprises, and massive deregulation of foreign investment flows and domestic economic activities. These institutional and policy changes have taken place despite severe macroeconomic difficulties, following massive external and fiscal shocks and successive attempts at macroeconomic stabilization that involved dramatic changes in the economy's rate of accumulation, external competitiveness, and public finances.

Despite almost a decade of stagnation and macroeconomic instability, the Mexican transition stands as remarkably rapid and smooth when compared to other adjustment experiences in Latin America. The

I am grateful for comments I have received from the editors of this volume, the participants at the June 1992 seminar on "Las dimensiones políticas del ajuste estructural en México" held in Mexico City, and to Ernie Bartell, Carlos Bazdresch, Rolando Cordera, José Antonio Ocampo, Víctor Urquidi, and Samuel Valenzuela. All remaining errors are entirely my own responsibility.

virtual absence of political tensions and resistance to change stands in sharp contrast to the experience of more reluctant reformers, such as Brazil, with similar macroeconomic difficulties. And when compared to countries such as Chile and Bolivia that are also well advanced in the reform process, the dislocation and adjustment costs (beyond those of macroeconomic adjustment to external shocks) appear to be strikingly small in the Mexican case. Moreover, recent economic trends—positive per capita growth for several consecutive years, successful inflation stabilization, and massive capital inflows since 1989—have turned Mexico's adjustment model into an example to be emulated by less eager reformers.

This chapter develops three main arguments. The first section argues that, precisely because it is a unique case, the smoothness and comparative success of the Mexican experience should be attributed to a number of singular features. The country's macroeconomic structure is particularly significant in this regard, although Mexico's no-less-peculiar pattern of state-labor relations and its presidentialist system, policy management, and geopolitical advantages have clearly played an important role. The chapter's second section characterizes structural reforms as a set of nontraditional instruments designed to overcome the growing costs, throughout the decade, of the macroeconomic adjustment process itself. It is these costs, as suggested by a "political economy model" of the reform process developed in this section, that explain the acceleration of the reform drive in the second half of the 1980s. And it is the very particular nature of the macroeconomic policy trade-offs, rather than the intrinsic merits of market reforms for the allocative and dynamic efficiency of the economy, that explains the sustainability of the reform package so far. Indeed, and this is the third point, the Mexican economy entered the 1990s severely weakened—rather than strengthened—by the adjustment process of the 1980s. One implication is that, despite some recent encouraging signs, we are unlikely to see a new Mexican economic miracle. In fact, there may be little in this adjustment model (certainly less than is generally believed) to be emulated by others.

SOME SINGULAR FEATURES OF MEXICO'S ADJUSTMENT PROCESS

The external shocks of the 1980s—the 1982 debt crisis and falling terms of trade for primary commodities—created severe imbalances in both the balance of payments and fiscal accounts of the primary exporters and highly indebted countries of Latin America. Indeed, the increase in debt service placed strain on both the balance of payments and government finances, due to the fact that the public sector was often the major external debtor within these countries. Similarly, the fall in export revenues also reduced fiscal incomes because a portion of those exports often accrued to the government in the form of export taxes or public enterprise profits.

It is convenient to visualize the main forces that, as a result of the fiscal and external dimensions of the shocks of the past decade, created a potential vicious circle of macroeconomic instability and stagnation (see figure 3.1). The foreign exchange crises following the external shocks triggered currency devaluations, which in turn often further weakened public finances. This happened in two ways. First, depreciations increased the domestic currency value of foreign debt and external interest payments, thus adding to fiscal stress. Moreover, in the presence of high indexation in the wage and price system, depreciations were followed by bursts of high inflation. The latter, combined with lags in tax collection, tended to erode the real value of tax revenues (the Olivera-Tanzi effect). Public investment cuts, resulting from weakened public finances, combined with the adverse effects of high inflation on private investments, leading to economic stagnation and capital flight.

This vicious circle was set in motion, to a greater or lesser degree, in all the major debtor countries in Latin America; once in motion, the process tended to perpetuate itself well after the initial external gap created by the shocks themselves had been eliminated. Moreover, the size of the external and fiscal shocks and the severity of credit rationing faced by governments created unprecedented constraints on economic policy and, as a common characteristic of these adjustment processes, sharply reduced the effectiveness of traditional macroeconomic policy instruments. Increasing public investments by issuing domestic public debt raised the prospect of higher domestic interest rates and, because of their impact on the fiscal deficit, an unsustainable accumulation of domestic debt. Monetary financing of these deficits would generate unsustainable losses of foreign exchange reserves and, eventually, further depreciations and inflation.

In sum, macroeconomic policies operated between the Scylla of a liquidity trap in the market for foreign assets and the Charybdis of an internal debt trap in the domestic bonds market.[1] Fanelli, Frenkel, and Rozenwurcel (1990: 47) illustrate the problem with an illuminating comparison to the Keynesian concept of a liquidity trap:

> When the entrepreneurs' expectations regarding the future evolution of the economy are pessimistic, this same pessimism induces them to allocate funds in

---

[1]For a detailed and formal analysis of the resulting ineffectiveness of fiscal and monetary policy, see Ros 1991a. The recent literature on three gap models has dealt extensively with this subject. See Bacha 1990; Carneiro and Werneck 1988; Fanelli, Frenkel, and Winograd 1987; Fanelli, Frenkel, and Rozenwurcel 1990; Ros 1991b; Taylor 1991; as well as the literature on external and internal transfer problems (in particular, Ortiz and Noriega 1988; Reisen and van Trotsenburg 1988).

FIGURE **3.1**

The Macroeconomic Instability-Stagnation Dynamic

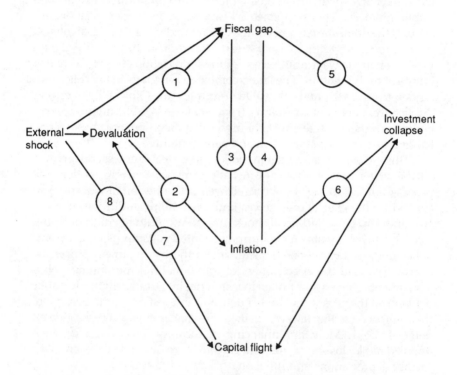

1. Depreciation-induced real wealth loss
2. Wage/price indexation
3. Monetization of fiscal deficits
4. Olivera-Tanzi effects
5. Fiscal constraints on public investment
6. Uncertainty and resource misallocation effects
7. Increased current account adjustment
8. Default risk and fiscal rigidities

financial assets and away from productive investment. In such a situation, as Keynes has shown, monetary policy is either inefficient or ineffective and cannot reverse pessimistic expectations. And this is so because the economy's problems lie in the state of the entrepreneurs' animal spirits. This analogy with the Keynesian liquidity trap, however, ends here. Traditional Keynesian medicine would not work in an open economy with the characteristics of Latin American economies. . . . In the present Latin American situation, the agents facing a highly unstable macroeconomic environment show an increased liquidity preference for foreign assets and consequently the demand for domestic financial assets is very low, a few percentage points of GDP in many Latin American countries. So, if the government sought to finance even a small increment in its deficit in the domestic financial market (its only possible choice since the foreign credit market is rationed), the pressure on the demand for the increased supply of financial assets would be so strong that it would induce a disequilibrium in the market which would ultimately foster capital flight.

Another aspect of the ineffectiveness of conventional macroeconomic policies emerged whenever the vicious circle, or spiral, entered into a high-inflation regime. As illustrated by figure 3.1, a regime of high inflation is characterized by multiple interactions among inflation, public finances, and monetary growth. Not only do inflationary pressures acquire a momentum of their own as indexation mechanisms become more and more entrenched in the wage and price formation systems, but they also come to exert strong influence on fiscal deficits (through Olivera-Tanzi effects, in particular, as already mentioned) and the financing of the fiscal deficit. They do so by affecting money demand and, more generally, the composition and term structure of the public debt. In these conditions, the money supply process becomes endogenous (in other words, it is jointly determined with the rate of inflation) and largely escapes the control of monetary authorities. Due to these interactions and the resulting inflation inertia, any one-dimensional approach to price stabilization—based on monetary, fiscal, exchange rate, or other particular policy instruments—is bound to be inefficient, and it is very likely to be ineffective as well. This is the basic insight of the heterodox literature on inflation and stabilization, and the case for employing an incomes policy to bring high inflation under control.

Overcoming the ineffectiveness of conventional policy instruments in the post-1982 period has been the central problem facing Latin

American governments, a problem many have yet to solve. The following discussion examines the Mexican experience from this perspective: Why and how did Mexico eventually escape from the vicious circle of macroeconomic instability and stagnation?

THE PRESENCE OF AN OIL RENT, THE ABSENCE OF A WAGE CONSTRAINT

The strength and perversity of the mechanisms and feedback effects described in figure 3.1, and the resulting constraints on domestic policies, varied substantially across Latin American countries depending on specific national characteristics. Mexico's macroeconomic adjustment problem combined two features: very severe balance-of-payments difficulties (a result of the debt crisis, as in other major debtor countries, but aggravated by the collapse of petroleum prices and the initial inelasticity of Mexico's exports) and a relatively minor fiscal adjustment problem, whose solution was greatly facilitated by the existence of a sizeable foreign exchange surplus in the government's income and expenditure accounts and the relative absence of policy constraints on the wage front.

Let us begin with the latter, the adjustment of public finances. In the Mexican experience, the existence of massive petroleum export revenues in the fiscal accounts (which more than offset interest payments on external debt) meant that currency depreciations, by increasing the domestic currency value of these foreign exchange earnings, had the effect of increasing the government's fiscal revenues. Just as in the case of copper revenues in Chile and coffee export tariffs in Colombia, petroleum revenues in Mexico (and Venezuela) turned the exchange rate adjustments required to restore external balance into an automatic mechanism of fiscal adjustment. The importance of this feature can hardly be exaggerated: devaluations of the peso in 1982 explain almost entirely the increase in Mexico's public savings that year (a real revaluation of the government's external surplus equivalent to 2 percent of GDP); currency depreciations in 1982 in Argentina and Brazil (which lacked such export/fiscal revenues) produced, respectively, a 5 percent and a 2 percent expansion of the fiscal deficit as a proportion of GDP.[2]

Mexico's initial conditions in product, labor, and financial markets — a tradition of moderate inflation, a low degree of indexation in the wage/price system, and substantial room for maneuver in wage policy — also tended to mitigate the inflationary repercussions of depreciations and to facilitate the adjustment of public finances, at least when compared to high-inflation countries with entrenched indexation mechanisms and

---

[2]The estimates for Brazil and Argentina are found in Reisen and van Trotsenburg 1988. They correspond to the depreciation-induced increase in the real value of external interest payments.

relatively demonetized financial systems. On the eve of the 1982 crisis, for example, official adjustments in wages were still made once a year, while wage adjustments in Brazil had already become semestral and Argentina was moving from quarterly to monthly settlements. Wage adjustments in Mexico during the critical year of 1983 fell to less than half of past price increases, and on average they have remained below past inflation since then. Financial disintermediation and demonetization were also far less advanced; cash balances in the first quarter of 1982 were 10 percent of GDP, compared to 5.8 percent in Brazil and 4.9 percent in Argentina (Reisen and van Trotsenburg 1988: table I.14).

These features had profound implications for fiscal adjustment, and they help explain why Mexico's record in this respect appears so outstanding in the aftermath of the debt crisis. As shown in tables 3.1 and 3.2, the large public-sector operational deficit in 1981 (10 percent of GDP) turned into a small surplus (0.4 percent of GDP) as early as 1983, largely as a result of a 5.5 percent contraction in public investment, a 2.3 percent real revaluation of oil export revenues (net of interest payments) in the fiscal accounts, and a fall in real salaries of public employees that accounts fully for the 1.5 percent decline in public consumption expenditures. Indeed, apart from the sharp cutback in public investment (the dirty and unsustainable component of the adjustment), fiscal adjustment was largely achieved through devaluations and wage policy-induced transfers of real income from the private to the public sector.[3]

Oil, however, was a mixed blessing because it exacerbated an already severe burden in the balance of payments. Like all the other large debtors except Chile, Mexico effected large financial transfers abroad—on the order of a third of total export revenues—between 1983 and 1989. These debt-related transfers were compounded with one of the largest terms of trade losses in Latin America; as a result of declining petroleum prices, especially after 1985, Mexico's terms-of-trade deteriorated by about 40 percent between 1981 and 1990. Moreover, the overwhelming presence of oil in the export structure (over 70 percent of total exports at its peak in 1982–1983) both reduced the supply elasticity of exports and exacerbated the contractionary effects of devaluation on

---

[3]In contrast, exchange rate adjustments and fiscal imbalances interacted perversely in other large debtors such as Brazil and Argentina: as the domestic currency depreciated, the higher exchange rate increased the domestic currency value of external debt service, thus worsening the fiscal accounts and exacerbating the size of the inflation tax required to close the fiscal gap in real terms. Combined with high indexation, increasing demonetization of the domestic financial system, and the erosion of tax revenues due to tax collection lags and high inflation (Olivera-Tanzi effects), this difference accounts for what is the most striking contrast in the adjustment experiences of these countries and Mexico: the much higher inflation rates in the former, by far more remarkable than any difference in growth performance. In fact, it is not necessary to go much beyond the destabilizing impact in one case—and stabilizing impact in the other—of exchange rate adjustments to explain the much faster acceleration of inflation and, eventually, the hyperinflation episodes in countries such as Brazil and Argentina.

TABLE 3.1
MACROECONOMIC INDICATORS IN THE 1980s

	1980	1981	1982	1983	1984	1985	1986	1987	1988	1989	1990	1991-P
Annual growth rates (in %)												
GDP per capita	5.4	6.3	-2.9	-6.3	1.4	0.4	-5.9	-0.3	-0.6	1.0	2.5	1.7
Consumer prices[1]	29.8	28.7	98.8	80.8	59.2	63.7	105.7	159.2	51.7	19.7	29.9	18.8
Real wages[2]	-0.8	3.5	-1.3	-21.0	-6.7	1.6	-5.6	0.7	-1.0	5.1	2.9	
GDP (constant 1980 pesos)	8.3	8.8	-0.6	-4.2	3.6	2.6	-3.6	1.7	1.4	3.1	4.4	3.6
Consumption	7.8	7.8	-1.9	-4.2	3.8	3.1	-2.0	-0.5	1.7	4.7	4.7	3.4
Private	7.5	7.4	-2.5	-5.4	3.3	3.6	-2.6	-0.4	2.1	5.7	5.2	3.7
Public	9.5	10.3	2.0	2.7	6.6	0.9	1.5	-1.2	-0.5	-0.7	1.7	1.9
Fixed investment	14.9	16.2	-16.8	-28.3	6.4	7.9	-11.8	-0.1	5.8	6.5	13.4	10.1
Private	14.0	11.5	-15.1	-22.1	7.9	12.2	-10.4	6.8	10.2	8.6	13.6	14.4
Public	17.1	22.5	-18.8	-36.0	4.1	0.9	-14.2	-12.3	-4.2	0.8	12.8	-1.9[3]
Exports	6.1	11.6	21.8	13.6	5.7	-4.5	4.2	10.7	5.0	3.0	5.2	5.9
Imports	31.9	17.7	-37.9	-33.8	17.8	11.0	-12.4	5.0	37.6	19.0	22.9	13.7
Indices (1978 = 100)[4]												
Real effective exchange rate	86.9	73.2	100.2	109.0	89.4	86.1	125.7	136.9	113.1	102.9	99.5	
Real exchange rate	86.7	78.9	118.7	124.6	107.6	104.1	129.1	127.8	102.2	97.4	91.1	
Relative unit labor cost	112.5	128.2	83.1	64.0	69.8	67.8	51.9	53.5	67.6	77.3	83.9	
Terms of trade (1971 = 100)		124.3	108.4	99.0	97.1	91.9	66.2	73.1	66.1	70.5	73.8	
In % of nominal GDP												
Primary deficit	3.0	8.0	7.3	-4.2	-4.8	-3.5	-2.1	-5.4	-7.6	-7.9	-7.5	
External interest payments	1.1	2.1	3.3	4.6	3.9	3.7	4.4	4.4	3.6	3.5	2.4	
Domestic real interest payments	-0.5	-0.1	-5.1	-0.8	1.2	0.6	0.1	-0.8	7.6	6.1	3.3	
Operational deficit	3.6	10.0	5.5	-0.4	0.3	0.8	2.4	-1.8	3.6	1.7	-1.8	
Economic deficit	6.6	13.0	15.6	8.1	7.2	8.0	14.4	14.4	9.3	4.8	2.3	
Financial intermediation	1.0	1.1	1.3	0.5	1.4	1.5	1.1	1.0	1.6	0.6	1.1	
Financial deficit	7.5	14.1	16.9	8.6	8.5	9.6	15.5	15.4	10.9	5.4	3.4	

[1] December–December. [2] Average real earnings in the manufacturing sector.
[3] Includes the effect of TELMEX privatization. [4] With the exception of terms of trade.

Sources: Banco de México, Indicadores económicos, and Presidencia de la República, Criterios Generales de Política Económica para 1982.

TABLE 3.2
EXTERNAL AND FISCAL ADJUSTMENTS IN THREE PERIODS

	Changes within the period		
	1981–84	1984–87	1987–91
Billions of U.S. dollars			
Trade balance[1]	19.9	–3.5	–18.4
Oil exports	2.0	–8.0	–0.2
Non-oil trade balance	17.9	4.5	–18.2
Non-oil exports[2]	2.2	4.9	9.4
Imports	–12.7	1.0	25.3
Consumer goods	–2.0	–0.1	5.3
Intermediate goods	–5.7	1.0	14.4
Capital goods	–5.0	0.1	5.6
Nonfactor services (net)[3]	3.0	0.6	–2.3
In % of nominal GDP			
Operational fiscal surplus	9.7	2.1	0.7
Public savings	4.2	0.7	0.0
External	2.3	–3.9	–0.8
Internal	1.9	4.6	0.8
Public investment	–5.5	–1.4	–0.7
Public consumption	–1.5	–0.7	–0.4
Internal disposable income (public sector)	0.4	3.9	0.4

[1] Includes nonfactor services.
[2] Includes *maquiladora* exports.
[3] Excludes *maquiladora* exports.

Sources: Presidencia de la República, *Criterios Generales de Política Económica*; Banco de México, *Indicadores Económicos*.

private expenditures. Currency devaluation eased fiscal adjustment because of petroleum export revenues accruing to the state. But because the foreign currency value of petroleum export revenues was unaffected, devaluation exacerbated the required adjustment in the non-oil current account. The same was true, for a given real exchange rate adjustment, of the overall reduction in domestic expenditure required to achieve a given current account adjustment.[4] It is not surprising, therefore, that the external imbalance was largely closed through a sharp import contraction in the period following the debt crisis (tables 3.1 and 3.2), and it was accompanied by one of the largest declines in the investment/GDP ratio in the region.

Analogous reasoning also explains why, when petroleum revenues were severely curtailed by the 1986 crisis, the external and fiscal adjust-

[4]The reduction of domestic spending was, in fact, *induced* by devaluation, for in those conditions the exchange rate was bound to affect the external balance through Hirschman and Díaz Alejandro effects (that is, through contractionary effects on private income and spending, which are simply the other side of devaluation's stabilizing effects on the fiscal accounts).

ments had to be very different from those in the preceding period (see table 3.2). Since both the private-sector trade deficit and the public-sector trade surplus were now smaller, the contractionary effects of devaluation on domestic spending were also less substantial. With a more elastic response of nonpetroleum exports—resulting from past devaluations and an exceptionally high real exchange rate in 1986–1987—the balance-of-payments adjustment could rely more on export expansion than on import contraction. It was also made less severe by the greater availability of external finance. On the other hand, because the positive fiscal effects of devaluation were smaller (as a result of reduced oil revenues) and public investment had already been reduced to very low levels, fiscal policy had no option but to rely on an increase in domestic public savings.

Nevertheless, the collapse of public and private investment that occurred in the wake of the debt crisis, and the increase in domestic public savings needed to compensate for the loss of foreign exchange revenues after the 1986 oil shock, had a longer-term cost above and beyond the stagnation of productive activity and the contraction of the population's real incomes: a sharp decline in the domestic private savings rate (see table 3.3). This remains one of the central problems facing economic policy makers in Mexico.

THE ROLE AND EFFICIENCY OF INCOMES POLICY

The Mexican labor market (that is, the formal labor market that plays a leading role in wage determination) is highly organized, with a number of "institutional rigidities" constraining labor mobility. At the same time, the labor market shows a high degree of real wage flexibility, largely as a result of a centralized corporatist system of wage determination that is strongly conditioned by government policies. This system of wage determination gives the Mexican government remarkable room for maneuver in its wage policy, a feature that is rooted in the linkages forged between the Mexican working-class movement and the state during and after the 1920s and the fact that Mexican labor unions have a weak base, with their general orientation influenced to a greater or lesser degree by official paternalism (see Noyola 1956).

The absence of a "wage constraint" (that is to say, the government's comparatively broad room for maneuver in the area of wage policy) has been one important factor softening the difficult policy trade-offs that other Latin American debtors faced in correcting external and fiscal imbalances. It also had other important implications.

Although fiscal constraints were less severe and indexation mechanisms less entrenched in Mexico than in many other Latin American countries, Mexico could not avoid a period of high inflation. With the 1982 devaluations, inflation accelerated sharply from its initial rate of

TABLE 3.3
INVESTMENT AND SAVINGS RATES, 1980–1991

	1980	1981	1982	1983	1984	1985	1986	1987	1988	1989	1990[1]	1991[1]
In % of GDP (at constant 1980 pesos)												
Fixed investment	24.8	26.5	22.2	16.6	17.0	17.9	16.4	16.0	16.8	17.3	18.8	20.0
Residential	7.7	7.8	7.8	6.7	6.9	7.1	6.7	7.0	7.3	7.5	NA	NA
Business and infrastructure	17.1	18.7	14.4	9.9	10.1	10.8	9.7	9.0	9.5	9.8	NA	NA
Net investment	16.2	17.9	12.7	5.0	6.2	7.4	4.8	4.6	6.3	6.9	NA	NA
Depreciation	8.6	8.6	9.5	11.6	10.8	10.5	11.6	11.4	10.5	10.4	NA	NA
Private	14.1	14.4	11.9	10.4	10.7	11.7	10.9	11.5	12.4	13.1	14.3	15.7
Public	10.7	12.1	10.3	6.2	6.3	6.2	5.5	4.5	4.4	4.2	4.5	4.3
In % of nominal GDP												
Domestic savings	22.2	21.4	22.4	24.7	22.5	22.4	17.8	22.3	20.1	20.7	17.7	17.6
Public savings	7.1	2.1	4.7	7.0	6.3	5.8	4.1	7.0	1.4	2.7	6.6	7.0
External	4.1	3.2	5.0	6.2	5.5	4.4	0.5	1.6	-0.2	0.0	1.3	0.8
Domestic	3.0	-1.1	-0.3	0.8	0.8	1.4	3.6	5.4	1.6	2.7	5.3	6.2
Private savings	15.1	19.3	17.7	17.7	16.2	16.6	13.7	15.3	18.7	18.0	11.1	10.6
Private disposable income	80.2	83.7	79.3	78.6	79.3	81.1	81.8	80.6	87.5	85.0	79.4	78.9
Average propensity to consume	.832	.787	.835	.807	.817	.818	.866	.848	.799	.794	.871	.871
Inflation tax	2.0	1.9	5.5	3.1	2.1	2.2	3.2	3.6	1.4	0.6	1.0	0.5
Real private income per capita (index 1980 = 100)	100.0	109.4	97.1	87.8	87.5	89.3	78.5	79.2	82.1	85.7	80.5	81.8
Capital-output ratio[1]	2.6	2.6	2.9	3.1	3.2	3.2	3.4	3.5	3.6	3.6	NA	NA
Capital-output ratio (nonresidential)[1]	1.5	1.5	1.7	1.8	1.8	1.9	2.0	2.0	2.0	2.0	NA	NA
Average age capital stock[2]	10.9	10.7	10.8	11.1	11.5	11.7	12.0	12.3	12.6	12.9	NA	NA

[1] Preliminary.
[2] Refers to gross capital stock.
NA = Not Available.
Sources: Banco de México, *Indicadores económicos*, and Presidencia de la República, *Criterios Generales de Política Económica*; A. Hofman, *The Role of Capital in Latin America* (ECLA Working Paper No. 4, 1991).

25–30 percent in 1981. Despite a massive fiscal turnaround following the debt crisis—which, as already mentioned, brought the public-sector operational balance into surplus in 1983—the very orthodox stabilization strategy pursued during this period failed to bring inflation down to target. Price increases stabilized at a high rate of around 60 percent per year in the second half of 1985. The ensuing oil shock left no option but to maintain a very high real exchange rate and sacrifice price stabilization objectives for at least a while. The cost was a higher rate of inflation, running at 160 percent in 1987 and accelerating in the last few months of that year. An increasing financial fragility, and two financial shocks followed by a new exchange rate crisis in December 1987 (see Ros 1992a), eventually caused policy makers to give renewed priority to price stabilization. These developments also stimulated a different approach to counterinflation policy.

What followed confirmed the insights of the heterodox approach to stabilization—and its case for incomes policy under high inflation—and illustrates, at the same time, how the efficiency of incomes policy was enhanced by the old corporatist, centralized system of wage determination. In December 1987, faced with generalized wage demands, the prospects of a further acceleration of inflation following a new foreign exchange crisis, and the threat of a further increase in the frequency of wage adjustments (which by then occurred every quarter, compared to only once in 1981), the de la Madrid administration (1982–1988) launched the Economic Solidarity Pact (PSE) in order to achieve rapid disinflation. The pact was a tripartite agreement comprising the following measures: an initial freeze on the exchange rate and public prices, together with further fiscal adjustment (the government's contribution to the program); wage restraint, including an initial wage freeze, on the part of labor unions; and a radicalization of the import liberalization program that had begun in 1985. Along with voluntary price restraint, this last element was the business sector's contribution to counterinflation policy.[5]

The pact, unlike previous stabilization attempts, fully achieved its targets. In fact, its target of 1–2 percent monthly inflation by the end of 1988 was reached in the first few months after its implementation. From 160 percent in 1987, the annual inflation rate was down to 20 percent by 1989 and, after a temporary flare-up in 1990, back to 18.8 percent in 1991. Disinflation took place without deepening the contraction of labor's real earnings, even despite a surge in consumer spending and business investments. The ensuing economic recovery, moderate at first, gained momentum in 1989–1991. The success of the program was such that, despite the continuous real appreciation of

[5]It should be noted that, although import liberalization did not contribute significantly to disinflation (Ize 1990), import tariff policy was indeed fine-tuned for a couple of years in accordance with the pact's price guidelines to the private sector.

the Mexican peso, the government was able over time to reduce the preannounced rate of daily devaluations.

The role of incomes policy in these developments should not be underestimated, as is often the case in orthodox views. Orthodox perspectives often portray incomes policy as a useful auxiliary component in a disinflation package, but not really as a necessary condition for its success. In this view, fiscal and monetary policy—the "fundamentals"—are the only necessary and sufficient conditions for curing inflation, even though the cure may be painful without the anesthetic provided by incomes policy. The Mexican experience does not fit well with these views, suggesting that incomes policy was far more than a convenient (and, indeed, very effective) anesthetic.

In fact, the Economic Solidarity Pact is a rare case of inflation stabilization without fiscal adjustment. From 1988 to 1991, the operational budget deficit was on average higher than in 1987, by about 2 percent of GDP. Despite an increase in the government's primary surplus (the budget excluding all interest payments on public debt), the higher operational deficit resulted from the high real interest payments on domestic public debt that the government transferred to the private sector in 1988 and 1989 (see table 3.1). But even after a decline in real interest rates, the operational budget surplus in 1991 had improved by only 0.7 percent of GDP with respect to 1987, less than can be accounted for by the effects of lower inflation on tax collection (the Olivera-Tanzi effect operating in reverse).[6] The basic reason for this lack of fiscal adjustment, as can be seen in table 3.2, is that the effects of the pact's fiscal measures—which, indeed, contributed to rising domestic public savings—were fully offset by declining external public savings resulting from the real appreciation of the peso and its effects on the domestic currency value of petroleum export revenues.[7]

Even if incomes policy was a necessary condition (and surely it was far more necessary than a nonexistent fiscal adjustment), this does not

---

[6]The Olivera-Tanzi effect was estimated at 0.9 percent of GDP in 1987. If other effects of inflation on the operational deficit—that is, on financial subsidies and the composition of the public debt—are included, their sum adds up to 1.2 percent of GDP (see Banco de México 1989). On the other hand, the financial deficit—the budget with no inflation adjustments at all—dropped sharply from 16 percent of GDP in 1987 to 1.3 percent in 1991. However, this reduction is fully attributable to the decline in the inflation rate (through, in particular, its effect on nominal interest rates).

[7]This analysis could be objected to on the grounds that *past* fiscal adjustment (leading to a sizeable primary surplus by 1987) helped reduce the government's solvency problems, permitting it to relax credit rationing and easing the initially tight capital account of the balance of payments. But this was, at most, a complementary factor. As developments in the second half of 1987 strongly suggested, without incomes policy-based stabilization, the turnaround in the capital account would not have taken place. In any event, the point remains that there was no additional fiscal adjustment (adjusted for inflation) after 1987.

mean that it was a sufficient condition for the success of the pact.[8] What the absence of fiscal adjustment means is that the effects of the fall in the inflation tax on aggregate demand (on the order of 3 percent of GDP) were not compensated by an equivalent reduction in government spending or an offsetting increase in noninflationary public revenues. The expansionary effects of the fall in the inflation tax—which, indeed, led to a rapid expansion of private spending, at rates of 4 percent in 1988 and 6 percent in 1989—were absorbed by the balance-of-payments current account, which rapidly turned from surplus to deficit in the course of 1988. The current account deficit led in turn to a severe loss of international reserves—close to U.S.$7 billion in 1988 (3.4 percent of GDP), about the size of the reduction in the inflation tax. These reserve losses could not have continued for much longer without compromising the pact's exchange rate policy rules and, with them, the sustainability of the stabilization attempt as a whole. At this point, other nonmacroeconomic instruments were introduced to soften the policy trade-offs and overcome the ineffectiveness of macroeconomic policy.

A POLITICAL ECONOMY MODEL OF STRUCTURAL REFORMS

Before looking at recent trends, it is necessary to step back and discuss what had occurred on the "structural reform" front. Mexico's path to macroeconomic stabilization and structural adjustment can be briefly summarized as follows. In the wake of the 1982 debt crisis, the government adopted a very orthodox, stabilization-first strategy in order to rapidly restore price and balance-of-payments stability. This was to be followed by a gradualist approach to structural adjustment that would promote an incremental process of resource reallocation in a stable and growth-oriented macroeconomic framework. This "high growth/slow structural adjustment strategy"—which prevailed as a policy stance during 1984 and part of 1985—was soon abandoned in favor of an increasing radicalization of market reform measures which, contrary to conventional wisdom and advice, took place within the highly adverse macroeconomic environment created by the 1986 oil price shock. At the same time, and after the failure of successive orthodox attempts at inflation control, macroeconomic policy shifted in late 1987 to a rather heterodox approach to stabilization. Despite the high priority given to price stabilization in this period—or perhaps because of it, as argued below—structural adjustment measures accelerated thereafter.

---

[8]There is, however, some truth to the point that the turnaround in the capital account after 1989 was itself a consequence of successful price stabilization. If this was so, then Mexico's macroeconomic structure featured in recent years a multiplicity of equilibria. In such conditions, the coordination of wage and price decisions by incomes policy becomes not only a necessary, but also a sufficient, condition to move the economy from the high-inflation to the low-inflation equilibrium.

Each of these successive waves of market reform often accelerated well beyond the original intentions of policy makers. In addition, as already noted, the timing and sequence of policy reform often ran counter to well-established orthodox principles (see, for example, Corbo and Fischer 1990). Many price controls were removed before trade liberalization began, and thus world prices could not serve as a guideline for domestic prices; trade policy reform took place in the midst of a severe external shock that magnified foreign exchange constraints, high inflation that distorted price signals, and an economic slowdown that exacerbated adjustment costs; and financial liberalization began before price stabilization was consolidated, and thus at a time of high real interest rates.

This section develops a model of the reform process that attempts to explain those two characteristics, the snowball effects in the reform sequence and policy makers' apparent irrationality in the timing of policies. The model shares the growing realization of some economists that an explanation for these phenomena must draw from the field of political economy. In discussing trade policy reform, Dani Rodrik (1992) has asked: "If a period of macro instability is the worst time to undertake a trade reform, why are so many countries doing it?" After discarding as an insufficient explanation the growing influence of some academic economists on policy makers, Rodrik offers the following reasons:

> First, a time of crisis occasionally enables radical re-
> forms that would have been unthinkable in calmer
> times. That it takes the prospect of a severe denouement
> to bring a nation to its collective senses is the aggregate
> version of an insight due to Samuel Johnson: "When a
> man knows he is to be hanged in a fortnight, it concen-
> trates his mind wonderfully." The quip seems to apply
> with equal force to nations in severe crisis, as some of
> the key cases of radical trade reform illustrate: Bolivia
> (in 1985), Mexico (since 1987), Poland (1990), Peru
> (1990). In all of these cases, a macroeconomic crisis of
> unprecedented proportions has led the leadership to
> embrace a wide range of reforms, of which trade liberal-
> ization was one component.
>
> The second reason has to do with the role of foreign
> creditors, and of the IMF and World Bank in particular.
> The 1980's were a decade of great leverage for these
> institutions vis-à-vis debtor governments, especially
> where poorer African countries are concerned. The
> trade policy recommendations of the World Bank were
> adopted by cash-starved governments frequently with

little conviction of their ultimate benefits. This accounts
for the high incidence of wobbling and reversal on the
trade front, once again especially in Africa. It also
indicates that we ought not to be too optimistic on the
sustainability of reform in many of these countries (p.
89).

There is, however, more to it than these useful insights suggest. An
adequate explanation should also clarify some unconventional links
between macroeconomic adjustment and market reforms, as well as
account for the very different pace of reform in countries with policy
makers of similar convictions.[9]

THE MODEL

The model encompasses the proximate determinants of the reform
process and two reaction functions, one for policy makers and the other
for foreign lenders and investors:

(1) $R = R\,(w_{pm},\ O,\ T_p)$
(2) $w_{pm} = w_{pm}\,(C,\ w_f)$
(3) $w_f = w_f\,(R,\ i,\ C)$

R = stage of the reform process
w_{pm} = willingness of policy makers to reform
w_f = willingness of foreign lenders to lend
T_p = policy trade-offs between stabilization and structural reform
O = domestic opposition to market reforms
i = market interest rate
C = costs of not obtaining external finance

Equation (1) expresses the stage of the reform process, or the degree
of implementation of structural reforms, as a function of the willingness
of policy makers to reform and the political obstacles they face (the
extent of domestic opposition to reforms), as well as the objective policy
trade-offs between stabilization and market reform. A well-known
example of such trade-offs concerns the exchange rate dilemmas that a
trade liberalization program faces in conditions of macroeconomic instability: price stabilization is likely to require a real appreciation of the

---

[9]Note also that the two reasons offered cannot be applied to the same country at the
same time: reform is either embraced by a heroic leadership that has finally come to its
senses, or it is undertaken by cash-starved governments with little conviction, as a result of
International Monetary Fund and World Bank pressure. Although the author probably did
not mean to apply both reasons to the same case, an explanation of the Mexican experience
along these lines would then have to rely on the first reason only. This would, in the
author's view, be a poor explanation.

domestic currency, while the trade program pulls the real exchange rate in the other direction in order to avoid an unsustainable expansion of imports. In the absence of a sufficient number of policy instruments, the package is inconsistent, and one or both of its objectives will not be achieved. The sharper these trade-offs, the greater the likelihood that trade liberalization will have to be reversed or slowed, no matter how eager policy makers are to undertake it. The "trade liberalization cum real appreciation" experiments in the Southern Cone during the late 1970s are often referred to as an illustration of this phenomenon.

The willingness of policy makers to reform is determined by their perception of the expected net benefits of reform. The incentives policy makers face are, in turn, a function of the costs of not obtaining external finance and the willingness of foreign lenders to lend, given those costs (equation 2). Because multilateral and commercial bank creditors make at least part of the potentially available external finance conditional upon the adoption of market reforms, the greater the costs of not obtaining foreign credit, the greater the incentive for policy makers to reform. Those costs may take the form of economic stagnation, high inflation, or an unmanageable degree of conflict introduced by other policy options (such as debt repudiation or capital controls). Given these costs, the benefits of reforming are also enhanced by foreign creditors' greater willingness to lend, which—as shown by equation (3)—is essentially the same as the response of foreign lenders to the implementation of reform, other things being equal. One could add to this function the size of the allocative and dynamic efficiency gains expected from the reform process. These expected benefits—which have been present in the Mexican experience, as we shall see later—are excluded for the time being in order to emphasize that, even if these benefits are not perceived, other conditions may end up inducing policy makers to accelerate the reform process. An alternative justification for not including these gains in the net benefit function would be to assume that policy makers are short-term maximizers (no heroic leaderships here). Because those gains are likely to take a long time to materialize and make a difference, short-term maximizers will discount them at such a high rate as to make them negligible.

Foreign lenders, on the contrary, are long-term maximizers and apply, say, the market interest rate to discount the long-term benefits of reforms. The repayment of their loans or the profitability of their investments depends on the long-term economic viability of the recipient country, and they perceive that market reforms will enhance this viability. Thus their willingness to lend depends on the stage of the reform process and, inversely, on the market interest rate that affects the discounted value of the future benefits of policy reform (equation 3). The expected viability of a given country is also affected by lenders' perceptions of the country's long-term growth potential and economic and political stability. Because these "country risks" (in bankers' jargon) are strongly correlated with policy makers' perceived costs of not obtaining external finance, the latter can serve as a proxy for the former (thus avoiding a proliferation of variables).

Taking the policy trade-offs (T_p), the costs of not obtaining external finance (C), internal opposition (O), and the market interest rate (i) as exogenous variables, the three-equation model can be solved for R, the stage of the reform process, and the willingness to lend and to reform $(w_f$ and $w_{pm})$. In this form, the model can be further simplified in two relationships: the foreign lenders function (equation 3, reproduced below) and, substituting from (2) into (1), the stage of reform (R) as a function of the willingness to lend and other (exogenous) variables (equation 4):

(3) $w_f = w_f (R, i, C)$
(4) $R = R^* (w_f, C, O, T_p)$

These equations determine simultaneously w_f and R. Both of these relationships are likely to be strongly nonlinear, as shown in figure 3.2. In the case of the foreign lenders function (the w_f (R) curve), this is because a critical mass of reforms may be necessary before foreign investors are convinced to step up their lending; yet beyond a certain point (when, say, the country already qualifies as a "market economy"), they may expect no further significant benefits from additional reforms. (Indeed, the willingness to lend, viewed as a permanent flow of foreign savings, may even decline at that stage.) Similarly, the reform process function (the R (w_f) curve corresponding to equation 4) is likely to step up slowly before a critical level of foreign lending makes it worthwhile to undertake reforms, then accelerate at intermediate levels of foreign lending, and become inelastic again at even higher levels because the marginal benefits of further reforms for policy makers diminish when the rationing of foreign credit is no longer a problem.

Figure 3.2 shows the determination of foreign lending and policy reforms in three different situations. In figure 3.2a, the particular form of the model shares some features with Schelling's (1978) "critical mass" model.[10] There are three equilibria, two stable (a high one at point A and a low one at point B) and one unstable, the intermediate one at point C. This last point represents a critical mass of both foreign lending and domestic reforms, beyond which the reform process will accelerate toward the high equilibrium at A. To visualize this, consider a point such

---

[10]There are some important differences too. A point on either curve reflects an optimizing behavior on the part of either foreign lenders or policy makers. In Schelling's model of the "dying seminar," one of the two curves is the 45-degree line stating the condition that in equilibrium expectations are fulfilled. The underlying reasons for the S shape of the other curve are, of course, completely different.

FIGURE **3.2**

The Determination of Foreign Lending and Policy Reforms

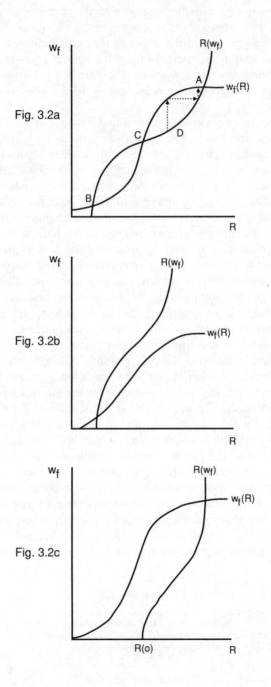

as D. At this point, the stage achieved by the reform process R (D) is such that lenders consider it worthwhile to step up their lending beyond w_f (D), moving toward their foreign lending function. This positive response in turn induces policy makers to accelerate policy reforms beyond R (D), triggering a further response on the part of lenders and so on. This process stabilizes at A, where no further benefits for lenders and policy makers justify additional policy reforms. Analogous reasoning would show that any departure from the reform process below C would trigger successive responses on the part of lenders and policy makers, tending to reverse policy reforms toward the low-level equilibrium at B.

The critical mass of reforms is determined by the shape and position of the two curves, and will thus be reduced by any leftward shift of the foreign lenders function or any rightward shift of the policy makers (and the reform process) functions.[11] In particular, a weaker internal opposition or a softening of policy trade-offs reduces the critical mass of reforms by shifting the policy makers function (and thus the reform process function) to the right, while a fall in the market interest rate has a similar effect by shifting the lenders function to the left. An increase in the costs of not obtaining external finance has, at first glance, an ambiguous effect by shifting both curves to the right; higher costs make policy makers more willing to reform, but they also mean that foreign investors are more reluctant to lend. The first effect is, however, likely to predominate under most conditions because lenders will generally spread these costs over a longer time horizon than policy makers. The critical mass of reforms will thus be smaller.

Multiple equilibria are not the only possible outcome. Figures 3.2b and 3.2c show unique equilibria at low and high levels, respectively. In figure 3.2b, reluctant policy makers—facing strong internal opposition or difficult policy trade-offs, or perceiving small costs in not obtaining external finance—will undertake a minimal amount of reforms. There is, therefore, no critical mass of reforms that will convince foreign investors to lend, and the process remains stuck at a low level of both foreign lending and policy reform. In figure 3.2c, enthusiastic reformers—facing little opposition at home and soft policy trade-offs—will undertake a large number of reforms even in the absence of foreign lending (R(0)), but this in turn will trigger a positive response from lenders and the reform process will accelerate well beyond the policy makers' minimal intentions, stabilizing at a high level of foreign lending.[12]

---

[11] The irony was totally unintended and unanticipated.

[12] In figure 3.2b or figure 3.2c, the curves could cross again at negative levels of foreign lending and reform, but such an intersection (not shown in the figures) would be unstable. Any positive departure from it would make policy makers and lenders realize that it is to their mutual advantage to move toward the higher-level (and the only stable) equilibrium.

THE UNCONVENTIONAL MACROECONOMIC ROLE OF STRUCTURAL REFORMS

The model can now be applied to explain the timing and sequencing of policy reforms in Mexico. Market reforms were, in fact, initially reversed during the 1982 crisis; the government introduced foreign exchange controls, and it kept direct import controls (which had been fully reestablished in 1981) almost intact until mid-1985. This reversal resulted from the sharp contraction in foreign lending (a shift to the right in the foreign lenders function) that prevailed until 1985, despite the massive fiscal adjustment that took place in 1982–1983. Thus, notwithstanding President de la Madrid's intentions to reform (comprehensively outlined in the 1983 National Development Plan), the reform process proceeded at a slow pace throughout 1983 and 1984.

Several new developments took place in 1985–1986. On the one hand, the Baker Plan can be seen as foreign lenders' heightened response to reform, and thus as both an exogenous shift to the left in the foreign lenders function and an increase in the expected net benefits of reform for debtors (a shift to the right in the policy makers function). That is, a major player announced the need to step up foreign lending in exchange for the adoption of market reforms. On the other hand, the mid-1985 foreign exchange crisis and especially the oil shock in early 1986 had two other important effects. By forcing the Mexican government to structure macroeconomic policy so as to provide unprecedented levels of "exchange rate protection" in 1986–1987, the highly adverse external environment had the paradoxical effect of softening the policy trade-offs involved in trade liberalization by facilitating the adjustment of industrial firms to a more open economy. For this reason, as well as because the high exchange rate and domestic recession subsumed the specific costs of trade liberalization into the broader and more apparent costs of overall macroeconomic adjustment, the oil shock also lowered resistance to change. This is a major reason for the smoothness—both economic and political—of the Mexican transition toward a liberalized trade regime.[13]

The second effect of the oil shock was to raise the costs to policy makers of not obtaining external finance, thus increasing their incentives to accelerate the reform process. At the same time, however, the oil shock reduced by half the exchange revenues derived from Mexico's main export product, thereby making foreign creditors more reluctant to lend. President de la Madrid's dilemma in early 1986—to declare a debt

---

[13]The other major reason, besides the general lack of domestic opposition, is probably Mexico's successful import-substitution experience in the past—in the sense that this strategy effectively modified the economy's pattern of comparative advantages in favor of manufacturing and the initially infant industries. This feature reveals itself in the fact that current trends in the trade pattern and industrial structure are with no major exceptions an extrapolation of the past. For further analysis, see below and Ros 1992b.

moratorium or to embrace the Baker Plan—was eventually resolved in favor of maintaining a course of structural reform. The government, which had first announced a comprehensive privatization program in early 1985, proceeded to close or sell many state-owned enterprises in 1986 and 1987 (although not yet the major ones). Similarly, a radical schedule of trade liberalization, announced in August 1985, was followed to the letter, and the deregulation of foreign investment flows gained momentum.

The reform process accelerated still further after 1988. As noted earlier, a comprehensive incomes policy had been essential to recovering price and financial stability, but the other causes of policy ineffectiveness were still in place. Even if private investment recovered, it was soon to become apparent that the sharp decline in private savings rates could make an economic recovery unsustainable. Without external finance, the sustainability of stabilization itself was in doubt (a point made clear by the reserve losses in 1988). To avoid a "stabilization without growth" scenario (or even worse, a return to high inflation), the government had to compensate for the legacy of the macroeconomic adjustment process—the severely depressed rates of investment and domestic savings—with a substantial increase in foreign savings. Under these circumstances, external finance was more necessary than ever before.

At the same time, all other incentives were in place for a big leap forward in the reform process. The Brady Plan, like the Baker Plan before it, was soon to offer a reduction in external transfers in exchange for further reforms (now in the more attractive form of debt relief), thereby increasing the net benefits of reform. The real exchange rate was at or near peak levels by the end of 1987 and, through "exchange rate protection" to domestic industry, it could provide a cushion for the dislocation costs of more radical trade reform. In fact, this occurred in late 1987 in the context of the stabilization program, as already noted. In May 1989, the Salinas administration overhauled foreign investment regulations (virtually repealing the 1973 law on foreign investment), thus opening new areas of the economy to foreign capital and establishing automatic approval for 100 percent foreign-owned investment projects fulfilling a number of conditions. The government also undertook financial liberalization and, more generally, a comprehensive deregulation of tertiary activities (including road transportation and telecommunications) after 1989. Privatization entered its more significant and complex phase with the sale of some of Mexico's largest state enterprises: the two airline companies (Mexicana de Aviación and Aeroméxico) in mid-1989, the two largest copper-mining enterprises (Compañía Minera de Cananea and Mexicana de Cobre), the country's largest telecommunications company (TELMEX, sold in late 1990 to a group of domestic and foreign investors), and the commercial banks (which had been nationalized in 1982 and were sold to local financial groups in 1991–1992).

It is worth noting in this context that the official case for reduced state participation was not based on microeconomic efficiency grounds. Rather, it was a macroeconomic argument, ultimately based on policy ineffectiveness, that made reference to very special conditions of the 1980s: a government whose access to credit markets was rationed at the same time that it faced pressing social needs, and a private sector with ample financial resources abroad, resources that could readily be invested in previously state-dominated activities that lacked a high social priority. Under such conditions, a clear comparative advantage argument could be made for privatization even if public enterprises had absolute efficiency advantages over private firms, because society as a whole would clearly gain from a reallocation of public investments from areas where social and private returns do not differ greatly to activities yielding a higher social/private returns differential.

Two other factors contributed to the acceleration of the reform process. So far this analysis has assumed that the costs of not obtaining external finance are exogenous (that is, they are independent of the reform process itself). Yet some policy reforms may have the effect of increasing such costs. Import liberalization, combined with a real appreciation of the peso after 1988, appears to be one such instance: import boom that followed was one of the main causes for the mushrooming trade and current account deficits that exacerbated the need for further external finance. In fact, the sequence of events clearly suggests that the acceleration of reforms in other areas—particularly the reprivatization of the banking system—was a means of alleviating (through capital inflows) a balance-of-payments position that was otherwise unsustainable partly as a result of recent trade and exchange rate policies.[14]

The other factor, also related to trade reform, was the smoothness of the transition itself in the 1985–1987 period. This had a feedback effect on the reform process because it encouraged policy makers to believe (mistakenly) that trade policy reform caused the boom in manufacturing exports before 1987 (see Peres 1990; Ros 1992b). As a result, this factor also generated exaggerated expectations about the long-term benefits of trade liberalization, which contributed to the further acceleration of trade reform in late 1987.[15]

---

[14]It was partly unsustainable because the large current account deficits in recent years also reflect the decline of the private savings rate, a consequence not of trade policy reform but of the past macroeconomic adjustment.

[15]I depart here from the assumption that policy makers are cynical and/or short-term maximizers.

The model has other interesting applications that also clarify some particular features of the Latin American experience. For example, the model could explain the sudden shift away from gradualism (and from whatever remains of the conventional wisdom concerning the correct sequencing of reforms) in the recent "big bang" experiences of Peru and Venezuela. By the early 1990s, partly as a result of past adjustments and failures, the costs of not obtaining external finance had become unbearable—and were clearly perceived to be so by policy makers. Moreover, in contrast to earlier periods, many other incentives are now fully in place. Taken together, these factors can cause a sudden acceleration of reforms, a shift from figure 3.2b to figure 3.2c.

On the other hand, the slower pace of reform implementation in Brazil can be viewed in part as a consequence of sharp trade-offs between stabilization and market liberalization. Unlike Mexico (or Venezuela), traditional exchange rate dilemmas are exacerbated in Brazil by a large external debt and the absence of export revenues accruing to the government. To the extent that trade liberalization increases the exchange rate adjustment necessary to reconcile internal and external balances, it adds to the fiscal adjustment required to compensate for the weakening of public finances that results from devaluation. This is probably why short-lived stabilization episodes in Brazil (and in Argentina, under similar conditions) were consistent only with highly overvalued currencies, and why the degree of real exchange rate variability in this adjustment process was so high. Under such circumstances, an accelerated transition in the trade policy regime would only increase the fiscal burden, and it could make policy reform unsustainable unless the fiscal accounts had initially overadjusted. As long as this harsh precondition is not met, and/or a massive reversal of external transfers does not take place, gradualism emerges as the only viable option in an already fiscally strangled economy. Similarly, with less past capital flight (than either Mexico or Argentina, in this case) on which to draw, the macroeconomic advantages of privatization become less obvious.

THE LEGACY OF ADJUSTMENT AND THE LONG-TERM CONSEQUENCES OF MARKET REFORMS

The collapse of public and private investments that took place in the wake of the 1982 debt crisis, and the loss of foreign exchange revenues after the 1986 oil shock, together with the stagnation of productive activity and the subsequent contraction of the population's real incomes, affected the Mexican economy's growth potential in at least two ways. First, these developments changed the structure and age distribution of the capital stock. Second, they produced a sharp decline in the domestic private savings rate.

THE STRUCTURE AND AGE DISTRIBUTION OF THE CAPITAL STOCK

Simply recording the huge contraction in gross investment would understate the implications of the decline in the rate of capital accumulation for the Mexican economy's growth potential. This is so for several reasons. Whenever gross investment falls, the greatest impact is on business and infrastructure investment (residential investment is strongly influenced by demographic factors) and net investment (on which the growth of capacity depends), rather than on depreciation, which depends on the slowly changing age distribution of the capital stock. Moreover, the burden that falls on net investment increases over time if its fall has been severe enough, all the more so if low investment rates persist over a prolonged period of time because the depreciation rate itself will tend to increase as a result of the aging of the capital stock.

These features are clearly observable in Mexico's adjustment process. As can be seen in table 3.3, while gross investment fell by 7.5 percent from 1980 to 1989, residential investment fell by only 0.2 percent. Thus the whole burden of the reduction fell on business and infrastructure investment, whose rate in 1989 was thus less than 60 percent of its value in 1980 (and around half of its value in the 1981 peak). The decline in net investment was even larger, over 9 percent of GDP. The 1982–1983 fall was so severe that, as a consequence, the average age of the capital stock started rising in those same years, and it has continued to do so since then (see table 3.3). This probably explains the increase in the depreciation rate from 8.6 percent of GDP in 1980–1981 to 10.4 percent of GDP in 1989 (after reaching a peak of 11.6 percent in 1983 and again in 1986), and it also explains why the fall in net investment was actually greater than the decline in gross investment. Another way of looking at the adverse consequences of these shifts in the composition of gross investment is to observe the increase in the capital-output ratio (from 2.6 in 1980 to 3.6 in 1989).

THE FALL IN THE PRIVATE SAVINGS RATE

Table 3.3 also shows the behavior of domestic savings, both public and private.[16] The most dramatic change was the sharp decline in the private savings rate (by around 5 percent of GDP) between the early 1980s and the early 1990s, which accounted for a similar decline in the domestic savings rate. (By 1991, public savings rates had recovered to their 1980 level.)

---

[16]These are presented in their "operational" definition, which excludes from private savings (and includes in public savings) the purely nominal component of interest payments representing a compensation for inflation's erosion of the value of existing public nonmonetary debt. In this definition, private savings can be expressed as: $s_p = (1-c)yd_p + ct_i$, where yd_p is private disposable income (operational definition), t_i is the inflation tax, and c is the average propensity to consume out of *real* private disposable income (excluding the inflation tax from the operational definition of disposable income). Each of these elements affecting savings is shown in the table.

As shown in table 3.3, the private savings rate (comprising both personal and business saving) suffered three negative shocks during this period—in 1982–1984, 1986–1987, and 1989–1990—from which it never fully recovered, so that each successive trough was always below the previous one. The first shock came with the debt crisis. The decline in private savings (as a fraction of nominal GDP) was largely the result of contracting private income (which fell by 2.9 percent of GDP between 1980–1981 and 1982–1984) and a moderate increase in the propensity to consume (from .81 to .82). The combined effect of these elements outweighed the impact of a rising inflation tax by 1.6 percent of GDP. The contraction in private disposable income—by far the most important factor in the reduction of private savings in this period—was the counterpart to increases in the proportion of public external savings (the public-sector foreign exchange balance in domestic currency) and foreign disposable income in the gross domestic product. Both increases were largely the result of the sharp peso devaluations that occurred in this period, a concrete representation of the contractionary effects already alluded to. These exchange rate adjustments also explain why the domestic savings rate did not fall in this period despite the reduction in private savings; the resulting income transfers from the private sector (with a relatively low propensity to save) to the public sector (with a relatively high propensity to save) tended, on the contrary, to increase the economy's average propensity to save. This was especially the case in 1983 (precisely when the real exchange rate was at its peak), and it is another way of appreciating the strong contractionary effects of devaluations in this period.

The second shock came with the collapse of oil prices in 1986. Initially the collapse represented a blow to public savings because it sharply curtailed public revenues. This is the reason why the share of private income in GDP actually increased in 1986. But through new exchange rate and fiscal adjustments, the shock was transmitted to the private sector; the 3.1 percent increase in public domestic savings in 1986–1987 (which almost offset the 3.4 percent loss in public external savings) caused the private savings rate to fall by 2.1 percent. The resulting decline in domestic savings was thus of a similar size. The major factor this time was a sharp increase in the propensity to consume, from .82 to .86, a shift that was largely due to the fall in the population's real incomes. As occurred in the previous period, this increase offset the impact of a larger inflation tax, although this source of government revenue was of declining value. (Despite a much higher inflation rate than in 1982–1983, the inflation tax was smaller in 1986–1987, by about 0.5 percent of GDP, because of the erosion of the corresponding "tax base"; the private sector's cash balances had declined from 3.1 to 1.9 percent of GDP between 1982 and 1987.)

In 1988, the first year of the Economic Solidarity Pact, private savings recorded an impressive recovery. However, this was temporary and largely associated with the spectacular increase in real interest payments on domestic government debt, which was in turn associated with extraordinarily high real interest rates during the stabilization period (30 percent in 1988). This had the double effect of increasing the share of private income in the gross domestic product[17] and reducing the propensity to consume, probably as a result of the distributional bias of the income increase. After 1989, as the initial uncertainty and credibility problems of the stabilization effort receded, the domestic real interest rate began to return to normal levels, and with this change both private income and the propensity to consume returned to their pre-1988 values. However, because the stabilization program has successfully reduced the inflation tax (by around 3 percent of GDP, compared to its 1987 level), the private savings rate has actually declined below its 1986–1987 value. And because public savings did not increase between 1987 and 1991 (as noted, the fiscal adjustments made during the stabilization program were offset by the fiscal effects of the real exchange adjustments that accompanied it), the overall domestic savings rate has continued its decline. This is, in effect, the counterpart of "stabilization without fiscal adjustment." The decline in the inflation tax led to an expansion of private consumption, and because this was not neutralized by an increase in public savings, it also caused a reduction in overall domestic savings.

Looking now at the three periods as a whole, the major factor behind the fall in the private savings rate has been the increase in the population's propensity to consume. The reduced share of private income in the gross domestic product, and the virtual elimination of the inflation tax by 1991, also contributed to the fall but in a much smaller proportion.

What accounts for the huge increase in the propensity to consume? As the previous analysis has already suggested, and as confirmed by table 3.3, the propensity to consume has been closely related to the behavior of private real income per capita. Its increase in the past decade appears to have been determined, in particular, by the sharp contraction in the population's real income that took place during the debt crisis and the 1986 oil price collapse.[18] The legacy of these two shocks, and the "lost decade" of economic stagnation that followed, was a sharp reduction in the private savings rate and, with it, in the economy's overall capacity to generate savings. Although much more empirical research is needed on this subject, preliminary evidence also supports the hypothesis that the decline in

---

[17] As tables 3.1 and 3.3 show, the increase in government interest payments (8 percent) was almost identical to the increase in private income (7 percent).

[18] For a more detailed defense of this very Keynesian explanation and a discussion of possible alternative hypotheses, see Ros 1992a. On the behavior of private consumption and savings in the 1980s, see also Alberro 1991; Arrau and Oks 1992. Alberro does not discuss the decline in the savings rate, but his estimates of consumption functions for the 1980s yield strikingly Keynesian results and are thus fully consistent with this chapter's interpretation. Arrau and Oks offer an excellent review of methodological and data problems in estimating savings. Their focus, however, is on the decline in private savings after 1987 and on the role in it of durable goods consumption (not a major factor up to 1989).

publicly provided services may have led to a substitution of private for public consumption during the 1980s, thus contributing to the fall in the measured private savings rate. As discussed in Ros 1992a, the decline in public consumption expenditures from 1980 to 1989 was accompanied by an increase (as a share of real private disposable income) in private spending on health care, education, entertainment, transportation, and communications (from 16.3 percent of GDP in 1980 to 18.4 percent of GDP in 1989).[19]

MARKET REFORMS, ECONOMIC EFFICIENCY, AND PRODUCTIVITY GROWTH

With comparatively low investment and domestic savings rates, Mexico's economic growth in the early 1990s was half of what it was during the oil boom. On present trends (around 3–4 percent per year) it will remain significantly below the long-term growth rate of the postwar period (6.5 percent per year). Despite a foreign savings rate well above historical levels, the Mexican economy currently invests a lower proportion of its output than at any time in the two decades before 1980. As a result, expansion of productive capacity occurs at a slower pace than in the past. The economy, in sum, emerges weaker, rather than stronger, from the years of crisis and adjustment.

At the same time a "great transformation" has taken place—if one can appropriate Polanyi's expression to describe events of a different scale. The far-reaching reform process raises two central questions. First, are market reforms likely to affect significantly the economy's productivity growth rate and external competitiveness so that, despite lower rates of accumulation, the economy may recover some of the growth potential lost during the crisis? Second, can the shift in the market/state balance bring about a permanently higher flow of external savings, significantly greater than historical rates, which would allow an increase in the rate of accumulation despite a sharp decline in the domestic savings rate? This section focuses on the first question, examining the available evidence on the subject. The concluding section addresses the second issue.

Some policy reforms, especially those affecting the domestic regulatory framework (concerning, for example, road transportation), were long

---

[19]The economic rationale for this effect is that, to the extent that consumers value such publicly provided social services as education and health care, private spending on these items will increase when public provision of these services declines or their quality deteriorates. The implication is that a part of the decline in public consumption did not contribute to the increase in overall domestic savings but was rather offset by a decline in the private savings rate. It is worth emphasizing that much more research is needed on this subject. Part of the increase in private spending on social services could be a result, for example, of long-term trends in the composition of private consumption that continued to operate during the 1980s independently of the fall in public consumption.

overdue and are clearly desirable on both efficiency and equity grounds.[20] Their adverse impacts have been limited (if present at all), and the benefits of regulatory changes in many areas have by and large exceeded the costs. These have not been the most radical reforms, however, nor those from which the greater benefits were to be expected. What follows focuses on the most important of them—trade and investment liberalization, privatization, and state reform—and on a preliminary evaluation of their effects.

The case for greater selectivity in state participation in the economy— indeed, for state disengagement in a number of productive activities—is also extremely powerful. But this is so, as already mentioned, because of macroeconomic reasons related to the special conditions of the 1980s. This particular argument has less significance for the long-term growth potential of the economy, beyond the promise of a considerable expansion in human capital investments that huge privatization revenues make possible.

There is also, of course, a microeconomic case for privatization based on the notion that greater private-sector participation will improve the overall efficiency of investment. If such efficiency gains are a positive function of the share of private investment in overall investment, then part (if not all) of the fall in the overall rate of accumulation could be compensated for by the shift in the composition of investment. And as table 3.3 shows, there has indeed been a dramatic shift in the composition of investment during the 1980s; the private-sector share of total fixed investment rose from 56 percent in 1980–1981 to 77 percent ten years later.

The first point to be made in addressing this issue is to recognize that the efficiency of overall investment does not depend only on its private/ public-sector composition, but also on the rate of investment itself. As already discussed, the rate of investment affects investment efficiency through its impact on the age distribution and structure of the capital stock (residential/nonresidential, net investment/depreciation). Now, as clearly shown in table 3.3, the shift in the private/public-sector composition of investment was a result of the absolute decline in the rate of public investment rather than of an absolute increase in private investment. In the early 1990s the latter was at approximately the same levels as ten years earlier (14–15 percent of GDP). If its share in overall investment had increased, this was only because of the collapse of public investment rates from around 11.5 to 4.5 percent. Unless the productivity of public investment was actually negative—and no one has argued this—the efficiency losses resulting from the absolute fall in the overall rate of investment are bound to outweigh any efficiency gains brought about by the shift in its composition. The rise in the capital-output ratio since 1982 is fully consistent with this conclusion.

---

[20]For a discussion of regulatory changes in domestic activities affecting road transportation, telecommunications, and the banking system, see Dávila 1988; Ramos Tercero 1988; San Martin 1988.

In addition, the relationship between the efficiency and the composition of overall investment is surely more complex than generally assumed. It is likely to have the shape of a Laffer curve (an inverted U), with low efficiency levels being consistent with both too high and too low shares of public investment. This is the case because, as much recent empirical research suggests, public investment itself affects the productivity of private investment. Thus at low levels of public investment, further reductions can bring about losses rather than gains in overall efficiency. Given the sharp contraction of public investments during the 1980s and the fact that the microeconomic efficiency gains and performance improvements of Mexico's newly privatized enterprises are yet to be seen in most cases, the question arises as to whether Mexico may have moved to the wrong side of this Laffer-type curve. In such circumstances, an increase in public investments in areas with high social returns and high positive externalities for the productivity of private investment is the best way of addressing the problem of investment efficiency.

The results of trade policy reform are also controversial. Let us turn first to the static efficiency gains expected by classical trade theory.[21] One striking feature of the Mexican transition toward a liberalized trade regime is the smoothness of the microeconomic processes of resource reallocation, which can be explained by the fact that at least up to 1987–1988 tariff reductions and the elimination of import licenses were effectively compensated by a high degree of "exchange rate protection." This facilitated the adjustment of industrial firms to a more open economy, and it prevented job losses, which at least until 1987–1988 were largely the result of contracting industrial demand rather than import penetration. Moreover, current trends in the trade *pattern* and industrial *structure* are largely an extrapolation of the past. As shown in table 3.4, with few exceptions (the growing export shares held by the wood products industry and, after 1985, by textiles and apparel) the 1980s witnessed an extrapolation of past trends in trade and industrial patterns, marked by the increasing importance of heavy intermediates, consumer durables, and capital goods. Since 1985 (the first year of radical trade reform) these trends have continued unabated and, in the case of consumer durables and capital goods, have if anything accelerated.[22]

The counterpart of this smoothness and of the lack of reversal in the direction of structural change in manufacturing is, however, that the classic

---

[21]For a detailed discussion of resource reallocation processes, see Ros 1992b and, in particular, Moreno 1988, who analyzes the most important aspect of these processes, the restructuring of the automobile industry and its role in the 1980s manufacturing export boom.

[22]The declining share of heavy intermediates between 1985 and 1989 was largely due to the falling share of petrochemicals, whose export boom was concentrated in the first half of the decade as the large expansion of productive capacity undertaken during the oil boom found no outlet in the domestic market. The share of heavy intermediates in 1989 was, nevertheless, well above 1980 levels.

efficiency gains expected from trade liberalization cannot possibly be very important. For those expecting a large, painful, but very beneficial reallocation of resources in favor of traditional (labor- and natural resource-intensive) exportable goods, the experience with trade liberalization to date should have been, in fact, greatly disappointing. Apart from the impact of a high exchange rate, one major factor explaining these developments is simply Mexico's past import-substitution experience and the advanced stage that intra-industry (and intra-firm) specialization and trade processes had already reached by 1980, precisely in those capital-intensive, large-scale manufacturing industries that were responsible for most of the export boom in the 1980s. The industrial policy reforms of the late 1970s, especially in the automobile industry, gave further impulse to those processes. Thus the incentives provided later by a very attractive exchange rate and by the mid-1980s trade reforms fell on already fertile ground. The outstanding export performance of Mexico's manufacturing sector in the 1980s was to a large degree, then, a legacy of the import-substitution period. In a very real sense it highlighted the success of import substitution, showing that, despite some costs, it led to an irreversible change in the economy's structure of comparative advantages.

What can be said about the dynamic effects of trade liberalization on productivity performance? Any attempt to answer this question at this stage must be considered tentative and preliminary. It is with these strong qualifications in mind that we now examine the available evidence on the manufacturing sector, beginning with labor productivity.

Overall labor productivity grew in the 1980s at 1.4 percent per year, well below historical trends (on the order of 3.5 percent per year). This was true for the years both before and after the 1985 trade reform. At the same time, productivity growth for manufacturing as a whole recovered in the post-trade liberalization period after 1985. This acceleration was largely concentrated in the automobile industry, basic metals, and food processing. In the first two industries, the evolution of import and export ratios suggests that productivity gains were most likely the result of increasing intra-industry (and intra-firm) specialization in foreign trade, associated in the case of automobiles with its special policy regime and international developments since the late 1970s.[23] In food processing, the fact that productivity increases took place in the midst of a slowdown in the

---

[23]In particular, the export-oriented investments of the late 1970s and early 1980s (following the 1977 automotive decree) must have made a significant contribution to the technical modernization of the industry, whose effects were only fully felt well into the 1980s as the new plants created by those investments came into operation and rapidly expanded their share in the industry's output (on this subject, see Moreno 1988). In the basic metals sector, the industry's rationalization is perhaps also related to a government program with precisely that goal, which included the closure or privatization of many public enterprises in a sector where these firms have traditionally accounted for a relatively high share of the industry's output (29.5 percent, compared to 7.2 percent on average for the manufacturing sector as a whole).

TABLE 3.4

OUTPUT AND PRODUCTIVITY GROWTH IN MANUFACTURING, 1980–1989

| | Annual Growth Rates | | | | Percentages | | | | | |
| | Labor Productivity | | Output | | Import Ratios[1] | | | Export Ratios[2] | | |
	1980–1985	1985–1989	1980–1985	1985–1989	1980	1985	1989	1980	1985	1989
Food processing[3]	0.7	1.3	2.5	1.8	12.9	4.4	10.2	12.0	11.8	15.5
Textiles, apparel, leather	0.3	-0.9	-0.3	-1.8	5.5	2.4	8.5	8.6	8.1	19.1
Lumber, wood, furniture	3.3	0.4	-0.5	-0.7	6.0	3.1	6.1	2.9	8.2	24.2
Paper	2.4	1.2	2.4	2.6	28.4	14.8	25.9	3.4	4.3	9.1
Chemicals	1.7	1.5	4.6	2.8	43.7	36.9	46.4	14.6	32.6	33.0
Stone, clay, glass	-0.2	0.5	1.1	1.7	6.2	3.1	5.2	4.1	12.1	17.0
Basic metals	-0.1	6.4	0.1	2.8	81.1	37.4	42.3	2.6	11.4	31.7
Fabricated metals, machinery, equipment	0.9	4.2	-1.6	2.2	99.2	56.1	93.9	8.5	23.4	46.3
Automobiles[4]	1.2	5.6								
Other manufacturing	0.3	-1.2	1.3	-1.2	67.6	48.2	75.4	7.3	16.0	28.3
Total manufacturing	1.2	1.8	1.2	1.6	40.5	22.9	36.4	9.0	16.7	26.3

[1]Ratio of imports to sector GDP (1980 constant pesos).
[2]Ratio of exports to sector GDP (1980 constant pesos).
[3]Includes beverages and tobacco.
[4]Terminal industry.

Source: INEGI, Sistema de Cuentas Nacionales.

industry's output growth also suggests a process of industry rationalization, but of a different nature altogether. In this case, industry rationalization was probably associated with rapid import penetration in the industry after 1988; indeed, by 1989 the import ratio in food processing was more than double its 1985 level. The rapid expansion of imports in the domestic market probably led to the shakeout of some parts of the industry, with the elimination of less efficient producers explaining both its rising average productivity levels and the deceleration of output growth in the midst of an overall economic recovery in manufacturing.

However, import penetration has had much more ambiguous consequences for productivity performance in other manufacturing activities. Table 3.4 shows that, despite the overall improvement in productivity, five of nine major manufacturing sectors had lower productivity growth rates after 1985 than in the early 1980s. Indeed, productivity actually fell in two sectors (textiles and a residual category of other manufacturing industries) after 1985. Moreover, the three worst performers (these two sectors and the wood products industry) all had declining output levels after 1985, reflecting the fact that imports displaced domestic production even more rapidly than national producers could take advantage of expanding export opportunities. These three sectors, as well as food processing, experienced the fastest rates of import penetration in the entire manufacturing industry; the almost fourfold increase in the import ratio for textiles was especially remarkable.[24]

It is very difficult to evaluate the dynamic efficiency gains from trade liberalization because other important factors must have also affected recent productivity trends. In particular, the low rate of capital accumulation (through endogenous technical progress effects) and the decline in social investments during the 1980s (through its effects on human capital formation) must have adversely affected the long-term trend of productivity growth. Nevertheless, one can conclude that, whatever the beneficial effects of reforms, they have to date been outweighed by the adverse developments just mentioned.

STATE REFORM AND THE TASKS OF DEVELOPMENT POLICY

The other dimension of market reform in Mexico has been the retreat and restructuring of the state. The neoliberal argument is that a smaller state is better able to perform its priority tasks. Some recent developments on the revenue and transfers sides of fiscal accounts are certainly encouraging in this regard; the efficiency of tax collection has improved, the tax base has expanded, several inequitable subsidies have been eliminated, and the inflation tax has practically disappeared. But many other

---

[24]The evidence on total factor productivity growth does not appear to be much more encouraging, despite some claims to the contrary. For a detailed discussion, see Moreno 1992.

changes on the expenditure side have been far less fortunate. Overall, Mexico's fiscal adjustment has not encouraged greater internal efficiency in the public sector, despite or perhaps because of its massive character. As already noted, fiscal adjustment after 1985 was achieved by and large through deep cuts in public investment and in the real salaries of public employees, which was hardly a useful means of improving the efficiency of the state and its bureaucracy. On the other hand, despite some positive recent trends in social spending, state disengagement has not served its main stated purpose: the expansion of social infrastructure. The main contribution of privatization revenues has been to support (very effectively, no doubt) recent stabilization efforts by temporarily compensating for the decline in the inflation tax and by strengthening the balance-of-payments capital account (the result of private investors' bringing financial assets back home to purchase the public enterprises offered for sale).

The Mexican state is now smaller but not necessarily more efficient. The implications of this are more important than generally acknowledged because the state's priority tasks—social policy, in particular—are far more formidable today than in the past. This is so for several reasons. First, there is an accumulated backlog of social needs that went unmet during the 1980s. Second, in the absence of strong social and regional policies, some social disparities are likely to be exacerbated in the future. This, of course, will depend very much on the long-term effects of current economic growth strategies. But holding this factor constant, there are at least two reasons why the present development pattern may have this effect: (1) the state's retreat from agriculture and the reform of the land tenure system may bring private capital and prosperity to some rural areas, while also inadvertently impoverishing large masses of rural workers over a more or less prolonged period; (2) the benefits of greater integration with the international economy are likely to be very unevenly distributed within the country. For example, these processes may deepen regional disparities between a prosperous north, increasingly integrated with the U.S. economy, and a poor and backward south, plunged into agricultural stagnation.

Finally, and no less fundamental, by abandoning trade and industrial policy instruments that worked successfully in the past without providing effective replacements, current development strategy encourages the exploitation of present rather than potential comparative advantages. The basic task of development policy—the task of changing and enhancing the present endowment of resources and gradually shifting the pattern of comparative advantages toward higher-value-added, technology-intensive activities—now, in the absence of industrial policy, falls fully upon social policies. A proportionate response to this challenge could actually make things better than they might otherwise be (that is, better than under an active industrial policy with little social policy). However, the point is that the challenge itself is now much greater, while no coherent response is yet on offer. A less than proportionate response would lead to freezing the present stage of development—remaining stuck in the relatively unskilled, low-paid production processes in capital-intensive industries. This is a far from desirable prospect for a country that needs both to grow fast and to raise rapidly the living standards of its nearly ninety million people.

CONCLUDING COMMENTS

If the efficiency and productivity effects of market reforms are unlikely to make up for the loss of growth potential that occurred during the 1980s, what can be expected of neoliberal reforms' impacts on external capital inflows and the prospects for increasing the rate of accumulation by these means? Since 1989, the reform process has brought huge capital inflows in the balance of payments and, from privatization revenues, billions of dollars into the Mexican treasury (a total of U.S.$16 billion between 1989 and 1992). The overall impact of market reforms on business confidence has been clearly positive. More than that, these reforms have seemingly created the sense of a new beginning among the local entrepreneurial class as well as among foreign investors. This has had positive practical effects, as witnessed by the large amount of capital repatriation since 1989 and, at another level, the financial restructuring of some leading Mexican conglomerates (whose prospects immediately after the 1982 crisis were not bright).

The reforms have recently reached at least a symbolic peak with the reform of the land tenure system and the negotiation of the North American Free Trade Agreement (NAFTA) with the United States and Canada. They are now in their final stage. Privatization entered its final phase in 1992, with the sale of the remaining banks, insurance companies, and parts of the operations of CONASUPO (the food distribution company) and SIDERMEX (Mexico's largest steel producer). This means that a substantial fraction of recent capital inflows is likely to disappear in the near future. Those inflows related to privatization revenues were clearly temporary in nature, and they began declining sharply in 1993.

All this leads to a final and most important aspect of the overall reform process. Does the change in entrepreneurial attitudes and behavior reflect the temporary euphoria of financial markets or, rather, a long-lasting revival of Keynes's "animal spirits" that could prove to be the major positive outcome of the reform process? This question is, in fact, part of a broader issue regarding the consequences of the shifting balance between market and state and the changing ideological climate. Is this change in ideology a sign that, once Mexico's economic backwardness had been reduced by state-sponsored industrialization, a different

set of ideas was more suitable for the new stage, a shift that is the natural
companion to the transition from Gershenkronian to Schumpeterian
entrepreneurship? Dealing with these questions falls outside the scope
of this chapter, and of the wisdom of its author. But on its answer
depends the size of the macroeconomic adjustment problem that lies on
Mexico's medium-term horizon, as well as its longer-term prospects for
rapid economic development.

What can be said is that the origins of Mexico's adjustment problems, and of the new problems created by the adjustment process, are
both macroeconomic in nature. This has two important implications.
First, the notion that the crisis was brought about by the exhaustion of
past development strategies should not be taken for granted, even
though it is quite clear that several key elements of past development
strategies required change. Second, the solution to the new obstacles
facing Mexico—the deterioration of growth potential as a result of
decreased investment efficiency and domestic savings, as well as the
decline in the provision of social services and public investments—is
likely to require new and better forms of state participation in the
economy. Very little attention is being given to these problems and to
what government policy can do about them. At the same time, too much
is expected from the efficiency gains of market reforms.

REFERENCES

Alberro, José L. 1991. "The Macroeconomics of the Public Sector Deficit in
    Mexico during the 1980s." Mexico City: El Colegio de México. Mimeo.
Arrau, Patricio, and Daniel Oks. 1992. "Private Saving in Mexico, 1980–90."
    Policy Research Working Paper. New York: World Bank.
Bacha, Edmar L. 1990. "A Three-Gap Model of Foreign Transfers and the GDP
    Growth Rate in Developing Countries," *Journal of Development Economics*.
Banco de México. 1989. *Indicadores Económicos*. Mexico City: Banco de México.
Carneiro, Dionisio, and Rogerio Werneck. 1988. "External Debt, Economic
    Growth and Fiscal Adjustment." Texto para Discussao No. 202. Rio de Janeiro:
    Departamento de Economia, Pontifícia Universidade Católica do Rio de Jan-
    iero.
Corbo, Vittorio, and Stanley Fischer. 1990. "Adjustment Programs and Bank
    Support: Rationale and Main Results." New York: World Bank, November.
    Mimeo.
Dávila, E. 1988. "La reglamentación del autotransporte público." Documento de
    Trabajo. Mexico City: ITAM.
Fanelli, José María, Roberto Frenkel, and Guillermo Rozenwurcel. 1990. *Growth
    and Structural Reform in Latin America: Where We Stand*. Buenos Aires: CEDES.
Fanelli, José María, Roberto Frenkel, and Carlos Winograd. 1987. *"Argentina,"*
    Stabilization and Adjustment Policies and Programmes. Country Study No. 12.
    Helsinki: WIDER.
Ize, Alain. 1990. *Trade Liberalization, Stabilization and Growth: Some Notes on the
    Mexican Experience*. Washington, D.C.: Fiscal Affairs Department, IMF.

Moreno, J.C. 1988. *The Motor-Vehicle Industry in Mexico in the Eighties.* Mexico City: ILET.

————. 1992. "Multifactor Productivity Growth in Mexico: Some Notes on Recent Research." Notre Dame, Ind.: University of Notre Dame. Mimeo.

Noyola, Juan. 1956. "El desarrollo económico y la inflación en México y otros países latinoamericanos." In *La economía mexicana,* vol. 2, edited by L. Solís. Lecturas de El Trimestre Económico, no. 4. Mexico City: Fondo de Cultura Económica.

Ortiz, G., and C. Noriega. 1988. *Investment and Growth in Latin America.* Washington D.C.: IMF.

Peres, Wilson. 1990. *From Globalization to Regionalization: The Mexican Case.* Technical Papers, no. 24. Paris: OECD.

Ramos Tercero, E. 1988. "Un análisis económico de la reglamentación de la actividad aseguradora en México." Mimeo.

Reisen, Helmut, and Axel van Trotsenburg. 1988. *Developing Country Debt: The Budgetary and Transfer Problem.* Paris: OECD Development Centre.

Rodrik, Dani. 1992. "The Limits of Trade Policy Reform in Developing Countries," *Journal of Economic Perspectives* 6:1 (Winter).

Ros, Jaime. 1991a. "Movilidad de capital y eficacia de las políticas ante una corrida del crédito," *El Trimestre Económico* 58:3:231 (July–September).

————. 1991b. "Fiscal and Foreign Exchange Constraints on Growth." Paper presented at the conference "New Directions in Analytical Political Economy," University of Notre Dame, March.

————. 1992a. "Ajuste macroeconómico, reformas estructurales y crecimiento en México." Prepared for the project "El Rol del Estado en América Latina," of the Fundación CEDEAL.

————. 1992b. "Mexico's Trade and Industrialization Experience since 1960: A Reconsideration of Past Policies and Assessment of Current Reforms." Prepared for the project "Trade and Industrialization Reconsidered," of the World Institute for Development Economics Research, Helsinki.

San Martin, J. 1988. *Transport in Mexico: A Comparative Analysis of Basic Indicators with Other Countries.* Mexico City: Secretaría de Comunicaciones y Transportes.

Schelling, Thomas C. 1978. *Micromotives and Macrobehavior.* New York and London: W W Norton & Co.

Taylor, Lance. 1991. *Income Distribution, Inflation and Growth: Lectures on Structuralist Macroeconomic Theory.* Cambridge, Mass.: MIT Press.

4

Political Liberalization and Uncertainty in Mexico

Soledad Loaeza

In the 1980s some analysts predicted the proximate collapse of Mexico's political system. Yet by the early 1990s, the most serious problems threatening the survival of postrevolutionary authoritarianism in Mexico appeared to have been favorably resolved. The state had reasserted its position as the fulcrum of political equilibrium; the institution of the presidency had been rehabilitated; and the "official" Institutional Revolutionary Party (PRI) had recovered its former electoral strength.

Despite the fact that these three core elements of the traditional system remain intact, Mexico's experiences during the last ten years include many contrasting developments (even contradictions) that qualify the impression that the regime has returned to the status quo ante. The most notable inconsistencies stem from the fact that remnants of authoritarianism in the state, the presidency, and the "official" party survive in a context of greater political pluralism and a significant shift in the country's development model. These changes are evident in the increase in independent participation, electoral and otherwise; in the intensification of competition among political parties; and in the combativeness of the federal Congress.

The severe economic crisis that afflicted Mexico after 1981—with its combination of external debt, recession, and inflation—was the starting point for an anti-authoritarian mobilization whose electoral expression

This chapter incorporates ideas inspired by the comments of Carlos Bazdresch, Marcelo Cavarozzi, Rolando Cordera, Luis Hernández, Julio Labastida, and José Luis Reyna on an earlier version of this essay presented at the conference from which this volume originated. Translation by Aníbal Yáñez.

in the 1980s threatened the PRI's virtual monopoly in many parts of Mexico. The temporal coincidence of this challenge with the end of military dictatorships in Argentina, Brazil, Chile, and Uruguay encouraged a false generalization. The trenchant questioning of Mexican authoritarianism and the strengthening of party-based political opposition (processes which culminated in the disputed presidential election of July 1988) appeared to be portents of regime change. Many viewed the weakening of the state as the beginning of a transition that would lead the country from an authoritarian to a democratic regime.

However, at the end of Carlos Salinas de Gortari's administration, the political readjustments that have occurred offer a rather different picture from that described by those who forecast that the days of Mexican authoritarianism were numbered (Barros Horcasitas, Hurtado, and Pérez Fernández del Castillo 1991; González Casanova 1991). It is certainly true that the Mexican political system is much more open today than it was in the 1970s, but it is still far from democratic. Both political participation and competition have increased, yet forces and tactics that are not part of the formal political process can still change outcomes. This means that Mexico has not taken the crucial step from authoritarianism to democracy, which consists of transferring power from a group of people to a set of rules (Przeworski 1991: 14). The low degree of institutionalization in postelectoral behavior is currently the most powerful obstacle to the development of democracy in Mexico.

As some authors have pointed out, recent Mexican experience is characterized most accurately as a process of political liberalization rather than democratization (Middlebrook 1986). It also confirms the view that there is no sequential relationship—much less a simultaneous one—between liberalization and democratization (Baloyra 1987; O'Donnell and Schmitter 1986).[1] In the Mexican case, as in others, liberalization has been a means of restoring political balance. However, Mexico's experience contradicts the belief that regime liberalization only has two possible outcomes: a hardening of authoritarianism (also called "normalization") or democratization (Przeworski 1991: 66; O'Donnell and Schmitter 1986: 6–7). Contrary to the widespread belief that liberalization is a transitional formula, Mexico's experience with political liberalization dates back more than twenty years. Its success has meant the cancellation of democratization, or at least its indefinite postponement.[2]

---

[1]This conclusion is valid in the terms in which O'Donnell and Schmitter (1986: 6–14) develop these concepts and the relationship between them.

[2]This is what Przeworski and O'Donnell and Schmitter argue. Although O'Donnell and Schmitter admit that there can be liberalization without democratization, they also argue that once essential citizenship rights are recognized, it is very difficult to contain rising demands. From their perspective, then, liberalization strengthens the demands for democratization. The expansion or intensification of these demands culminates either in the elimination of authoritarianism or an authoritarian regression.

In Mexico, successive presidential administrations have since the early 1960s opened institutional channels to independent participation, especially through different electoral reforms that have recognized political forces opposed to the PRI. If democratization were the result of a cumulative process of liberalizing measures, Mexican authoritarianism would have been dismantled long ago. Yet on the other hand, there is no denying that during more than two decades the Mexican political system has opened significantly. This suggests that the differences between liberalization and democratization may be so great that these two paths are negatively correlated, as indeed seems to be the case in Mexico. That is, a successful liberalization is not necessarily one that results in democratization. Rather, the success may lie in its becoming a permanent arrangement that obeys its own logic.

This chapter seeks to analyze the Mexican liberalization experience as a long-term formula with its own distinctive characteristics. It will identify the reasons why this strategy has succeeded, allowing the governing elite to maintain control over the process of political change. The discussion will focus primarily on developments during the 1980s, without forgetting that since the 1960s the Mexican political system has responded to social groups' demands for effective participation with gradual, carefully calculated liberalizing reforms. The first section discusses the differences between liberalization and democratization. The next section analyzes the country's most recent transformations in light of both the current political situation and the structural limits that have consistently shaped political change in Mexico—and whose existence long predates the crisis of the 1980s.

LIBERALIZATION AS AN ALTERNATIVE TO DEMOCRATIZATION

In a transition—that is, in a general process of dismantling authoritarianism and creating a democratic regime—liberalization and democratization may appear to be sequential, even parallel, processes. More important, they have been considered related and mutually conditioning processes. However, each exhibits unique characteristics that may profoundly differentiate one from the other, and which may explain why one process can proceed quite independently of the other.

Liberalizing an authoritarian system implies far-reaching changes—including, for example, those stemming from the dissolution of mechanisms that control participation and the resulting increase in pluralism. Such changes may be necessary to dismantle authoritarianism, but they are not sufficient because they do not automatically guarantee greater control by the ruled over the rulers. This step does not even guarantee a greater competition for power. One of the defining characteristics of regime liberalization is that the governing elite maintains control over the process of change, so that even when changes may occur in response to demands from below, it is also a project directed from above.

Thus liberalization can be an option for authoritarian elites who want to remain in power and who respond to the demands for political liberalization by broadening spaces for the free action of individuals and groups. Hence, liberalization enlarges the social bases of the regime. For those in power, this type of limited change is attractive for at least two reasons. First, the elite does not abdicate its power to direct change and it retains the possibility of reversing the process—which is a powerful negotiating card vis-à-vis mobilized groups or individuals. Second, to the extent that liberalization is seen as a transitional formula, it offers a wide margin for pragmatic and ad hoc solutions. Both the group in power and those who are mobilized can make use of this margin for maneuver.

In contrast, democratization is a process whose rules appear to be more clearly defined. It concerns a specific institutional arrangement whose mechanisms and actors are well identified in terms of the rights and obligations that lie behind the "citizenship principle" (O'Donnell and Schmitter 1986: 7–11).

From this one can infer that the most notable difference between liberalization and democratization is that the latter's path is relatively predictable, even given the uncertainty inherent in democratic processes (Przeworski 1991: 10). The degree of uncertainty in regime liberalization is greater insofar as it is an open process subject to the impact of pragmatic actions. In democratic competition, participants know the rules of the game as well as the resources committed to the game; the only uncertainty is the outcome (Przeworski 1991: 12–13). In contrast, in a liberalized environment, the degree of uncertainty regarding the institutional framework and the resources that the participants put into play may be greater than that surrounding the outcome of competition itself. This is so because the authoritarian elite has not surrendered the privileges of power, and consequently it may or may not subject itself to rules and institutions. Mobilized actors, for their part, will want—and to a certain extent will be able—to do the same. Thus a low degree of institutionalization distinguishes a liberalization process from a democratization process, and the degree of uncertainty in the former is greater than that in the latter, especially with regard to the end point of the process. So, for example, in the early 1990s, countries that experienced democratization in the 1980s—including Argentina, Brazil, Chile, and Uruguay—face problems of democratic consolidation, while Mexico is still struggling with the dilemmas of a political opening whose evolution is uncertain.

Mexico's liberalization experience is by no means new. The country first attempted liberalization in 1963, when the López Mateos administration (1958–1964) introduced a party deputy system to channel middle-class political discontent through existing political parties. Unheeded, this discontent could have threatened the system's stability (Loaeza 1988). Giving dissatisfied minorities an increased presence in the federal Chamber of Deputies through a proportional representation formula was a means of institutionalizing protest without modifying the system's essential features.

Since then, liberalization has operated in different ways. It has helped to "institutionalize" several interest groups, trade unions, and political parties that have managed to gain entry into the system. Thus one effect of these reforms has been to increase the size of the political arena, with more players and more issues subject to political debate. In 1970 President Echeverría proposed a "political opening" in order to mitigate the effects of the 1968 student uprising. This proposal was an important step toward recognizing the legitimacy of the opposition, but the reforms it introduced were more attitudinal (greater tolerance of criticism and of the diversity of public opinion) than institutional. Subsequent openings in the form of electoral reforms (in 1977, 1986, and 1989) gradually expanded the channels for independent participation and representation.

From a long-term perspective, these successive liberalization measures may appear to be part of a coherent, long-term reformist project. However, on closer examination they seem instead to have been isolated measures, part of a pattern of system response to conjunctural conflict. From this perspective, successive liberalizations in Mexico appear to be a conditioned reflex, the reaction of an authoritarian structure that is activated when that structure encounters mobilized opposition.

The fragmented nature of these different liberalization episodes stands out if we consider the characteristics of the different political conjunctures that set the mechanism in motion. For example, the 1977 Law on Political Organizations and Electoral Processes (LOPPE) enlarged the arena for party competition, thus integrating leftist political organizations into the system and inducing them to renounce extra-parliamentary forms of action. On the other hand, the 1986 Federal Electoral Code responded to middle- and upper-class demands for effective representation in a context of severe recessionary policies and the moral bankruptcy of the state.

These examples suggest that what has spurred liberalization in Mexico time and again is the drive to preserve the system, not a supposed democratic imperative. The efficacy of this response pattern has produced confusion over its real meaning. Because the governing elite has resorted to it frequently and with considerable success, its recurrent use could be mistaken for continuity. The difference between recurrence and continuity is important: recurrence reveals authoritarianism's ability to survive and to restrict political change; continuity tends to confer an almost biological democratic nature on the Mexican system, one that naturally directs its development without having to rely on significant modifications.

THE EXPERIENCE OF THE 1980S

Mexico's political stabilization experience during the 1980s is yet another example of a critical situation that was resolved by liberalizing certain forms of participation for specific groups. In contrast with previous instances, liberalization in this case (which initially consisted of reducing fraud in local elections and acknowledging the resulting opposition victories) was the price that the de la Madrid administration (1982–1988) was willing to pay in order to implement a severe adjustment program concurrent with structural reforms aimed at replacing the country's prevailing development model. This period of anti-authoritarian mobilization was also distinguished by the fact that it was a response to the country's worsening economic situation, and to the belief that Mexico's political formula was as exhausted as its pattern of growth. Moreover, the most significant changes took place in the context in which political institutions operated, not in the institutions themselves.

The 1980s will enter Mexican history as a period of shifts in the regime born of the 1910–1920 Mexican Revolution. During this decade, many government initiatives departed so far from traditional policies that it is tempting to speak of rupture rather than change. The de la Madrid administration abandoned the import-substitution model and opened the Mexican economy to international competition. It also made the private sector and market forces the principal engine of growth, with the state retaining residual responsibility for guiding the development process.

Because de la Madrid's reforms centered on economic and administrative issues, political changes seemed to echo the ruptures, compromises, and readjustments occurring in these two areas. The state's new role in the economy inevitably influenced the overall political balance by altering the positions of other political actors. Thus, for example, the key role assigned to private enterprise in promoting economic growth increased the political weight of business organizations. They then tried to extend their leadership role in economic activities to the electoral arena. Well-known businessmen embraced electoral politics, and their organizations openly participated in the National Action Party (PAN), the main beneficiary of the private sector's new-found political vocation. On the other hand, these same economic policies aggravated trade unions' traditional weakness and subordination.

The impact of economic reform on the power structure precipitated the readjustment of actors' positions, but discontinuity in the political arena was not as pronounced as it was in the economy. There were important changes, the most notable of which concerned the role of political parties and elections. Nevertheless, the reform of the state did not significantly modify the basic constitutional provisions that have defined the organization of political power since 1917.

The preservation of the prevailing institutional arrangement is even more noteworthy given the fact that authoritarianism was under attack by the middle and upper classes. Important anti-authoritarian opposition groups appeared within these class formations and within the private sector. These groups advocated electoral democracy, and they decried the country's economic decline and the state's apparent incapacity to guarantee growth and public order. Opposition groups voiced their discontent in a series of electoral mobilizations (which until July 1988 centered around the PAN) that effectively challenged the PRI in several regions.

At first, government authorities met this challenge with unprecedented tolerance toward opposition electoral advances at the local level (Martínez Assad 1985). Then, when this strategy seemed risky, they attempted to reestablish traditional forms of electoral control, provoking angry confrontations in a politically charged atmosphere. In response, the de la Madrid administration resorted to a regulated political opening, which produced the 1986 Federal Electoral Code. Although increased independent electoral participation can destabilize an authoritarian system that rests on conformity, the mere act of holding regular elections also provides an escape valve for tensions and allows for the expression of protests within an institutional framework, thereby neutralizing their disruptive potential. From 1983 onward, local-level opposition victories shook the PRI's traditional predominance and altered the terms of political competition. But at the same time, the fact that pressure for change was concentrated in the electoral arena and in existing organizations (nine parties participated in the 1985 federal elections) let the system absorb protest and permitted the governing elite to maintain ultimate control over the process.

In this case, however, liberalization had to respond to much more than demands for participation, and it was no longer the conferred democracy that had been characteristic of previous reforms. This liberalization episode was a necessary readjustment of political institutions to the demands of a changed society. The distance between this social context and that of the past is measured in the contrast between de la Madrid's affirmation that the 1986 Federal Electoral Code responded to society's changing demands, and the way in which then-Minister of the Interior Jesús Reyes Heroles introduced the LOPPE in 1977, which he said reflected the fact that President López Portillo was "committed to a political reform to activate progress in Mexico" (Reyes Heroles 1977: xv).

The electoral insurrection of the 1980s was the most palpable manifestation of the changing context in which the state, the presidency, and the "official" party operated. The increase in independent electoral participation reflected transformations within Mexican society, whose internal complexity had grown dramatically over the previous twenty years as a result of increasing urbanization and rising educational levels. This increasingly heterogeneous society could no longer be easily assimilated in a single political framework—no matter how flexible that arrangement might be—as the PRI had done for more than four decades.

In spite of the differences outlined above, the results of this liberalization experience were not very different from those of the past. They consisted mainly of an enlarged political arena, with a broader repertoire of issues open to political discussion and a greater number of players in the game. There was a pluralization of political forces and of ideological currents acting within political parties and/or through opinion and interest groups. Greater complexity in political dynamics reflected a deeper phenomenon: the fact that public opinion now counted in the political balance. This change raised the threshold of tolerance for political differences and increased the efficacy of independent participation, while at the same time setting certain limits to the impunity with which elites might exercise public authority.

The strengthening of party oppositions—especially the PAN, which was supported by business organizations and the discontented middle class—engendered a gradual transformation in the meaning of the vote. In preceding decades the vote had served to validate the democratic essence of the Mexican regime. But during the 1980s, voting also became a means of protest. In the end, the vote became what it is today: a negotiating card, which may or may not express political preferences.

The new meaning of the vote has introduced a crucial change in Mexican politics: relative uncertainty. Long absent from Mexican elections, uncertainty is now a factor in shaping the liberalization process. It has, moreover, increased ambivalence within the PRI, which now oscillates between functioning as a machine for promoting electoral mobilization and as an apparatus for controlling participation, with all that this implies in terms of the party's identity and operation. The unpredictability of electoral outcomes also results from increased formal and informal monitoring of elections and greater party competition, especially at the local and state levels. In the past, nomination by the "official" party was a sure way to power, but this is no longer the case in important regions of the country. Even the PRI's electoral recovery in the August 1991 federal elections was possible only because of intense campaigning.

Nevertheless, these changes have not altered the political system's authoritarian essence. Even though relations between the PRI and government authorities throughout this period were marked by friction and barely disguised tensions, the privileged relationship between the "official" party and the state endures. By virtue of these ties, the PRI does not compete with other parties on an equal basis. Moreover, the centralization of power inherent in Mexican presidentialism has not given way. Its characteristic arbitrariness underlies the uncertainty that permeates the multiple levels of electoral competition.

Strong presidentialism contains a crucial limitation on democratization: the predominance of the executive over the legislative branch, which in Mexico remains in the hands of a docile PRI majority. Moreover, the strength of the presidency has compromised advances in the electoral field, not so much because it unconditionally supports the "official" party, but because as supreme arbiter of electoral competition the president can cancel electoral outcomes (as in Guanajuato and San Luis Potosí in 1991 and in Michoacán in 1992). In all of these cases, negotiations between the opposition and the presidency voided the election of PRI candidates in order to quiet opponents' accusations of electoral fraud. The president's informal intervention in these postelection conflicts altered the voters' mandate, at least as it had been established according to prevailing rules. These extra-institutional arrangements unmasked the fact that laws and legal codes can be subordinated to the survival needs of part of the political elite (elements who must have concluded that these concessions cost less than abiding by the law).

Thus, although electoral competition has intensified, government authorities retain a considerable margin of arbitrariness. The institutionalization of electoral processes remains low, despite the changes made when the lengthy, complicated Federal Electoral Code was exhaustively debated by all political parties in 1989.

THE REASONS BEHIND MEXICO'S LIBERALIZATION

If indeed liberalization has been the survival option for authoritarianism over the past three decades, then we must necessarily examine its foundations and the reasons for its success. Many analyses of Mexico's different liberalization episodes have concentrated on short-term factors: those that trigger a liberalization response, and those that stand in its way. The type of protest, the demands, and the political strength of mobilized groups are important factors in defining the responses adopted. Conservative resistance within the government or the PRI, divisions within the political elite, and presidential leadership are all significant factors, but they are insufficient explanations—especially in light of the fact that liberalization has been a recurring response. Put differently, if gradual and controlled change had in every instance been the result only of conjunctural factors, then it is very likely that these measures would have had a cumulative effect and perhaps led to democratic change. The fact that this has not happened suggests that there are deeper reasons why liberalization has in each case offered satisfactory responses to the challenges posed by opposition mobilization, and that these reasons have to do with structural elements in the organization of political power in Mexico.

There have been two bases for liberalization policy: immediate or conjunctural, and structural. The former comprise the sources of opposition protests, their objectives, and their form, all of which are variable. The structural bases are permanent or evolve very slowly, as is the case with changes in social structure.

Liberalization in the 1980s was guided by both types of factors. Among the conjunctural factors the most important were the roots of protest, the type of anti-authoritarian mobilization that was organized, its protagonists, and its objectives. The structural factors shaping political change were social inequality, the prevailing institutional framework, and Mexico's relationship with other countries, especially the United States.

Unlike events in other Latin American countries—where anti-authoritarian protests in the 1980s stemmed from a generalized repudiation of the regime—in Mexico opposition mobilization had a more limited origin: the economic crisis. It began in March 1981, when international lenders abruptly suspended credit to the Mexican government. The nationalization of the banks—decreed by President López Portillo in September 1982, a few weeks before he left office—made matters worse. The bank nationalization profoundly weakened the traditional alliance between the Mexican state and the private sector, and the latter responded by denouncing authoritarianism as the cause of recession, inflation, and the bleak economic outlook. The fact that the starting point for the anti-authoritarian mobilization was the state's inability to guarantee economic growth implied that if the state could recover that ability, this would suffice to satisfy the demands for change. It implied that the sources of discontent would disappear once the recession faded and inflation eased.

The most significant political protests prior to 1988 coalesced around electoral and party mobilizations, as noted earlier. This feature is important because the initiative for change on these occasions came from mobilized portions of the middle and upper classes, whose purposes were not to transform the structure of social domination but simply to set limits on the exercise of governmental authority. Moreover, the main characteristic of these groups' leadership was a preference for electoral protest. If the initiative for change had been in the hands of trade unions or the popular classes, it is likely that the direction of change would have been very different (Loaeza 1990).

The mobilization of broad popular groups around Cuauhtémoc Cárdenas's presidential campaign in 1988 was very different from the mobilizations that dominated the political dynamics of earlier years. The repercussions of that presidential election explain President Salinas's and the PRI's subsequent behavior, as well as the creation of the National

Solidarity Program (which will undoubtedly be identified as the Salinas administration's most effective political instrument) and the composition of the political forces that dominate end-of-the-century Mexico. But these developments must not obscure the fact that mobilization preceding the 1988 presidential succession defined the profile of liberalization, because it determined the forms of protest and established its parameters and dynamics. By so doing, it oriented the character of liberalization itself.

Discussion of the characteristics of this electoral mobilization inevitably leads to a consideration of the second set of factors that structured Mexico's liberalization. This is so because one consequence of the economic crisis of the 1980s was that it uncovered the very foundations of the Mexican system, so that conjunctural factors appeared more than ever as projections of the deep-seated bases of Mexican authoritarianism. In this regard, the three structural variables mentioned above stand out: social inequality, Mexico's institutional framework, and its relations with the United States. These factors limited change, but they also acted as retaining walls in a fragile, potentially explosive situation.

THE MOBILIZATION OF THE PRIVILEGED

The upper- and middle-income groups that participated in the anti-authoritarian mobilization of the 1980s were among those benefiting from Mexican development. Between 1963 and 1977, middle-income groups made up 30 percent of the population but received 49 percent of total family income. Throughout those years the proportion of income going to these groups increased steadily, while the proportion going to lower-income and even higher-income groups decreased in relative terms (Aspe and Beristáin 1984: 31–58). This means that during the years immediately preceding the economic crisis, these groups had enjoyed a period of unprecedented prosperity that accentuated their privileged position. Their demand for political autonomy was one consequence of their increasing prosperity. Thus, for example, the rich states of Chihuahua, Sinaloa, and Sonora—which until the 1980s registered high voter abstention rates—became the stage for some of the most powerful challenges to the PRI's virtual political monopoly.

Prosperity also catalyzed a developing culture of participation. Numerous political newspapers and magazines appeared. Between 1980 and 1987, the number of radio listeners in Mexico increased from sixty million to eighty million, and the number of television viewers almost doubled, from thirty million to more than fifty-five million. Large social groups gained exposure to all kinds of national and international information. Their interest in public affairs grew, and it nurtured attitudes of responsible citizenship and self-confidence, especially among the economically favored.

Confronting a poor economic outlook and an apparently ineffective state apparatus, Mexico's privileged groups may have resorted to electoral insurrection in self-defense. This impression is borne out by the relative paralysis of the popular classes, who were hurt most by the deteriorating economic situation and the government's recessionary policies.

One of the most revealing clues to the privileged position of those groups that mobilized in the 1980s may well be the leading issues they articulated. Despite a decline of more than 40 percent in the real minimum wage during the first three years of the de la Madrid administration, the mobilized groups targeted state authoritarianism and the excesses of public power. Their main demand was respect for democratic freedoms, not an end to adjustment policies. A second important indicator of the class character of this mobilization was its main beneficiary, the PAN, which had never strayed from its liberal, Catholic, and anti-state origins. It was not the parties of the left, such as the Mexican Unified Socialist Party (PSUM), the Socialist Popular Party (PPS), the Trotskyist Revolutionary Workers' Party (PRT), or the Socialist Workers' Party (PST), that benefited from this anti-authoritarian mobilization. This confirms that the mobilized groups' interest was focused elsewhere. As long as the essential fact of the Mexican political order—the structure of social domination—was not in question, the middle and upper classes would concentrate their efforts in the terrain of party politics.

THE INSTITUTIONAL FRAMEWORK

The 1982 crisis shook Mexican institutions but did not destroy them. Unlike the situation in other Latin American countries, where the end of military regimes seemed to open limitless possibilities, liberalization in Mexico did not mean a new beginning.[3] The institutional arrangement set down in 1917 remained relatively intact. The republican, federal, presidentialist regime and its division of governmental powers have not changed significantly despite important reforms regarding municipal organization and elections, such as proportional representation and the explicit inclusion of political parties in the Constitution as public interest entities. Basic continuity in this area contrasts with the very significant and frequent changes made in other constitutional articles, such as those dealing with education, the agrarian sector, labor, or the state's role in the economy.

---

[3] In terms of institutional limitations, liberalization in Mexico would be midway between the breakdown of democracies and the end of authoritarianism, in the way that O'Donnell and Schmitter (1986: 19) described when they contrasted the limits that seem fatalistically to guide the destiny of unsuccessful democracies and "many moments of the transition— namely, the exultant feeling . . . that the future is open, and that ideals and decisions count as much as interests and structures."

The regime's definition of itself as democratic and pluralist did not prevent it from being authoritarian in practice—that is, for the centralization of power in the hands of the executive to translate into a limited pluralist and nonparticipatory system (Linz 1978: 205–66). Nevertheless, unlike other instances of authoritarianism, Mexican authoritarianism claimed a democratic legitimacy derived from its revolutionary origins: it had been born to realize popular demands, not to repress them.

The Mexican system's alleged pluralist vocation expressed itself in the regularity of elections to renew local and national government authorities. Elections traditionally took place in an atmosphere of generalized indifference, given that PRI candidates always won, often by overwhelming margins. But the PRI's exercise of hegemony did not produce an explicit renunciation of a multiparty system. Nor did authoritarian practices close the door to other forms of organization and interest representation. This led to the formation of a dense network of groups and associations, independent of political parties, that have also played a key role in maintaining the system's stability even when they were not part of the PRI.

The importance of this structure of interests lies in the fact that when the 1982 crisis hit, Mexican society had a relatively complex, autonomous organizational network in place that could buffer political tensions. Discontent and protest were directed through established channels. Once again the government could define the problem as one of "malfunctions" in existing institutions. The problem could be resolved through changes in personnel and in political conduct—and by adjusting electoral legislation. Liberalization, then, was limited in its scope.

THE INTERNATIONAL CONTEXT AND RELATIONS WITH THE UNITED STATES

Most political analysts have concluded that international factors play a minor role, if any, in processes of regime transition (see, for example, Baloyra 1987; O'Donnell and Schmitter 1986). In the Mexican experience, however, even if international factors do not bring about political change, they definitely condition it. More so during the 1980s than on previous occasions, Mexico's relations with other countries (and with the United States in particular) were central to the process of political change. The Echeverría and López Portillo administrations initially increased Mexico's openness to the international environment, heightening its vulnerability to external pressures. Later, Mexico's overwhelming external debt and grave internal situation gave rise to fears of political instability whose effects would reach far beyond its borders.

Territorial contiguity with the United States introduces a central distinction between Mexico and the other Latin American countries. This geographic proximity has consistently cast its shadow over Mexico's political options, so much so that some authors maintain that stability in both countries requires a minimum degree of compatibility between their respective policies (Knight 1987).

Geography places Mexico in an important position within the United States' national security sphere. During the 1980s, a number of factors heightened Mexico's strategic value to the United States. First, Mexico was a closer and more secure source of petroleum than any other country. Second, Mexico's external debt jeopardized the stability of international financial markets—particularly the stability of the U.S. banking system—because it represented 44 percent of the capital of the nine most important U.S. banks (Kraft 1984). Third, bilateral trade had grown by a factor of 3.5 since the mid-1970s. Fourth, according to 1980 U.S. census data, more than half of the two million undocumented aliens living in the United States were Mexicans (García y Griego and Verea Campos 1988). And finally, increased drug-trafficking and Mexico's role as producer and/or transit point for drugs bound for the U.S. market underscored Mexico's strategic importance to the United States.

Together these issues created a network of interactions and interdependencies whose contradictions became more acute as a result of conflicts in Central America (on which the U.S. and Mexican positions differed radically). In Washington's eyes, these considerations made Mexico a high-risk zone, a kind of "soft underbelly" in the region,[4] giving the United States cause to become involved in seeking solutions to Mexico's problems.

For many in the United States, the Mexican crisis was a time bomb at their very doorstep. Generalized instability in Mexico could unleash a huge wave of migration, to mention only one recurring U.S. concern regarding its southern neighbor. In Washington there was "a feverish preoccupation with Mexico's corrupt, dysfunctional and old-fashioned political and economic system and the threat that this represented to U.S. interests" (Bagley 1989: 49).

U.S. worries about Mexico's immediate future had two effects on the bilateral relationship: they were a source of conflict because they presaged intervention in Mexico's internal affairs, and they inspired policies of cooperation, especially regarding the foreign debt.

The points of conflict centered on Mexico's domestic policies and its policy toward Central America. The U.S. media, members of Congress, and government authorities pressured for political change in Mexico. These pressures did not fall directly on the Mexican government; if they had, the de la Madrid administration would probably have resorted angrily to a defense based on the right of self-determination. However,

---

[4]Here I borrow the phrase used in Europe at the end of the nineteenth century to refer to the Balkan states. Europeans believed that the weakened condition of these countries presented a risk to their neighbors, and that any explosion there would produce destabilizing aftereffects throughout the region.

U.S. views regarding the need to reform the PRI, or to open the way for the development of a two-party system built around the "official" party and the PAN, influenced Mexican public opinion and, consequently, entered Mexico's internal political dynamic (Buzenberg 1987; González Valderrama 1987).

Cooperation, on the other hand, was evident on the debt issue. Mexico's foreign debt exposed the interdependence between the two countries and laid bare Washington's interest in preventing potentially explosive consequences. The asymmetry between the two countries was clearer than ever before, but so was their mutual vulnerability. The impact of Mexico's debt on the stability of the U.S. financial system explains the emergency rescue that U.S. financial authorities, in collaboration with the International Monetary Fund, orchestrated in August 1992.[5] It also explains why the U.S. Department of the Treasury intervened in negotiations in 1986 between Mexico and international banks, supporting a sizeable reduction in interest rates and an extension of payment periods from eight to nineteen years after Mexico's finances suffered from another decline in petroleum prices (Domínguez 1989). It is very likely that the Mexican case inspired both the 1985 Baker Plan of "Adjustment with Growth" and the 1989 Brady Plan, which sought to reduce the total amount of debt as a condition for fostering growth in debtor countries (Buira 1990).

Thus the United States played a very important role in the Mexican transformation of the 1980s. It validated and strengthened the demands of mobilized groups at the very moment when the Mexican government desperately needed the United States' goodwill to help solve its most urgent problems (Loaeza 1987). The U.S. factor also helped contain a potentially explosive situation.

THE UNCERTAINTY OF LIBERALIZATION

Can liberalizations be consolidated political solutions whose evolution is an open-ended process? To explore this possibility, this chapter has examined the conjunctural factors that precipitated the Mexican crisis of the 1980s and the structural parameters that oriented and limited its outcome. The pragmatic nature of the solutions produced by liberalization is clear, especially after 1988. The Salinas administration's efforts to resolve the imbalances and conflicts that had arisen in the Mexican regime only served to underscore the inadequacy of existing institutions. Under these conditions, the behavior of political actors and the

---

[5]Thanks to this support, the Mexican government obtained a loan that enabled it to enter into negotiations with its international creditors. In exchange, it was to sell petroleum to the United States for its strategic reserve under terms highly unfavorable to Mexico (Kraft 1984: 16–17).

effect of electoral codes seemed as unpredictable as the results at the ballot box.

The sense of uncertainty regarding Mexico's future is greater still if we move from the terrain of elections and political parties to the foreseeable effects of economic policy on some fundamental aspects of the political balance. For example, during the 1980s, the "official" party was one of the first victims of cutbacks in public spending. The shortage of funds had a negative impact on the public services for which the PRI has traditionally served as broker, but it also eroded the party's organizational and mobilization activities. The Economic Solidarity Pact (PSE)—signed in 1987 and renewed several times in subsequent years—increased the subordination of trade unions to the state and probably stimulated the proliferation and strengthening of interest groups that prefer to remain outside the "official" party.

On the other hand, the Salinas administration launched reforms that may deepen liberalization—especially changes in the land tenure system and the structure of primary and secondary public education, as well as the National Solidarity Program (PRONASOL), which some analysts consider to be the main obstacle to rehabilitating the PRI. These innovations may stimulate the rise of autonomous local-level organizations, for example, by altering the power structure at the state level. Similarly, signing the North American Free Trade Agreement (NAFTA) with the United States and Canada altered the balance of forces within the business sector by strengthening those elements linked to export activities.

The impact of these developments is unpredictable. Salinas's leadership underscored the point that liberalization is an open-ended process. The disputed 1988 presidential elections decisively conditioned government policies; they were the touchstone for President Salinas's determination to build up his personal popularity in order to erase the memory of what many still see as his theft of the presidency. He largely achieved this objective.

Salinas's leadership itself intensified the pragmatic nature of political liberalization in Mexico. This was so because the president exercised a double leadership: proactive with regard to the economy, and reactive with regard to politics (Cerny 1988). Thus economic modernization kept to a well-designed plan, one with clearly sequenced stages. But as far as politics was concerned, the responses were more intuitive, following shifts in opinion (obsessively traced via public opinion polls) with almost millimetric fidelity. They did not conform to a long-term modernizing project. Under these conditions, the most recent experience with political liberalization in Mexico takes the form of a proposal whose development seems more uncertain than ever.

REFERENCES

Aspe, Pedro, and Javier Beristáin. 1984. "Toward a First Estimate of the Evolution of Inequality in Mexico." In *The Political Economy of Income Distribution in Mexico*, edited by P. Aspe and Paul E. Sigmund. New York: Holmes and Meier.

Bagley, Bruce. 1989. "La interdependencia y la política de Estados Unidos hacia México: la década de los ochenta." In *México-Estados Unidos, 1987*, edited by Gerardo M. Bueno and Lorenzo Meyer. Mexico City: El Colegio de México.

Baloyra, Enrique A. 1987. *Comparing New Democracies. Transition and Consolidation in Mediterranean Europe and the Southern Cone*. Boulder, Colo.: Westview.

Barros Horcasitas, José Luis, Javier Hurtado, and Germán Pérez Fernández del Castillo. 1991. *Transición a la democracia y reforma del Estado en México*. Mexico City: Universidad de Guadalajara/FLACSO/Porrúa.

Buira, Ariel. 1990. "Evolución de la estrategia de la deuda." In *Interdependencia. ¿Un enfoque útil para el análisis de las relaciones México-Estados Unidos?*, edited by Blanca Torres. Mexico City: El Colegio de México.

Buzenberg, William E. 1987. "The 1985 Elections and the North American Press." In *Electoral Patterns and Perspectives in Mexico*, edited by Arturo Alvarado. Monograph Series, no. 22. La Jolla: Center for U.S.-Mexican Studies, University of California, San Diego.

Cerny, Philip G. 1988. "The Process of Personal Leadership: The Case of De Gaulle," *International Political Science Review* 9:2 (April).

Domínguez, Jorge I. 1989. "Una dialéctica en las relaciones entre México y Estados Unidos: estructuras, individuos y opinión pública." In *México-Estados Unidos, 1987*, edited by Gerardo M. Bueno and Lorenzo Meyer. Mexico City: El Colegio de México.

García y Griego, Manuel, and Mónica Verea Campos. 1988. *México y Estados Unidos frente a la migración de los indocumentados*. Mexico City: Coordinación de Humanidades, UNAM/Porrúa.

González Casanova, Pablo. 1991. *Primer informe de la democracia*. Mexico City: Siglo Veintiuno.

González Valderrama, Rodolfo. 1987. "Fifteen Days That Shook the United States—Uselessly." In *Electoral Patterns and Perspectives in Mexico*, edited by Arturo Alvarado. Monograph Series, no. 22. La Jolla: Center for U.S.-Mexican Studies, University of California, San Diego.

Knight, Alan. 1987. *U.S.-Mexican Relations, 1910–1940. An Interpretation*. Monograph Series, no. 28. La Jolla: Center for U.S.-Mexican Studies, University of California, San Diego.

Kraft, Joseph. 1984. *The Mexican Rescue*. New York: Group of Thirty.

Linz, Juan J. 1978. "Una teoría del régimen autoritario. El caso de España." In *Política y sociedad en la España del siglo XX*, edited by Stanley G. Payne. Madrid: Akal.

Loaeza, Soledad. 1987. "El factor americano," *Nexos* 10:110 (February).

———. 1988. *Clases medias y política en México. La querella escolar 1959–1963*. Mexico City: El Colegio de México.

———. 1990. "Derecha y democracia en el cambio político mexicano: 1988," *Foro Internacional* 30:4 (April–June).

Martínez Assad, Carlos, ed. 1985. *Municipios en conflicto*. Mexico City: GV Editores/Instituto de Investigaciones Sociales, UNAM.

Middlebrook, Kevin J. 1986. "Political Liberalization in an Authoritarian Regime: The Case of Mexico." In *Transitions from Authoritarian Rule. Latin America*, edited by Guillermo O'Donnell, Philippe C. Schmitter, and Laurence Whitehead. Baltimore: Johns Hopkins University Press.

O'Donnell, Guillermo, and Philippe C. Schmitter. 1986. *Transitions from Authoritarian Rule. Tentative Conclusions about Uncertain Democracies*. Baltimore: Johns Hopkins University Press.

Przeworski, Adam. 1991. *Democracy and the Market. Political and Economic Reforms in Eastern Europe and Latin America*. Cambridge: Cambridge University Press.

Reyes Heroles, Jesús. 1977. "Palabras en la iniciación de los trabajos de la Comisión Federal Electoral." In *Comisión Federal Electoral, Reforma política*, no 1. Mexico City: Comisión Federal Electoral.

PART III

Political Parties and Elections

5

Embellishment, Empowerment, or Euthanasia of the PRI? Neoliberalism and Party Reform in Mexico

Denise Dresser

The politics of economic adjustment in Mexico raises some important questions regarding the future of the country's "official" political party. Will the Institutional Revolutionary Party (PRI) wake up one morning as a social democratic force along the lines of Western European parties? Or will it resist modernization and wage a battle to the death against neoliberal policies that undermine its corporatist structure and hegemonic status? In order to address these questions, this chapter analyzes the impact of economic liberalization and adjustment policies on this long-dominant party.

Since the onset of the Mexican economic crisis in 1982, the country's leaders have sought to stabilize (and liberalize) their economy through a series of reforms, including deregulation, privatization, and dramatic public spending cuts. Many of these policies, geared toward reducing the state's presence in key areas, illustrate what Miles Kahler has called "the orthodox paradox," the attempt to use state agencies and personnel to reduce the scope of the state (Callaghy 1989: 116).

This dismantling process affected the PRI dramatically. As a corporatist structure based on the organized inclusion of industrial labor and agricultural workers,[1] the party suffered three key impacts: (1) unable to meet the demands of corporate sectors accustomed to a flow of material benefits, the PRI lost representativeness among its bases; (2) displaced

---

[1]The term "inclusion" is used here to describe the political incorporation of lower-class groups that took place in Mexico during the 1930s. For an analysis of this process in comparative perspective, see Hewlett and Weinert 1982.

by a technocratic team intent on implementing economic reform, the party was increasingly marginalized from the decision-making process; and (3) powerless to guarantee electoral victories, the PRI lost ground as a legitimator of the regime.

However, in order to continue the economic reform program, state elites need political bases that can legitimize this path. Their strategy for reconstructing such a legitimizing base is to prod the PRI to "modernize." Economic liberalization has thus propelled the party to a critical threshold: it can renew itself and prevail by adjusting to the demands and constraints of economic restructuring, or it can retrench and possibly be rendered irrelevant by social forces and state managers pushing for change.

LOSING TOUCH WITH THE BASE

Mexico faced a severe economic crisis at the end of 1982, after a period of unprecedented economic growth (8 percent annually from 1978 to 1981). The incoming administration of Miguel de la Madrid inherited a recession, financial bottlenecks, unemployment, large public spending cuts, lack of access to financial markets, and an anticipated economic growth rate between 0 and -5 percent. In response, the new government instituted a change of course: an ambitious structural adjustment program designed to surmount the crisis and bring the country up to date with changing international economic circumstances. From import-substituting industrialization, Mexico would move to export-led growth; from protectionism to competitiveness; from state protection to state promotion. In order to achieve these goals, the state would deregulate the economy, invite foreign investment, place the private sector center stage, and go beyond the country's borders for new markets, partners, and technology. In other words, Mexico would "exchange the labyrinth of solitude for the supermarket of world integration" (Aguilar Camín and Meyer 1989: 289). But the country would first have to undergo a severe stabilization program that would lay the foundations for the future economic order.

Following an international trend, Mexico embarked on programs to broaden the scope of market forces as a counterpart to downsizing the state's economic role. De la Madrid's team sought to replace the overweight, subsidizing state of the 1970s with the lean, realistic, administratively modern state of the 1980s.

This transition marked a sharp break with the past. Since the 1930s no economic, social, or political field in Mexico had been free of state intervention. The state had direct control of the railroads and the petroleum, energy, and telecommunications sectors. Through ad hoc decisions, state elites had created or acquired a formidable complex of enterprises producing a wide spectrum of goods and services, from automobiles to movie theaters and cabarets. On the eve of the 1982 economic crisis there were 1,155 state-owned enterprises (Romero and Méndez 1990: 193). The state mediated relations between labor and capital, provided health care for over 50 percent of the population, and controlled half of the arable land through the ejido system. By 1982, government expenditures represented 46.1 percent of gross domestic product (GDP) (Newell and Rubio 1984: 380).

This ubiquitous state intervention gave way under the new program. Many of the reforms linked to the adjustment strategy — such as rationalization of public-sector investment programs, reduced subsidies for public utilities and publicly distributed commodities, privatization of state enterprises, and cuts in public-sector employment — derived from a radical critique of state management of the economy. State contraction during the de la Madrid administration underwent ebbs and flows, particularly regarding the depth and scope of privatization measures. Throughout the entire period, however, state elites maintained tight austerity, holding domestic resource use below production by an average of 4.8 percent of GDP from 1983 through 1988. As a result, as late as 1989, GDP per capita was 9 percent below its 1980 level, average real wages in manufacturing were down 24 percent, and real minimum wages were down 49 percent (Sheahan 1991; IDB 1990: 28; ECLAC 1990: 27).

As the de la Madrid *sexenio* unfolded, it became increasingly apparent that the restructuring program was undermining Mexico's populist and statist tradition. The country's economic strategies had passed through many stages since the Lázaro Cárdenas presidency (1934–1940), but until the 1980s they maintained an "inclusionary" kind of corporatism (O'Donnell 1973). This entailed support for and control of wages, social security and public health services, institutionalized channels for negotiation with both peasants and workers, extensive subsidies for basic foods, and support prices for peasant producers (Sheahan 1991).

Economic restructuring cut to the core of Mexico's redistributive coalitions and system of inclusionary corporatism. The shift from a protected to an open market, and from a state-centered to a private-led economy, affected Mexicans from all walks of life. The de la Madrid team's policies to set the economy on the track of renewed growth depended on wage controls, a reduced budget for social programs, the elimination of subsidies, and the stifling of labor demands. Peasants and blue-collar workers, middle-class professionals and inefficient industrialists, government bureaucrats and unemployed marginals all felt the strains of adjustment to a new development model. The "official" party soon became a target of the government's modernizing turn.

The PRI came of age in the 1930s as a party of corporatist groups and functioned successfully until 1982 as a pragmatic coalition of interests. It embodied the multiclass character of the Mexican Revolution, uniting into a single political force the interests of most social groups: conservatives and revolutionaries, peasants and agroindustrialists, workers and employers. The corporate structures granted control to the state but also gave tangible benefits to the sectors. Thanks to pragmatic negotiations and plentiful resources, there was always the possibility that every group would get something. As state resources dwindled in the 1980s, important segments within the PRI coalition—such as organized labor and bureaucrats—stopped receiving their usual shares of the economic pie. What had been at least a conciliatory (if not harmonious) relationship between party leadership and sectors soon turned into an acrimonious haggle over scarce resources, unfulfilled promises, and betrayed loyalties.

The economic crisis eroded the PRI's credibility among the bottom rungs of its corporatist structure. As wages and living standards fell, the PRI entered a "crisis of representation." Paradoxically, this was not because there were no ties between the party and social classes, but rather because the links between party and society had become so strong. Leaders in each sector had developed entrenched interests; patron-client relations formed an intricate web that acted as a filter against demands from groups located at the base. These groups now felt that their interests were no longer adequately represented.

The problem of representation was not new to the PRI. Over the past fifty years, representation was gradually deformed by the party's corporatist characteristics. The PRI became an electoral machine, providing political posts to members of the corporatist structure and, in the process, inhibiting the development of democratic avenues of representation. Party leaders justified this system by arguing that it guaranteed social rights and the permanent material progress of the population. But as the Mexican state grew leaner, the control that traditional power contenders exercised over the public budget weakened.

PRI leaders soon discovered that the party had no militants. Party identification was based more on pragmatic than emotional grounds. Party followers had little party loyalty or feelings of solidarity.[2] As an adviser to the PRI's secretary general commented:

> People say "I'm for the PRI because the PRI brought
> water and electricity." People derive their militancy from
> the concrete responses they get to their demands. They
> don't care about ideology or politics. Now that we don't
> have money because of the crisis, we tell them to wait,
> to practice self-discipline. Other groups come and tell
> them the opposite. When they vote for the opposition,
> they are simply following a natural inclination. People

---

[2]John Waterbury (1977: 329–42) argues that as patronage links become more specific in purpose, hard-nosed calculations of reciprocity may displace effective loyalty. This seems to have occurred in Mexico.

don't care whether the PRI modernizes or not, veers to
the left or to the right. They just want it to respond
(author interview, November 1, 1989).

The municipal reform implemented under de la Madrid illustrates
how budget cuts and changes in resource allocation affected the PRI's
traditional links with society. Before the reform, municipalities had been
dependent on funds doled out to them by the federal and state governments. Under the reform, municipal authorities gained broad discretion
over municipal budgets, as well as the power to channel credit and
administer resources. Each municipality would now outline its development projects and annual expenses. Following a strategy designed to
achieve better control over public spending, the federal government
would then evaluate the projects and fund those it considered viable.

Mexico's governors responded less than enthusiastically to the municipal reform, since it implied a substantial cut in their own resource
base. Besides the political discontent it generated among the governors,
the reform also heightened popular discontent because it often failed. If
government evaluators did not approve a municipality's projects, that
municipality received no public funding. Moreover, poor states like
Oaxaca, Chiapas, and Hidalgo banked most of their funding, paralyz-
ing municipal works for the entire *sexenio*. The people blamed the PRI.

The party also bore the costs of economic austerity on other fronts.
State managers' attempts to dismantle patronage systems and inject
efficiency into parastatal entities produced confrontations with organized labor, undermining support for the PRI. This was particularly
evident in the oil workers' union. As minister of budget and planning
under de la Madrid, Carlos Salinas de Gortari announced that PEMEX,
the state petroleum company, would no longer grant building and
shipping contracts to the union; contracts would be awarded on a
competitive basis in order to control costs and allow private-sector
participation. These measures were a direct assault on the union's
patronage machine, and the PRI paid the price in the 1988 presidential
elections when the union leadership instructed its members to vote for
an opposition candidate.

The economic crisis thus became a political crisis, in which the PRI's
new role was to muffle and demobilize discontent. The end result was
the erosion of ties with the party's base. Nationwide public opinion
studies in 1983 and 1987 revealed that support for the PRI had dropped
from 55.3 percent to 29.6 percent. And the number of those who did not
identify with the ruling party had increased from 26.1 percent to 46.7
percent (Basáñez 1990: 211–47).

As living standards declined and corporatist organizations were less
able to prevent further impoverishment of wage earners, new social
actors (like the rural poor) and new forms of organization (like the

coordinating committees and neighborhood assemblies) gained strength (Carr and Anzaldúa Montoya 1986; Foweraker and Craig 1990). The challenges that Mexico's burgeoning social movements posed to the politics of austerity, and their demands for state relief, soon propelled them into the political arena. Their struggles for the recovery of real wages and welfare benefits became a challenge to those in power, thrusting urban and rural workers and their organizations—willingly or not—into political battles. This growing political presence of social movements in the 1980s took place against the backdrop of declining PRI fortunes vis-à-vis alternative political forces. As a result of the PRI's limited fiscal resources, organizations lost their incentive to remain loyal to the party and gained reasons to support opposition groups that appeared more responsive to their needs (Tamayo 1990).

The PRI was also unable to reconstitute its support bases among social groups outside of the party's corporate structure, such as urban middle classes, professional associations, civic groups, and entrepreneurs. As the de la Madrid *sexenio* advanced, opposition forces aligned with the right-wing National Action Party (PAN) gained strength, particularly in northern states.[3] When the PRI sought to counter the appeal of the right by selecting local entrepreneurs as its candidates, it won a couple of elections but also further undermined its corporatist base. By July 1988, the PRI seemed unable to extend a convincing political offer to old allies or potential new ones.

SHOWDOWN AT THE PRI CORRAL

The PRI's failure as a legitimate representative was only one of its problems. The party also faced a "crisis of rationality," that is, the de-linkage of the political elite from the party apparatus (Conaghan 1987). The PRI's rationality problems emerged in three forms: (1) a growing rift between the administrative spheres of government, namely, the economic cabinet and the PRI; (2) the splintering of the party and the defection of the Cardenista faction; and (3) the emergence of rival groups within the PRI, known broadly as the "renovators" and the "dinosaurs," each struggling to control the party's future course.

The PRI's marginalization from key levels of government and policy making was the result of a shift in elite composition. The central theme of de la Madrid's administration was economic recovery through political prudence and economic realism. He believed his goals could only be achieved by placing loyal allies in key government posts. As a result, de la Madrid's cabinet was one of the most unbalanced in Mexico's history:

---

[3] As of the 1985 federal deputy elections, the PRI had fallen to below 70 percent of the vote in Baja California, Chihuahua, Coahuila, the Federal District, Durango, Guanajuato, Jalisco, México, Sonora, and Veracruz. Up until 1982 the PRI usually garnered far more than 70 percent (Klesner 1991). For an account of the PAN's growing influence, see Story 1987; Loaeza and Segovia 1987; Loaeza 1989, 1992.

administrators and financiers prevailed at the expense of traditional politicos. Out of the fourteen initial members of his cabinet, only three had begun their political life in the PRI (Hernández Rodríguez 1987). Of the seven cabinet members who belonged to de la Madrid's inner circle, six were longtime personal friends. In addition to their ties of friendship, these individuals were linked by having reached the same diagnosis of Mexico's economic ills: the cause of the crisis lay in the abandonment of the "stabilizing model of development." The key to recovery was to reinstitute two aspects of that model: successful collaboration between the state and the private sector, and the retreat of the state to a role of simple guidance.

Nelson et al. (1989) and others have argued that government leaders generally seek a high degree of elite cohesion when they are attempting to implement economic adjustments. This was certainly true of de la Madrid. His goal was to implement a stabilization policy that would solve problems left by previous administrations, and he believed he could only achieve this goal with a homogeneous, cohesive elite. This strategy, independent of its merits, contributed to the erosion of a historic alliance between the executive and the "official" party. The ascent of de la Madrid's team to power meant the displacement of important sectors of the political class—factions within the PRI, organized labor, and the bureaucracy that had opposed his candidacy. Longtime politicos resented being replaced by young politicians with little knowledge or experience. As a disgruntled PRI official complained:

> The technocrats gained access to the political class, not through the wide door of political struggle, but through the narrow door of technical expertise—thanks to palace coups, not mass mobilization; thanks to cabinet desk jobs, not public speeches (author interview, September 6, 1989).

With this shift in leadership composition, the locus of political decision making moved from the political areas of government (the Ministry of the Interior, the PRI) to the financial and planning areas (the Ministries of Finance and of Budget and Planning) (Centeno and Maxfield 1989). During his presidential campaign, de la Madrid placed men he trusted in key positions on the PRI's National Executive Council. This imposition of the "president's men" on the party revealed a trend that was confirmed throughout his administration: the concentration of decision making in the hands of an administrative elite, and the consequent marginalization of the PRI.

The exclusion of party leadership from effective participation in decision making culminated in what observers called "the crisis of the political class": the defection of Cuauhtémoc Cárdenas and Porfirio

Muñoz Ledo, and the creation of the Democratic Current within the PRI. The debate over de la Madrid's successor and the imposition of Salinas as the PRI's candidate despite party opposition drove a final wedge between the PRI and an already disaffected group within the political class. According to a PRI official:

> A group of marginalized politicians saw that the arrival of [Salinas] to power would extend their own marginalization for another six, if not twelve, years. The Democratic Current emerged to prevent the Salinas candidacy. De la Madrid did not know the party. He did not realize how much discontent there was. He was convinced that Salinas assured the continuity of his project. A real politician would have named someone else as his successor (author interview, November 14, 1989).

In the name of economic restructuring and continuity, de la Madrid broke the traditional balance of forces within the political class and revealed the multiplicity of contending forces within the PRI. The party's rationality crisis reached its zenith with the creation of the Party of the Democratic Revolution (PRD), which became an outlet for those opposed to the PRI's alienation from the executive. The Cardenista/PRD movement was quick to capitalize on the PRI's retreat from its distributive commitments. Cárdenas defended state intervention in the economy, vowed to defend small and medium-sized firms, demanded the immediate suspension of debt payments, and promised to rescue privatized firms that had been sold by a "treacherous regime and a party that defends foreign interests" (*La Jornada*, September 18, 1988).

For years the PRI had successfully contained opposition by using the corporatist structures of the political system first to isolate dissenters (such as unionized workers and teachers in 1958, physicians in 1964, and students in 1968) and then suppress them. After the more or less violent elimination or neutralization of counter-elites, the government poured resources into the areas whence opposition had sprung and the PRI then proceeded to co-opt the new leadership (Stevens 1974). The economic crisis rendered the traditional mechanisms of PRI control obsolete. Declining state resources made it more difficult for the party to buy off and "neutralize" burgeoning opposition.

The effects of the PRI's unresponsiveness to the demands of its base and the party elites' inability to resolve conflicts among themselves were felt with full force in the 1988 presidential election. For the first time in Mexico's history, a PRI candidate won the presidency with little more than an absolute majority (50.7 percent of the vote), while a broad coalition of intellectuals, university students, workers, residents of low-income neighborhoods, and grassroots organizations delivered nearly one-third of the vote (31.1 percent) to an opposition candidate.

President Salinas entered office with the legacy of a demoralized and divided party, an invigorated opposition, and a presidential institution tainted by claims of illegitimacy. The party's corporatist machine, which had proved incapable of delivering legitimizing votes—especially in urban areas—was pronounced "dead on arrival."[4]

One of Salinas's first attempts at reconstruction and reconciliation was the designation of his cabinet. In an effort to restore balance within the political class, Salinas incorporated old PRIístas and even officials linked with his challengers for the presidency. This strategy bought political support and rebuilt ties with the old guard. With Salinas pushing and prodding, the Mexican political class began to regroup and close ranks.

Salinas also recognized that the PRI had to change if it was to survive. Even though economic restructuring policies had weakened historical alliances between the party and its sectors, government leaders recognized that the PRI's corporatist pact still resolved important problems. Anti-inflationary pacts would be unworkable without the support of the labor movement, and wage cuts and adjustment would be difficult to implement without a subordinated unionism. The party's corporate structures had to be rescued, albeit in modified form.

The 1988 elections were the PRI's wake-up call. Sectoral leaders would have to relinquish their monopoly on interest representation and open channels for effective base participation. To survive as a majority party in a more competitive and demanding environment, the PRI would have to institute radical changes in the process of selecting its candidates, leaders, and administrators. A PRI official and member of IEPES, the PRI's think tank, noted: "The party was at a crossroads; it either modernized or it died" (author interview, October 31, 1989).

Thus the PRI entered a new phase in its history. The "moderniza-tion" effort began with Salinas's designation of Luis Donaldo Colosio as PRI president. Colosio embodied the changing profile of the party's leadership: young, with little grassroots experience but with a graduate degree from abroad. Colosio assembled a team of men with similar characteristics, who soon became known as the neo-PRIístas.

---

[4]Guadalupe Pacheco's (1989) study indicates that in urban districts with large work-ing-class and popular sectors, the PRI vote was reduced by the competitiveness of the opposition in about 85 percent of the cases. In mixed (urban-rural) areas the PRI obtained favorable votes in 67 percent of those districts with popular-sector voters and in 60 percent of those with working-class voters. In rural districts the PRI faced a less competitive situation in 90 percent of all cases. Pacheco concludes that working-class and popu-lar-sector votes for the PRI suffered major setbacks in big cities but that the "official" party was able to compensate its losses through the rural vote. She also notes that 1988 signaled a collapse in the efficiency of the PRI's corporatist sectors as a means of securing pro-PRI votes.

Neo-PRIísmo is based on the assumption that the PRI of the past is dead. The party's corporatist structure no longer works as a mechanism of political support. The PRI needs to construct a new electoral base within a participatory society, and this depends on a reform of the candidate selection process that would promote the election of local, more representative leaders.

The party's rationality crisis is perhaps most visible in the presence of a large segment of leaders who oppose the modernizing trend. Most of the PRI's old guard began their political careers in a period of party hegemony and stability. Most still cannot believe what is happening. The ranks of the dissenters include influential politicians who feel that they are being attacked on two fronts: by the president's economic reforms and by the PRI's modernization. Labor leaders are being offered continued wage austerity *and* party reform. Politicos/entrepreneurs are being offered the modernization of distributive, productive, and marketing apparatuses that effectively undercut their monopolies *and* party reform.

The struggle over modernizing the PRI in many ways reflects the broader battles being waged across Mexico. Contending factions within the PRI's National Executive Council have constituencies that extend far beyond the party's offices in Mexico City. The neo-PRIístas are perhaps the most vocal and visible faction because of their nationwide media campaign to revamp the party's lackluster image. Nevertheless, their visibility by no means reflects their real power within the party, where leadership is measured in terms of mass support, not newspaper columns. The neo-PRIístas also face problems of effective commitment within their ranks. Many donned modernizing masks simply because they believed that political winds would blow in that direction. They have adopted the discourse of party modernity but, when put to the test, would probably support the PRI's old methods.

These multiple factions within the PRI all looked to the party's Fourteenth National Assembly (which took place in September 1990) to resolve their uncertainties. However, the assembly left many questions unanswered, particularly regarding the relationship between the PRI and Salinas, as well as the viability of effective party reform. A PRI delegate described the event thus:

> The assembly was the catharsis of a PRI displaced by the growing technocratization of the political elite, marginalized by Salinas, and divided by the neoliberal direction of Mexican economic policy. The assembly was a kind of psychoanalytic session in which the PRI diagnosed itself as the sick man of the political system and offered possible treatments to achieve a speedy recovery (author interview, September 5, 1990).

Participants rebelling against traditional political cures and wishing to experiment with new formulas passed two key reforms at the PRI assembly. The first lifted a rule at the core of Mexican corporatism: PRI members would no longer be forced to join party-affiliated unions. Prior to the assembly, the PRI had defined itself as a party of "sectors and citizens." The new statute changed the preferential order and placed the citizenry—not the sectors—center stage. Second, local-level party officials would no longer be imposed from above; they would be elected by the membership. Even the PRI's presidential candidate, previously anointed by the outgoing president, would be chosen by a new National Political Council (Pereznieto Castro 1990). Optimistic analysts hailed a new era of concertation and negotiation within the party, and they argued that the council could become a forum where all currents within the party could voice their concerns (Pereznieto Castro 1990; Gómez 1990; Rubio 1990).

Nevertheless, gaping loopholes remained. The assembly did not make statutory modifications that would have put an end to the PRI's old practices. Under the revised statutes, primary elections would take place "except in cases where [the council] decides otherwise" (Bailey, Dresser, and Gómez 1990). The council would hold ample discretionary powers, such as the authority to determine when "exceptional circumstances" dictate that popular consultation should not take place. And in all likelihood, those exceptional circumstances would be based on the president's evaluation of local political conditions. During his closing speech at the assembly, Salinas warned that democracy had its limits. Opening up the party, he said, "does not mean conceding to our adversaries . . . what the citizens have not given them." The assembly's end result seemed to be increased subordination of the PRI to presidential control, accompanied by acute dissatisfaction among pro- and anti-reform groups over the ambiguous nature of the new statutes. Following the assembly, the party appeared to be drifting, waiting for a clear definition of what exactly "modernization" meant.

LOSING TOUCH WITH THE EXECUTIVE

Continued political infighting paralyzed the PRI, rendering it unable to respond effectively to changing electoral circumstances. It intensified the PRI's crises of representation and rationality and contributed to the emergence of a third problem: the party's alienation from the executive. In his first State of the Nation address, Salinas lambasted a state that supported captive markets, public enterprises, protectionism, corruption, and, above all, privileged bureaucracies. By attacking the state, Salinas was also attacking the PRI, the instrument through which the state had administered its power since the 1930s. Beneath his critique of the PRI's clientelist practices, however, lay a more fundamental criticism. For Salinas, the PRI was at fault not because of its corporatist structure, but because that structure was no longer able to give legitimacy to the presidency.

With the PRI failing as a legitimator, Salinas placed the responsibility for generating consensus on the presidency itself—on the president's capacity to conciliate interests, resolve controversies, and recreate legitimacy. He did so by reviving the strategies associated with one of Mexico's oldest political formulas: presidentialism.[5] Presidentialism was a natural and logical outcome of the Mexican Revolution. The Mexican Revolution had triumphed over the old order, but it still needed to institute a revolution "from above" to achieve social justice. This could only be assured by a strong government. The Constitution institutionalized presidentialism by granting extensive powers to the executive: the permanent authority to intervene in and regulate property relations according to the public interest and the authority to arbitrate conflicts between labor and capital.

Until the early 1970s, leaders exercised varying degrees of presidentialism in order to consolidate their power and implement reforms, including nationalizations and the creation of public enterprises. They did so in close alliance with the PRI. Until the Díaz Ordaz administration (1964–1970) there had always existed a close and operative relationship between the president and the PRI. Presidents began their political careers in the party and had usually served in a variety of political posts. They were familiar with the party's corporatist structures, they had participated in its internal power struggles, and they knew the unwritten rules.

When import-substitution industrialization lost momentum and civil society began to protest the disparities in wealth created by "stabilizing development," the party/president alliance faltered. The demise of the "Mexican miracle" severed the bond between the executive and the PRI. Luis Echeverría (1970–1976) responded by inaugurating the modern-day version of presidentialism, characterized by a certain distrust of traditional politicians and the centralization of power in the executive office, not in the PRI/presidency duo. Echeverría thus initiated a trend: in economic crisis the president would bypass the party and establish a direct, personal relationship with the corporatist structure itself. In troubled times, the president could go beyond the party and exercise a "personal style of government."

Almost twenty years later Mexicans are witnessing the resurrection of that personal style. An analyst of the Echeverría period noted that:

> From the moment [Echeverría] began the electoral battle, he used a political style that Mexicans had never seen before. . . . He visited places that no other candidate had visited. . . . From the very beginning he spoke

[5]Carpizo (1979) discusses the emergence, consolidation, and tactics of presidentialism. For an analysis of its manifestations in the Echeverría and López Portillo administrations, see Cosío Villegas 1974; Zaid 1987.

of a "democratic opening." In time, people began to trust him; certain labor sectors even began movements to overthrow corrupt leaders who had traditionally controlled them, with the hope that they would be backed by the new government (Córdova 1989: 261).

Candidate Salinas followed a similar strategy, cultivating the image of a "man of the people" in an attempt to rebuild a presidential image tarnished by economic crisis. As president, Salinas visited all parts of Mexico in order to soften popular resentment over severe wage cuts implemented as part of de la Madrid's stabilization policies. Popular groups began to believe that they had access to the president. As one specialist on the Mexican political elite noted:

> This image of accessibility has become a mechanism of national security. If Salinas had locked himself up in the presidential palace and attempted to govern from there, Cárdenas would have burned the country. The president is generating legitimacy with his presence, monopolizing the generation of consensus. The central axis for creating legitimacy in this country used to be the party; now this has changed (author interview, November 22, 1989).

This "Echeverría-ized Salinismo" did not augur well for the party. Echeverría's brand of presidentialism had marginalized the PRI from important aspects of the political process. In a worsening economic context, that trend could only become accentuated.

The PRI's legitimacy had traditionally resided in its capacity to accommodate interests and reconcile differences among key social groups. De la Madrid and Salinas wrested this capacity away from the party through the Economic Solidarity Pact (PSE).[6] Designed as a concerted effort among productive sectors to curb rampant inflation and stabilize the economy, the pact soon underwent a metamorphosis. What began as a purely economic measure became a political instrument for governance in the hands of the president, a mechanism capable of generating concentric circles of legitimacy around the institution of the presidency. Under the pact, the president and his economic team map out goals, negotiate their timing and implementation with representa-

---

[6]Government officials, business leaders, and labor agreed on the Economic Solidarity Pact in December 1987. The pact called for a combined effort (concertation) to limit price and wage increases in order to combat spiraling inflation. Though it was renamed the PECE in 1989, its substantive goals remained basically intact. For a definition and analysis of concertation, see Lembruch 1984. The Mexican case is discussed in Kaufman, Heredia, and Bazdresch 1992.

tives of business associations, and then use the institutional arena provided by the pact to inform labor of agreed-upon decisions. Thus the pact has displaced the traditional apparatuses of corporate decision making and control concentrated in the PRI. Concertation took away labor leaders' power to negotiate wage increases and placed it in the executive branch (the economic cabinet). Although the pact's quasi-corporatist arrangement gave labor an institutional entrée into the executive branch, labor has not been able to halt the trend toward increasingly centralized decision making by the president and his economic team. The power and influence of sectoral leaders is eroding under the emergence of a new kind of "elitist corporatism." In effect, the president and his economic team have taken over the alliances forged by the PRI.

However, the PRI's alienation from the executive branch cannot be attributed solely to the use of concertation to overcome Mexico's economic difficulties. The prevailing political culture is receptive toward acts of presidentialism but ambivalent regarding the PRI. As one analyst observed: "Mexican political culture is fascinated with power. It is significant when people view Salinas as playing political hardball" (author interview, November 14, 1989). Salinas won this reputation through a series of preemptive strikes against the "leviathans" of the Mexican state.[7] By arresting the leader of the powerful oil workers' union and by forcing the head of the teachers' union into early retirement, Salinas scored points among constituencies opposed to corruption and clientelism. By pursuing "untouchables" within the system, which was publicly perceived as a haven for powerful, corrupt, and privileged leaders, the president further distanced himself from the PRI.

The PRI experienced a parallel marginalization in the decision-making process. The relationship between PRI leaders and the economic cabinet became almost nonexistent. As one resentful member of the old guard declared:

> The Salinistas act superior to all of us in the PRI, especially regarding technical expertise. They believe that their "macro" knowledge is superior to our "micro" knowledge of how to govern a municipality. The technocrats constantly question the PRI's behavior. Many high-ranking officials have even declared themselves non-PRIístas and have been reluctant to pay their party membership dues. They argue that they don't owe the party anything (author interview, October 12, 1989).

---

[7]Reyes Heroles (1987) coined the term "internal Leviathans" to refer to entrenched leaders within some of Mexico's most powerful and wealthy unions. Over time, these leaders had developed interests that did not always accord with those of the executive branch.

The position of the technocrats within the government seemed to be to move ahead with the economic reform program, regardless of its impact on the party. As a PRI militant noted: "Many of us who campaign across the country are constantly being questioned about the government's economic orientation. With each wage freeze we lose support out there" (author interview, October 6, 1989). After the 1989 elections in Baja California, where the PAN won the governorship, a growing perception emerged within the party that the PRI was being sacrificed whenever or wherever the president and his team needed to shore up support for the president's program.

REBOUND OR RESPITE?

Despite these trials, the PRI rebounded in the 1991 midterm elections, winning over 60 percent of the vote. The party won an absolute majority in all states except the Federal District and even recovered in contested urban areas. This victory restored PRI hegemony in the Chamber of Deputies and gave the party virtual legislative independence.[8] The PRD, the big winner in 1988, lost over four million votes in 1991, and the PAN could not rise above its historic limit of 18 percent of the national vote. Given the PRI's renewed ability to construct an electoral majority in a competitive atmosphere, analysts augured a return to the PRI's traditional predominance.

The PRI's comeback indicated that it was successfully addressing its crisis of representation. Prior to the elections, the PRI had engaged in an all-out effort to promote the vote, particularly among PRI sympathizers. According to a party candidate: "We went for the sure vote in PRI districts, and we stopped canvassing PAN districts, where we knew we would lose anyway" (author interview, June 8, 1992). Mass meetings gave way to door-to-door canvassing by party officials, and weekly polls measured levels of support. PRI efforts were assisted by massive government campaigns to revamp the voter registry and distribute voter credentials.

To shore up its representativeness, the party also sought a new type of candidate. In many regions (especially the Federal District) the PRI groomed and then ran locally well known leaders, culling those with broad appeal through public debates and primaries. With the labor sector's ability to influence candidate selection weakened, and with the PRD "exit option" appearing less palatable, sector leaders had little choice but to acquiesce to the PRI's candidate choices. In the 1991 midterm elections, 17 percent of PRI candidates came from the business sector, and businessmen continue to figure prominently as PRI candi-

---

[8]In the 1991–1994 legislative period, the PRI's congressional strength (it controlled 61 of 64 seats in the Senate and 291 of 300 seats in the Chamber of Deputies) meant that the PRI no longer needed PAN support to pass legislation.

dates, members of the party's finance committee, and supporters of PRI organizations (Ortega Pizarro 1992).

The PRI also rebuilt its ties with urban popular movements by exchanging votes for material benefits and promises of economic improvement via resources from the National Solidarity Program (PRO-NASOL). PRONASOL became the backbone of a neocorporatist strategy to address the immediate needs of the lower middle class and the informal sector. PRONASOL was designed to construct new patronage networks with the country's low-income constituencies, especially marginal groups in urban areas with electoral weight. Solidarity's propaganda, resources, and organization have enabled the PRI to resume its traditional role as a welfare machine (Dresser 1991). PRONASOL has also provided the PRI with a new generation of leaders and candidates; with their new-found popularity, in 1991 these PRONASOListas won by even greater margins than other PRI candidates.

Despite these changes, doubts persist as to whether the PRI has overcome its crisis of representation. The party's electoral rebirth may have been due to factors independent of the PRI's "modernization." Its triumph could be more mirage than reality, more ephemeral and conjunctural than long term. The combination of a popular and effective president, effective economic policies that are fueling expectations of better living standards, and a social program that caters to the needs of many low-income voters constitute a powerful political mix, a mix which aided the PRI but was not developed within the party (Cornelius 1991; Sánchez Susarrey 1991).

Nevertheless, the PRI's rebound was marred by turmoil in Guanajuato and San Luis Potosí, where election irregularities bespoke the thinness of the reform veneer. Salinas himself selected the 1991 gubernatorial candidates in both states, in an effort to distance himself from local-level party dinosaurs. But the PRI paid a high cost in lost credibility and internal cohesion.

The elections in Guanajuato and San Luis Potosí demonstrated that opposition to change persists within the party *and* its leadership. On the one hand, opening up political spaces to local and regional PRI bosses via primaries risks jeopardizing the national leadership's control over the pace and timing of "modernization" (Sodi 1992). On the other, avoiding internal primaries in order to maintain unity within the PRI family generates local conflicts. Bringing external pressure to bear on regional disputes and imposing candidates from Mexico City provoke demands for regional autonomy.

According to many base PRIístas, the only thing that has been "modernized" within the PRI is the "*dedazo*" (candidate imposition from above). The electoral victory of 1991 served as a temporary bond, but the persisting conflicts among PRI members in Oaxaca, Tabasco, Michoacán, and Guanajuato underscore that the party's crisis of rationality is far from over. At its heart is the perception among PRI members that the party is no longer fulfilling its purpose as a system of power sharing and elite recruitment.

In an interesting twist, the 1991 elections did not mark increased PRI alienation from the executive. Rather, they signaled the party's greater subordination to it. Salinas set the tone, pace, and limits of the party's transformation. As one analyst noted: "Change within the PRI will reflect what the president wants of the PRI" (author interview with Carlos Ramírez, June 6, 1992). Salinas wanted to promote change within the party to sustain the economic reform, but no more. Consequently, the PRI will function less as a political party than as an instrument of governance. Measures will be taken to avoid ruptures within the political class and to maintain acceptable levels of PRI support, but the maxim appears to be, "loosen the reins as little as possible and only when forced to." Government elites will not relinquish any space if it weakens their control over the party.

Opening up the PRI to internal (and external) competition could jeopardize the economic restructuring effort. An internal struggle within the PRI or among contending parties might become a governability problem. Consequently, primaries and initiatives to create a more level playing field among parties must be temporarily discarded and/or diluted. Salinas endorsed certain PRI candidates for gubernatorial races (and vetoed others) in order to create a "Salinista" political class, supportive of the government's economic policies. But beyond the imperative of maintaining and extending central control, what occurs within the PRI appears to be of secondary importance compared to Mexico's economic reform program.

Thus the PRI's future is closely tied to the economic restructuring model. This linkage explains why some of the most unyielding obstacles to greater political liberalization do not lie in the PRI's dinosaurian strongholds but in the presidency itself. Salinas viewed economic reform as a formula for strengthening the PRI and weakening the opposition. Economic growth has become Mexico's containment policy for the 1990s. Insofar as the government obtains good economic results, popular discontent with the PRI will evaporate and alternative parties may appear less attractive. Guided by the philosophy of "social liberalism," the PRI can continue to shore up its questionable electoral legitimacy through legitimacy via the provision of welfare benefits.[9] Therefore, even reformist voices in the political class have little incentive to relinquish power, given that such a choice might jeopardize the country's economic recovery. Within these limits, the chosen route for the PRI is a "managed transition" that allows the party to remain as the centerpiece

---

[9]For a definition of "social liberalism," see Sánchez Susarrey 1992a, 1992b; Aguilar Villanueva 1992.

of a more competitive party system, similar to those of Japan, Sweden, and Italy.[10] The reform of the PRI has been designed to achieve a "modernized" form of dominant party rule whereby the PRI wins elections in a less corrupt and more competitive fashion. The PRI will not be sacrificed for the uncertain goal of democracy, particularly given that a largely technocratic political elite owes its survival and is staking its continuity on the party's predominance (Coppedge 1992). According to this logic, "to place democracy at the front of the train that is transforming the economy would be equivalent to suicide; we would end up like the ex-Soviet Union" (Rubio 1992: 47).

CONCLUSION

Mexico's economic crisis led to a reorientation of the state's role in the economy and, as a result, to the adoption of policies that ended traditional sources of patronage at all levels of the political economy. Strategies adopted for governing during the crisis broke down old collective identities and the institutions to which they were bound. The effects of economic restructuring have been felt with particular force within the state party. As the corporatist structures that had sustained it began to give way, the PRI lost its legitimizing capacities. As the PRI passed through crises of representation and rationality, Salinas and his economic team increasingly viewed the party as an obstacle to the economic reform program. The severity of the economic crisis introduced a new phenomenon on Mexico's political horizon: severe tensions emerged between state managers and the PRI apparatus. The crisis interrupted the perfect communication and continuity that had previously prevailed between the state and its party, and it led to a new differentiation of functions. Bureaucratic elites concentrated on designing formulas for overcoming the crisis, while the party was given a "blotter" role, absorbing the costs of unpopular decisions associated with crisis management, as well as the Herculean task of winning elections in a context of economic adjustment. The crisis not only delinked the development apparatus from the consensus apparatus, but it also shifted the latter from the PRI to the executive. Salinas established himself as supreme arbiter, unencumbered by traditional institutions like the PRI, and also drew on presidential power to reform the party.

Strategies designed to enhance presidential power at the cost of subordinating the PRI are evidence of an attempt to insulate economic policy makers from societal pressures and to increase their autonomy. Analysts have described the Mexican state as the expression of a particular pact of domination that also behaves like a corporate actor, with an organization and interests of its own. Oftentimes these interests conflict since state managers are likely to be divided on substantive

---

[10]I borrow the term "managed transition" from Rubio 1992.

goals (Cardoso 1979). Various authors have pointed to "relative state autonomy" as a precondition for effective economic intervention (see, for example, Evans and Rueschemeyer 1985). Such autonomy is closely related to the capacity of state institutions to implement a given policy choice (Hall 1987). In order to formulate and implement collective goals, the state must mitigate the conflicts created by its role as a corporate actor, turn a deaf ear to the demands of particular groups, and even shed traditional allies. Contexts of economic crisis tend to intensify state managers' quest for autonomy. The imperatives that crises create (the need to cut public spending and subsidies, for example) produce conditions that encourage state elites to opt for more exclusionary forms of decision making. When shrinking economic capabilities take from the state its role as resource distributor, it ceases to be an arena for political compromise or, alternately, for political conflict. Actors that used to develop from state tutelage are now "disincorporated." Consequently, the more state managers strive for insulation and autonomy, the more they risk alienating political factions.

Recent trends in Mexican political life point to a redefinition of the distances between the state's economic managers and a party that paved the way for their access to power. This redefinition raises important questions regarding the role of the PRI and its membership in future pacts of domination. The party seems to be on the threshold of a critical juncture, a sharp discontinuity in a given historical-developmental process (Collier and Collier 1991). A critical juncture opens new avenues of change and closes others in a way that shapes politics for years to come. Technobureaucrats who have gained access to key levels of the state are not experienced in corporatist politics. They would like to end corruption and clientelism, political intermediaries, and subsidies. In other words, they want to revamp the old formulas that constituted the backbone of the PRI's hegemony and transform the PRI into a "modern" party based on individual affiliation and militancy. Even if this were possible, the problem of generating consensus for state actions would still remain unresolved. Current ad hoc reliance on the presidency as a legitimizing agency would still have to be institutionalized. To dismantle the PRI would be to dismantle crucial segments of Mexico's institutional framework that rest on the party's corporatist structure. For over forty years, that structure supported a specific form of political and economic domination that now seems to have fallen out of step with the imperatives of structural adjustment. Corporatist organization of interests via the PRI permitted state supervision of key social groups, but it also assured stable arenas of political support. If the party withers, government officials will have to devise new forms of control and legitimation.

Faced with the task of linking economic modernization and institutional change, Mexico's political elites have opted to "stay the course," to maintain sectoral representation while the PRI is being redefined as a competitive electoral entity (Cornelius 1990). But the political elite cannot afford to lose control over an increasingly diverse and electorally volatile civil society in the meantime (Rubio 1990). In the midst of an ambitious economic transformation, Mexico's leaders have chosen an unusual survival strategy: the transformation of the "official" party while it is still in power. The "structural refounding of the party" means creating one party within the other, while using economic growth to assure political predominance. Factions within the PRI are being simultaneously embellished, empowered, and partially euthanized by the government. However, if the ultimate goal is that a "modernized" PRI join the select club of dominant party democracies, many items remain on the party's reform agenda.[11] Mexican elections still lack the credibility and level playing field that distinguish dominant party democracies in Japan, Italy, and Sweden (see Pempel 1990). Unless state elites have the political will and vision to make needed changes, Mexico may not move into the privileged realm of exceptional democracies but will remain ensconced in the discredited category of exceptional authoritarianisms.

REFERENCES

Aguilar Camín, Héctor, and Lorenzo Meyer. 1989. *A la sombra de la Revolución Mexicana*. Mexico City: Cal y Arena.
Aguilar Villanueva, Luis. 1992. "La última reforma es mental," *Examen* 3:35 (April).
Bailey, John, Denise Dresser, and Leopoldo Gómez. 1990. "XIV Asamblea del PRI: balance preliminar," *La Jornada*, September 26.
Basáñez, Miguel. 1990. *El pulso de los sexenios: 20 años de crisis en México*. Mexico City: Siglo Veintiuno.
Callaghy, Thomas M. 1989. "Toward State Capability and Embedded Liberalism: Lessons for Adjustment." In *Fragile Coalitions: The Politics of Economic Adjustment*, by Joan Nelson et al. New Brunswick, N.J.: Transaction Books.
Cardoso, Fernando Henrique. 1979. "On the Characterization of Authoritarian Regimes in Latin America." In *The New Authoritarianism in Latin America*, edited by David Collier. Princeton, N.J.: Princeton University Press.
Carpizo, Jorge. 1979. *El presidencialismo mexicano*. Mexico City: Siglo Veintiuno.
Carr, Barry, and Ricardo Anzaldúa Montoya, eds. *The Mexican Left, the Popular Movements, and the Politics of Austerity*. Monograph Series, no. 18. La Jolla: Center for U.S.-Mexican Studies, University of California, San Diego.
Centeno, Miguel Angel, and Sylvia Maxfield. 1989. "The Marriage of Finance and Order: Origins and Implications of Change in the Mexican Political Elite." Paper presented at the conference "Mexico: Contrasting Visions," Institute for

---

[11]These changes include transparency in party financing, equal media access for all parties, candidate selection through internal primaries, promotion of a participatory and democratic civic culture, sanctions on party operatives who commit electoral fraud, and so on.

Latin American and Iberian Studies, Columbia University, New York, April 23.

Collier, Ruth Berins, and David Collier. 1991. *Shaping the Political Arena: Critical Junctures, the Labor Movement, and Regime Dynamics in Latin America*. Princeton, N.J.: Princeton University Press.

Conaghan, Catherine. 1987. "Party Politics and Democratization in Ecuador." In *Authoritarians and Democrats: Regime Transition in Latin America*, edited by James Malloy and Mitchell Seligson. Pittsburgh, Penn.: University of Pittsburgh Press.

Coppedge, Michael. 1992. "Prospectos de reestructuración económica y política en México," *Este País* 14 (May).

Córdova, Arnaldo. 1989. *La revolución y el Estado mexicano*. Mexico City: Era.

Cornelius, Wayne A. 1990. "Mexico: Salinas and the PRI at the Crossroads," *Journal of Democracy* 1:3 (Summer).

———. 1991. "Las elecciones de 1991," *Cuadernos de Nexos* 40 (October).

Cosío Villegas, Daniel. 1974. *El estilo personal de gobernar*. Mexico City: Joaquín Mortiz.

Dresser, Denise. 1991. *Neopopulist Solutions to Neoliberal Problems: Mexico's National Solidarity Program*. Current Issue Brief Series, no. 3. La Jolla: Center for U.S.-Mexican Studies, University of California, San Diego.

ECLAC (Economic Commission for Latin America and the Caribbean). 1990. *Preliminary Overview of the Economy of Latin America and the Caribbean, 1990*. Santiago: CEPAL.

Evans, Peter B., and Dietrich Rueschemeyer. 1985. "The State and Economic Transformation: Toward an Analysis of the Conditions Underlying Effective Intervention." In *Bringing the State Back In*, edited by D. Rueschemeyer, P. Evans, and Theda Skocpol. London: Cambridge University Press.

Foweraker, Joe, and Ann L. Craig, eds. 1990. *Popular Movements and Political Change in Mexico*. Boulder, Colo.: Lynne Rienner, in association with the Center for U.S.-Mexican Studies, University of California, San Diego.

Gómez, Leopoldo. 1990. "El PRI y los tigres de papel," *Cuadernos de Nexos* 26 (August).

Hall, Peter. 1987. *Governing the Economy: The Politics of State Intervention in Britain and France*. London: Polity Press.

Hernández Rodríguez, Rogelio. 1987. "Los hombres del Presidente de la Madrid," *Foro Internacional* 109:28 (July–September).

Hewlett, Sylvia Ann, and Richard S. Weinert, eds. 1982. *Brazil and Mexico: Patterns in Late Development*. Philadelphia, Penn.: Institute for the Study of Human Issues.

IDB (Inter-American Development Bank). 1990. *Economic and Social Progress in Latin America*. Washington, D.C.: Johns Hopkins University Press, for the IDB.

Kaufman, Robert, Blanca Heredia, and Carlos Bazdresch. 1992. "The Politics of the Economic Solidarity Pact in Mexico: December 1987 to December 1988." Paper presented at the conference "The Political Economy of Democratic Transitions," World Bank, Washington, D.C., May 4–5.

Klesner, Joseph L. 1991. "Modernization, Economic Crisis and Electoral Realignment in Mexico." Paper presented at the Sixteenth International Congress of the Latin American Studies Association, Washington, D.C., April 4–6.

Lembruch, Gerhard. 1984. "Concertation and the Structure of Corporatist Networks." In *Order and Conflict in Contemporary Capitalism*, edited by John Goldthorpe. Oxford: Clarendon.

Loaeza, Soledad. 1989. *El llamado a las urnas*. Mexico City: Cal y Arena.

—————. 1992. "The Role of the Right in Political Change in Mexico, 1982–1988." In *The Right and Democracy in Latin America*, edited by Douglas Chalmers, Maria do Carmo Campello de Souza, and Atilio Borón. New York: Praeger.

Loaeza, Soledad, and Rafael Segovia, eds. 1987. *La vida política mexicana en la crisis*. Mexico City: El Colegio de México.

Nelson, Joan, et al. 1989. *Fragile Coalitions: The Politics of Economic Adjustment*. New Brunswick, N.J.: Transaction Books.

Newell, Roberto G., and Luis F. Rubio. 1984. *Mexico's Dilemma: The Political Origins of Economic Crisis*. Boulder, Colo.: Westview.

O'Donnell, Guillermo. 1973. *Modernization and Bureaucratic Authoritarianism: Studies in South American Politics*. Berkeley: Institute of International Studies, University of California, Berkeley.

Ortega Pizarro, Fernando. 1992. "Los empresarios, poderosa fuerza en el PRI, aunque no sean sector," *Proceso* 800 (March 2): 21.

Pacheco, Guadalupe. 1989. "Los perfiles electorales de 1988: los sectores del PRI y el entorno distrital urbano." Paper presented at the Fifteenth International Congress of the Latin American Studies Association, Miami, December 4–6.

Pempel, T.J., ed. 1990. *Uncommon Democracies: The One Party Dominant Regimes*. Ithaca, N.Y.: Cornell University Press.

Pereznieto Castro, Leonel. 1990. "Algunos cambios probables del PRI, de acuerdo a las resoluciones de la XIV Asamblea Nacional." In *El partido en el poder: seis ensayos*. Mexico City: IEPES.

Reyes Heroles, Federico. 1987. "Los desconciertos fundamentales de finales de siglo." In *Contrahechuras mexicanas*. Mexico City: Joaquín Mortiz.

Romero, Miguel A., and Luis Méndez. 1990. "La reestructuración de la industria paraestatal." In *México en la década de los ochentas: la modernización en cifras*, edited by Augusto Bolívar and Rosa Albina Garavito. Mexico City: Universidad Autónoma Metropolitana-Azcapotzalco.

Rubio, Luis. 1990. "¿Es reformable el PRI?" *Cuadernos de Nexos* 28 (October).

—————. 1992. "La transición administrada," *Nexos* 174 (June).

Sánchez Susarrey, Jaime. 1991. "El porqué de una votación tan elevada en una elección intermedia," *Epoca* 12 (August 26).

—————. 1992a. "El liberalismo social," *Epoca* 42 (March 23).

—————. 1992b. "Liberalismo social: nuestro cambio," *Examen* 3:35 (April).

Sheahan, John. 1991. *Conflict and Change in Mexican Economic Strategy: Implications for Mexico and for Latin America*. Monograph Series, no. 34. La Jolla: Center for U.S.-Mexican Studies, University of California, San Diego.

Sodi, Demetrio. 1992. "¿Democracia priísta?" *La Jornada*, June 5.

Stevens, Evelyn P. 1974. *Protest and Response in Mexico*. Cambridge, Mass.: Massachusetts Institute of Technology Press.

Story, Dale. 1987. "The PAN, the Private Sector, and the Future of the Mexican Opposition." In *Mexican Politics in Transition*, edited by Judith Gentleman. Boulder, Colo.: Westview.

Tamayo, Jaime. 1990. "Neoliberalism Encounters *Neocardenismo*." In *Popular Movements and Political Change in Mexico*, edited by Joe Foweraker and Ann L.

Craig. Boulder, Colo.: Lynne Rienner, in association with the Center for U.S.-Mexican Studies, University of California, San Diego.

Waterbury, John. 1977. "An Attempt to Put Patrons and Clients in Their Place." In *Patrons and Clients in Mediterranean Societies,* edited by Ernest Gellner and J. Waterbury. London: Duckworth.

Zaid, Gabriel. 1987. *La economía presidencial.* Mexico City: Vuelta.

6

Party System and Political Transition in Mexico: A Pragmatic Approach

Jorge Alcocer V.

Since 1985—the year that Mexico entered the General Agreement on Tariffs and Trade (GATT)—Mexico has been undergoing a deep, widespread, and seemingly irreversible transformation of the structural foundations of its economy. The main component of that transformation has been the transition from an economy oriented toward the domestic market—overprotected and with a high degree of direct state intervention—to one in which foreign markets (primarily that of the United States, for geographic-historical reasons) have become the driving force of the economy. This transition coincided with rapid economic liberalization and the state's retreat from all areas of the economy except those constitutionally defined as its exclusive domain.

This economic adjustment process generated important changes in Mexico's political life, in its political parties, in the government, and in society itself. The following discussion refers generally to Mexico's three main political parties, the Institutional Revolutionary Party (PRI), the National Action Party (PAN), and the Party of the Democratic Revolution (PRD). These three parties are the indispensable reference point for any analysis of the future development of the Mexican political system.

Strictly speaking, Mexico does not have a party system, if by that we mean a set of political organizations that are the vertex around which the politico-electoral system, the struggle for public power, and the formation of the government in a broad sense are organized. This is the case because the state that arose out of the Mexican Revolution obtained its

Translated by Aníbal Yáñez. An earlier version of this essay benefited from the comments and criticisms of participants in the seminar from which this volume took form.

legitimacy and built consensus through extra-electoral mechanisms. Until well into the 1970s, Mexican elections were, in the best of cases, ritual events, a way to legitimize a transfer of power imposed from the apex of the "revolutionary family." Where elections are mere ritual, it is impossible for political parties to develop.

No country has equaled Mexico's success in building a strong and durable political system that is formally multiparty but is in fact a single-party system. Mexican election results from 1920 to 1976 chronicle that reality. For decades, Mexico's politico-electoral life consisted of the dominant party (PRI), a tolerated token opposition (PAN), and the occasional appearance of groups that adopted party form in order to compete in a specific election and then disappeared almost without a trace. During most of this time, the Communist Party subsisted at the margins. (Founded in 1919 but outlawed in 1946, it did not recover its legal standing until 1978.)

However, in 1985 the PRI enjoyed its last year of guaranteed electoral triumph at the national level. Of the three hundred congressional seats in question, 292 went to the PRI, which, when combined with the PRI's absolute control of the Senate, ensured that party's uncontested control of the legislature for another three years. This occurred despite signals of growing voter discontent in northern Mexico in 1983–1984, when the PAN won important municipal victories in Chihuahua and Durango.

Until the mid-1980s, the composition of electoral forces in Mexico was practically static: the PRI was by far the majority party, although it was beginning to lose support in large and mid-sized cities; the PAN was consolidating its second-place position, capitalizing on Mexico's increasing urbanization; and, finally, the left was a distant third, with a maximum of one million votes. Nevertheless, something had begun to change. The 1982 devaluation and the events that followed opened the way to what would be Mexico's worst economic crisis. A society that was now predominantly urban saw its hopes for economic improvement dashed.

In several electoral contests in northern Mexico in 1986 (the most important one being in Chihuahua), the middle classes used their votes to express their growing discontent. With no economic palliatives to offer, and keenly aware of the approaching presidential succession, the administration of Miguel de la Madrid (1982–1988) played a new card: electoral reform to broaden the spaces for the opposition and close off those for future internal dissidence. In 1986 the Mexican Constitution was amended to increase the total membership in the Chamber of Deputies to five hundred, with all new seats assigned on the basis of the proportion of the national vote captured by each party. Additionally, an electoral tribunal was created and a new federal electoral code was passed.

The entire opposition voted against the constitutional reform, and most opposition parties (including the PAN and the Mexican Unified Socialist Party, PSUM) voted against the electoral code. Their basic reason was a "governability" clause introduced in the reform, as well as the recomposition of the top electoral authority, the Federal Electoral Commission (CFE), which beginning in 1987 ceased to have parity representation of political parties and adopted a proportional formula that gave the PRI a direct majority on the commission.

However, for this embryonic political crisis to develop into a fully expressed social movement required an internal split in the ruling elite. Only after cleavages developed within the PRI would it be possible for a new politico-electoral picture to emerge in Mexico. The 1988 presidential elections, in which the PRI candidate won by the slimmest of margins, substantially modified Mexico's party system and opened up a (still incomplete) process that has been called the "Mexican transition toward democracy."

Immediately following the 1988 elections, incoming president Carlos Salinas de Gortari undertook a series of actions to legitimize and consolidate his precarious position. The first was to issue calls for a new politico-electoral reform and for a dialogue with all opposition forces. Another Salinas initiative was to open the way to a new process of reform and reorganization within the "official" party, culminating in the PRI's Fourteenth National Assembly in 1990.

The main targets of Salinas's actions were the PAN and the National Democratic Front's presidential candidate, Cuauhtémoc Cárdenas. How these two opposition forces responded to the president's initiatives largely decided the fate that each would face in the following months and years. During early 1989, measures Salinas took in the areas of economic policy and the administration of justice helped him regain the support of vast groups of citizens who had mobilized in protest against electoral fraud a few months earlier. But an even more important outcome of the president's actions was that they fostered a split in the opposition front that had formed after July 6, 1988, as the two main opposition groups adopted different positions in response to the electoral reform initiative.

In May 1989, the Mexican Socialist Party (PMS, a fusion of the PSUM and the Mexican Workers' Party, PMT) dissolved in order to form the Party of the Democratic Revolution (PRD). A few weeks later the CFE approved the change of the PMS name and revisions in its founding documents, paving the way for the new party's legal status. In a legal and historical sense, the PRD inherited the electoral registry won by the Mexican Communist Party (PCM) ten years earlier.

Meanwhile, beginning in late 1988 the PAN concentrated its efforts on recovering its position as the second-ranked electoral force. While it initially made common cause with the PRD on electoral reform issues, as time went on the PAN increasingly distanced itself from PRD radicalism. With a vision less influenced by recent disputes, the PAN discovered that the PRD's radicalism and Mexico's transformed political situation presented the PAN with the opportunity to become the government's primary interlocutor.

When the government began adopting longtime PAN demands as part of its own economic program, the PAN leadership decided to risk internal changes that would open up key spaces to a new group within the party leadership. This new group, the "neo-PANistas," strove to refashion the PAN's image as a party with the potential to govern. It would not attack the government's key economic policies; rather, it noted that they constituted the administration's "recognition"—late, but recognition nonetheless—of the validity of the PAN's principles and program.

The PAN thus presented itself as the party able to bring about a negotiated transition. This culminated with its decision to support constitutional reforms on electoral matters, leaving the PRD as the sole opponent of the reforms. By its action, the PAN hoped to win its demand for the reprivatization of the banks that had been nationalized in 1982.

The pattern was repeated in 1989–1990 when a new electoral law (the COFIPE) was drafted and discussed. The PRD and the PAN started out as allies, outlining a point-by-point agenda of issues to be won. But in the end, the PAN opted to go it alone and reached its own agreements with the PRI and the government.

The PRD, meanwhile, failing to factor in the changes that had taken place in 1988 and 1990, found itself politically and socially isolated. As the governability crisis that some PRD leaders had predicted became increasingly unlikely, the PRD's discourse became more radical and the party's isolation deepened. Sartori's observation that "it is likely that an opposition is less responsible the less hope it has of governing" (1980: 176) closely describes this stage of the PRD's life. The PRD took on the features of an "antisystem" party, not those of a "revolutionary party," as they are described by Sartori (1980: 165–69). PRD leaders lived through the two paradoxes that Sartori describes: "Voters may protest at the same time that party activists become alienated. Analogously, the party leadership may have ideological motivations, while the rank and file simply has no bread."

In order to understand the PRD's behavior, it is necessary to recall the systematic campaign of government and PRI attacks, including murder, carried out against the PRD during this period. And the PRD—in the person of its presidential candidate and party leader, Cuauhtémoc Cárdenas—was the direct target of the electoral fraud perpetrated by the PRI/government at the national level in 1988 and later at the state level in Tabasco and Michoacán. The PRD's confrontational stance during 1989 and 1990 was directly shaped by these events.

The government has followed a two-pronged approach in dealing with its opponents. With the PAN it has maintained cordial relations (even an open alliance), and it has either recognized the PAN's legitimate victories or taken drastic actions to remedy grievances, as in the cases of Guanajuato and San Luis Potosí. With the PRD the government's position has been one of aggression: slander campaigns orchestrated by the president's press office; tolerance of continued fraud against the PRD; indifference toward physical abuse and murder perpetrated by regional caciques. The litany of injuries is long.

However, the PRD's approach toward the government, and particularly toward the president, began to change. Statements by some PRD leaders are evidence of this new tack, in which the results of the 1991 federal elections undoubtedly played a part. By August 1991 the turbulence in Mexico's political system had subsided, to the point where there seemed to be a return to the hegemonic party system. The PRI had garnered over 60 percent of the total vote; the PAN remained steady at 17 percent; and the PRD captured only 8 percent of the total. This outcome gave the "official" party a comfortable majority in the Chamber of Deputies and enabled it to regain one of the four Senate seats it had lost in 1988. With its control over "satellite" parties, the PRI had the two-thirds majority it needed to pass constitutional reforms without having to call on either of the two leading opposition parties, the PRD and the PAN.

The situation was different at the local level. The PRI continued to lose ground in medium-sized and large cities, which cost it the governorships of Baja California and Guanajuato. And there was an unprecedented number of northern and central-highland municipalities in the hands of the (mostly PAN) opposition. These results suggest that no party can assume it controls the urban vote. Urban voters will continue to evaluate their own circumstances and expectations when determining how to cast their votes.

Although the August 1991 national election results signaled an important recovery for the PRI over 1988, they also marked the continued decline of the PRI from its historical levels of support. This key point suggests that electoral competitiveness has gained entry into the Mexican political system and will advance over time from the local to the state and national spheres.

Over the last few years the PRI has confronted the most serious set of contradictions to affect it since its founding by Calles in 1929. Government actions since 1985, but most clearly since 1989, have left the party without a programmatic and ideological foundation. This is not only the result of the discontinuities from one *sexenio* to the next, but of something that goes deeper: a rupture in the party's traditional points of reference that enabled it to maintain its identity across administrations.

Salinismo swept away these points of reference by breaking with the political and legal institutions inherited from the government of Lázaro Cárdenas (1936–1940) and by abandoning the economic policies established under Miguel Alemán (1946–1952). There is only one comparable episode in the history of the PRI: Cárdenas's break with Calles in 1935, which led to the party's change of name from the Revolutionary National Party (PNR) to the Party of the Mexican Revolution (PRM) and to the reorganization of the party based on the sectors and the corporatist structure that sustain it today.

Had it not been for the 1987 rupture within the PRI, the party might already have changed its name and ideological-programmatic reference points. But when the PRD challenged the PRI for the "legacy" of the Mexican Revolution and the mantle of Cardenismo, the PRI responded pragmatically by preserving the party's old reference points officially but ignoring them in practice. This strategy allowed the PRI to maintain a high degree of cohesion by giving the old guard a doctrinal pretext for not following the Democratic Current faction out of the party.

Between 1989 and 1992, the PRI decided to concentrate its efforts on recapturing the urban vote by drawing on President Salinas's increasing popularity, rather than by attempting to redefine the party. A deal struck during the PRI's Fourteenth National Assembly secured cohesion within the party in exchange for maintaining the substance of the PRI's basic documents and for reforming the internal selection methods for party leaders and candidates. However, this deal was effectively vetoed by Salinas. A forceful presidential speech against internal dissidents, whom Salinas branded "new reactionaries," was followed by the annulment in practice of the reforms affecting electoral procedures. "Unity candidates" replaced internal elections, and single candidacies to leadership posts replaced consultation with the rank and file. By 1992 the critical voices were reduced to a minimum, and the PRI was able to "elect" its new leader through the same procedure of presenting a single candidate who would then win by acclamation in a duly sectoralized and controlled assembly.

This does not mean that the PRI has experienced no change in recent years. However, the changes that did take place did not affect its core features: its character as an "official" party completely subordinated to presidential decisions, fused and confused with the state apparatus, financially dependent on the illegal transfer of public resources, perfected as the electoral machinery of the government, and atrophied as the ideological glue of the group in power.

Changes to the PRI have been of another order. The party began modifying its sectoral structure, with the ultimate aim being to do away with it altogether. The transformation of the National Confederation of Popular Organizations (CNOP) into the National Union for Citizen Linkage (UNE) as a "front of citizens and movements" was the most radical measure up to that point, and for this reason it offered the most interesting and complex clue to the possible transition in the PRI structure that might result from future internal reform.

The PRI's recent electoral successes have come at the expense of perpetuating skepticism among the citizenry and the opposition parties. At present the Mexican electoral system faces no greater challenge than that of credibility. This factor will be crucial in defining the behavior, decisions, and interactions of the three main political parties in the run-up to the federal elections of 1994. The 1994 juncture will not only produce an electoral outcome but will also define the future course of the Mexican party system. We can envision a number of alternative scenarios for the evolution of the major parties.

The PRD will be challenged to renew its ties with the middle-class electorate in Mexico's urban centers, ties that were weakened by the leftism of PRD discourse and practice. To meet this challenge successfully will require a pronounced change in the party's perspective on the process of economic reform. The Cardenista leadership has thus far opposed the reform and its principal measures, failing to heed the broad support that the reform has among majority sectors of the population.

The PRD has been characterized by its uncompromising stance toward the North American Free Trade Agreement (NAFTA), toward the privatization of state firms, toward the reform of the land tenure system, and toward the government's economic policies in general. As for its own proposals, the PRD's position on economic issues is a mix of the positions of Lázaro Cárdenas in the 1930s and Luis Echeverría in the 1970s. Although PRD strength has weakened in urban areas, Cuauhtémoc Cárdenas still retains strong appeal and exerts significant influence. However, as of 1994 he has been on the campaign trail for six years, leading one to question whether he can once again build an electoral front that is a powerful pole of attraction for broad sectors of the voting population.

The most likely scenario is that the PRD, with Cárdenas as its candidate, will seek to unite the whole range of parties and groups on the left of the electoral spectrum. In order to do this, Cárdenas will have to carry out a delicate operation: making programmatic changes to attract sectors that have distanced themselves from Cardenismo, without disrupting his coalition's fragile internal cohesion. Absent a broad front built around its candidate, the PRD seems condemned to remain the third-ranked electoral force in Mexico, far behind the PRI and the PAN.

The PAN also has problems to address before the 1994 federal elections. Despite efforts to minimize internal conflict, in October 1992 there was a split in the PAN when two former party chairmen and former presidential candidates, one former general secretary and former parliamentary coordinator, and several longtime cadres left the PAN.

The PAN's strategy is based on a medium-range course that can be summed up in terms of its two objectives: to consolidate its privileged role as interlocutor and co-participant in the tasks of government by winning governorships and to regain the second-place position in federal elections that it lost to the PRD in 1988. Despite overtures from the PRD to form alliances in San Luis Potosí and Durango, evidence thus far indicates that a broad alliance with the PRD is not on the PAN's agenda.

If the PRD and the PAN effectively address their respective challenges, the 1994 federal-level elections will see three political alternatives seeking to differentiate themselves before the electorate. Regardless of the results of the elections, the process itself will be positive for the party system, for it will permit progress toward a panorama marked by tripartism, with increased competitiveness based on the regional influence of the two opposition forces.

As regards the Mexican Congress, competition in the Chamber of Deputies will center on gaining seats. The situation in the Senate will depend on the reform process: without reform, the PRI will suffer minor losses; with reform, a much larger number of seats will go to the opposition. In any case, control of the presidency will most likely coincide with an absolute majority in both chambers of Congress, although no party will reach a two-thirds majority in the Chamber of Deputies.

Among the many scenarios to be considered, there is one in particular worth mentioning: a possible alliance between the PAN and the PRD in 1994. It is possible that Cárdenas would be willing to step aside to make way for a "third" (non-PAN) candidate acceptable to both forces and attractive to broad groups of citizens. Many factors operate against this possibility, among them reluctance on the part of the PAN leadership. But it is a possibility that should not be dismissed out of hand.

The PRI, meanwhile, will continue its attempt at internal reform. In this process it will meet resistance from the labor sector (the CTM), which sees a move away from the sectoral organization of the party as one more blow against labor's declining presence within the "official" party. Although there are still some who anticipate further splits in the ranks of the PRI, the evidence points to appreciable internal stability. Ultimately the PRI's unity will depend on how the party carries out its transformation.

The PRI's internal reform effort has raised an interesting issue: whether to change the name of the "official" party. Although a name change is welcomed in the highest spheres of government, it may well be that the advantage of identity will far outweigh the advantage of change in 1994, and that we will have "PRI" for the remainder of the Salinas administration.

Whatever changes are implemented, the reform is not likely to touch two central aspects of the PRI: its financing mechanisms, and the subordination of the PRI majority in Congress to the executive. With or without internal reform, the PRI's existence as an "official" party, its symbiotic relationship with the state apparatus, and its absolute dependence upon the president will continue to be its distinguishing features. This seems to confirm that it is virtually impossible to implement radical reforms in parties of this type, in which case the alternatives are either to endure or to disappear.

The most favorable scenario for the PRI in 1994 would be a three-way contest because, like any party in government, it would benefit from a divided opposition vote. In this scenario, the PRI would continue its long-term decline even though it won the election. Rather than a precipitous collapse, the PRI would face the perspective of a slow extinction.

In contrast, the most troublesome scenario for the PRI would be a PAN-PRD alliance, which would lead toward total confrontation, a battle at close quarters in which the PRI would stand alone. In this situation, the system of power that has maintained a monopoly of government since the end of the Mexican Revolution would face the greatest challenge in its history.

Whatever direction the evolution of the party system takes, one essential condition must be met in order for this process to transpire under conditions of social peace and relative economic stability: clean elections. The credibility of the process and of its results together form the keystone of Mexico's political future.

REFERENCE

Sartori, Giovanni. 1980. *Partidos y sistemas de partidos. Marco para un análisis.* Madrid: Alianza Editorial.

7

Realignment or Dealignment? Consequences of Economic Crisis and Restructuring for the Mexican Party System

Joseph L. Klesner

Carlos Salinas de Gortari brought more fundamental change to Mexico than any president since Lázaro Cárdenas in the 1930s. Salinas's bold restructuring of Mexico's economy, which led him to revise key aspects of Mexico's postrevolutionary constitution, required that he confront powerful political forces. Salinas's economic policies threatened the interests of organized labor, the long-term beneficiaries of Mexico's agrarian reform program, supporters of Mexico's state-owned enterprises, and economic nationalists, all of whom traditionally supported the ruling Institutional Revolutionary Party (PRI).[1] The very postulation of Salinas as the PRI's presidential candidate in 1988, after he had begun to implement the neoliberal economic restructuring program as President Miguel de la Madrid's minister of budget and planning, provoked a

I wish to thank Luis Aguilar, Roderic Camp, and the editors for their comments on an earlier version of this chapter. I, of course, remain responsible for any errors or omissions.

[1]This listing of PRI supporters does not imply that the working class or the peasantry actually benefited from PRI rule. Most analysts agree that during the past three decades or so the working class has actually suffered under PRI rule. Whether the peasantry has really benefited from agrarian reform and the recreation of the ejido is a subject of considerable debate. That organized labor's leaders and the caciques who dominate the countryside have benefited from the PRI's rule is less contested. This essay does not examine whether the peasantry or working class have good reasons to support the PRI. As noted below, in many cases peasants' and workers' actual evaluations of the PRI have little to do with their voting decisions.

split in the PRI. As a result, opposition candidates received unprece-dented numbers and percentages of votes in the 1988 election, the most contested presidential election in modern Mexican history and an election the real results of which remain in serious doubt.

The results of the 1988 election and the controversy surrounding that election have led many to ask whether Mexico is entering a new political era.[2] Many political analysts argue that the economic crisis of the 1980s both strained the legitimacy of the governing elite and created bitterness among those who have suffered as the result of the post-1982 economic crisis and the economic restructuring that de la Madrid and Salinas pursued as the solution to that crisis. In this context we might ask whether Mexico has reached what Ruth Berins Collier and David Collier (1991: 27–29) have labeled a critical juncture, a time during which fundamental political alignments will be reconsidered and new political coalitions formed. Or, to use the terminology of electoral analysts, was the 1988 election a realigning election? If not, should we nevertheless expect a critical realignment in the next electoral cycle? There are striking similarities between the current period in Mexico and those periods in the United States described by Walter Dean Burnham (1970: 10) as "eras of critical realignment": Mexico has suffered "abnormal stress in the socioeconomic system." "Politics as usual" has not integrated political demands, as should be evident considering the emergence and popu-larity of the campaign of Cuauhtémoc Cárdenas, the defector from the ruling PRI who may have actually polled more votes than Salinas in the 1988 presidential race. Issue-distances between major challenges have grown by postrevolutionary Mexican standards. Indeed, the neoliberal-ism of de la Madrid and Salinas marks a major departure from the interventionist strategy of development followed by postrevolutionary Mexico, and the Cárdenas reaction has been strongly motivated by the demand that Mexico not abandon its revolutionary heritage of an interventionist, economic nationalist state. The undetermined issue, though, is whether there has been a reorganization of the mass bases of Mexican politics. And, if there has not been such a realignment, why not? These questions define the focus of this essay.

These questions provoke more than academic interest. If competi-tive electoral democracy is to arrive in Mexico, its parties of opposition must make deep inroads into the foundations of the ruling elite's monopoly on power. Mexico has a formally democratic political struc-ture, which uses an electoral process to choose successors for Mexico's president and state governors, none of whom can stand for reelection. Thus the principal challenge to Mexico's opposition parties is to win elections for key offices. Winning those elections means overcoming the advantages held by the PRI, the ruling elite's electoral machine. One of

---

[2]The following three paragraphs are drawn from Klesner 1993.

the most intimidating of those PRI advantages has been solid electoral support from Mexico's masses. To really challenge the PRI electorally, and to thereby convert Mexican politics into the competitive but constitutional politics we recognize as democracy, will require detaching the PRI's mass support bases from automatic electoral support for the ruling party. That is, at a minimum, electoral dealignment is a must for competitive politics to emerge in Mexico. Given the advantages held by the PRI due to incumbency and its support among the mass media (especially the broadcast media), realigning the Mexican electorate so that significant social sectors can be counted on to vote for the opposition may be the only long-term way to ensure competitive elections. However, the conclusion of this essay is that realignment is still a distant possibility.

ALIGNMENT, REALIGNMENT, AND DEALIGNMENT

Those who study electoral politics in the United States and Europe have identified much of the postwar period—an era marked by political stability—as consisting of "normal" elections, in which partisan alignments remained stable. However, partisan dealignment has clearly occurred in the past two decades or so, as shifts in party identification and changes in the social structure of industrial democracies have eroded the social bases of early postwar party alignments. We do not know whether partisan realignment has yet occurred, or whether it will occur at all, in the United States and Europe. Although changes in the cleavage structures of these societies may be leading voters to change their party identification, changes in the functions of political parties (due to changes in communications technology, among other things) may frustrate the future possibility of parties with strong bases of social support. In other words, in many advanced industrial societies, dealignment is a reality; realignment remains only a possibility.[3]

Certain assumptions underlie the concept of stable partisan alignments and the possibility that they may come to an end through dealignment or realignment. First, the concept assumes that a voter forms a partisan attachment to a relatively permanent political party, and that under normal circumstances he or she will continue to vote for that party's candidates in every election. Second, the concept generally refers not to strong personal allegiance to a particular political party, but to the alignment of an entire group (or at least some significant majority of a group) sharing some socioeconomic, ethnic, regional, or demographic characteristic. Dealignment is said to have occurred when the groups that have regularly supported a particular party no longer do so. Realignment implies that within the electorate the group basis of support

---

[3]See Dalton, Flanagan, and Beck 1984 for a survey of the literature and several important case studies.

for major political parties has been reorganized, perhaps—but not necessarily—with the result that the party or parties that previously tended to dominate (or at least to win more frequently) no longer do so. Third, realignments are not everyday occurrences; indeed, they may happen only at intervals of several decades. If they occurred more frequently, the concept of stable electoral alignments would be meaningless. So for the average voter, alignment with a particular political party is a lifelong attachment.

TABLE 7.1

FEDERAL DEPUTY ELECTION RESULTS, 1961–1985

(PERCENTAGE OF TOTAL VALID VOTES[1])

Year	PAN	PRI	PPS	PARM	PDM	PCM PSUM PMS PRD	PST PFCRN	Other
1961	7.6	90.3	1.0	0.5	—	—	—	—
1964	11.5	86.3	1.4	0.7	—	—	—	—
1967	12.5	83.8	2.2	1.4	—	—	—	—
1970	14.2	83.6	1.4	0.8	—	—	—	—
1973	16.5	77.4	3.8	2.0	—	—	—	—
1976	8.9	85.2	3.2	2.7	—	—	—	—
1979	11.4	74.2	2.7	1.9	2.2	5.3	2.2	—
1982	17.5	69.3	1.9	1.3	2.3	4.4	1.8	1.3
1985	16.3	68.2	2.1	1.7	2.9	3.4	2.6	2.9
1988	18.0	50.4	9.2	6.1	1.3	4.5	10.2	0.5
1991	17.7	61.4	1.8	2.1	1.1	8.3	4.3	3.1

[1]Annulled votes have been excluded from these totals.

The PRI's regular and overwhelming victories in the postwar period are evidence of extraordinary partisan stability in Mexico. Table 7.1 shows the results at the national level of federal deputy elections since the 1960s. With the exception of the 1988 elections, the PRI's victories have been commanding, at least as expressed in official statistics.[4] The election of 1988 was much

---

[4]The veracity of official electoral statistics is, of course, in question in Mexico. Thus an analysis of electoral behavior based on these statistics, such as that performed here, does not necessarily imply that the electoral strength credited to different parties by electoral authorities is a direct measure of the underlying mass political support for those parties. Yet so long as elections are the means by which political succession occurs in Mexico, those who accumulate the most counted votes will take office. Thus both real and invented votes count in contemporary Mexico, and those that disappear before they are counted do not. If the regime's law and order break down, the real bases of support will probably be better able to express themselves. This essay does not explore the real bases of political support and opposition to the regime, only that which is expressed electorally. One should note, however, that official electoral statistics have quite closely approximated electoral support as measured by opinion polls in recent elections.

closer, and the official results were strongly challenged both by members of the opposition and by other, neutral observers. Many thus asked, "Was the election of 1988 a realigning election?" (see, for example, Gómez and Klesner 1988; Molinar Horcasitas and Weldon 1990). If so, the likelihood of competitive elections in the future is high, and we may soon be able to include Mexico among the world's competitive democracies. The outcome of the 1991 elections, however, suggests that those who saw realignment as a key result of electoral challenges from the right and the left in 1988 were premature in their judgments.

SOCIAL BASES OF PRI ELECTORAL DOMINANCE: THE POLITICAL ECONOMY OF ONE-PARTY HEGEMONY

The most noted aspect of postrevolutionary Mexican politics has been the PRI's hegemony. It dominated other political forces for such a long time that observers felt justified in calling the party system a one-party or a hegemonic party system. How has this electoral record been accomplished? Certainly electoral shenanigans and electoral violence have played a role, but Mexico's revolutionary heritage and the political

TABLE 7.2

CORRELATIONS BETWEEN ELECTORAL SUPPORT FOR THE PRI AND SELECTED SOCIAL AND ECONOMIC VARIABLES, 1967–1991[1]

Variable	1967	1970	1982	1985	1988	1991
% in localities of > 2,500	−.68	−.73	−.76	−.73	−.71	−.65
% in localities of > 20,000	−.59	−.65	−.78	−.77	−.68	−.72
% born out of state (immigrants)	−.57	−.65	−.64	−.57	−.55	−.60
% with no schooling	.62	.61	.62	.59	.49	.48
% with post-primary education	−.68	−.76	−.74	−.69	−.58	−.62
% EAP[2] in primary sector	.74	.80	.74	.70	.60	.62
% EAP in secondary sector	−.63	−.73	−.79	−.72	−.64	−.69
% EAP in tertiary sector	−.72	−.75	−.44	−.43	−.32	−.35
Urban upper class	NA	NA	−.67	−.63	−.52	−.86
Urban middle class	NA	NA	−.22	−.19	−.12	−.19
Urban working class	NA	NA	−.80	−.75	−.66	−.66
Urban service workers	NA	NA	.76	.73	.63	.67
Rural popular classes	NA	NA	.82	.78	.67	.71
Rural nonmanual workers	NA	NA	.12	.13	.17	.12

NA = Not Available.

[1]Zero-order Pearson Correlation Coefficients. N varies because of missing data and changes in electoral districts. Range of N = 159 to 290. All correlations statistically signifant at the .02 level. All correlations > .24 significant at the .001 level. The 1970 census did not divide occupational categories into sufficiently detailed groups to make it possible to compare class categories with these in the 1980 census, so class categories are excluded from the analysis for 1967 and 1970.

[2]EAP = economically active population.

economy of its development experience have also been crucial to PRI electoral hegemony. Table 7.2 offers a statistical summary of the socio-economic correlates of PRI electoral support in several recent federal elections. At this point we are interested in representative "normal" elections toward the end of the era of "stabilizing development," such as the elections of 1967 and 1970. Explaining the basis for each of the statistically significant correlation coefficients provides an insight into the political economy of PRI hegemony, but it also suggests the sources of partisan dealignment in contemporary Mexico.

Most fundamentally, PRI electoral support has been strongly positively correlated with various measures that tap Mexican ruralness. There are strong positive correlation coefficients linking PRI voting with the primary sector of the economy and with rural manual occupations, and there are strong negative correlations between PRI voting and urbanization (if the converses of the measures of urbanization were shown, equally strong positive correlation coefficients would have emerged). Rural Mexico has been the PRI's bastion for six decades. In rural districts the PRI's candidates have infrequently faced challengers, and when they have, they have usually won with greater than 90 percent of the vote.

The factors explaining this electoral success are well known. Mexico's 1910–1920 revolution was fought, among other reasons, to win justice for campesinos. Mexico's most revered postrevolutionary president, Lázaro Cárdenas, delivered on the revolutionary promise of land reform in the 1930s. Through land reform, Mexico's rural sector was reorganized to reincorporate the ejido, the traditional community-based collective farm in which ownership of land titles remained in community hands. Land reform beneficiaries have been grateful to the revolutionary party for its efforts on their behalf, efforts of which they have frequently been reminded, especially at election time.

But even if some peasants began to doubt the beneficence of the ruling party, other structures have ensured their electoral support for the PRI. The PRI has been vigorous in creating campesino organizations at the national level, in co-opting those that emerge at the local and regional levels, in placing PRI militants in control of those organizations, and in urging the membership to vote for PRI candidates at election times. Moreover, the ejido also has sometimes had undemocratic characteristics. Ejidos have often been dominated by caciques who have been able to deliver the *ejidatarios'* votes to the PRI; *ejidatarios'* need for credit has often placed them in debt to caciques; and caciques, with their connections to the PRI, have often been the real enforcers of political order in the countryside. When the higher levels of illiteracy or very rudimentary education typical of rural areas are added to the aforementioned characteristics, the PRI's advantages in the countryside are clear.

So the PRI has supported a pattern of rural development that has led to *caciquismo*, which itself is beneficial to the PRI at election time.

It is less easy to use aggregate data to sort out patterns of partisan alignment among urban dwellers because neighborhoods exhibiting different class characteristics are intermixed within individual electoral districts. The PRI has clearly been less dominant in urban areas than in rural areas. Yet it should not be forgotten that until only recently the PRI won a majority of the votes in urban areas. As table 7.3 shows, as late as 1979 the PRI polled a majority in even the most urban districts.

TABLE 7.3

ELECTORAL SUPPORT FOR PARTIES, STRATIFIED BY
LEVEL OF URBANIZATION

	Average Vote for PRI in Federal Electoral Districts				
Level of Urbanization	1979	1982	1985	1988	1991
>95% urban	54%	50%	44%	30%	48%
75–94% urban	60%	62%	53%	42%	54%
50–74% urban	71%	68%	61%	50%	61%
25–49% urban	85%	78%	72%	57%	68%
<25% urban	84%	82%	78%	64%	71%
	Average Vote for PAN in Federal Electoral Districts				
>95% urban	19%	28%	24%	27%	23%
75–94% urban	24%	24%	27%	31%	29%
50–74% urban	15%	20%	21%	23%	22%
25–49% urban	6%	12%	12%	13%	14%
<25% urban	8%	10%	9%	10%	11%
	Average Vote for Left in Federal Electoral Districts				
	PSUM 1982	PSUM 1985	PMS 1988	LEFT 1988	PRD 1991	LEFT 1991
>95% urban	9%	6%	8%	42%	10%	25%
75–94% urban	4%	3%	4%	26%	4%	13%
50–74% urban	4%	3%	3%	26%	7%	13%
25–49% urban	3%	2%	2%	29%	9%	15%
<25% urban	2%	2%	3%	24%	9%	16%

In urban areas, the PRI's strength has usually been attributed to the urban "pillars" of the party, the unionized labor force and the so-called popular sectors. In the absence of survey evidence from the 1960s and early 1970s, it is hard to demonstrate statistically that this view reflects electoral reality. There is abundant anecdotal evidence to suggest that union bosses exerted significant pressure over their members to vote for the PRI. Support for the PRI from neighborhood associations whose leaders were co-opted by the PRI is well documented (Cornelius 1975). Although not well documented, it is generally assumed that state-sector employees (many of whom owe their jobs to political contacts) also provide electoral support for the ruling party; the state-sector employees' union, the Federation of Public Service Workers' Unions (FSTSE), has, along with the teachers' union, been one the largest constituent members of the PRI's "popular sector."

Whether the PRI actually received electoral support from the membership of these party-affiliated worker and "popular sector" organizations is not certain. Indeed, Kenneth Coleman's 1973 survey evidence from Mexico City suggested no major decline in the propensities of voters to support the PRI as incomes increased; in fact, high-income voters were more inclined to report that they had voted for the PRI than were low-income voters. Both lower-income and higher-income voters chose the PRI by large majorities, at least when asked to report their past electoral behavior.[5] Mexico City may have been unusual in the extent to which popular classes were relatively free from control by PRI bosses, but one must take seriously the likelihood that by the 1960s all voters in large urban areas could freely cast their votes against the PRI. Whether those votes would have been counted for the PAN or other opposition parties is another question.

The greatest support for opposition parties in the 1960s and 1970s came from the middle class. Until the 1980s, this opposition had its only real outlet in the National Action Party (PAN), a center-right party rooted in Catholic social reformist traditions similar to Christian Democratic parties elsewhere (Mabry 1974). The PAN grew in popularity until about 1973; since then, its official vote tallies nationally have leveled off at between 16 and 18 percent of the vote (see table 7.1). However, the PAN has done much better in more urban areas (see table 7.3). Certainly its successes in municipal and other elections in northern states and in Yucatán during the past decade indicate that not all PAN voters are from the middle class (see Barraza and Bizberg 1991; Guillén López 1989). Yet the PAN has had its most public base in the middle class, as the audience at PAN functions in the 1980s showed.

What could have changed this pattern of alignment in which the PRI's complete dominance of the countryside, its probable majority support from unionized labor and state-sector employees, and its continued support from a significant share of the middle class ensured that the PRI gained more than 70 percent of the votes in most national elections? The success of the development model pursued by the Mexican government in

---

[5]Coleman 1975: 504. See also Davis and Coleman (1982), who present survey data suggesting no major difference in the voting propensities of the lower and upper classes in Mexico City in the 1960s and early 1970s.

the 1940s, 1950s, and 1960s was one factor that began to detach voters from the PRI. The failure of this development model in the 1970s, and especially in the 1980s, is the other factor producing dealignment and the possibility of realignment.

THE CONSEQUENCES OF SUCCESS

"Stabilizing development" produced remarkable economic growth rates in the 1950s and 1960s, growth concentrated in the industrial and services sectors of the economy. Hence, by the early 1970s Mexico's hegemonic party had begun to encounter challenges similar to those that Samuel Huntington suggests all such one-party systems, totalitarian or authoritarian, must eventually face:

> In the third, adaptive phase, the party deals with legal-rational challenges to its authority which are, in large part, the product of its earlier successes. The creation of a relatively homogeneous society and the emergence of new social forces require the party to redefine its roles within that society. Four developments which the party must come to terms with are: (1) the emergence of a new, innovative, technical-managerial class; (2) the development of a complex group structure, typical of a more industrial society, whose interests have to be related to the political sphere; (3) the reemergence of a critical intelligentsia apart from and, indeed, increasingly alienated from the institutionalized structures of power; and (4) the demands by local and popular groups for participation in and influence over the political system (Huntington 1970: 32–33).

The Mexican political elite had long counted on the PRI to manage such difficulties. Its corporatist structure was supposed to deal with the demands of interest groups, satisfying some but constraining even more of them. Those seeking an opportunity to participate in politics were to be recruited into the party through its clientelistic system of camarillas, and their attitudes were to be changed by a heavy dose of party socialization and significant opportunities to enrich themselves by appropriating public funds. The governing elite also counted on the party to co-opt intellectuals. Public administrators were expected to join the party if they sought to advance in their careers.

Yet by the early 1970s the PRI had begun to fail at all of these tasks. Although it was able to constrain working-class and campesino demands, the PRI proved less capable of mediating and limiting the demands of the growing middle class. The successes of the 1968 student movement proved that the PRI could be bypassed by those intent upon nonelectoral forms of participation, and the events of the Echeverría *sexenio*—instances of guerrilla insurrection, urban terrorism, continued student unrest, and open conflict between the government and the private sector—confirmed that the PRI was not effectively channeling demands for participation. By the early 1970s intellectuals increasingly rejected the PRI, preferring to form their own, as yet illegal, political groups and becoming increasingly strident in their criticism of Mexico's rulers. Finally, a split became apparent between *políticos* and *técnicos*. *Políticos*, who operated mostly within the PRI, grew concerned that they were being ignored by the *técnicos* who occupied more and more key positions in the state apparatus.

The government responded to these challenges by engineering an electoral reform in 1977 that facilitated the legalization of several political parties (mostly on the left), with the expectation that additional participation would be channeled into futile efforts to win election races. These efforts were bound to be frustrated, but opposition parties' reward would be token representation in the Chamber of Deputies. Of course, President López Portillo hoped that the benefits of petroleum-produced prosperity would undercut the appeal of more radical elements on the left, and both he and Minister of the Interior Jesús Reyes Heroles thought it better to have such radical elements operate within the sphere of open contestation than to force them to work outside it. They also wagered that, despite the fact that Mexican society had become more complex, the growth of new social groups less disposed to support the "official" party had not advanced so far that these groups outweighed traditional bases of PRI support. Indeed, they assumed that some of the previous protest vote (which had generally been directed to the PAN) would be redirected to the new parties, thus dispersing the vote to various opposition parties—some old, some new— in a classic divide-and-conquer strategy. Finally, Reyes Heroles apparently thought that by creating new sources of competition from more ideologically challenging parties, and by no longer permitting the PRI to rely on fraud and coercion to create the appearance of party vigor, the PRI rank and file would be forced to renovate itself, producing new and better local leaders to replace decrepit caciques, new candidates who could win on their merit rather than through fraud and threats of violence (see Klesner 1988).

The social trends discussed above led to a gradual decline in the PRI's margin of victory and in the growth of the PAN's electoral support. The PAN polled especially well in urban areas. In 1973, for example, the PRI received only 51.8 percent of the vote in the Federal District, and it did relatively poorly in the more urbanized states such as Jalisco, México, and Puebla. The degree of electoral competitiveness in individual districts increased (see table 7.4). By 1973, there was two-party competition in more than 20 percent of all electoral districts. With the appearance of the new, independent parties on the left in 1979, over a fourth of all districts evidenced two-party or multiparty competition.[6]

TABLE 7.4

ELECTORAL COMPETITIVENESS IN FEDERAL DEPUTY ELECTIONS

(PERCENTAGE OF ALL ELECTORAL DISTRICTS)

Year	Monopoly	Strong Hegemony	Weak Hegemony	Bipartite	Multi-partite	Opposition Victory
1964	28.1	52.2	4.5	14.0	—	1.1
1967	24.2	61.2	3.6	9.7	—	1.2
1970	27.0	53.9	1.7	17.4	—	—
1973	18.7	51.3	4.1	21.8	1.0	3.1
1976	35.8	44.6	6.7	11.9	0.5	0.5
1979	9.4	48.0	12.3	6.3	22.7	1.3
1982	1.3	51.7	6.3	26.1	14.0	0.3
1985	3.3	41.7	9.0	21.0	21.3	3.7
1988	1.0	19.0	15.0	8.3	34.0	22.7
1991	—	21.7	16.0	18.0	41.0	3.3

Source: Reproduced from Leopoldo Gómez and John Bailey, "La transición política y los dilemas del PRI," *Foro Internacional* 31:1 (July–September 1990): 69. The figures for 1991 were calculated by the author.

Yet these trends were primarily a function of changes in Mexican social structure, especially the decline in the proportion of the economically active population engaged in agriculture and the increase in the share of the electorate living in urban areas. They did not indicate political realignment, or even dealignment. At the aggregate level, there was little evidence of partisan dealignment before 1988. Indeed, partisan alignments seemed relatively stable, as a comparison of the columns in table 7.2 for the years 1967 and 1970, on one hand, and 1982 and 1985, on the other, would suggest.

Another way of making the same point is through multiple regression analysis.[7] Table 7.5 presents the standardized regression coefficients (beta weights) from ordinary least squares (OLS) regressions in which the dependent variable is the percentage of the valid vote received by the PRI in each federal deputy election since 1967, and the independent variables are measures of industrialization (percentage of the economically active population in the secondary sector), urbanization (percentage of the population living in settlements of more than 20,000 people), education (percentage of

---

[6]The 1976 election was an exception to the trend. In 1976 the PAN suffered a serious internal division and did not nominate a presidential candidate, with the consequence that PAN congressional candidates also suffered.

[7]Multiple regression analysis improves on simple correlation analysis by permitting one to control for the interactive effects of independent variables.

the population with no schooling), and electoral participation (percentage of the potential electorate casting ballots). It is notable that a very high percentage of the variance in voting for the PRI (shown by R^2) can be predicted by these four variables alone, and that almost all of the regression coefficients are statistically significant throughout the time period being studied. The regression analyses for the period from 1967 through 1985 indicate that the PRI did poorly in districts with higher levels of industrialization and urbanization (with each having a strong and independent effect). It did better in districts in which the population was relatively uneducated, and it usually did better in districts in which the election turnout was high.

TABLE 7.5

MULTIPLE REGRESSION ANALYSIS OF DETERMINANTS OF
PRI ELECTORAL SUPPORT[1]
(STANDARDIZED REGRESSION COEFFICIENTS)

Year	Industriali- zation	Urbani- zation	No School	Participation	R^2	F	N
1967	.00 (.564)	-.44 (.000)	-.00 (.000)	.22 (.001)	.43	30.94	157
1970	.00 (.646)	-.48 (.000)	-.00 (.000)	.18 (.001)	.55	49.28	157
1973	-.44 (.000)	-.14 (.029)	.30 (.000)	-.04 (.366)	.61	72.53	183
1976	.12 (.046)	-.45 (.000)	.17 (.030)	.15 (.010)	.49	45.90	184
1979	-.52 (.000)	-.21 (.000)	.17 (.000)	.07 (.061)	.67	140.05	287
1982	-.49 (.000)	-.33 (.000)	.12 (.004)	.00 (.916)	.72	181.74	287
1985	-.37 (.000)	-.41 (.000)	.12 (.013)	.11 (.003)	.67	19.98	287
1988	-.36 (.000)	-.39 (.000)	.00 (.961)	.01 (.866)	.49	67.43	287
1991	-.38 (.000)	-.45 (.000)	-.04 (.500)	-.05 (.251)	.56	91.30	287

[1]Independent variable = % of valid (non-annulled) votes for PRI in federal deputy elections. Standardized regression coefficients from ordinary least squares (OLS) regression. Level of significance of the regression coefficients displayed in parentheses; coefficients in *italics* are statistically significant at the .05 level. Variables measured at the level of the federal electoral district.

These results take on added importance when considered in the context of changes in Mexican society. Structural social change was eroding the PRI's base. The share of the population in the countryside was declining, as was the unionized proportion of the working class. These were the

PRI's strongholds. Conversely, the social bases of opposition parties—industrialized urban areas with more educated populations—were growing in size. A continuation of these trends would have led to further declines in the PRI's share of the total vote, but it is important to emphasize that the decline would have been gradual.

There was also some realignment within the opposition ranks, especially on a geographical basis: the PAN's support base became more and more northern, and beginning in 1979 some of its traditionally strong bases in Mexico City and cities in central Mexico shifted toward the new leftist opposition parties. This, too, can be shown by multiple regression analysis. It is crucial to recognize here that Mexico's regions vary in their levels of economic modernization (measured by industrialization, urbanization, and education). Tables 7.6 and 7.7 (displaying the

TABLE 7.6

MULTIPLE REGRESSION ANALYSIS OF DETERMINANTS OF
PAN ELECTORAL SUPPORT[1]

(STANDARDIZED REGRESSION COEFFICIENTS)

Year	Industriali- zation	Urbani- zation	Immi- gration	No School	Partici- pation	R^2	F	N
1979	*.60* (.000)	−.14 (.061)	—	*−.21* (.001)	−.08 (.074)	.42	51.08	287
1979	*.64* (.000)	−.12 (.112)	.08 (.282)	*−.21* (.001)	−.07 (.126)	.43	42.24	287
1982	*.57* (.000)	.07 (.285)	—	*−.20* (.000)	−.05 (.259)	.57	93.56	287
1982	*.63* (.000)	.10 (.127)	−.11 (.061)	*−.21* (.000)	−.02 (.599)	.58	79.12	287
1985	*.30* (.000)	*.19* (.010)	—	*−.23* (.000)	*−.16* (.001)	.43	53.28	287
1985	*.45* (.000)	*.26* (.000)	*−.31* (.000)	*−.28* (.000)	*−.10* (.037)	.47	50.66	287
1988	*.35* (.000)	*.21* (.006)	—	*−.15* (.016)	−.06 (.223)	.39	44.89	287
1988	*.57* (.000)	*.29* (.000)	*−.45* (.000)	*−.22* (.000)	.02 (.726)	.47	50.83	287
1991	*.32* (.000)	.15 (.063)	—	−.13 (.059)	*.10* (.050)	.29	29.61	287
1991	*.47* (.000)	*.20* (.016)	*−.29* (.000)	*−.18* (.009)	*.12* (.019)	.32	27.67	287

[1]Independent variable = % of valid (non-annulled) votes for PAN in federal deputy elections. Standardized regression coefficients from ordinary least squares (OLS) regression. Level of significance of the regression coefficients displayed in parentheses; coefficients in *italics* are statistically significant at the .05 level. Variables measured at the level of the federal electoral district.

TABLE 7.7

MULTIPLE REGRESSION ANALYSIS OF DETERMINANTS OF ELECTORAL
SUPPORT FOR INDEPENDENT PARTIES OF THE LEFT[1]
(STANDARDIZED REGRESSION COEFFICIENTS)

Year	Industriali-zation	Urbani-zation	Immi-gration	No School	Partici-pation	R^2	F	N
1979	.22 (.001)	.49 (.000)	—	-.04 (.477)	-.00 (.935)	.48	63.39	287
1979	.10 (.171)	.45 (.000)	.24 (.000)	.01 (.905)	-.03 (.430)	.50	57.13	287
1982	.48 (.000)	.19 (.007)	—	-.04 (.524)	.12 (.011)	.43	52.94	287
1982	.10 (.187)	.45 (.000)	.18 (.014)	-.00 (.998)	.09 (.057)	.44	44.96	287
1985	.24 (.000)	.43 (.000)	—	-.04 (.553)	.06 (.213)	.43	52.54	287
1985	.13 (.083)	.39 (.000)	.24 (.001)	.00 (.992)	.02 (.623)	.46	47.87	287
1988	.30 (.000)	.18 (.029)	—	-.05 (.445)	.21 (.000)	.28	28.23	287
1988	.10 (.204)	.10 (.191)	.42 (.000)	.01 (.828)	.15 (.004)	.36	32.39	287
1991	-.13 (.128)	.17 (.071)	—	.21 (.009)	-.08 (.167)	.04	3.54	287
1991	-.26 (.008)	.14 (.154)	.25 (.005)	.25 (.002)	-.10 (.091)	.06	4.38	287

[1]Independent variable = % of valid (non-annulled) votes for independent leftist parties in federal deputy elections. Standardized regression coefficients from ordinary least squares (OLS) regression. Level of significance of the regression coefficients displayed in parentheses; coefficients in *italics* are statistically significant at the .05 level. Variables measured at the level of the federal electoral district. Parties included: 1979: PCM; 1982: PSUM and PRT; 1985: PSUM, PRT, and PMT; 1988: PMS and PRT; 1991: PRD.

results of the same regression model used in table 7.5, this time with the PAN's and the left's results serving as the dependent variables) show that the regions with higher levels of economic modernization tended to vote for the PAN or parties of the left.[8] Figures 7.1 and 7.2 indicate the regional aspects of Mexican opposition voting, controlling for the effects

[8]Tables 7.6 and 7.7 show the results for the period from 1979 to 1991 for two different regression models. The first model uses the same independent variables used to explain PRI voting in table 7.5. The second model adds the independent variable "percent born out of state," a measure of immigration, to the other independent variables. (For an important study of urban migrants' political behavior, see Cornelius 1975. See Molinar Horcasitas and Weldon 1990 for an ecological study of Mexican electoral behavior in which immigration is a key variable.) Regression analyses of PRI voting using the second model found the immigration variable to be statistically insignificant, so those results are not reported.

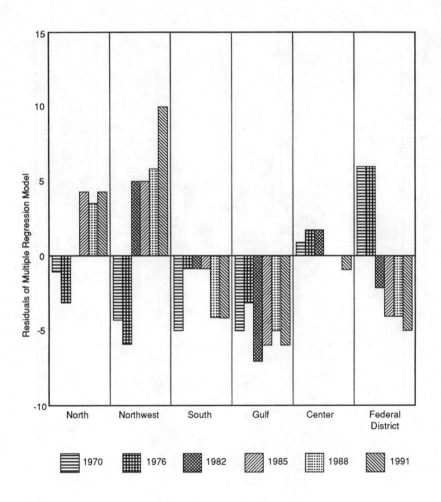

FIGURE **7.1**

Regionalism in Mexican Elections
Voting for PAN, 1970-1991

FIGURE **7.2**

Regionalism in Mexican Elections
Voting for Independent Left, 1970-1991

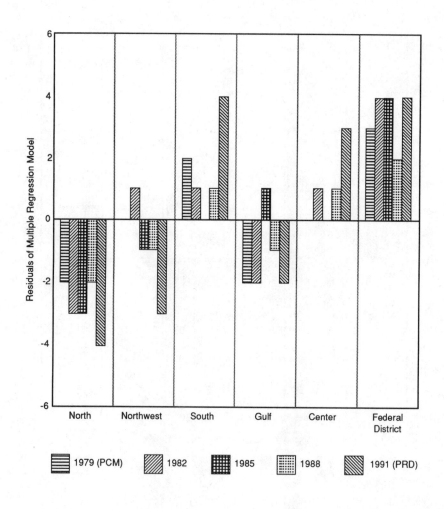

of industrialization, urbanization, education, and participation.[9] Figure 7.1 indicates that the PAN had overperformed in the Federal District up until 1976, but that since then it has done more poorly than it would be expected to, considering the level of modernization there. Conversely, figure 7.2 shows that independent leftist parties perform better in the Federal District than would be predicted on the basis of the level of modernization. The reverse is true for the north and northwest (as defined in Smith 1979: 68). Nevertheless, regional realignment in opposition voting was also of modest proportions from 1979 to 1985, although the PAN's spectacular victories in major cities in several northern states in late 1982 and early 1983 indicated that the movement of voters away from the PRI threatened to become serious. It is important to note, though, that these developments occurred after the onset of economic crisis.

THE COLLAPSE OF THE DEVELOPMENT MODEL: POLICY FAILURE AND ECONOMIC CRISIS

As noted in the preceding section, electoral change had taken place very gradually in Mexico. Much of that change had occurred in a period of economic prosperity. Only in the latter part of the Echeverría *sexenio* (1970–1976) did Mexico begin to experience economic difficulties, and even these problems seemed temporary when Mexico's petroleum boom arrived under Echeverría's successor, López Portillo (1976–1982). The petroleum boom, however, did not last. The dramatic fall in oil prices (and with them, export revenues) in the early 1980s occurred at the same time that many of the loans Mexico took on in the late 1970s came due, leading to the financial crisis of the 1980s. The PAN's electoral challenge in the north in 1982–1983, in the gubernatorial elections in Sonora and Nuevo León in 1985, and again in Chihuahua in 1986 indicated that the PRI faced an unprecedented challenge to its hegemony. The Democratic Current's break from the PRI in 1988, the results of the 1988 presidential election, and the controversy surrounding that election strongly suggested that the economic conjuncture of the mid-to-late 1980s might lead to political realignment and an end to PRI hegemony.

Statistical analysis of aggregate data from the 1988 election indicates that there was some change in partisan alignment in Mexico, at least

---

[9]Technically, this is an analysis of the residuals of the regression analyses reported in tables 7.6 and 7.7. A residual is the difference between the actual value of the dependent variable and the value predicted by the regression equation. Thus a positive residual indicates that the vote for the PAN (in figure 7.1) or the left (in figure 7.2) is greater than one would expect based on the values of the independent variables (measuring modernization and participation) alone. In figures 7.1 and 7.2, the residuals are grouped by election year and by region, and each bar represents the *mean* residual (essentially a percentage of the total vote) for the region and the election year. The regression model used here excludes the immigration variable. Note that to save space, the regression equations for the PAN for 1970 and 1976 are not reported in table 7.6, even though their residuals are graphed in figure 7.1.

temporarily. However, a single election provides insufficient evidence to say with certainty that firm new alignments had been formed.[10] The correlation coefficients in table 7.2 suggest that some change had occurred; note that the size of the correlation coefficients between PRI voting and both economic sector variables and social class variables generally declined. Table 7.5 also shows that the regression coefficients for the education variable and for participation were both statistically insignificant, suggesting that after controlling for the impact of urbanization and industrialization, education no longer had an independent effect on voting for the PRI. This remained true in 1991. High levels of participation did not give a significant advantage to the PRI in either 1988 or 1991, contrary to much previous experience.

Table 7.8 presents correlation coefficients for voting for leftist parties in recent elections. Note that the correlation coefficients between total left vote and the education variables declined in magnitude between 1985 and 1988. Moreover, the left's traditional strength in urban middle- and upper-class districts declined, as did its traditional weakness among campesinos. These correlation coefficients indicate that the left did better in 1988 in districts with higher concentrations of the poorly educated and peasants than it had ever done before. Table 7.3 presents similar information. In previous elections the left's support dropped off considerably as districts became more rural, but in 1988, although that drop-off outside the most urban districts remained, the left's support was relatively large in rural areas and did not decline from the second-most-urban to the least-urban category. Among leftist parties, it is notable that for the two that showed greatest growth in electoral strength between 1985 and 1988—the Party of the Cardenista Front for National Reconstruction (PFCRN) and the Authentic Party of the Mexican Revolution (PARM)—it is impossible to find any statistically significant correlation with social structural variables (Klesner 1993). Thus we might conclude that the over 11 percent of the vote going to the PFCRN in the 1988 congressional elections came at the expense of the PRI, as did the over 6 percent going to the PARM. Now the independence of these two parties can certainly be questioned, and the growth in PFCRN support was certainly due in good measure to the use of "Cardenista" in its name. Yet these parties' performance in 1988 indicates that some substantial percentage of the PRI's social base had become free to vote for other parties. This indicates dealignment, if not realignment.

Miguel Basáñez has presented survey evidence indicating a similar trend toward loosening partisan attachments in the mid-1980s. He

---

[10]This was made doubly difficult because of Cárdenas's candidacy. The extent to which Cárdenas's extraordinary challenge was due solely to association with his father is still unclear. Whether a leftist candidate other than Cárdenas would perform even remotely as well as Cárdenas did in 1988 remains an open question. Were leftist voters in 1988 one-time voters for the left? The question cannot be answered at this time.

TABLE 7.8

CORRELATIONS BETWEEN ELECTORAL SUPPORT FOR LEFTIST PARTIES AND
SELECTED SOCIAL AND ECONOMIC VARIABLES, 1982–1991[1]

Variable	Total Left 1982	Total Left 1985	Total Left 1988	Total Left 1991	PSUM 1985	PRD 1991
% in localities of > 2,500	.59	.46	.40	.31	.53	−.01
% in localities of > 20,000	.60	.46	.32	.28	.53	−.04
% born out of state (immigrants)	.52	.45	.40	.28	.46	.00
% with no schooling	−.37	−.28	−.18	−.05	−.34	.18
% with post-primary education	.54	.41	.22	.21	.48	−.06
% EAP[2] in primary sector	−.39	−.30	−.19	−.08	−.37	.18
% EAP in secondary sector	.47	.39	.27	.15	.45	−.11
% EAP in tertiary sector	.17	.11	.03	−.09	.14	−.22
Urban upper class	.49	.37	.16	.14	.43	−.10
Urban middle class	.12	.08	.00	.02	.09	−.08
Urban working class	.47	.37	.27	.16	.43	−.13
Urban service workers	.56	.42	.28	.24	.48	−.07
Rural popular classes	−.50	−.39	−.26	−.18	−.46	.13
Rural nonmanual workers	−.13	−.15	−.13	−.11	−.13	−.08

[1]Zero-order Pearson Correlation Coefficients. N = 290. All correlations > .24 significant at the .001 level; > .10 significant at the .05 level.

[2]EAP = economically active population

shows that over 20 percent of the population moved into the nonaligned camp between 1983 and 1987, so that nearly half of all Mexicans no longer sympathized with a particular party (Basáñez 1990: 225). The PRI, meanwhile, lost about 25 percent of the population to other parties and the nonaligned. A Gallup poll conducted before the 1988 election indicated that about a third of those polled had voted for the PRI in 1982 but intended to defect in 1988 (Domínguez and McCann 1992a). Coming over a month before the actual elections, this was probably a conservative estimate of actual defection.

From whom did the parties of the left gather their votes in 1988? Correlation analysis of growth in the left's share of the vote between 1985 and 1988 (using the various social structural variables listed in tables 7.2 and 7.8) produced no strong, statistically significant results. The lack of strong, significant correlations between social structural variables and growth in leftist voting suggests that this vote was obtained from across most social groups. In contrast, growth in the PAN's percentage of the vote (1985–1988) was most highly correlated with the share of the workforce in urban upper-class occupations (r = .22), and it showed statistically significant negative correlations with the share of the workforce in rural, manual occupations (r = -.16) and in the primary sector (r = -.14). In 1988, the PAN seemed to move even further out of the countryside and away from popular classes, although this was not necessarily true in northern states (Barraza and Bizberg 1991).

The preceding analysis provides some indication why the PRI has feared the left more than the PAN, and why it was willing to concede defeat to the PAN in gubernatorial elections in Baja California in 1989 and in Chihuahua in 1992, but not to the Party of the Democratic Revolution (PRD) in elections in Michoacán in 1989 and 1992.[11] In essence, the PRI and the PRD (and other parties on the left) seemed to compete for the same portions of the electorate, whereas PAN voters were firmly in the PAN camp and were a sufficiently small part of the electorate that it was safe to concede them to the PAN. It was not safe for the PRI to lose to the PRD if that only increased the credibility of the PRD among the PRI's own electoral bases. Domínguez and McCann's study (1992a) of the 1988 Gallup poll results indicates that a strong indicator of defection from the PRI was the sense that another party could win (or that the PRI could lose). This only reinforced the need to defeat the most dangerous challenger.

In the 1988 elections, the PRI as usual performed strongly in the more rural, southern states, gaining its highest presidential vote percentages in the Pacific south and in the Gulf states, including the Yucatán peninsula. In congressional races the PRI performed strongly in the Pacific south and the Gulf even after controlling for the effects of those regions' lower levels of economic modernization (see figure 7.3). These regions have historically been PRI territory. The PRI's extra efforts in the north (Chihuahua, Nuevo León, and Coahuila, among other states) and the Pacific north (Sinaloa, Sonora, the Baja Californias) produced an unexpectedly high PRI vote share there in 1988. In the relatively urbanized regions of the center and in the Mexico City area, the PRI's performance lagged. In the presidential race, Cárdenas did particularly well in Mexico City and in some center states (especially Michoacán). The twenty-nine federal deputy seats that the National Democratic Front (FDN) won were concentrated in Michoacán, the state of México, and Mexico City. The PRI's determination to retake Michoacán and México in state elections in 1989 and 1990, respectively, again reflected great concern about losing to a party on the left. The PAN's thirty-eight seats were concentrated in urban areas, especially in Mexico City, Ciudad Juárez, León, and the Guadalajara area, all within the PAN's traditional geographical bases.

---

[11] The PRI initially claimed victory in the 1992 Michoacán gubernatorial election, but the PRI governor-elect subsequently stepped down because of mass demonstrations against PRI fraud.

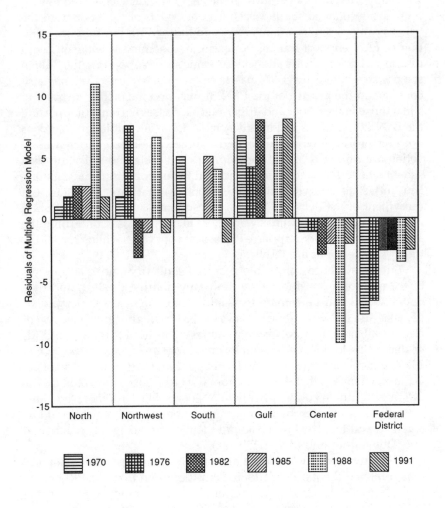

FIGURE **7.3**

Regionalism in Mexican Elections
Voting for PRI, 1970-1991

Residuals of Multiple Regression Model

North   Northwest   South   Gulf   Center   Federal
                                                 District

1970   1976   1982   1985   1988   1991

There is evidence that clear distinctions are forming among opposition parties' social bases and their supporters' policy preferences. Gallup's May 1988 pre-election poll and a *Los Angeles Times* poll conducted in August 1989 both showed that, whereas those preferring Salinas in the 1988 presidential race did not differ significantly across levels of socioeconomic status, those who planned to (and apparently did) vote for Cárdenas clustered more toward lower socioeconomic levels, and those who supported Manuel Clouthier, the PAN candidate, clustered toward high socioeconomic status levels. The defection of the poor from the Salinas campaign was a dangerous sign for the PRI, but the concentration of PAN support among upper socioeconomic levels (again, with disaffected voters across all socioeconomic strata supporting the PAN in some states where the PAN has been particularly effective) has also constrained the growth of the PAN. It may become more constraining still if those in the upper and upper-middle classes currently supporting the PAN defect to the PRI in order to block the left, although that does not seem to have occurred in 1991. These class-based differences in voting are mirrored in socioeconomic policy preferences. Polling data show that Cardenistas are more inclined to support economic nationalism and state intervention in the economy than are PANistas. On repayment of the debt and foreign investment issues, those indicating support for President Salinas were more like PANistas. Concerning the sale of state-owned enterprises, PRIístas are not yet as willing to yield to the private sector as are PANistas.

Survey evidence points to one crucial similarity among supporters of the political opposition: they uniformly distrust the PRI, and they doubt that it can be transformed into a more democratic party. Cardenistas and PANistas do not believe the PRI has legitimately won recent elections. Nor do they believe that Salinas either tried to reform the PRI, or that he could do so if he really wanted to (*Los Angeles Times* 1989: 8, 23). The most striking finding in Domínguez and McCann's study of the Gallup poll data is that defectors from the PRI (those who voted for the PRI in 1982 but voted for either the PAN or the FDN in 1988) were most strongly characterized by their sense that the political regime could be changed and that the PRI's 1988 presidential candidate was not a good one (Domínguez and McCann 1992a).

In many ways, the evidence just presented suggests that a political realignment did not occur in 1988. Some defection from the PRI's ranks took place at both elite and mass levels, but more would have to occur at the mass level to achieve a critical realignment. As of 1988, the axis of electoral politics still turned on the issue of the regime, not public policy. Juan Molinar Horcasitas argues that two axes of political cleavage have coexisted recently in Mexico, an ideological axis and a strategic (system-antisystem) axis. In his analysis, "The refusal to liberalize electoral policy led to a bloc movement away from the political center and toward increased polarization along the strategic axis. Strategy replaced ideology as the key to party-system organization. The opposition party leaders' perception that their counterparts in government would not heed election results has led to a profound split between the two groups" (Molinar Horcasitas 1989: 280). It is hard to imagine that such a system-antisystem cleavage could exist for long without producing a violent rupture. Interestingly, Cardenistas are much more inclined to believe that such a rupture is in Mexico's future than are PANistas (*Los Angeles Times* 1989: 25).

Salinas de Gortari, notably, rejected the inevitability of either political rupture or political realignment. His challenge upon taking office—especially because he did so under the cloud of alleged electoral fraud—was to bring about the fundamental economic change he favored while avoiding both political rupture and political realignment.

ECONOMIC RESTRUCTURING AND ITS CONSEQUENCES FOR PRI ELECTORAL SUPPORTERS

Salinas and his economic team believed that in the long run the economic changes they launched would be to the nation's economic benefit and, presumably, to their political benefit. The economic reforms they introduced were profound, and they will take some time to have full effect. In the meantime, Mexicans of all social strata have experienced great adjustments in their everyday lives. The burden of adjustment has not fallen equally on all Mexicans. Some have benefited and others have suffered as a consequence of neoliberal reforms. Have there been electoral repercussions?

Mexico's economic restructuring began before Salinas came to office. His predecessor, Miguel de la Madrid, administered an austerity program whose burden fell largely on wage earners. Wage restraint was a key element in the program, as were taxes on end-of-year bonuses and a 50 percent increase in the sales tax (Bortz 1986: 42–43). The de la Madrid administration also began to liberalize Mexico's economy by entering the General Agreement on Tariffs and Trade in 1986, reducing tariffs, inviting foreign investors to reconsider Mexico, and selling some state-owned enterprises. The social consequences were momentous. Lorenzo Meyer writes:

> It is clear that the social cost was enormous; during the de la Madrid *sexenio* social spending was reduced, salaries lost half their purchasing power—salaries went from representing 36 percent of gross domestic product to 29 percent—the GDP stagnated, inflation was not contained (it was 80 percent in 1983 and 159 percent in 1987) and the informal economy grew because of the impossibility of the formal sector generating the em-

ployment demanded by the demographic expansion of the working-age population (1991: 31).

Salinas accelerated the restructuring process when he came to power in December 1988. "Salinastroika" had five main pillars: a rapid opening to the international economy; the sale of most state-owned enterprises; the reduction or elimination of government subsidies for many formerly subsidized basic consumption items, part of a general reduction in government spending and a general freeing of prices; a crackdown on some labor leaders generally judged to be corrupt, as a means of weakening organized labor; and legislation changing the constitutional status of Mexico's ejidos. Each of these measures entailed significant adjustment burdens. Each could, therefore, erode electoral support for Salinas's party, the PRI.

The principal features of Mexico's opening to the international economy included the drastic reduction of tariff barriers, the liberalization of rules constraining direct foreign investment, and agreement to create a North American free trade area with the United States and Canada. In terms of winners and losers, the winners were Mexicans able to buy imported goods (especially the middle and upper classes), those likely to be employed in enterprises created as a result of new foreign investment, and those philosophically committed to free trade. These are not large groups, although satisfying consumers can generate a feeling of general prosperity. Losers included those workers who joined the ranks of the unemployed as the result of increased competition from foreign products, and rural producers who saw their traditional markets flooded with imported foodstuffs.[12] Economic nationalists were generally distraught over the North American Free Trade Agreement (NAFTA) and a more favorable government attitude toward foreign capital. The losers can be quite vocal groups.

Where is the balance among winners and losers? Opinion polling data suggest that the majority of the Mexican population favors economic opening.[13] Enrique Krauze argues: "Economic nationalism has been one of the main themes of the Mexican Revolution, but it has never been a deep, sincerely felt attitude in the Mexican people. Their expecta-

---

[12]Hence prices of agricultural products and peasant incomes have fallen. The dramatic increase in food imports was due in part to an overvalued peso. See Reding 1991: 271–73.

[13]The *Los Angeles Times* October 1991 poll revealed that 50 percent of those surveyed favored encouraging foreign investment, while only 32 percent favored restricting it. These results mirrored almost exactly those from the *Los Angeles Times* August 1989 poll. On the issue of trade negotiations with the United States, 61 percent of those sampled favored the potential free trade arrangement (20 percent "totally" and 41 percent "somewhat"), while only 15 percent opposed it (6 percent "totally" and 9 percent "somewhat"). Regarding the consequences of free trade, 48 percent of respondents thought it would be mainly good for Mexico, 18 percent felt that it would be mainly bad for Mexico, and 22 percent thought that it would be neither good nor bad. See *Los Angeles Times* 1991: 7, 20.

tions, their fears [about the trade agreement] are more pragmatic than ideological" (Boudreaux 1991). If Krauze is right, Salinas's opening of the economy may yield more benefits than costs for his party, provided of course that the measure succeeds in generating employment and economic growth.

The divestment of state-owned enterprises was a major pillar of Salinas's effort to introduce competition into the Mexican economy. Divestment has different meanings, however. It can mean the sale of a state-owned enterprise to the private sector or to a union, or it can mean transferring ownership to a state or local government, liquidation of a firm through bankruptcy proceedings, or the merger of a firm with other enterprises in the state-owned sector. Some of Mexico's largest state-owned firms, with the largest payrolls, were among those sold to private investors, but many firms (perhaps a majority) were liquidated (*Latin American Special Report* 1991).

Here, again, potential winners and losers can be predicted, but the balance between them is hard to determine. The biggest losers were those put out of work as a result of bankruptcies or downsizing, those whose consumption had been subsidized by some state-owned firms, and those strongly committed to state ownership of basic industry. Those gaining from privatization may include consumers (if the inefficiencies of state monopolies are not reproduced by private owners), those few who have been able to buy into formerly state-owned firms, and those employed because of the expansion of newly privatized firms. Advocates of capitalism will enjoy ideological satisfaction. In the short term, losers are more easily identified than winners. Yet survey evidence suggests that those who believe privatization will help people like themselves outnumber those who believe it will do harm.[14]

Prices of a broad array of basic consumer items long subsidized by the Mexican state began to rise under de la Madrid. Part of Salinas's effort to lower inflation was the Pact for Stability and Economic Growth (PECE). Despite the anti-inflation rhetoric of the PECE and efforts under it to curb unions' demands for real wage increases, on several occasions the prices of basic commodities rose faster than the overall consumer price index (*Latin American Regional Report* 1990; *Latin American Weekly Report* 1990). Poor workers and consumers bore the brunt of this anti-inflation policy. It is to be expected that they might hold Salinas and the PRI responsible, and a widely held view of the PRI's difficulties in 1988 attributes Salinas's relative unpopularity as a PRI presidential candidate to the country's poor economic performance. Yet when asked about their

---

[14]In one poll (*Este País* 1991: 16), 39 percent of respondents thought that privatization would be helpful to people like themselves (14 percent thought it would help much, 25 percent that it would help a little), while 29 percent of those surveyed thought it would be harmful (10 percent thought it would harm others like themselves much, 19 percent thought it would do a little harm), and 17 percent thought it would have no effect.

personal economic situation over the previous three years, Mexicans' views were almost evenly split over whether their situations had improved, stayed the same, or worsened.[15] It is interesting, however, that the same poll found that over three-quarters of the respondents felt that Salinas's handling of the economy was good or very good (*Los Angeles Times* 1991: 9). Again, gauging the balance between those who might hold the PRI responsible for the price increases with which they have been forced to cope, and those who seemed willing to go along with Salinas's general liberalization of the economy in hopes of long-term benefits, is difficult.

One of Salinas's first acts upon coming to power was to confront powerful union leaders. Although this measure was presented as a crackdown on corruption, it was also a means to weaken the power of organized labor and thereby hold down wage increases, thus helping to control inflation. Furthermore, confronting and defeating powerful union bosses was an effort to weaken traditionally powerful forces within the PRI, those most likely to oppose Salinas's efforts to restructure the party. Again, Salinas undoubtedly created animosity among the supporters of organized labor by these actions, even while demonstrating that he was a strong leader.

Perhaps Salinas's most fundamental change in the structure of the Mexican economy was legislation ending Mexico's agrarian reform program and permitting the sale of ejido land. This plan, long lurking in the shadows, was not unveiled until after the 1991 federal congressional elections. Proponents of dismantling the ejido argue that by allowing Mexican peasants to buy and sell land, some peasants will accumulate sufficiently large landholdings that they can greatly increase overall agricultural productivity. Moreover, the end of the ejido may eliminate the power bases of many rural caciques and thereby end their exploitation of campesinos. Critics of the plan argue that if villages lose control of land titles, Mexico's revolutionary heritage will be betrayed, and that agribusinesses will accumulate very large landholdings and exploit the former landowners now forced to seek employment as rural workers. Salinas's decision to wait until after the 1991 elections to initiate this reform may reflect good political sense; a November 1991 survey indicated strong opposition to the sale of ejido land, with a strong majority of respondents holding the belief that the law prohibiting the sale of such land had been beneficial to Mexico (*Este País* 1992: 34).

In sum, those likely to bear the adjustment costs associated with restructuring are more visible than the likely beneficiaries, especially in the short term. Whether the losers perceive themselves to be losers,

---

[15]In the *Los Angeles Times* poll taken in late September and early October 1991, 36 percent of those surveyed said their personal economic situations were better than three years earlier, 33 percent judged that they were the same, and 30 percent reported they were worse (*Los Angeles Times* 1991: 6).

though, is not so clear. Certainly the leaders of groups identified as likely losers perceive themselves to be losers; whether their followers have that perception depends in part on how happy they might be to be freed from domination by union bosses or caciques. Salinas received strong acclaim from the Mexican people for his bold leadership. Some of that acclaim may have rubbed off on his party, too.

PRI VICTORY DESPITE ECONOMIC CRISIS AND RESTRUCTURING?

No one expected the PRI to respond to the electoral challenge of 1988 by simply rolling over and dying. Nor was Salinas expected to destroy the PRI or allow it to expire. Nevertheless, in light of the opposition parties' advances in 1988 and the social costs of economic restructuring since then, the PRI performed far better in the 1991 federal congressional elections than would have been predicted a year or two earlier. Compared to its 1988 performance, the PRI regained over 10 percent of the vote from opposition parties (see table 7.1). Why? In a pair of penetrating essays, Jorge Alcocer (Alcocer 1991; Alcocer and Morales 1991) argues that the following factors accounted for the PRI's success: (1) "inertial fraud," (2) "fraud designed and executed to guarantee triumph in those zones of high risk for the PRI," (3) votes won because of a PRI strategy focused on polling places and city blocks in the most populous urban areas of the country, and (4) votes freely cast for the PRI. Alcocer's categories usefully organize the following discussion of the PRI's strategy to avoid a feared realignment of the electorate.

Inertial fraud refers to the difficulty of curbing practices that local PRI organizations have used for decades to ensure the *carro completo*— that is, the sweep of all available elected positions by PRI candidates. In 1991, the political opposition was particularly vocal about the PRI's declared victories in gubernatorial races in the states of Guanajuato and San Luis Potosí. Some suggested this reflected a disinterest in democracy on the part of Salinas and the PRI leadership, a disinterest they were forced to reconsider in light of the huge opposition protests against electoral fraud in those two states. Wayne Cornelius (1991) provides a different view:

> A more persuasive explanation for what happened in Guanajuato and San Luis Potosí is that lower-echelon leaders in many parts of the far-flung PRI apparatus no longer automatically obey directives from the center. There is a basic conflict of interest between the party's entrenched state and local machines, which are concerned with maintaining their traditional share of power and perks, and the modernizing national political elite in Mexico City.

Salinas's decision essentially to void the Guanajuato and San Luis Potosí elections by forcing the PRI governors-elect to step down helped him take further action against *caciquismo* and state and local party organizations' continued use of electoral fraud. In essence, it potentially allowed Salinas to engineer a kind of electoral dealignment—detaching from automatically voting for the PRI those individuals who had been unable to resist the demands of caciques, as well as eliminating phantom voters improperly listed on electoral rolls. Those provisions of the 1990 federal electoral law that mandated the complete re-registration of all eligible voters, required voter identification cards carrying the voter's picture, signature, and fingerprint, permitted parties access to the Federal Electoral Commission's computers during the vote count, required the immediate release of preliminary election results, should all make it much more difficult for local PRI machines to carry out fraud. If this analysis is correct, in the future local PRIístas will have to produce their majorities the hard way: through effective public policy and the nomination of winning candidates.

It has also been charged that the central party leadership, perhaps including the Salinas inner circle, may have engaged in more targeted fraud in districts where the PRI had been weak. In particular, critics noted that in the process of re-registering the electorate (in conjunction with the 1990 national census) and issuing voter identification cards, some three million individuals who requested cards did not receive them, and about six million of the voting-age population apparently did not request identification cards (Castañeda 1991). Basáñez's polling data indicate that those expressing no party sympathy were less likely to have been registered—and even less likely to have received their voting credentials—than PRI or opposition supporters (Basáñez 1991: 5). The suspicion is widely held that the distribution of voting credentials was slowed so as to disqualify some potential supporters of opposition parties.

However, what is more likely to have contributed substantially to the PRI's resurgence in 1991 was a massive effort (begun in 1989) to create a network of get-out-the-vote promoters coordinated by the PRI's state organizations, with connections down to the lowest level of Mexican society. The plan targeted the 115 most important cities in the country. It used a system of national surveys designed to permit the PRI organization to tailor its candidates and their campaigns to meet the demands of particular districts. Furthermore, these surveys helped considerably in getting out the vote (see Berrueto Pruneda n.d.). Although the PRI has always been able to mount a far larger and more richly funded campaign than its opposition, this was an unprecedented effort to reclaim the grassroots. As Alcocer and Morales (1991: 30) conclude, such a massive effort could have been undertaken only with the support of government resources. Whether the PRI played fair in this effort or not, it produced results.

Finally, we must recognize that in 1991 a larger share of the Mexican electorate may have freely voted for the PRI's candidates than in the recent past. Several factors may have contributed to this outcome. First, the left (especially the neo-Cardenista PRD) was a less attractive alternative in 1991 than in 1988, when Cuauhtémoc Cárdenas was its presidential standard bearer. The left did not maintain its unity after 1988; indeed, some parties that constituted the Cardenista alliance left the coalition shortly after the presidential election was over. Furthermore, the PRD had its own internal divisions. In this context, many voters who had voted for Cárdenas in 1988 may have decided that the PRD was not the best option in 1991 (Domínguez and McCann 1992b: 13–14).

Second, despite the costs of adjustment, the Mexican economy had experienced robust economic growth, great increases in investment, and a rapid decrease in inflation. This was achieved by a PRIísta president leading a PRI-dominated congress. Reported sympathies with the PRI in 1991 were up 50 percent over 1989, while sympathies for the PRD declined by half.[16]

Third, the Salinas administration embarked on a large, complex program, the National Solidarity Program (PRONASOL), aimed at ameliorating the costs associated with economic restructuring. This program was supposed to target those areas where poverty and the costs associated with the economic crisis were most severe. Its major initiatives included building health care facilities in rural areas, extending telephone service to remote villages, and refurbishing schools. It was a form of welfare for the less fortunate, but one that emphasized self-help through neighborhood committees that were supposed to participate in the selection of projects and supervise their implementation. In the process, poor people not only benefited materially but, some analysts suggest, they were organized for, among other things, voting for the ruling party (see Dresser 1991).

What did this mean for patterns of electoral alignment? First, the PRI's relative strengths in nonindustrialized, nonurban settings did not change despite the campaign's supposed concentration on voters in cities (see the regression coefficients in table 7.5). Nonetheless, as table 7.5 also shows, the PRI's former advantage in districts with high percentages of uneducated people (which disappeared in 1988) was not regained in 1991. This means that either the PRI was more effective at appealing to better educated voters, or opposition parties cut into the PRI's base among the uneducated, or both. Table 7.7 would suggest that

---

[16]In August 1989, 32 percent of the respondents to the *Los Angeles Times* poll sympathized with the PRI; in October 1991 the figure was 48 percent. The PRD's support fell from 15 percent to 7 percent (*Los Angeles Times* 1991: 24).

the left, in this case the PRD, made inroads in districts with high percentages of uneducated voters.

Indeed, the most interesting statistical findings about the 1991 election concern the PRD's support groups. Overall, the same statistical model that successfully explains PRI and PAN voting (shown by R^2) is a very poor predictor of PRD voting in 1991 ($R^2 = .04$). Adding immigration (those born out of state) as an independent variable improves the power of prediction only slightly ($R^2 = .06$). Indeed, as the last column in table 7.8 shows, no socioeconomic variables are strongly correlated (either positively or negatively) with PRD voting in 1991. This is an indication of dealignment in the electorate, specifically a lack of alignment of key social groups with the principal party of the independent left. In the regression model in table 7.7, it is important to note that for the first time the regression coefficient for industrialization is negative. The statistically significant positive coefficient for the uneducated is also important. The regression coefficient for immigration remains positive and statistically significant. The coefficients for these three variables suggest that the PRD became more effective in districts with concentrations of the poor and the uneducated than the left had ever been before, but again this is a weak relationship.

A second statistical finding is that the regionalization of opposition voting observed in 1988 increased in 1991. Figures 7.1 and 7.2 indicate that the PAN did even better in the north and northwest than would have been expected given the levels of economic modernization in those regions, and that in 1991 the PAN strengthened its support in the northwest. Conversely, the PRD did particularly poorly in those two regions in 1991, compared with the performance of independent leftist parties in 1988 and earlier years. The PRD, though, surged in the south and center in 1991 and consolidated its relative strength in Mexico City. The regionalization of the PRI vote observed in 1988 did not reappear in 1991; instead, the PRI regained its historical levels of electoral performance in various regions (see figure 7.3). These results are consistent with survey evidence indicating that in 1991 both the PAN and the PRD became less national and more regional in their appeals (Domínguez and McCann 1992b: 12–13).

Because of opposition parties' strong performance in 1988 and their apparent capacity to draw voters from the PRI's various social bases, and because of changes in the PRD's support bases in 1991, it seems safe to conclude that some dealignment of the Mexican electorate occurred during this period. Indeed, Basáñez's survey data for the early 1990s reported that the majority of the electorate had no partisan sympathy (Basáñez 1991: 3). Given an appealing opposition candidate for whom to vote, Mexican voters may again vote against the PRI, as they did in 1988. Given an appealing PRI candidate, however, Mexican voters may again return to the PRI fold, as they did in 1991. Nevertheless, the Mexican electorate is less securely under the PRI's control than it has ever been. Less than 40 percent of electoral districts can now be defined as under PRI monopoly, strong hegemony, or weak hegemony, in contrast to 1982 when nearly 60 percent of all districts fit those categories (table 7.4). Yet no large and easily identified group of Mexican voters has been captured by the opposition, making it hard to conclude that realignment of the Mexican electorate has occurred.

CONCLUSIONS: REALIGNMENT OR DEALIGNMENT?

Successes by the PRI in 1991 do not necessarily indicate that the PRI has permanently recouped the voters it lost in the 1980s. They certainly indicate that neither the PAN nor the left has realigned the Mexican electorate other than perhaps a realignment of the opposition electorate on regional grounds. The 1988 elections did show that certain social groups have become uncoupled from the PRI—that electoral dealignment has occurred. Past efforts to reform the PRI were motivated in large part by a desire to reinvigorate the party at its mass base, so as to maintain the patterns of partisan alignment that had long ensured the PRI's hegemony. Those reforms generally failed, and the electorate has become more and more free to vote as it wishes. Some loosening of the electorate from PRI bonds is due to changes in social structure associated with modernization. As Mexico continues to urbanize and as its population becomes more educated, the PRI may see a substantial number of children of its past supporters voting for the opposition. Economic crisis, including unpopular aspects of the economic restructuring program begun under de la Madrid and accelerated by Salinas, suddenly produced widespread rejection of the PRI, a party that no longer seems to stand for revolutionary causes. But the Salinas administration and the PRI leadership actually seem to have reinvigorated the party to some extent.

Yet it is quite likely that the tight, secure bonds of electoral support the PRI enjoyed in the past will never be recreated by a Mexican political party. Parties have come to serve new and different functions. They are no longer the major intermediaries between government and the electorate. The mass media and interest groups also serve crucial linkage roles. The PRI's corporatist structure is a vestige of the past, and the PAN and PRD will never have corporatist structures. Hence, voters will surely be much more able to defect from political coalitions in the future. This shift will likely inflate the role of the media and place a premium on the art of campaigning. In both of these realms, the PRI is currently far ahead of its challengers, as its success in 1991 showed. The PRI may have the disadvantage of being associated with the difficult economic consequences of the Salinas administration's economic development program, and it may suffer much discredit for past indiscretions, but it has a far more skilled, better funded campaign organization than its opponents. Moreover, the mass media, especially television, have been very supportive of PRI candidates. These remain large barriers that the PAN and PRD will have to overcome if they wish to govern Mexico.

REFERENCES

Alcocer V., Jorge. 1991. "Cifras desentrañadas," *Proceso* 774 (September 2): 32–37.
Alcocer V., Jorge, and Rodrigo Morales M. 1991. "Mitología y realidad del fraude electoral," *Nexos* 166 (October): 27–33.
Barraza, Leticia, and Ilán Bizberg. 1991. "El Partido Acción Nacional y el régimen político mexicano," *Foro Internacional* 31:3 (January–March): 418–45.
Basáñez, Miguel. 1990. *El pulso de los sexenios: 20 años de crisis en México.* Mexico City: Siglo Veintiuno.
———. 1991. "Encuesta electoral 1991," *Este País* 5 (August): 3–6.
Berrueto Pruneda, Federico. n.d. "Las elecciones de 1991 y el Partido Revolucionario Institucional: organización electoral y la estructura partidista." Forthcoming.
Bortz, Jeffrey. 1986. "Wages and Economic Crisis in Mexico." In *The Mexican Left, the Popular Movements, and the Politics of Austerity,* edited by Barry Carr and Ricardo Anzaldúa Montoya. Monograph Series, no. 18. La Jolla: Center for U.S.-Mexican Studies, University of California, San Diego.
Boudreaux, Richard. 1991. "Mexicans Favor Trade Pact," *Los Angeles Times,* October 22.
Burnham, Walter Dean. 1970. *Critical Elections and the Mainsprings of American Politics.* New York: Norton.
Castañeda, Jorge G. 1991. "The New Science of Electoral Engineering," *Los Angeles Times,* August 13.
Coleman, Kenneth M. 1975. "The Capital City Electorate and Mexico's Acción Nacional: Some Survey Evidence on Conventional Hypotheses," *Social Science Quarterly* 56:3 (December): 502–09.
Collier, Ruth Berins, and David Collier. 1991. *Shaping the Political Arena: Critical Junctures, the Labor Movement, and Regime Dynamics in Latin America.* Princeton, N.J.: Princeton University Press.
Cornelius, Wayne A. 1975. *Politics and the Migrant Poor in Mexico City.* Stanford, Calif.: Stanford University Press.
———. 1991. "Victory from the Jaws of Fraud," *Los Angeles Times,* September 6.
Dalton, Russell J., Scott Flanagan, and Paul Allen Beck, eds. 1984. *Electoral Change in Advanced Industrial Societies: Realignment or Dealignment?* Princeton, N.J.: Princeton University Press.
Davis, Charles L., and Kenneth M. Coleman. 1982. "Electoral Change in the One-Party Dominant Mexican Polity, 1958–73: Evidence from Mexico City," *Journal of Developing Areas* 16:3 (July): 523–42.
Domínguez, Jorge, and James A. McCann. 1992a. "Whither the PRI? Explaining Voter Defection in the 1988 Mexican Presidential Elections," *Electoral Studies* 11:3.
———. 1992b. "Shaping Mexico's Electoral Arena: The Construction of Partisan Cleavages in the 1988 and 1991 National Elections." Paper prepared for the

1992 Annual Meeting of the American Political Science Association, Chicago, September 3–6.

Dresser, Denise. 1991. *Neopopulist Solutions to Neoliberal Problems: Mexico's National Solidarity Program.* Current Issue Brief Series, no. 3. La Jolla: Center for U.S.-Mexican Studies, University of California, San Diego.

Este País. 1991. "Encuesta: Privatización del sector público." No. 9 (December): 16–17.

———. 1992. "Encuesta: el ejido ante la opinión pública." No. 10 (January): 34–35.

Gómez, Leopoldo, and Joseph L. Klesner. 1988. "Mexico's 1988 Elections: Beginning of a New Era of Mexican Politics?" *LASA Forum* 19:3 (Fall): 1–8.

Guillén López, Tonatiuh. 1989. "The Social Bases of the PRI." In *Mexico's Alternative Political Futures*, edited by Wayne A. Cornelius, Judith Gentleman, and Peter H. Smith. Monograph Series, no. 30. La Jolla: Center for U.S.-Mexican Studies, University of California, San Diego.

Huntington, Samuel P. 1970. "Social and Institutional Dynamics of One-Party Systems." In *Authoritarian Politics in Modern Society: The Dynamics of Established One-Party Systems*, edited by Samuel P. Huntington and Clement H. Moore. New York: Free Press.

Klesner, Joseph L. 1988. "Electoral Reform in an Authoritarian Regime: The Case of Mexico." Ph.D. dissertation, Massachusetts Institute of Technology.

———. 1993. "Modernization, Economic Crisis, and Electoral Alignment in Mexico." *Mexican Studies/Estudios Mexicanos* 9:2 (Summer).

Latin American Regional Reports. 1990. "CTM Threatens to Pull Out of 'Pacto'," *Latin American Regional Reports: Mexico and Central America*, August 23, pp. 6–7.

Latin American Special Report. 1991. "Mexico: More of a Roll-Back than a Sell-Off." *Privatisations: A Regional Survey*, April, pp. 4–5.

Latin American Weekly Report. 1990. "Pact and All, Prices are Running Away," December 20, p. 3.

Los Angeles Times. 1989. *Los Angeles Times Poll*, no. 192, press release.

———. 1991. *Los Angeles Times Poll*, no. 258, press release.

Mabry, Donald J. 1974. *Mexico's Acción Nacional: A Catholic Alternative to Revolution.* Syracuse, N.Y.: Syracuse University Press.

Meyer, Lorenzo. 1991. "El límite neoliberal," *Nexos* 163 (July).

Molinar Horcasitas, Juan. 1989. "The Future of the Electoral System." In *Mexico's Alternative Political Futures*, edited by Wayne A. Cornelius, Judith Gentleman, and Peter H. Smith. Monograph Series, no. 30. La Jolla: Center for U.S.-Mexican Studies, University of California, San Diego.

Molinar Horcasitas, Juan, and Jeffrey Weldon. 1990. "Elecciones de 1988 en México: crisis del autoritarismo," *Revista Mexicana de Sociología* 52:4 (October–December): 229–62.

Reding, Andrew. 1991. "The Crumbling of the 'Perfect Dictatorship': Mexico's Democratic Challenge," *World Policy Journal* 8:2 (Spring): 255–84.

Smith, Peter H. 1979. *Labyrinths of Power: Political Recruitment in Twentieth-Century Mexico.* Princeton, N.J.: Princeton University Press.

PART IV

SOCIAL ACTORS AND THE STATE

8

The Restructuring of State-Labor Relations in Mexico

Enrique de la Garza Toledo

This chapter assesses changes in Mexico in the course of the shift from a social-authoritarian to a neoliberal-authoritarian "style" of development. The chapter examines important changes in the relationship between unions and the state, as well as the recent restructuring of production and its consequences for labor—for employment, wages, industrial relations, and collective bargaining. It also offers some observations concerning the relationship between corporatism and neoliberalism in Mexico.

THE TRANSFORMATION OF MEXICO'S DEVELOPMENT STYLE

The concept of development "style" refers here to the links between a particular regime of capital accumulation and the set of relationships developed among social classes, the state, and the economy. Capital accumulation always rests upon particular socio-technological bases—that is, specific configurations of the technological base, workplace organization, and labor relations (de la Garza 1992a, 1992b). The socio-technological configuration underlying the productive process in Mexico from 1940 to the 1970s (the period of import-substitution industrialization) was based on Taylorism-Fordism in assembly and machining operations and on the initial automation of continuous flow processes. Labor relations in Mexico have been characterized by state tutelage of labor affairs, unions' control over rank-and-file workers, and limited protection of employment, wages, and working conditions (de la Garza 1990).

Translated by Aníbal Yáñez.

Transforming the socio-technological base of the productive process allowed Mexico's core industrial sectors to expand significantly. In the 1940s, capital accumulation still relied on the reduction of real wages. By the 1960s, accumulation was based on productivity increases (de la Garza 1991). However, it is not sufficient to have modern means of capital accumulation if the commodities that are produced cannot be purchased by consumers. The regime of accumulation associated with Mexico's social-authoritarian development period had four major flaws: (1) although manufactured goods were exported during this period, the export path could not sustain high rates of economic growth; (2) in the 1960s the new middle class and the upper strata of the working class comprised the principal market for consumer durables, but these groups were far too small to constitute an adequate domestic market; (3) the country's capital goods industry failed to develop satisfactorily; and (4) beginning in the late 1960s, the agricultural sector (which was an important source of export earnings) entered a period of crisis as a result of unequal exchange with the industrial sector (de la Garza 1988).

The social-authoritarian style of development implied state intervention in the economy and a specific kind of relationship (corporatism) between the working class and the state. Public spending drove market and investment activities, as well as the reproduction of the labor force. Through spending and regulation, the state mediated relations between capital and the working class. This mediation between capital and labor is what is understood as corporatism.

Corporatism implies that the state is a privileged arena for resolving disputes between capital and labor. Moreover, from the moment that unions agree to share responsibility for the workings of the state, labor relations at the level of the firm become subordinated to major state policies. The subordination of labor organizations to the state does not mean that there is a lack of bargaining, representation, or profit for all participants in the "pact." The categories that Schmitter developed in defining corporatism (monopoly of representation guaranteed by the state, elimination of alternative leaderships, and so forth [in Schmitter and Lehmbruch 1979]) outline the steps involved in implementing this corporatist form of domination. But these formal features should not hide the fact that corporatism is an asymmetrical relationship between a dominant and a subordinate actor. Furthermore, the corporatism of the Keynesian state also has its rationality in economics and production, not just in the social order.

The crisis of Mexico's social-authoritarian development style began as a crisis in the agricultural sector, which had been exhausted by long-term unequal exchange with the industrial sector. It was further expressed as a public-sector fiscal crisis after the state borrowed heavily to cover its increased spending. The burden of debt financing had repercussions in the domestic market and within the corporatist pact. Moreover, the productive process entered into a prolonged crisis (lasting through the 1970s and 1980s) that was exacerbated by the globalization of the Mexican economy. This crisis affected the domestic market, state regulation of and intervention in the economy, and the corporatist pact. Beginning in the mid-1980s, changes in the productive process were expressed as a rapid restructuring whose features pointed toward a new, neoliberal-authoritarian style of development.

This neoliberal-authoritarian development style has four main features: (1) polarization of the productive apparatus between a restructured export-oriented sector and a backward sector oriented toward the domestic market (de la Garza 1992c); (2) low wages; (3) capital accumulation based on private and foreign investment, not public spending; and (4) a contradictory relationship between unions and the state.

The power of organized labor in Mexico derives from the corporatist network of relations linking unions with the state. These links are reaffirmed through the connections among workers, "official" labor organizations, the state, and a patrimonial-bureaucratic culture. The principal features of this complex array of corporatist relations are:

- Union participation in the political system (particularly the Institutional Revolutionary Party [PRI] and various government agencies). Union involvement in this area has declined in recent years, and unions' ability to deliver votes has been called into question. Nevertheless, within the PRI's sectoral and territorial structure, unions continue to receive their quota of elected posts. Labor continues to look toward the political system and the government in fashioning its survival strategies.

- Union participation in institutions involved in the reproduction of the labor force. Union leaders sit on the governing boards of organizations such as the Mexican Social Security Institute (IMSS). Although unions have never been decisive in setting these institutions' agendas, during periods of economic prosperity unions have found ways to press for more and improved social services for workers. Above all, unions have been able to secure services for workers as part of a system of patronage administered by union leaders.

- Union participation in economic policy making. Although unions have not been decisive at this level either, they have often been called upon to form "pacts" with the state because of their ability to control wages and strikes, two elements that can complicate the implementation of incomes policies.

- Union support for the state system of labor-management conciliation and arbitration. State-supported labor leaders are part of the state leadership and share responsibility for the workings of the state—not because they are subordinated to it, but because they have a genuine interest in supporting the system. At the same time, while "official" unions could not exist without state support, the state also needs them to maintain peace in the workplace and to implement the state's economic policies, especially wage controls.

In other words, corporatism is a form of interest representation in which interests are mediated by the state. It is also a form of top-down, authoritarian representation in the sense of having limited plurality, little competitiveness, and infrequent turnover of those in positions of power. Another dimension of corporatism as a framework of relations between unions and the state can be found in union culture. Traditional union culture in Mexico has four elements: the concentration of decision-making authority in the top leadership (passive consensus); a patrimonial relationship between the union leadership and the rank and file; a faith in solutions that come from the state; and "guarantees" regarding the availability of jobs and the steady improvement of wages and benefits.

Mexico's state-subsidized labor organizations also have a bureaucratic component. This component has grown in importance as unions have expanded in number and increased their participation in policy implementation, and as links between trade union bureaucracies and state agencies have become stronger. However, Mexico's labor organizations are not fully "modern." They function through an informal network set up to resolve conflicts and negotiate worker benefits. This informal network takes on patrimonial characteristics from the moment its leaders are invested with special powers (contacts and influence) vis-à-vis workers and when the system fails to function efficiently unless these contacts and influence are brought to bear. In this culture, power is not purely abstract; it is partly personal, and it is partly related to an individual's post. Union culture, in turn, is embedded in a larger statist culture rooted in the ideological tradition of revolutionary nationalism and its confused equation of social justice and democracy.

Job security was guaranteed through labor contracts for indefinite time periods, seniority-based promotions, and restrictions on management's ability to transfer workers at will. In effect, job security meant job rigidity. The union's role in the production process had nothing to do with productivity. Instead, the union was one more element in the web of relations surrounding the worker. Union leaders determined work loads, justified absences, and controlled hiring and firing.

The restructuring of Mexican corporatism has had important implications for labor organizations. In general, labor organizations have seen their participation in the political system, their control over the labor force, and their role in shaping economic policy and in arbitrating disputes significantly reduced. Restructuring undermined unions' ability to influence the course of national labor policy and threw into crisis their ability to fashion a discourse that could confront the new neoliberal discourse of state officials. At the same time, economic restructuring affected "official" unionism because new productive arrangements undermined patron-client networks in the workplace. Changing patterns of collective bargaining also affected the system of economic benefits and unions' ability to intervene in the work process. Finally, should the restructuring process generate a reduced number of wage earners and increase the number of more politically independent unions, this could also contribute to the crisis or restructuring of authoritarian unions themselves.

NEOLIBERALISM AND CORPORATISM, THEORY AND MEXICAN PRACTICE

Neoliberalism and corporatism appear in theory to be mutually exclusive. Liberalism was born as an alternative to feudal privileges, but it was not associated with egalitarianism. Liberalism views society as made up of individuals, not social classes. The general welfare is a product of the welfare of each individual, and the social order is self-regulating (Macpherson 1964). Social justice as a conscious policy of income redistribution is alien to the classic liberal form; inequality is neither just nor unjust because the market is not voluntary. Even more, inequality is associated with innovation and science; to equalize unequals in the marketplace would hinder progress. This is true both for social welfare policies and for redistributive corporatist pacts that voluntarily link economic growth to social peace (King 1987).

There is, then, a logical tension between liberalism and corporatism. In part this is because they correspond to different historical periods. Liberalism is associated with laissez-faire and the illegality of the working class, its organizations, and its conflicts. Corporatism, on the other hand, is associated with the Keynesian-interventionist and welfare state, the social state. Corporatism as a pact among classes that is mediated by the state is counterposed to the free market and the free interplay among the factors of production. Corporatist arrangements distort the tendency toward equilibrium (Lehmbruch and Schmitter 1982). Under corporatism, interest associations are also integrated into state policy (Pike and Stritch 1974). In its West European variant, corporatism regulates conflicts between classes through income distribution and the mediation of industrial relations. The corresponding economic policy is based on consensus building within the political system.

The social state and its corporatist component are counterposed to the liberal state from the moment that society is no longer conceived in terms of individuals, but rather is envisioned as comprising social classes which can enter into conflict. In the case of conflicts between classes, the state attempts to resolve them through rules and institutions rather than declare them illegal. Implicit here is an assumption that the market alone cannot achieve "social justice," nor can equilibrium be achieved spontaneously. In other words, the economic theory that most closely approximates corporatism would be Keynesianism.

As a response to the crisis of the social state, neoliberalism dismantled or limited post-World War II corporatist arrangements. The costs of the crisis fell on workers, and under these conditions corporatist pacts could no longer be maintained (Baglioni 1987). However, the entire welfare state was not dismantled, nor did the pacts disappear entirely. For instance, social security was not entirely privatized except in extreme cases, such as in Chile under military rule. The end result was not nineteenth-century laissez-faire, although the state now has less influence and control over the economy.

The social-corporatist state seeks to link economics and politics through public spending as part of a grand pact between corporate actors, and to reconcile capital accumulation with peace and social order. The emergence of neoliberal states has produced a number of changes in corporatist arrangements and in industrial relations systems: the state's commitment to activist social policy has declined, as has the bargaining power of unions; national accords have become less frequent; unions have had to engage in increasingly defensive tactics; the gap between the state, on one hand, and the working class, unions, and political parties, on the other, has increased. In addition, one finds falling unionization rates, a declining number of strikes, and a crisis of representation within unions (Baglioni 1987).

But the new neoliberal consensus is not fully formed. The world of industrial relations is torn between a neoclassical liberalism that seeks to let the market regulate factor allocation, on the one hand, and the search for a "post-Fordist" consensus on the shop floor, on the other. The cultural poverty of neoliberalism has led to the appearance of such hybrids as economic neoliberalism, political neoconservatism, and authoritarian neoliberalism—that is, free markets with traditional social values (Hinkelammert 1984).

In Mexico, this hybrid has been dubbed "social liberalism." Social liberalism seeks to reclaim the tradition of nineteenth-century Mexican liberalism and the political values associated with the Mexican Revolution. In this sense, the state is to be less proprietary while remaining strong. The state deregulates and privatizes, but not totally. Social justice as a state-led voluntary process is not egalitarian but compensatory. From the perspective of social liberalism, democracy is not limited to the individual; it includes space for corporatist organizations (as in Salinas de Gortari's [1992] statement that "the PRI is a party of citizens and of organizations and sectors").

▪ Mexican social liberalism is not, nor can it be, pure neoliberalism. The Salinas administration's National Solidarity Program (PRONASOL) compensated somewhat for the market's "imperfections" or "lags" by assisting groups living in extreme poverty. Mexico's social liberal state is less proprietary, but it does not renounce economic regulation through pacts. It limits the power of corporatist organizations, but it does not abolish them or totally exclude them from decision making. In other words, it is neoliberalism with a strong state—strong both politically and vis-à-vis labor. It liberalizes the economy but subordinates labor relations to its conception of economic development. In this transition, unions have been impotent to halt the fall in wages and the decline in social spending (other than that which occurs through PRONASOL). Nor have they been able to resist the increasing flexibility demanded in collective bargaining agreements. At the same time, unions' influence within the ruling party has declined, and they face greater challenges from workers themselves.

How can we explain the continued existence of unions in light of their deteriorating relationship with both the state and the rank and file? Are they likely to disappear when market reforms are complete? Will corporatism be compatible with an open market economy, or will a new type of corporatism arise?

UNIONS, THE CHANGING ROLE OF THE STATE, AND ECONOMIC RESTRUCTURING

The corporatist pact between unions and the state in Mexico has been significantly affected by changes in state policy and economic restructuring. These transformations have also altered unions' management of the labor force in important areas.

UNION REGULATION OF WAGES

As table 8.1 shows, in the 1980s all forms of wages reported in official statistics declined as never before. Although wages recovered somewhat in 1991 and 1992, they were still far below 1980 levels.

Wages in the *maquiladora* sector and in the manufacturing industry fell less rapidly than in other activities, but wage declines were nevertheless very significant across the board. Because these data are averages, they may disguise a wide gap between high- and low-end wages. Table 8.2 reports data from the ongoing survey conducted by the Metropolitan Association of Industrial Relations Executives (AMERI). These data indicate that in 1989–1991 (when real wages recovered somewhat) the standard deviation in wage increases was small (3.2 in 1989, 2.2 in 1990, and 1.6 in 1991). One possible explanation is that increased benefits compensated for wage cuts. However, table 8.2 shows that this was not the case in Mexico; fringe benefits added only modestly to increases in

TABLE 8.1

CHANGES IN REAL WAGE LEVELS DURING THE 1980s

Change in the national minimum wage, 1982–1990	−54%
Change in contract wages in firms under federal labor jurisdiction, 1982–1990	−43%
Change in average remunerations per person employed in the manufacturing industry, 1982–1990	−30%
Change in average wages in the *maquiladora* industry, 1982–1990	−28%
Percent by which average contract wages exceeded the national minimum wage in 1990	59%
Percent by which the *maquiladora* wage exceeded the national minimum wage in 1990	67%
Average contract wages as a percent of average *maquiladora* wages in 1990	95%

Note: In all categories, nominal wages were deflated by the annual rate of inflation (annual changes in the national consumer price index).

Source: Carlos Salinas de Gotari, *Segundo Informe de Gobierno: Anexo* (Mexico City: Presidencia, 1990).

TABLE 8.2

ANNUAL VARIATION IN CONTRACT WAGES AND FRINGE BENEFITS, 1989–1991

Year	Average Contract Wage Increase	Standard Deviation in Annual Wage Increases	Average Change in Contract Wages and Fringe Benefits	Difference between Average Contract Wage Increase and Inflation Rate (with ± range of variation among firms)
1989	NA	3.2	18.0%	3.6 (±3.2)
1990	18.1%	2.2	22.2%	−.1 (±2.2)
1991[1]	21.3%	1.6	25.6%	5.3 (±1.6)

NA = Not Available

[1]January–September average

Source: AMERI enterprise servey (n = 1000)

workers' total compensation. Even so, workers' compensation did increase in real terms in 1989 and 1991. In 1990 the average variation for firms with upper-limit increases (see the last column in table 8.2) was also slightly positive.

Another possible explanation for the observed pattern of wage variation is that there were notable differences in wage reductions between small and large firms. Table 8.3 indicates that the drop in wages between 1980 and 1985 was greatest in large firms. Although remunera-

TABLE 8.3

AVERAGE REMUNERATION PER EMPLOYEE BY FIRM SIZE
IN THE INDUSTRIAL SECTOR, 1980–1985
(000S OF 1980 PESOS)

| | Firm Size (number of workers) | | | | | | |
	1–5	6–25	26–50	51–100	101–250	251–500	> 500
1980	47.1	76.7	90.2	99.1	110.5	128.1	160.8
1985	52.1	78.2		77.3	89.4	106.1	118.2
% Change, 1980–1985	+ 10.7	− 5.9		22.0	− 19.1	− 17.2	− 26.5

Source: Author's calculations based on INEGI industrial censuses for 1980 and 1985.

tions were higher the larger the size of the firm, during this five-year period remunerations in large companies tended to flatten out toward the levels prevailing in small firms.

It is also possible that salaries (*sueldos*) may have followed a different trajectory than wages (*salarios*). Table 8.4 shows a rise in real wages and salaries in manufacturing between 1988 and 1991, but salaries increased at nearly twice the rate of wages. This had the effect of reducing wages as a portion of total remunerations (a category that includes salaries).

Finally, the drop in public-sector wages generally mirrored that which occurred among all wage earners. However, in certain sectors (such as in education and the petroleum industry), wages declined more from 1981 to 1989 than indicated by the figures reported earlier.

Mexico's minimum wage is clearly not a living wage. However, as many as 22 percent of Mexican workers (those enrolled in the Mexican Social Security Institute, IMSS) earned the minimum wage in 1990, and in 1991 about 60 percent of employed workers earned less than two times the legal minimum wage.

Can wage differentials be explained by differences in productivity? In the Mexican case, it appears that falling wages do not reflect changes in productivity. Tables 8.5 and 8.6 show that from 1980 to 1990 there was no strong positive correlation between productivity and remuneration in the manufacturing sector.

Instead, wages fell during the 1980s because unions were ineffective at negotiating wage increases for workers. (Indeed, remuneration actually rose more quickly for nonunion than for unionized workers.) And unions had little influence on the government's minimum wage and public-sector wage policy. All unions suffered, especially those in large firms. Although after 1989 the Confederation of Mexican Workers (CTM) did win more substantial wage increases than other major labor organi-

Table 8.4
Real Wages, Salaries, and Benefits in the Manufacturing Industry, 1988–1991
(000s of 1978 pesos)

	Average Wage per Worker	% Change in Average Wage per Worker	Average Salary per Employee	% Change in Average Salary per Employee	Average Benefits (all personnel)	% Change in Benefits (all personnel)	Wages as % of Total Remunerations	Average Manufacturing Wage ÷ National Minimum Wage
1988 (January)	2.5		5.2		1.3		37.9	1.9
1990 (January)	2.7	8	6.8	30.7	1.7	27.8	33.7	2.1
1991 (September)	3.5	29.6	9.3	36.8	2.3	35.3	32.7	3.0
January 1988–September 1991		40		78.8		72.9		

Note: The first two categories in this table refer, respectively, to earnings by blue-collar workers (wages) and white-collar employees (salaries).

Source: INEGI, monthly industrial surveys.

TABLE 8.5

PERCENT VARIATION IN PRODUCTION, EMPLOYMENT, AND REAL WAGES IN THE MANUFACTURING INDUSTRY, 1980–1989

Activity	Employment	Production	Wages
Food, beverages, and tobacco	2.0	25.1	16.9
Textiles, clothing, and leather	–19.7	–1.8	–15.2
Wood and wood products	–17.3	7.6	–22.1
Printing and publishing	– 6.1	21.8	–23.8
Chemicals, petroleum derivatives	– 8.0	32.2	– 2.5
Nonmetallic minerals	–14.4	2.8	–17.9
Basic metals	–10.8	13.1	– 2.5
Metal products, machinery and equipment	–24.9	25.9	–15.8
Other manufacturing industries	– 6.3	37.0	5.0
All manufacturing activities	–11.8	19.8	–14.6

Source: Enrique Hernández Laos, "Identificación de factores que obstaculizan la movilidad de la mano de obra en el sector industrial mexicano" (Mexico City: Secretaría de Trabajo y Previsión Social, 1991). Mimeo.

TABLE 8.6

AVERAGE ANNUAL PRODUCTIVITY AND REMUNERATIONS IN THE MANUFACTURING INDUSTRY, 1980–1990

Year	Productivity per Person[1]	Average Annual Remuneration[2] per Person
1980	100.0	304.9
1981	101.6	318.3
1982	100.9	250.6
1983	100.1	215.6
1984	103.0	210.1
1985	105.9	208.1
1986	102.3	161.6
1987	104.3	145.1
1988	107.5	200.7
1989	112.1	219.1
1990	117.9	220.2
1991[3]	NA	231.7

NA = Not Available

[1]Coefficient of the index value for the physical volume of production divided by the index of persons employed (for both indices, 1980 = 100).

[2]Daily remunerations in constant (1978) pesos.

[3]January–June

Source: Carlos Salinas de Gortari, *Segundo Informe de Gobierno: Anexo* (Mexico City: Presidencia, 1990).

zations (especially more politically independent unions), the differences were not significant enough to indicate different wage trends. Many workers' wages fell below the level of a living wage. Yet unions were unable to increase their members' earnings relative to nonunionized employees, nor could they win increased benefits to compensate for the drop in wages. Neither were they able to link wage increases to productivity gains. Thus unions lost control over wage policy, the key variable in "official" unions' management of the workforce.

UNION CONTROL OVER EMPLOYMENT

Controlling employment has also been an important union prerogative, helping unions consolidate their patrimonial domination of the workforce. The available data on employment expansion show that wage labor grew by only 63 percent between 1980 and 1990, while the working-age population (fifteen years and older) increased 133.3 percent over the same period. During the 1980s wage labor increased in all sectors except in services and mining. However, not every wage earner was unionized. Only about 28 percent of those wage earners above the age of fourteen were unionized in 1980. This proportion varied widely by industry (see table 8.7).

Unions have been concentrated in industry and in the public sector; they have had only a limited presence in services, commerce, and agriculture. According to a Mexican government monthly industrial survey (the Encuesta Industrial Mensual), employment declined in most branches of the manufacturing sector during the 1980s. However, there were increases in the electrical power generation, petroleum, and government sectors.

Within the manufacturing sector, small and medium-sized firms had employment growth of 6.6 percent during the 1980s, while total employed personnel declined by 13.6 percent in firms with more than 250 workers. One might suppose, therefore, that if large firms were most affected by unemployment, unions were also strongly affected since they are concentrated in large firms. Yet public-sector employment increased during this period, except in state-owned firms in manufacturing and in the agriculture, forestry, and fishing industries. The beneficiaries included some national industrial unions and especially the Federation of Public Service Workers' Unions (FSTSE) (see table 8.8).

Temporary workers were most affected by unemployment. Temporary workers as a percentage of all workers enrolled in the IMSS in the Federal District fell from 18.9 percent in 1980 to 11.5 percent in 1990. This had a dual impact on unions. On the one hand, unions that did not include temporary workers in their membership were better able to protect the jobs of unionized workers. On the other hand, unions whose

TABLE 8.7
UNIONIZATION RATES BY INDUSTRIAL ACTIVITY, 1980

Activity	Rate of Unionization[1] (%)	% Increase in Number of Employees, 1980–1990
Food, beverages, and tobacco	15.6	7.6
Textiles, clothing, and leather	26.6	–18.5
Wood and wood products	3.7	–14.3
Paper, paper products, printing and publishing	5.5	– 1.4
Chemicals, petrochemical and coal derivatives, rubber, plastics	6.9	5.1
Nonmetallic minerals	4.1	– 0.8
Basic metals	32.3	–23.5
Metal products, machinery and equipment	1.6	–22.0
Electrical power generation	93.3	20.5
Mining	70.5	–61.2
Petroleum	71.5	38.1
Government (excluding state-owned companies)	63.7	38.3
National total[2]	28.0	

[1]The rate of unionization was calculated by dividing the number of unionized workers by the wage-earning population over the age of fourteen.

[2]The national total includes other activities not listed in the table.

Sources: Carlos Zazueta and Ricardo de la Peña, *La estructura del Congreso del Trabajo: Estado, trabajo y capital en México* (Mexico City: Fondo de Cultura Económica, 1984); Mexican population and housing censuses for 1980 and 1990; Carlos Salinas de Gortari, *Tercer Informe de Gobierno: Anexo* (Mexico City: Presidencia, 1991).

membership included temporary workers ran the risk of losing some patrimonial control, inasmuch as union leaders can more easily drag temporary workers into clientelist practices.

Finally, nonwage employment has grown faster than salaried employment in recent years, with a resulting decline in union membership. Moreover, there have been relatively high growth rates in services and commerce, two sectors that are not heavily unionized (Salas Páez 1992).

Although these data are inconclusive regarding the loss of employment in unionized sectors and the decline of union affiliation, one could propose the following hypotheses: (1) Union federations and national industrial unions may be losing their ability to preserve jobs for union-

TABLE 8.8

PERCENT CHANGE IN THE NUMBER OF PUBLIC-SECTOR EMPLOYEES BY
ECONOMIC ACTIVITY, 1981–1990

Activity	% Change
Forestry, agriculture, fishing	−70.6
Mining	15.6
Manufacturing	−48.0
Construction	0
Electricity, gas, water	20.5
Commerce, restaurants, hotels	8.5
Transportation, storage, communications	20.8
Financial services, insurance, real estate	97.5
Community, social, and personal services	20.4
Petroleum	38.1
Government (except state-owned companies)[1]	38.3
National average	17.4

[1]1980–1989

Source: Carlos Salinas de Gortari, *Tercer Informe de Gobierno: Anexo* (Mexico City: Presidencia, 1991).

ized workers in large industrial firms. (2) A new industrial proletariat is emerging in the *maquiladoras*, with union relationships that differ from traditional forms. (3) The number of union jobs is holding steady among public employee unions.

UNION MANAGEMENT OF INDUSTRIAL RELATIONS

There are two reasons why the management of workplace relations is important for labor corporatism in Mexico. First, union influence in this area permits it to negotiate favorable wage and employment terms, as well as contract provisions regulating the distribution of the workforce on the shop floor. Regulating the use of labor in the work process traditionally takes the form of limiting the employment of temporary workers, limiting the use of subcontractors, restricting the hiring of nonunionized supervisory workers,[1] and restricting the dismissal of rank-and-file workers.[2] A union's intervention in the work process can also take the form of detailed job descriptions, complemented by multicategory wage scales, restrictions on internal mobility, union par-

[1]Labor legislation in Mexico distinguishes between rank-and-file workers, who can be organized in a union, and supervisory employees (*empleados de confianza*), who may not unionize.

[2]Restrictions in this last area can take the form of higher indemnity payments to fired workers than the terms established by federal labor law.

ticipation in worker disciplinary procedures, and union involvement in training, health, and safety programs. In traditional labor relations contexts, wages are based on job categories and promotions are based on seniority.

Second, union intervention in the management of the labor force establishes the context for bureaucratic-patrimonial relations between labor leaders and the rank and file. Several forms of intervention (in hiring, in the work process, or in wage issues) entail collective patrimonial protection in exchange for consensus, or personal favors for workers in exchange for their loyalty to the leadership.

Labor relations, therefore, have an important informal aspect not covered by written regulations. Both formal and informal aspects must be taken into account when discussing union management of industrial relations. However, for the unionized sector (which is the sector in Mexico that is most extensively covered by collective contracts), modifying contract terms can have important consequences for the union's patrimonial management ability.

Over the last ten years (beginning with the first attempt to modify the collective contract at Diesel Nacional's automobile manufacturing plant), the negotiation or renegotiation of collective bargaining agreements in Mexico has been governed by the concept of increased flexibility. Management has sought the authority to make rapid adjustments in employment, in the use of the labor force, and in wages, depending on day-to-day production requirements. Moreover, policies adopted by both management and state labor authorities have encouraged more flexible use of the workforce.

The move toward increased flexibility in labor contracts has affected unions' patrimonial use of their terms. However, the degree of flexibility negotiated in collective contracts has not been uniform, nor has it affected all unions in the same way. The degree of flexibility and its impact depend on what previous contract conditions were, how important a flexible labor force is for the firm involved, what tactics the union has adopted in response, and management and worker cultures with regard to industrial relations.

The contracts most affected by the push for more flexibility (and therefore the unions that have been hardest hit by this process) are in nationally important industries, mainly state-owned companies that are being privatized or restructured, and in large, export-oriented firms. These were precisely the types of firms where the contractual model typical of postrevolutionary state-labor relations (highly formalized and complex workforce protections) existed in its purest form. In these firms, the push for greater flexibility in collective agreements also collided with a statist culture and a culture of job rigidity. For these reasons, the trend toward labor flexibility has provoked conflict, with unions sometimes accepting and sometimes opposing flexibility. In general, union efforts to resist have been defeated.

In small and medium-sized firms, as well as in large firms with so-called white unions (management-controlled unions), workers were generally less protected by their contracts and less used to rigidity than were workers in large state-owned firms. As a result, the substance of their collective agreements has changed less, and in general these unions have not resisted demands for increased labor flexibility, except in sectors controlled by politically independent unions.

Finally, Mexican labor law does not permit government workers to negotiate collective contracts; instead, they are covered by a special section (Apartado B) of the federal labor law. In many instances, government workers are regulated by special laws for public employees and by "general conditions of work" (*condiciones generales de trabajo*) that regulate tasks in each government agency. These conditions or guidelines have no legal standing and are often imposed unilaterally by the employer, although the unions representing government workers may propose new hires, help define job categories, and prevent workers from being removed from their jobs. In other words, within this largely unilateral situation there is an element of rigidity resulting from federal laws that so far remains unchanged (de la Garza 1992c).

WORKER-EMPLOYER CONFLICTS

There is no direct relationship in Mexico between strikes and wages. There have been periods when falling wages correlated with increased strike activity, and others when the opposite occurred. It could not be otherwise in a country where worker-employer relations are a matter of state policy. To this extent, the state's willingness to allow strikes is an important factor in explaining the ebb and flow of strike movements. The Cárdenas (1934–1940) and Echeverría (1970–1976) administrations were periods of rising real wages and increased strike activity. The Avila Camacho (1940–1946) and López Portillo (1976–1982) administrations were periods of declining wages and an increased number of strikes. The Alemán administration (1946–1952) and the second half of the de la Madrid administration (1982–1988) saw declining wages and a decrease in strike activity.

There is no information on the total number of strikes since 1984. However, in the 1980s the number of strikes under federal jurisdiction reached highs in 1982 and 1986. The number then remained low but stable after 1986. In contrast, worker-employer disputes that did not result in strikes increased dramatically. Individual worker grievances filed before conciliation and arbitration boards rose from 4,875 in 1980 to 27,776 in 1990, the vast majority of them filed by workers who sought to bypass their union leadership.

The volume of disputes over issues of union democracy has not declined. In general, however, politically independent union forces have not made significant advances in recent years. The number of such disputes reached a high point in 1983, dropped off substantially in 1985, and then recovered in 1990 (see table 8.9).

UNIONISM, THE PRI, AND NATIONAL PACTS

Mexico's 1988 federal elections revealed "official" unions' weakened ability to mobilize their members on behalf of the PRI. Important union leaders running as PRI candidates for Congress were defeated by candidates from the Cárdenas-led National Democratic Front (FDN). In the aftermath of this defeat, unions remained in the PRI's labor sector, but reforms to the party's organizational structure have significantly undermined their power. In 1991 the CTM had only one representative on the PRI's National Executive Committee under the party's combined sectoral and territorial structure. Moreover, party officials proposed making the number of sectoral delegates proportional to the number of union members. The CTM reacted vigorously, threatening to counsel its affiliates to vote their preferences, to ally with the opposition, and even to launch another party. Although the CTM ultimately did none of these things, these threats showed that PRIísta unions were on the political defensive.[3]

Unions have continued to participate formally in major national negotiations, but without a political or economic project of their own. The national economic pacts negotiated since December 1987 marked the high points of this union participation. Established as major tripartite agreements to contain inflation and permit growth, they have hardly meant real concertation. Union leaderships were invited more to ratify agreements already reached between business and the state than to take part as active participants in the negotiations. Union leaders have been called upon to carry out the difficult task of containing workers' wage demands—but with little to offer workers in exchange.

Nonetheless, the implementation of the state's new economic policy cannot occur without the unions. Unions have been the new policy's main supporters, although their support often seems coerced. Despite their apparent acquiescence on economic policy, the unions' power has not completely eroded, as shown by the CTM's veto of PRI reform.

---

[3]The CTM only represented 6.52 percent of registered voters nationally in 1988. During the PRI's sixteenth national assembly, the CTM was barely able to fend off its attackers as it rejected criticisms from members of the PRI's "Critical Current," vetoed changes in the party's statement of principles, and succeeded in having decisions taken by a streamlined national executive committee.

TABLE 8.9

STRIKES, ACTS OF VIOLENCE, AND WORKER STRUGGLES
FOR UNION DEMOCRACY, 1970–1990[1]

Year	Strikes	Acts of Violence	Struggles for Union Democracy[2]
1970	4	3.6	8.3
1971	20	33.6	24
1972	48	22.4	38
1973	60	39.2	55
1974	64	61.6	43
1975	94	33.6	54
1976	100	90	83
1977	92	100	75
1978	44	56	27
1979	48	56	38
1980	40	28	39
1981	36	25	60
1982	64	33.6	90
1983	12	45	100
1984	4	67	50
1985	12	28	36
1986	4	83	56
1987	84	72	80
1988	98	100	44
1989[3]	69	11	24
1990	NA	NA	100

NA = Not Available

[1]Index values are calculated in reference to the year(s) in which most actions of a given type occurred (1976 for strikes; 1977 and 1988 for acts of violence; and 1983 and 1990 for struggles for union democracy).

[2]Struggles for union democracy are those struggles that challenge "official" union leaderships in an effort to break or weaken corporatist control.

[3]January–July (excluding February).

Sources: Enrique de la Garza Toledo, "Independent Trade Unionism in Mexico: Past Developments and Future Perspectives," in *Unions, Workers, and the State in Mexico,* edited by Kevin J. Middlebrook. La Jolla: Center for U.S.-Mexican Studies, University of California, San Diego, 1991; *Entorno Laboral,* various years.

RESTRUCTURING LABOR CORPORATISM IN MEXICO

Criticism of labor corporatism abounds in Mexico, coming as much from government ideologues as from business. These critics view corporatism as a holdover from the old interventionist, welfare, and controlling state that took shape in the decades after the Mexican Revolution. From their perspective, the postrevolutionary state is giving way to a neoliberal state that privatizes, deregulates, and intervenes in the economy less frequently than before. Furthermore, they say, corporatist unions are unnecessary, costly, and unproductive because they are based on patrimonialism and the politicization of labor relations at the level of the state.

In an effort to confront the problems associated with their declining influence, "official" labor organizations have adopted two positions on economic restructuring and changing state policy.

THE NEOCORPORATIST STRATEGY: PRODUCTION AS A SPACE FOR NEGOTIATION

Several large national industrial unions were among the first to perceive the need for a change in strategy as a result of economic restructuring and changes in the state's role. Among other things, they have advanced the view that unions must themselves undergo restructuring. The first important union to accept this challenge was the Mexican Telephone Workers' Union (STRM). Identifying productivity as a space for negotiation was part of this union's plan to create a new corporatist relationship to replace the old corporatism. In the words of Francisco Hernández Juárez, STRM secretary general, "The modern Mexican state requires a labor movement in which both labor leaders and workers have current information on firm productivity" (Hernández Juárez 1990). In other words, the STRM proposed a new kind of corporatist unionism, one that mobilizes for production and advances proposals instead of engaging in confrontation. From this perspective, the modernization process is an arena of struggle, but any conflicts that occur should serve to shape a new social and political pact and a new labor policy.

The telephone workers' strategy has also been adopted by other national industrial unions. Since 1985, some unions that were part of the "official" structure yet operated somewhat independently have joined to confront the advancing process of industrial restructuring. These initiatives eventually resulted in the formation of the Federation of Goods and Services Unions (FESEBES) in 1990, comprising unions representing workers in the telecommunications, electrical power generation, airline, tramway, and movie industries.

President Carlos Salinas de Gortari's May Day 1990 speech summed up the new alliance between unions and the state. In their new form, unions would participate in agreements to modernize production, pursue a kind of productivity that would distribute wealth, improve working conditions, expand the knowledge base, and involve workers in company administration and ownership. Two other changes would also be necessary. Wages would be based on productivity and training, and the state would have to respect union autonomy in order to create a model of labor relations that was participatory, democratic, and based on concertation (not conflict and confrontation), while recognizing that regulated conflict can help drive social change [STRM 1990]).

The creation of the FESEBES demonstrated that part of the "official" labor movement understood that in order to survive as an interlocutor between workers and the state, it had to accept the challenge of capitalist restructuring—especially the need to increase productivity. Because it is the labor organization most experienced in the area of restructuring, the telephone workers' union served as the political or strategic axis within FESEBES. The union's willingness to ally with capital in a joint quest for higher productivity and quality earned it recognition as a valid interlocutor in proposals concerning these issues.

TRADITIONAL CORPORATISM: PASSIVITY WITH UNILATERAL FLEXIBILITY

More traditional "official" labor organizations, especially the CTM, suffered significantly from the change in official discourse. The CTM struggled through most of the 1980s to develop a coherent response to the new, neoliberal direction of the Mexican economy. Traditional unions continued to maintain that economic recovery should start with the domestic market, and that the external market was at most a complementary factor. From this perspective, wage payments would be the principal stimulus to reactivate the domestic market, and this in turn would revitalize investment. Revitalization would bring increased benefits, profit-sharing, and unemployment insurance, as well as a fiscal reform that increased taxes on capital. The whole process of economic reactivation would be led—and heavily regulated—by the state.

The CTM's program was clearly quite traditional. It sought to preserve corporatism and statism at the same time that the state's role and economic production were being restructured. Some minority sectors within the CTM began in the 1980s to look toward the production sphere, proposing, for example, the establishment of technical committees at the level of production units. These committees would discuss and negotiate production plans, the union's right to information, the introduction of technologies to humanize work, worker education, and new norms to protect workers (Martínez 1988). Some of these proposals were later put into practice.

CONCLUSIONS

Mexican corporatism has changed. For most "official" labor organizations, this change has meant a loss of influence in politics, economic and social-security policy making, conflict management, and industrial relations, all areas where these organizations were once key players. For other unions, the change brought discovery of the production process as an arena for negotiation. It also brought a shift in the character of the relationship between unions and the state: a shift away from the PRI and various state institutions, toward a more direct relationship between unions and the presidency.

The material and institutional conditions and the social networks that once were the foundation of traditional corporatism have been undermined, and extralegal conflicts have increased. Given the loss of corporatist protections and the ineffectiveness of independent union resistance, workers are choosing individual and family survival strategies that do not rely on unions. Cortés and Rubalcava (1992) have shown that during the 1980s families compensated for falling wages by increasing family income, combining traditional wages with informal employment and increasing the number of family members who worked. According to Reygadas (1989) and Leyva (1991), ineffectiveness has cost the unions legitimacy. Although their organizational control has not been broken, such control now rests on a weaker foundation than ever before.

The restructuring of corporatism in Mexico had its beginnings in shifts in the state's role and changes in the organization of production. Only later did corporatist restructuring reflect the efforts by a minority of "official" and more politically independent unions to promote change. However, Mexico's neoliberal state still needs "official" labor organizations to control wages and employment as part of a macroeconomic policy that places a priority on fighting inflation and attracting foreign investment. In this sense, the state's relationship with unions is authoritarian, with less real negotiation than before. In this way, "social liberalism" becomes authoritarian neoliberalism when it is applied to unions. Huntington and Moore (1970) and Huntington and Nelson (1976) discussed this kind of hybrid, one which emerges under single-party rule when authoritarian controls are needed to resolve tensions in the difficult transition to advanced industrial democracy.

Meanwhile, the prospects for Mexican unions in an open economy are unclear. The foreign investment that Mexico needs prefers weak unions because companies can therefore maximize flexibility unilaterally. This situation can increase heterogeneity in labor relations and in the restructuring of corporatism. Although corporatism does not formally disappear, it functions in a dramatically different way in new industries, as evidenced in the *maquiladora* sector along Mexico's northern border (Quintero 1992).

A new, reformed corporatism is emerging, albeit not everywhere. The new corporatism differs from the old in that it opens the arena of production to firm-by-firm negotiation, even if this occurs under state tutelage. This space can weaken patrimonial and union influence and force the decentralization of power down to the departmental level. It also encourages union leaders to be more proposal- and consensus-oriented. This "neocorporatism" retains some elements of the old (subordination to the state), but at the same time it is more in tune with new industrial relations practices at the level of the firm.

Contradictions in the corporatist restructuring process can also open new spaces for political action. These contradictions include: greater state authoritarianism toward labor vs. the decentralization of decision making to the shop floor in order to increase productivity; the multipolarity of union structure (Goldthorpe 1988) vs. federations organized along national lines; continued centralization of union power at the top vs. the need to involve workers in production; verticalist and authoritarian managerial cultures vs. worker involvement. In any case, the future of corporatism in Mexico will be tied to the economic development style and state configuration that prevail—and to the collective actions that extreme tensions and the collective will may unleash.

REFERENCES

Baglioni, Guido. 1987. *Stato, politica, economica e relazioni industriali in Europa.* Milan: Franco Angeli.

Cortés, Fernando, and Rosa María Rubalcava. 1992. "Cambio estructural y concentración: un análisis de la distribución del ingreso familiar en México, 1984–1989." Paper presented at the conference "Social Effects of the Crisis," University of Texas at Austin, April 23–25.

de la Garza, Enrique. 1988. *Ascenso y crisis del Estado social autoritario.* Mexico City: El Colegio de México.

———. 1990. "Reconversión industrial y transformación del patrón de relaciones laborales en México." In *La modernización en México*, edited by Arturo Anguiano. Mexico City: Universidad Autónoma Metropolitana-Xochimilco.

———. 1991. "Los ciclos del movimiento obrero en México en el siglo XX." Los Angeles: Program on Mexico, University of California, Los Angeles. Mimeo.

———. 1992a. "El estilo neoliberal de desarrollo y sus alternativas." In *Sujetos y proyectos económicos en México*, edited by Enrique de la Garza. Mexico City: Universidad Nacional Autónoma de México/Porrúa.

———. 1992b. *Reestructuración productiva y respuesta sindical en México.* Mexico City: Universidad Autónoma Metropolitana-Ixtapalapa.

———. 1992c. "La polarización del aparato productivo en México," *El Cotidiano* 45 (January–February): 3–9.

Goldthorpe, John H. 1988. "El fin de la convergencia: tendencias corporativas y dualísticas en la sociedad occidental moderna." In *Ordine e conflitto nel capitalismo moderno*, edited by John H. Goldthorpe. Milan: Il Mulino.

Hernández Juárez, Francisco. 1990. "Insostenible la alianza tradicional del gobierno y los sindicatos," *Excélsior*, June 5.

Hinkelammert, Franz. 1984. *Crítica a la razón utópica.* San José, Costa Rica: Departamento Ecuménico de Investigaciones.

Huntington, Samuel P., and Clement H. Moore. 1970. *Authoritarian Politics in Modern Society: The Dynamics of Established One-Party Systems.* New York: Basic Books.

Huntington, Samuel P., and Joan M. Nelson. 1976. *No Easy Choice: Political Participation in Developing Countries.* Cambridge, Mass.: Harvard University Press.

King, Desmond S. 1987. *The New Right.* Chicago: Dorse.

Lehmbruch, Gerhard, and Philippe C. Schmitter. 1982. *Patterns of Corporatist Policy-making.* Modern Politics Series, vol. 5. Beverly Hills, Calif.: Sage.

Leyva, M.A. 1991. "Modernización y sindicalización en Ferrocarriles Nacionales de México, 1970–1988." Master's thesis, Instituto J.M. Luis Mora, Mexico.

Macpherson, C.B. 1964. *The Theory of Possessive Individualism: Hobbes to Locke.* Oxford: Oxford University Press.

Martínez, Tomás. 1988. "Lineamientos fundamentales de la estrategia de la CTM." In *El movimiento obrero ante la reconversión productiva*, no. 2. Mexico City.

Pike, Frederick B., and Thomas Stritch, eds. 1974. *The New Corporatism: Sociopolitical Structures in the Iberian World.* Notre Dame, Ind.: University of Notre Dame Press.

Quintero, Cirila. 1992. "Reestructuración sindical en las maquiladoras mexicanas, 1970–1988." Ph.D. thesis, El Colegio de México.

Reygadas, Luis. 1989. "Corporativismo y reconversión industrial en minería." Master's thesis, Universidad Nacional Autónoma de México.

Salas Páez, Carlos. 1992. "¿Pequeñas unidades económicas o sector informal?" *El Cotidiano* 45 (January–February): 29–33.

Salinas de Gortari, Carlos. 1992. "El liberalismo social," *Perfil de la Jornada*, March 5.

Schmitter, Philippe C., and Gerhard Lehmbruch. 1979. *Trends toward Corporatist Intermediation.* Beverly Hills, Calif.: Sage.

STRM (Sindicato de Telefonistas de la República Mexicana). 1990. "XV Convención Nacional Ordinaria del STRM: Informe de la Comisión de Modernización." Mexico City: STRM, September.

9

From Bank Nationalization to State Reform: Business and the New Mexican Order

Francisco Valdés Ugalde

INTRODUCTION

A new period in Mexico's economic development opened in 1982, bringing to an end the clearly distinguishable "postrevolutionary" period (1940–1982). Nineteen eighty-two will long be remembered as the year when the Mexican presidency executed its last expropriation (the nationalization of Mexican banks) and immediately thereafter began constructing an economic and political order with characteristics that broke from the country's postrevolutionary past. The bank nationalization was the last attempt to shore up the power of Mexican presidentialism on the "doctrinal" bases of the Mexican Revolution.

President Miguel de la Madrid (1982–1988) initiated the transition toward a new relationship between the state and society—moving away from the ideology of the Mexican Revolution and toward a reconceptualization and reformulation of the relationships of real power. The government that succeeded him, that of Carlos Salinas de Gortari (1988–1994), had the task of establishing the principles on which Mexican society would be reordered, carrying out essential reforms, and creating the institutions that would make the reforms viable, and, most important, irreversible. The driving forces during this period were economic reform and reform of the state. Despite differences with previous policies, both

The author thanks Cecilia Gayet for her help in obtaining materials, and Eusebio Hidalgo for his help with data processing. Translated by Aníbal Yáñez.

types of reform were presented as furthering the advances of the Mexican Revolution.

Because of the 1980s economic crisis and reforms undertaken by the state, Mexico has experienced a change of unprecedented magnitude in the arrangement of its economic actors and an adjustment of its political system that would have been impossible to imagine just a few years ago. Mexico's private sector has been one of the constituent agents of the new order. The surprising convergence between this sector's historic demands (which were intensely renewed following conflicts with the government in the 1970s) and the political-economic criteria for the state's restructuring of the Mexican economy is not a coincidence. Rather, it is the crystallization of a reform that envisions the private sector as the axis of economic dynamics and which assumes that the state should not intervene except to preserve the stability that the economic process requires and to preserve national sovereignty. This convergence has transformed the business sector's relations with the state and with other social sectors.

This chapter makes the assumption that in critical situations such as the recent period in Mexico, social actors sharpen their senses and the instruments through which they both guide their own actions and influence those of other actors and institutions. The result is an intense struggle to (re)arrange society's material resources and patterns of authority. The strategic initiatives that actors employ in hopes of influencing the order that organizes these material resources and sources of authority is, consequently, a vital subject for social analysis. This chapter will address this issue, taking as its point of reference the Mexican business class.

AFTER THE BANK NATIONALIZATION

Surprisingly, the Mexican business class persisted in its oppositional, even belligerent stance toward the government following the bank nationalization, even though the government made heroic efforts to heal the wounds that the September 1982 nationalization left in the business community. A review of press accounts and statements by business organizations at the start of the de la Madrid administration reveals a continued awareness of the offense taken, an anti-statist drive, and above all a search for strategies to modify the regime of formal and informal relationships that framed business-government interactions in the preceding historical period (Luna, Tirado, and Valdés 1987: 15–18).

There appear to be several main reasons for the business sector's stance. The most obvious is the unstable business climate that prevailed in the months following the bank nationalization. Another seems to be uncertainty regarding the policies that the de la Madrid administration would implement to normalize its relations with the private sector. A third is a mistrust of how consistent the public sector would be in applying the medicine of structural adjustment to resolve the country's economic crisis.

In the three months between the bank nationalization and de la Madrid's inauguration, Mexico's business organizations engaged in an intense effort to recover their historical memory. However, that memory was neither homogeneous nor universally shared. The business community is divided into at least two major factions, moderates and radicals (see table 9.1).[1] In the context of this chapter (whose primary goal is to assess the political positions that induced a reordering of the Mexican state), the discussion of distinctions between moderates and radicals is limited exclusively to (1) the political positions that business organizations with national coverage and influence took as a result of the bank

TABLE 9.1
NATIONAL BUSINESS ORGANIZATIONS' POLITICAL ATTITUDES
TOWARD THE REGIME

Modern Faction				Radical Faction
Unconditional support		Moderate criticism	Strong criticism	
I	II	III	IV	V
CNPP	CANACINTRA	CANACO-MEX	CONCAMIN	COPARMEX
CNCPC		CNG	CCE	CONCANACO
		AMIS	CAMCO	
		CMHN	CNA	
		AMCB		

AMCB: Asociación Mexicana de Casas de Bolsa
AMIS: Asociación Mexicana de Instituciones de Seguros
CAMCO: Cámara Americana de Comercio
CANACINTRA: Cámara Nacional de la Industria de Transformación
CANACO-MEX: Cámara Nacional de Comercio de la Ciudad de México
CCE: Consejo Coordinador Empresarial
CMHN: Consejo Mexicano de Hombres de Negocios
CNA: Consejo Nacional Agropecuario
CNG: Confederación Nacional Ganadera
CNCPC: Confederación Nacional de Cámaras del Pequeño Comercio
CNPP: Confederación Nacional de la Pequeña Propiedad
CONCAMIN: Confederación Nacional de Cámaras Industriales
CONCANACO: Confederación Nacional de Cámaras de Comercio
COPARMEX: Confederación Patronal de la República Mexicana

Source: Matilde Luna, Ricardo Tirado, and Francisco Valdés, "Los empresarios y la política en México 1982–1986," in *Las empresas y los empresarios en el México contemporáneo,* edited by Ricardo Pozas and Matilde Luna (Mexico City: Grijalvo, 1991).

[1]Jacobo, Luna, and Tirado (1989) referred to them as the technocratic and liberal-conservative factions. They added a third group, the protectionist faction, which defined itself in the context of Mexico's trade liberalization. A detailed account of this process can also be found in Luna, Tirado, and Valdés 1991.

nationalization, and (2) the struggle unleashed by this event to establish new parameters for participating in economic policy making and shaping the norms governing state-society relations. For reasons that will become clear later, this distinction is relevant between 1982 and 1988, up until the time that the Economic Solidarity Pact (PSE) went into effect. In this sense, the purpose of this chapter is not to provide an exhaustive description of the political positions taken by the entire Mexican business class, which is very heterogeneous, or of the economic groups that have benefited from or been hurt by the policies of adjustment and macroeconomic restructuring. Rather, this chapter seeks to explain the nature of the sociopolitical activities engaged in by business organizations in relation to a new political arrangement in Mexican society.

Despite the violent shake-up that the bank nationalization provoked, not all businessmen protested or denounced the measure. Bankers obtained a legal injunction against the expropriation; industrialists carefully differentiated between the measure's legal implications and their hope that banking resources would be channeled toward industry; the merchants' association (CONCANACO) and the employers' association (COPARMEX) condemned it in absolute terms, seeing it as the advent of socialism through the "state-ization" of society. Even the Private-Sector Coordinating Council (CCE), an umbrella organization encompassing key business associations (headed at the time of the nationalization by one of the best-known representatives of the radical business faction, Manuel Clouthier), was not able to guide business responses in a single direction. The previous years of harmonious relations with the government, the petroleum boom of the late 1970s and early 1980s (whose benefits were unequally distributed among different groups and sectors), and the political advantage enjoyed by the business class during the preceding "good years" all conditioned a response that fell far short of what was needed to neutralize or counteract the nationalization (Millán 1988: 144–58).

Another reason for the business sector's tepid reaction was the nationalization's popularity among leftist and union sectors, whose support for the nationalization reinforced the president's decision and politically undermined the bankers. The expropriated bankers, for their part, did not adopt a confrontational position. Instead, their reaction was characterized by caution and discretion. The United States might have become one force in opposition to the measure. However, the main U.S. reaction was to concur that the nationalization had saved Mexico's banks from impending insolvency. As with any shake-up of this magnitude, the consequences of the nationalization would only become clear in the medium and long term.

While the moderate groups (primarily comprising organizations of industrialists and financiers from central Mexico) chose to negotiate with the government and establish links with the new administration, the radicals (organized through COPARMEX and CONCANACO, with strong influence in Monterrey, Puebla, Guadalajara, Culiacán, Hermosillo, and Ciudad Obregón, as well as some organizations in the capital) took advantage of this opportunity to mobilize middle- and upper-class groups throughout the country and to organize a movement called Mexico in Freedom. For moderates, the main challenge was to reconstruct relations with the government; bankers (and later the stock brokerages and other non-bank firms that had remained under bank control) negotiated with the de la Madrid administration to set the conditions under which they would receive indemnification (Maxfield 1990: 156–62). What was most important to the radicals was the fact that the state had broadened its economic intervention in a way that was directly opposed to Mexico's trajectory under the López Portillo administration (1976–1982). Despite the differences between business factions and their various representative organizations, businessmen unanimously rejected the bank nationalization on the grounds that it contradicted every private-sector statement over at least the previous ten years.

ADJUSTMENT AND PRESIDENTIAL AUTHORITY

The new direction taken by the de la Madrid government was perhaps to be expected, but it was not preordained. The administration began in seeming support of the principles that had produced the bank nationalization: state rectorship of the economy; reaffirmation of the tripartite relationship among the public, private, and social sectors,[2] which had been eclipsed somewhat in the preceding administration; and ratification of the primacy of the federal executive in economic matters by outlining strategic areas of exclusive state responsibility.

Indeed, in December 1982 President de la Madrid sent a constitutional reform bill to the Mexican Congress. The central feature of the reforms was the creation of an economic "chapter" in the Constitution which would more precisely define the principles that govern state economic activities. For the private sector, this initiative was a contradiction in terms—making explicit and reinforcing the very principles that had generated friction between the private and public sectors, affirming the same executive authority to intervene in economic affairs that had been used against the private sector only a few months before.

The key constitutional reforms (to Articles 25, 26, 27, and 28) established or reinforced (1) the state's economic rectorship; (2) a mixed economy with three sectors—public, private, and social; (3) exclusive state responsibility in strategic areas, including communications, petroleum and basic petrochemicals, nuclear energy, electricity, railroads, and banking; (4) economic planning under state control; and (5) increased

---

[2]The "social sector" consists of worker-owned companies, small producers' associations, and member-operated enterprises such as cooperatives.

delegation of responsibility for economic planning to the legislative branch (*Diario Oficial*, February 3, 1983).

Some analysts viewed the executive's "cession" of legislative authority to Congress as a way of promoting the restoration of business-sector confidence by introducing a "dose of rationality" into economic management, as opposed to the habitual use of discretionary power (Arriola Woog 1988: 215). Under conditions prevailing at the time, it was difficult for businessmen to notice that rationality. However, over a longer period this reform could be seen as fostering bipartisanship by inviting the private sector's direct participation through political parties and its indirect participation through contact with legislators. In the long run this measure seems to have achieved its aim; the participation of private-sector leaders and representatives in the federal Chamber of Deputies and in state legislatures has increased.

The controversy over the nature of this constitutional reform turns on the question of how a government that was clearly committed to structural economic adjustment (and willing to face its consequences) introduced principles identified with greater state intervention and a populist style, principles that one would expect to have been discarded in the transition toward a more fully market-driven economy. Although no definitive explanation is possible, this reform may make sense in light of the uncertain situation that prevailed at the time. The economy was in crisis and prone to volatility; politics was polarized; and presidential authority had been eroded. Presidential authority, the apex of the political system, had to be strengthened.

But underlying these visible signs of instability was another factor, which in the long run could (and did) have even more significant consequences: the policy of economic adjustment and reorganization rested on assumptions squarely opposed to those that had sustained the traditional economic policies of postrevolutionary governments. The break with now-demonized "populism" had the potential to fracture the governing coalition contained within the Institutional Revolutionary Party (PRI). An adjustment policy whose rationale was based on both control over macroeconomic performance and microeconomic, market-oriented reform would necessarily lead to the disarticulation of the vast network of political links that had arisen from the state and spread throughout the economy, politicizing it. Thus, the disintegration of the old model could have catastrophic consequences. For this reason it was necessary to send clear signals that the operation would be done by a capable surgeon, with sufficient anesthetic to relieve the pain—indeed, with enough resources to reattach amputated organs if they were to regenerate after being severed from the body. Nevertheless, one of the best known traits of the de la Madrid government was its lack of resolution when it came to ending the vestiges of the postrevolutionary pact and clearing the way for economic modernization. Businessmen saw de la Madrid's hesitation, and their resulting concerns to a large extent explain their continuing politicization during this entire period.

A CONTRADICTORY RECONCILIATION

The private sector, especially the radical faction, saw the constitutional reforms as prolonging statism and renewing the patterns of corporatist negotiation that reinforced or updated the links between different social sectors and the state, thereby perpetuating society's weakness and dependency on the state. Rejecting this model, business organizations called for a minimal, "subsidiary" state, a state that carries out only those economic responsibilities that cannot be adequately discharged by society. They also urged the state to withdraw from these activities as soon as society could take them over.

Private organizations' opposition to the constitutional reforms could not have been more definitive (see Millán 1988: 165–74; Luna, Tirado, and Valdés 1991: 51–59). Even though economic policy measures had favored business throughout the de la Madrid administration, in 1988 COPARMEX and CONCANACO issued the following joint statement:

> Beginning in 1980, the year that government planning was established as the determining factor in decision making, *the key concept underlying development plans is that the government, in the guise of the state, is empowered to be the direct agent of development and the engine driving the national economy, which gives the government an excessive leadership role. In practice, this turns society and the governed into spectators or simple complements or instruments of bureaucratic planning and activity* (COPARMEX and CONCANACO 1988: 3; emphasis added).

In response to the government's initiative to define consultation and concertation mechanisms around the centrality of the state in the economic process, the private sector advanced its own proposal to make *civil society* the axis of the economy. Beginning in 1982, private-sector organizations undertook various media campaigns aimed at identifying "private enterprise" with "civil society," in opposition to "government" and "bureaucracy." This identification of civil society with a market economy and a diminished role for the state became widespread. The business sector would be at the core of this civil society, substituting for the state as the hub of economic activity (Valdés 1987, 1988). But in addition to disseminating the values of private enterprise through the media, the private sector had to convert this idea into a principle guiding decision making in the economy. In their search for additional channels for their message, businessmen rediscovered politics, understood as the arena where social actors take shape and counterbalance other social forces. Business discourse characterized the prevailing relationship between state and society in Mexico in terms of four features: (1) ideological rigidity, (2) a government-dependent leadership system, (3) a crisis in the capacity to bring demands to the executive branch, and (4) the absence of a multiparty system (Millán 1988: 179–80).

Business organizations argued that vindicating civil society vis-à-vis the state required replacing a political system based on negotiation between classes and an arbiter-government with a political system in which social interaction defines economic space and the state only intervenes in a complementary way. Their demand, in sum, was for the creation of institutional forms that recognize the autonomy of social groups, among which the private sector occupies a privileged place because of its differential ability to mobilize both material and authority resources.

But the de la Madrid government, far from taking further steps to "state-ize" society (as most business organizations had feared), began an extensive privatization program. Between 1982 and 1988, a total of 743 public-sector firms were sold. Of these, 492 were firms with a majority state ownership, 78 had a minority state ownership, 160 were public trusts, and 13 were decentralized agencies. By 1988, only 412 enterprises remained in the hands of the federal government, out of a

TABLE 9.2
THE EVOLUTION OF STATE-OWNED ENTERPRISE,
DECEMBER 1982–FEBRUARY 1992

	1982	1983	1984	1985	1986	1987	1988	1989	1990	1991	1992
Decentralized organizations[1]	102	97	95	96	94	94	89	88	82	77	77
Firms with majority state ownership[2]	744	700	703	629	528	437	252	229	147	119	112
Public trusts[3]	231	199	173	147	108	83	71	62	51	43	43
Firms with minority state ownership[4]	78	78	78	69	7	3	0	0	0	0	0
TOTAL	1155	1074	1049	941	737	617	412	379	280	239	232

[1]Self-governing firms or institutions within the state sector.
[2]Firms with majority government ownership but with some private participation.
[3]Firms promoting economic development.
[4]Firms with minority government ownership.

Source: Unidad de Desincorporación, Secretaría de Hacienda y Crédito Público, *El proceso de enajenación de entidades paraestatales* (Mexico City: SHyCP, 1992).

total of 1,155 in 1982 (see table 9.2). Furthermore, the government launched an economic liberalization process that eventually covered almost all products; it promoted domestic and foreign private investment; and it supported the consolidation of old and new bankers in stock brokerage houses.

PROBLEMS OF REPRESENTATION

Is there an explanation for the ongoing conflict between the business sector and the state throughout the de la Madrid administration? Some authors attribute these tensions to a transformation of the model of business representation. From this perspective, the appearance of two political factions within the business community would be but one expression of new forces seeking to negotiate an arrangement that differed from those of the past. This new arrangement would have three main axes: (1) the establishment of "social corporatism"—that is, a monopolistic form of aggregated representation from the bottom up, with greater autonomy vis-à-vis the government and with enhanced private-sector influence; (2) the elimination of the tripartite representation characteristic of the mixed economy and its replacement with a bipartite relationship in which labor would be excluded from key decisions; at the same time, decisions would be insulated from labor's influence and placed in the hands of the public and private techno-bureaucratic complex (Luna 1990); (3) reform of the state apparatus, simplifying it and giving it a techno-economic rationale in order to separate it from political processes, whose flows would be diverted to other channels. The main objections to the consolidation of such a model emphasize its exclusionary character with regard to other social groups (including broad tiers of the business sector) and the absence of representational forms which in the long run could replace the economic and symbolic rewards that Mexico's established system of tripartite corporatism offered participants in exchange for their political subordination.

But the fact is that these processes are already under way, and they have helped provoke a crisis in the political representation of business as it existed prior to the 1982 conflict. Elsewhere (Luna, Tirado, and Valdés 1987) reference has been made to one feature of this earlier model: businessmen were excluded from party politics as a formal sector, but in exchange they were granted a privileged position in the formation of public policy through their own organizations, chiefly CONCAMIN and CONCANACO (which are legally considered "consultative organs" of government). It is precisely this representational arrangement mechanism that entered a period of crisis beginning in the 1970s and 1980s, mainly because it proved too narrow to encompass a more expansive view of private-sector social action as being able to occupy the spaces vacated by a shrinking public sector. In this sense, the 1982–1988 period marked the beginning of a transition in the model of business representation. This transition has not yet come to an end, in part because important changes may result from the North American Free Trade Agreement (NAFTA) which Mexico signed with the United States and Canada. Similarly, it remains uncertain whether a scheme such as that outlined above can be fully consolidated in the Mexican political context. A central feature of the new system of business representation is its changed appearance, reflecting the advent of new organizations over the last three decades. These organizations are not taken into account in the legal framework that pretends to govern them or in the formal rules of the Mexican political system.

The dynamic of private-sector representation has evolved since the creation of the Private-Sector Coordinating Council (CCE) in 1975. The CCE introduced to the business sector a form of corporatist representation not controlled by the state under existing law. The CCE is a civil association with which member organizations are affiliated on a voluntary basis. Its membership includes the most influential business organizations in Mexico: the CMHN, AMCB, AMIS, ABM, CNA, COPARMEX, CONCANACO, and CONCAMIN (which includes CANACINTRA). Legislation requiring mandatory employer affiliation with business "chambers" only applies to two of them, CONCANACO and CONCAMIN; the others are civil associations (except for COPARMEX, which is legally considered an employers' union). Nevertheless, CONCANACO and CONCAMIN have the largest number of individual members. Other employer organizations (AMCB, AMIS, ABM) are made up of firms, and the CMHN is comprised of thirty-seven individuals. The CCE groups all these organizations (Luna and Tirado 1992: table 8). Organizations affiliated with the CCE have both voice and vote on all matters considered by its board of directors, including the selection of the body's chairman. However, these organizations have very unequal numbers of members, which results in asymmetric representation. The most recent conflicts have arisen precisely because of the concentration of power that exists within the CCE:

> The CMHN, the AMIS, and the AMCB together account for . . . 42 percent of the representation within the CCE, although these three organizations together only include 121 (barely 1 percent) of the more than 900,000 CCE members (Luna and Tirado 1992: 95).

The degree of representational monopoly within the CCE is clear. This situation has generated growing discontent among organizations that have been marginalized from the decision-making process, leading them to demand repeal of legislation that makes affiliation with specialized business "chambers" obligatory and then groups them within the CCE in pyramidal fashion. However, were this demand to be met, organizations on the bottom would increase their influence while those at the top (CMHN, AMIS, AMCB, and the new bankers' association formed after banks were privatized) would lose their ability to control business organizations (Luna and Tirado 1992: 99–100). Also, the government would face a proliferation of negotiating arenas. What may happen in the future is still uncertain, but it seems likely that a highly oligarchic business structure (one that evidences signs of sclerosis and will eventually face a severe crisis of representation) will survive.

The threat of a representational crisis surfaced with great intensity in 1987, following the signing of the Economic Solidarity Pact. As Agustín Legorreta was about to step down from the CCE presidency, the potential for conflict reached unprecedented levels. Absent sufficient consensus to elect a successor, Rolando Vega was chosen to serve as the CCE's interim president. During his term members reached an agreement to institute a rotating presidency, an arrangement in which each affiliated body would hold the post for one year, with the possibility of a single one-year extension. This decision guaranteed that organizations with more affiliates but less decision-making influence at the apex of the business hierarchy would have a turn in the CCE's presidency. However, it also strengthened corporatist mechanisms and forestalled the move toward the more pluralist arrangements sought by small and medium-sized businessmen (who are more numerous but have less weight in the existing system of representation).

THE 1988 ELECTIONS AND THE BEGINNING OF THE SALINAS ADMINISTRATION

Except for death, nothing strikes greater fear in the heart of Mexican big business than the specter of Lázaro Cárdenas (president from 1934 to 1940). The sudden appearance of his son, Cuauhtémoc Cárdenas, as leader of the most important opposition group to split from the PRI in recent times set off alarms, and it led the PRI to look anew at business's criticism of and opposition to the regime. Almost simultaneously there was a new crisis in the Mexican economy, evident in the October 1987 stock market crash and the signing of the Economic Solidarity Pact later that year.

The appearance of the dissident Democratic Current (CD) within the PRI, Cuauhtémoc Cárdenas's candidacy for the Mexican presidency, and the July 1988 election results increased business's political opposition. As Federico Muggenberg, director of the CCE's Center for Social Studies, noted (*La Jornada*, March 3, 1988), the presidential candidacy of businessman Manuel Clouthier for the PAN became an additional source of division within the business class. Although the most radical sectors (in particular, the regional civic and business organizations) supported Clouthier's candidacy, the CCE and key firms softened their criticism of the de la Madrid administration and moved to close ranks with each other and with the government behind the PRI's presidential candidate, Carlos Salinas de Gortari.

Within this context of pre-election tension, there was a severe drop in the stock market and a dangerous resurgence of inflation, which threatened to derail the economic adjustment plan implemented over the preceding five years. The de la Madrid administration responded with the Economic Solidarity Pact, which aimed at stabilizing the economy. The PSE seemed to restore the primacy of tripartite concertation mechanisms, suggesting that earlier constitutional reforms (regarding the participation of the social sector in economic policy formulation and the leading role of the state) would finally become a reality. However, even though the labor and peasant sectors of the PRI signed the pact in the hope of gaining some benefit from it, the private sector was the real beneficiary. Then-CCE president Agustín Legorreta made it clear that the pact was an accord between "the president in a presidentialist system with a very comfortable little group of three hundred people who make the economically important decisions in Mexico" (*Unomasuno*, May 19, 1988). Legorreta continued,

> We gave the government a deadline to clean up its finances. It has met that goal. It has fulfilled the verbal promises it made to the business sector even earlier (which were not part of the pact), *such as the liquidation and dissolution of nationally important firms like Aeroméxico and Cananea* (emphasis added).

Legorreta added that the authorities "understood that if in July inflation was running close to 1000 percent, they risked losing power. Since holding onto power is of paramount importance to them, they agreed to the conditions imposed by the three hundred people comprising the business elite."

Two points are significant about these statements. First, they divulge to what degree economic decisions are controlled by an oligarchy, and they reveal the existence of an informal arrangement for negotiation and deal making that overrides the formal mechanisms established by law. Second, they make it clear that of all the alternatives discussed for reducing inflation, the one chosen was increased privatization of public enterprises, the option demanded by the private sector.[3]

Thus, the PSE operated as the institutional basis for stabilizing relations between the government and private enterprise, encouraging

---

[3]The most radical privatization effort would be carried out later, under Salinas de Gortari.

anti-inflationary behavior by granting business elites the concessions they demanded. Legorreta's statements are also revealing in that they show that businessmen were not satisfied (at least as of December 1987) with the program for reprivatization outlined by the de la Madrid administration, and that they feared something like the bank nationalization could still occur unless the constitutional norms adopted in 1982 were overturned. The successive renewals of the Economic Solidarity Pact reaffirm its role in controlling inflation and holding wages steady, two endeavors which (like privatization) more closely reflect elite decision making than the creation of a more autonomous market space in accordance with the liberal formulas guiding government policy.

THE SALINISTA REFORM AND THE PRIVATE SECTOR

Throughout his election campaign, Salinas de Gortari voiced the need to modernize Mexico, especially the economy. His proposals included increased privatization as well as trade opening, renegotiation of the foreign debt, repatriation of flight capital, increased foreign investment, fiscal reform, and a free trade agreement with the United States and Canada. Despite Salinas's announcement in the aftermath of the 1988 elections that "the era of what is practically a one-party system is over," the truth is that during most of the Salinas presidency there was no real political reform. The Salinas government concentrated on implementing economic changes and some administrative reforms.

For Salinas, economic reform took precedence over political reform, although many of the administration's economic reforms had important political consequences. The most significant one related to state intervention in the economy. In moving from intervention based on a public-enterprise system to a system of regulation and control of economic actors and processes, the state left important productive activities in the hands of the private sector. But at the same time, it created restrictions that regulated private-sector activities. Key developments in this regard included tax reform (which elicited strong reactions from business) and the new banking law.

A prominent feature of the Salinas administration was the rapid recovery of business confidence, obtained thanks to the government's ambitious efforts to privatize nonstrategic public enterprises,[4] its cleanup of public finances, the expansion of opportunities for private investment (including in agriculture, as a result of reforms to Article 27 of the Constitution), and the negotiation of NAFTA. All of these measures had a dual character: they satisfied long-deferred or long-denied private-sector demands, while actively supporting business expecta-

---

[4]The Salinas administration reclassified the list of strategic enterprises (specifically in the petrochemical industry), removing certain activities from the strategic category so that they could pass into private hands (Taniura, Schatan, and Máttar 1991: 95–96).

tions concerning the restructuring of the economy. Economic instability, private-sector pressure, and impending crisis in the PRI limited de la Madrid's autonomy in decision making, but Salinas knew how to maintain the initiative—staying well ahead of the expectations and demands of the business community, harvesting the fruits of a successful stabilization program, and accepting the Cardenista split from the governing elite as an accomplished fact.

In August 1989, nine months into his term, Salinas began to outline his project for state reform. As a central motif of presidential discourse, it synthesized what Salinas viewed as the essential tasks of his mandate: to reduce the size of the state (creating a state that is less proprietary) in order to devote more attention and resources to eradicating extreme poverty and addressing the acute needs of poor communities (bringing about a "solidaristic state"). This ideological operation was basically a way to legitimize the government's privatization program. In a key speech (delivered at the annual meeting of the Business Round Table, in Washington, D.C., on June 10, 1990) in which Salinas defined what he meant by reform of the state, he listed four structural changes at the core of his economic program: economic liberalization, economic deregulation, promotion of foreign investment, and an ambitious privatization policy. On this last point, Salinas noted that the economic crisis of the 1980s clearly demonstrated that increased state ownership was not the appropriate means to meet the needs of the population. On the contrary, the optimal path was the sale of such public enterprises as steel plants, airlines, mines, the telephone company, and banks. Privatization of the banks required a constitutional amendment, and this, in turn, required a two-thirds vote in Congress. According to Salinas, it was necessary to win the support not only of some opposition parties, but also of members of his own party who had voted for the bank nationalization eight years before. To achieve the political consensus necessary to carry out the privatization program, Salinas had to broaden its social impact. For this reason, he decided to link the revenues resulting from the sale of state enterprises with the satisfaction of social demands through the National Solidarity Program (PRONASOL), such that,

> Those who have the least recognize that privatization means an improvement in their living standards.
>
> This is why these programs have achieved a social consensus that will make them permanent. The better the results we obtain in social terms, the greater the popular demand for these programs to become permanent.
>
> Linking the resources that come from privatization to PRONASOL created a positive environment for pro-

grams that only two years ago would have been incon-
ceivable in Mexico (speech to the Business Round Table,
Washington, D.C., June 10, 1990, quoted in Gayet 1992).

Until 1982, the ideology of the Mexican Revolution articulated by
consecutive presidencies accepted that Mexico needed a private sector,
but this sector was to remain subordinate to the public sector. The
credibility of political authority rested on something quite different than
the supremacy of the private sector over other social forces. Political
legitimacy was based on the permanent tension caused by disequilibrium among different social groups and on state intervention in economic production. In contrast, government policy under Salinas aimed
at changing this form of legitimacy for another, one that corresponded to
a different style of economic intervention. This new legitimacy was
based on the withdrawal of the state from production activities and the
creation of conditions under which private enterprise becomes the
driving force for both economic and social activity. Paralleling this, the
state redefined its role as organizer of subordinate social sectors, adopting a scheme that seemed to diverge from traditional corporatism.[5] It is
important to emphasize that this transformation in the basis of the state's
legitimacy is sure to expand the private sector's sphere of action and
influence, making this formerly unrecognized sector a superordinate
factor in national life.

ECONOMIC CONCENTRATION AND PRIVATIZATION POLICY

Certain economic data are of cardinal importance in the realm of politics.
This is certainly true of economic power that has become concentrated
within key private-sector groups and firms. Although there are no
precise data available concerning the degree to which enterprise ownership and wealth are concentrated in Mexico, it is possible to estimate the
dimensions of these structural aspects of the Mexican economy. According to *Expansión*'s 1991 report on the performance of Mexico's principal
economic groups,

Significant economic concentration is still present. . . .
Companies that occupy the top ten positions in the total
of 119 principal groups—Telmex, Vitro, Grupo Industrial Alfa, Cifra, Valores Industriales, Desc, Cemex,
Bimbo, Grupo Industrial Minera de México, and Indus-
trias Peñoles—generated 56 percent of total sales, mo-

---

[5]The effects of economic restructuring undermined the PRI's traditional sectors. Also,
PRONASOL may eventually generate new organizational forms that can become bases of
government support. However, there are not yet enough elements available to permit an
evaluation of this program's long-term effects.

bilized 61 percent of total assets, and represented 53.7 percent of employment (*Expansión*, September 4, 1991, p. 139).

It should be noted that the businessmen who control these groups also participate in brokerage houses and insurance companies, have influence beyond Mexico's borders, and have played a preponderant role in the acquisition of privatized state-owned firms (table 9.3). It is clear that the concentration of wealth and the predominance of a few powerful business groups remain fundamental characteristics of the Mexican economy.

Something similar occurs in brokerage houses. Of twenty-five brokerage houses, only three (Operadora de Bolsa, Accival, and Inverlat) accounted for 40 percent of all stock market operations in 1989 (Luna 1990: 8). It is in the brokerage houses that the "new generation" of bankers has been formed, and their economic power is reflected in their participation in these firms and in the acquisition of the reprivatized banks. Frequently associated with these financiers are the owners and directors of the most dynamic exporting firms, such as producers of cement, beer, steel, glass, and televisions, who together form the nucleus of the business elite reconstituted by Salinas's privatization and business promotion policies. Moreover, members of this elite hold the key decision-making positions in the major business organizations discussed earlier, including the CMHN, AMIS, AMCB, and the new bankers' association. Altogether there are some 121 individuals who control the principal representational channels within the private sector, as well as this sector's capacity to negotiate with the government and with other social groups.

This part of the business sector is clearly emerging as the most dynamic and economically powerful in Mexico. However, it will not necessarily contribute to resolving national problems such as employment, as evidence from the three nations of North America indicates. The five hundred largest firms in Canada generate 12.5 million jobs, while the top five hundred companies in the United States account for 2.4 million jobs. Yet the five hundred largest Mexican firms generate only about 750,000 jobs. In Canada these firms account for 18.5 percent of that country's economically active population. The corresponding figure for the United States is 10.4 percent, while the figure for Mexico is only 2.8 percent (*Expansión*, August 21, 1991, p. 312). Although these countries differ in their history and economic position, such comparisons are still illustrative.

According to the data in table 9.3, the major privatizations carried out between 1989 and 1992 equaled 6.5 percent of Mexico's 1991 gross domestic product (GDP), an indication of the extent to which the most powerful private-sector groups were strengthened by this policy. *Expan-*

TABLE 9.3
THE PRIVATIZATION OF PUBLIC ENTERPRISES, 1989–1992

Purchaser	No. of firms	Economic sector	Company name	Purchase price (millions of US $)	% partic- ipation
Grupo Carso Southwestern Bell France Cable				4,559.1	24.78
STRM (4.4% A)	19	communications	Telmex	335.5	1.82
Accival	1	finance	Banamex	3,218.0	17.49
Vamsa	1	finance	Bancomer	2,839.4	15.43
Obsa	1	finance	Banca Serfín	937.5	5.09
Inverlat	1	finance	Multibanco Comermex	897.2	4.88
Inverméxico[1]	1	finance	Banco Mexicano Somex	609.4	3.31
GBM[1]	1	finance	Banco del Atlántico	477.1	2.59
Mexicana de Cananea S.A.	1	mining	Cia. Minera de Cananea S.A.	437.2	2.38
Estrategia B[1]	1	finance	Banoro	369.5	2.01
Finamex[1]	1	finance	Banca Promex	348.9	1.9
Banco Cédulas Peniche y Cantarel	1	finance	Hipotecarias	291.2	1.58
Abaco	1	finance	Banca Confía	295.8	1.61
Multivalores	1	finance	Banca Cremi	248.1	1.35
Icaro Áerotransportes	1	communications and transport	Aeronaves de México	263.8	1.43
Probursa	1	finance	Multibanco Mercantil de México	202.6	1.1
Siderúrgica del Pacífico	6	metalworking	Las Truchas & others	200.6	1.09
Mexival	1	finance	Banpaís	180.7	0.98
Grupo Acerero del Norte	13	metalworking	Ahmsa & others	148.7	0.81
Rojas, Padilla y Guadarrama	1	finance	Bancreser	140.9	0.77
Grupo Xabre	3	communications and transport	Cia. Mexicana de Aviación Aeropuertos y Terrenos Datatronic	144.5	0.79
Operadora Metro- politana de Lac- teos	4	agriculture	Conasupo, U. Inds. Ags., U. Inds. Chih., & others	87.1	0.47
Grupo Margen	1	finance	Banorie	74.0	0.40
Grupo Beta San Miguel	4	agriculture	Ing. Quesería, Ing. P. Arriaga, Fom. Az. Centro, Ing. A. Obregón	82.1	0.45

TABLE 9.3 (CONTINUED)
THE PRIVATIZATION OF PUBLIC ENTERPRISES, 1989–1992

Purchaser	No. of firms	Economic sector	Company name	Purchase price (millions of US $)	% particip- ation
Unilever	1	food/dairy	Tultitlán plant	70.3	0.38
Cia. Industrial Sucrum	4	agriculture	Ing. J. M. Martínez, Ing. L. Cárdenas, Ing. Independencia, Ing. El Dorado	58.3	0.32
Consorcio "G"	4	automotive	Dina & 4 subsidiaries	57.3	0.31
Consor. Ind. Escorpión	3	agriculture	Ing. Calipán, Ing. Plan de S.L., Imp. Cuenca, Papaloapan	54.4	0.30
Ahorrinox	1	na	Mexinox	45.1	0.25
SIPCSCRM	2	petrochemicals	Fertimex & 2 subsidiaries	40.1	0.22
Grupo Inv. de Annermex	3	agriculture	Cia. Ind. Azucarera, Ing. Plan de Ayala, Ing. San Gabriel	42.0	0.23
Frisco	3	mining	Minera Lampazos, Química Fluor, Minera Real de los Angeles	41.1	0.22
Alfa	3	metalworking	Alambres y Derivados, Barros de Acero Corrugados	26.5	0.14
Ispat Mexicana	4	metalworking	Sider. del Basas & subsidiaries	25.2	0.14
Unión Productora de Caña	3	agriculture	Ing. Melchor Ocampo, Ing. San Sebastián, Ing. Santa Clara	26.7	0.15
Sertel	1	communications	Servicio de Telerreservación	23.0	0.12
Mexabre/Pesq. California	4	fishing	Prod. Pesqueros —de Sinaloa —de Matancitas —de Topolobampo —del Pacífico	22.5	0.12
Ing. Santos	4	agriculture	Ing. Alianza Popular, Ing. Pedernales, Ing. Purjarán, Cia. Azuc. del Ing. Bellavista	26.4	0.14
Corp. Mexicana de Aviación	2	na	Datronic (50%) Turborreactores	19.4	0.11
Grupo Sokada Industrias	1	transport	Astilleros Unidos de Veracruz	18.2	0.10

TABLE 9.3 (CONTINUED)
THE PRIVATIZATION OF PUBLIC ENTERPRISES, 1989–1992

Purchaser	No. of firms	Economic sector	Company name	Purchase price (millions of US $)	% partic- ipation
Agroindustrias Int. del Norte	1	agriculture	Monterrey plant	19.1	0.10
Aceros Grales./ J. Woldenberg	1	metalworking	Tubacero	18.4	0.10
SUBTOTAL	111			18,023.0	97.94
PRIVATE-SECTOR SUBTOTAL	109			17,647.4	95.90
SOCIAL-SECTOR SUBTOTAL	2			375.7	2.04
OTHER PRIVATE SECTOR[2]	79			348.3	1.89
OTHER SOCIAL SECTOR[2]	9			30.0	0.16
TOTAL	199			18,401.3	100.00

Sources: Based on Unidad de Desincorporación, Secretaría de Hacienda y Crédito Público, *El proceso de enajenación de entidades paraestatales* (Mexico City: SHyCP, 1992).

NA = Not Available.

[1]Taken from *El Financiero*, April 24, 1992.

[2]Groups of firms in this subtotal were not listed individually because they represent a very small proportion of the total.

sión magazine, in its 1991 report on business groups, notes that, "While in 1989 the state accounted for 23.9 percent of the direct investment in the 104 groups included in this report, by the end of 1990 this proportion had declined to 12.9 percent. In other words, it fell by 42.1 percent in nominal terms" (*Expansión*, September 4, 1991, pp. 158–61).

Indeed, Salinas's privatization program was undoubtedly the most aggressive ever undertaken in Mexico. De la Madrid began the process late in his administration—a program of disincorporation that was set in motion in 1985 (Vera 1988) and which was intensified in 1987 after the signing of the Economic Solidarity Pact. The program expanded radically under Salinas (see tables 9.2 and 9.3).

One aspect of this privatization policy that deserves special comment is the disincorporation of the banks. In May 1990, President Salinas sent to Congress a bill that amended Articles 28 and 123 of the Constitution. The legislation eliminated paragraph 5 of Article 28, which stipulated the state's exclusive control over banking services. It restored a "mixed" banking regime in which private parties can own up to 100 percent of bank stock. Article 123 was modified in order to shift labor unions in the banking industry from section "B" to section "A" of the federal labor code—that is, from the sphere of public administration to the sphere of private-sector labor relations. A new banking law was later drafted to regulate banking services. The actual process of disincorporation did not begin until June 1991, when the first sale took place. By April 1992, the assets of fifteen banks had been entirely or partly sold, almost all of which were purchased by capital associations headed by brokerage houses. Sale of the banks produced more than 80 percent of the total income generated by privatizing major state-owned enterprises (see figure 9.1).

According to analysts who have closely followed developments in privatized firms, privatization occurred on the basis of informal agreements between the seller and the buyer (Garrido and Quintana 1990). These agreements did not always respect the formalities of the legal process, despite the Ministry of Finance's insistence on transparency in the process (Aspe 1990; Unidad de Desincorporación 1992). Among the cases that showed evidence of irregularities were the sales of Aeroméxico (for which the company was illegally declared to be bankrupt) and the Cananea copper mine (which was sold to Jorge Larrea, whose offer was not the highest presented in the public bidding). There were frequent demands from the private sector itself for transparency in the privatization process. A noteworthy case was the accusation made by the academic director of the Free Enterprise Research Center (CISLE) that "high-tech political clientelism" governed the privatization process (Luna 1990: 10).

It should be noted that the privatization process embraced more than the sale of firms in state hands. The Salinas government's political project went further—seeking to create a favorable environment for the private sector in all aspects of social life. One aspect of this is the private sector's place in rural Mexico following the reforms to Article 27 of the Constitution. This reform empowers peasant communities to decide whether to keep their land under the ejido regime or turn it into private property. The ejido also becomes subject to private law—that is, once the transition process established in the agrarian law comes to an end, the regular judicial system will have jurisdiction in disputes over the ownership of land (see *Diario Oficial*, January 6 and February 26, 1992). Although it is still too early to evaluate the effects of this policy, it is likely that the importance of the private sector in rural areas will increase enormously, radically modifying the features of the national agricultural sector.

FINAL CONSIDERATIONS: A MODEL FOR THE PRIVATE SECTOR

Although the business sector's protest against the state began with a call for all of society ("civil society") to modify the arrangements and

FIGURE 9.1

Privatization by Economic Sector
1989-1992

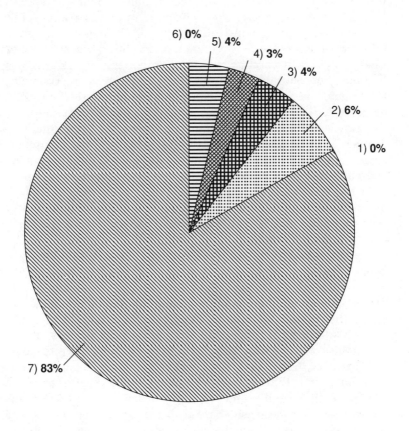

1) **Automotive**
2) **Communications and transportation**
3) **Mining**
4) **Metalworking**
5) **Agriculture**
6) **Petrochemicals**
7) **Finance**

NOTE: This figure presents the percentage of acquisitions by economic sector as outlined in table 9.3.

structure of public authority, society's complacence with the new arrangements entailed in Salinas's policies brings to mind Hegel's identification of civil society with bourgeois society, which finds its full realization in the state.

Contrary to what one might expect, the new order alluded to in the title of this chapter is not the one that liberalism claims to represent—that is, it is not the passage from a preponderant state to a predominant market. What we find instead are the consequences of significant transformations in Mexico's economic and political order, whose structural principles have changed in an important way. Whereas state hegemony once rested on the public enterprise system, economic protectionism, and corporatist arrangements that included broad segments of the working population, today regime legitimation depends on a state that privileges regulatory mechanisms, opens Mexico to international competition, and selectively distributes "solidarity" resources.[6] In this context, the most noteworthy features are the overarching agreements and pacts that carry considerable weight in the operation of the economy. It is worth asking whether resources can be efficiently allocated given the existence of institutional mechanisms that protect a social power structure that is highly unfavorable to the participation of more diverse economic actors.

At the same time, the presidentialist character of the Mexican political system has become more clearly visible. Old institutional arrangements that once mediated relations between the state and subordinate social groups have lost their former importance, while the mechanisms that permit the federal executive to exercise its concentrated power are stronger now than at few other times in Mexico's history.

In this context, sociopolitical actions by businessmen and the policy measures that the Salinas government implemented in favor of the most powerful parts of the business sector have permitted the private sector to occupy (both explicitly and implicitly) a privileged position among social actors. Businessmen share with the government elite decision-making power over national affairs. These groups have constructed a new alliance aimed at exorcising the ghosts of conflicts dating from the 1970s and 1980s and capable of meeting the challenges posed by the collapse of the post-World War II development model. In this pact, the private sector becomes the social actor with the greatest capacity to mobilize available economic resources and command authority. The inevitable question this poses is, how does the rest of society fit in?

---

[6]Despite presidential rhetoric to the effect that the resources obtained by making the state less of a "proprietor" would go to increase "solidarity," the proportion of resources channeled to PRONASOL decreased steadily over time. In 1989 PRONASOL spending represented 72.4 percent of revenues from the sale of state-owned firms. This figure fell to 45.5 percent in 1990 and 31 percent in 1991 (Gayet 1992).

REFERENCES

Arriola Woog, Carlos. 1988. *Los empresarios y el Estado, 1970–1982*. Mexico City: Coordinación de Humanidades, Universidad Nacional Autónoma de México/ Miguel Angel Porrúa.

Aspe, Pedro. 1990. Speech at the VI Reunión Nacional de la Banca, August 13, *El Gobierno Mexicano* 21 (August): 189–96.

COPARMEX and CONCANACO. 1988. *Propuestas del sector privado*. Mexico City: COPARMEX/CONCANACO.

Garrido, Celso, and Enrique Quintana. 1990. "La privatización oligárquica." Mimeo.

Gayet, Cecilia. 1992. "La reforma del Estado en México bajo la gestión de Carlos Salinas de Gortari 1988–1991." Master's thesis, Facultad Latinoamericana de Ciencias Sociales.

Jacobo, Edmundo, Matilde Luna, and Ricardo Tirado, eds. 1989. *Empresarios de México: aspectos históricos, económicos e ideológicos*. Guadalajara: Universidad de Guadalajara.

Luna, Matilde. 1990. "La estructura de representación empresarial en México: la década de los noventa y los cambios en las estrategias corporativas." Mexico City: Instituto de Investigaciones Sociales, Universidad Nacional Autónoma de México. Mimeo.

Luna, Matilde, and Ricardo Tirado. 1992. *El Consejo Coordinador Empresarial, una radiografía*. Mexico City: Instituto de Investigaciones Sociales, Universidad Nacional Autónoma de México.

Luna, Matilde, Ricardo Tirado, and Francisco Valdés. 1987. "Businessmen and Politics in Mexico, 1982–1986." In *Government and Private Sector in Contemporary Mexico*, edited by Sylvia Maxfield and Ricardo Anzaldúa Montoya. Monograph Series, no. 20. La Jolla: Center for U.S.-Mexican Studies, University of California, San Diego.

———. 1991. "Los empresarios y la política en México, 1982–1986." In *Las empresas y los empresarios en el México contemporáneo*, edited by Ricardo Pozas and Matilde Luna. Mexico City: Grijalvo.

Maxfield, Sylvia. 1990. *Governing Capital*. Ithaca, N.Y.: Cornell University Press.

Millán, René. 1988. *Los empresarios mexicanos ante el Estado y la sociedad*. Mexico City: Siglo Veintiuno/Instituto de Investigaciones Sociales, Universidad Nacional Autónoma de México.

Taniura, Taeko, Claudia Schatan, and Jorge Máttar. 1991. *Intra-Industry and Intra-Firm Trade between Mexico and the United States: The Autoparts, Electronics, and Secondary Petrochemical Industries*. Joint Research Programme Series, no. 76. Tokyo: Institute of Developing Economies.

Unidad de Desincorporación SHyCP. 1992. *El proceso de enajenación de entidades paraestatales*. Mexico: Secretaría de Hacienda y Crédito Público.

Valdés, Francisco. 1987. "Ensayo sobre la convocatoria social de los empresarios. ¿Hacia un nuevo liderazgo sociopolítico?" *Estudios Sociológicos* 15 (September–October): 433–54.

———. 1988. "Los empresarios, la política y el Estado," *Cuadernos Políticos* 53 (January–April): 47–69.

Vera, Oscar. 1988. "The Political Economy of Privatization in Mexico." Presented at the conference "The Privatization of Public Enterprises in Latin America," University of California, San Diego, La Jolla.

10

Political Change in Mexico's New Peasant Economy

Jonathan Fox

INTRODUCTION

The Mexican state is recasting its long-standing leading role in the national economic development process. The postrevolutionary state balanced the competing challenges of economic growth and political stability by closely regulating the distribution of both income and property. This model of regulation framed Mexico's political development until the economic crisis of 1982. Since then, Mexico's presidents have been restructuring the nature of state intervention in the economy, gradually dismantling much of the "revolutionary nationalist" legacy in favor of increased integration into the international market.

The new official ideology of "social liberalism" calls for the state to encourage private sector-led economic development by largely withdrawing from most of its past regulatory and productive activities, while continuing its commitment to social justice through more efficient and less paternalistic distributive reforms. Like past Mexican policy makers, however, the social liberals base much of their political legitimacy on their success at encouraging both growth and distribution. And since both Mexico's contested 1988 presidential election and the Gorbachev experience underscored how democratic political competition could complicate efforts toward economic change, Mexican policy makers have worked largely within the existing political system to carry out their economic reform project.

I would like to thank the volume editors, as well as Luis Hernández, Sergio Zermeño, Judy Harper, and an anonymous government official for their helpful comments. This essay was completed in September 1993.

In spite of the relatively slow pace of change in national political institutions, economic and social policy reform has dramatically altered the context within which much of Mexican politics unfolds. Policy change alters the structure of political opportunities available to contending actors, just as political conflict conditions the viability of competing policy options. This chapter explores one dimension of this interactive process by analyzing how changing economic policy has affected politics in one important arena of Mexican society: the countryside.

Mexico has been a predominantly urban society for over two decades, but agriculture still accounts for more than one-quarter of the economically active population. The "rural" share of the national population is significantly larger, though underrepresented in national census data. Mexico's most extreme poverty is still concentrated in rural areas, but so is electoral support for the ruling party. If political competition in the countryside were to become as open as it has become in Mexico's larger cities, the overall national political balance would look very different. If the long-precarious peasant economy becomes increasingly unviable for large numbers of producers, how will it affect a regime that has long depended on social peace and predictable electoral outcomes in the countryside?

Poverty in the peasant economy is a long-standing problem. Agrarian reform parcels were often too small or too poor in quality to support a family, and have since been successively subdivided with population growth. The agricultural frontier can no longer absorb land-hungry peasants, and redistribution of large private holdings virtually ended in the mid-1970s. Most of those who remained on the land combined agriculture with migration and wage labor to survive (Grindle 1988). For landholders, government production support programs were uneven in coverage, unreliable in quality, and often conditioned on political subordination (Fox 1993). But if in the past the key rural development policy question was whether the terms of state intervention would favor peasant producers, today the question is whether there will be any significant economic support for the peasant economy at all.

Top agricultural-sector policy makers have predicted that the combination of subsidy cuts, trade opening, and privatization of the agrarian reform sector is likely to reduce the rural population by *one-half* within a decade or two.[1] So far, the rural political response has been muted, but as the new policies "trickle down" from Mexico City's newspaper head-

---

[1] See Undersecretary of Agriculture Luis Téllez's remarks, cited in Golden 1991. At a May 1992 Harvard forum, Dr. Téllez followed up with the prediction that the economically active population in agriculture would probably fall from 26 percent to 16 percent in the coming decade. Government critics made comparable predictions of massive rural proletarianization two decades ago, but they greatly underestimated the peasantry's capacity to resist full displacement. Protest drove renewed state intervention to subsidize the better-off third of the ejido sector, and campesino identity turned out to be more resilient than predicted. Recently, however, the prospects for state intervention have changed greatly, and perhaps peasant identity as well, at least among the younger generation with significant migration experience.

lines and reach inside hundreds of thousands of farm gates, will they open a political Pandora's box?

Analysts from across the spectrum agree that rural social and economic polarization is increasing, but the political implications are still far from clear.[2] It is difficult to generalize about rural politics because the Mexican countryside is made up of a diverse mosaic of contrasting scenarios. This chapter explores the principal political trends that are unfolding during this open-ended period of transition, and argues that the main cleavage in peasant politics will be between "voice" and "exit." Will peasants mobilize to make family farming economically viable, or will they decide to join long-standing city-bound and northward migrant streams? The chapter focuses on the diverse political actions of the rural poor, not because they will necessarily be their principal response, but because they are the actions most likely to affect the political system more generally.

The chapter begins with an overview of state economic intervention in smallholder agriculture in Mexico, followed by a focus on the principal political trends in the countryside since the national economic crisis began in 1982, including: rural electoral politics, ideological context, political conflicts over rural policy reforms, and changing patterns of rural social organization.

STATE INTERVENTION AND THE RURAL SOCIAL PACT

The land reform of the 1930s that laid the foundation for rural political stability was an uneven patchwork. In some regions the national state made pacts with local elites rather than redistribute land, ceding autonomy in exchange for political subordination (Sanderson 1981). The social pact with land reform beneficiaries involved a similar deal, as the state offered the "politics of promises" — the hope of access to social and economic supports in return for political subordination. This arrangement eroded significantly by the late 1960s, leading to a broad wave of land invasions throughout the country and the rise of guerrilla movements in the state of Guerrero. While security forces responded with repression, reformists within the state offered rural development programs to placate unrest. The state responded to pressure from below with an increasingly elaborate array of agricultural support programs from the mid-1970s until the 1982 crisis, but in the absence of accountability mechanisms they were largely turned to the advantage of rent-

---

[2] According to a study sponsored by the prominent Private-Sector Coordinating Council (CCE), "the modernization [of the countryside] is following two paths: the economic and political integration of the producers with access to the international market, and the economic exclusion of the majority of the unproductive peasants, who are still under tutelar control [of the government], have restricted access to resources, and are ideologically subordinated" (Varela et al. 1991: 2).

seeking bureaucratic entrepreneurs within the growing state agencies (Fox 1993).

Mexican agriculture is highly polarized. Most producers fall into one of two categories: either they are medium- and large-scale farmers, usually with irrigation, or they are nonirrigated smallholders with less land than needed to provide the equivalent of a full year's employment even at minimum wage (CEPAL 1982). Mexico also has a significant intermediate segment of market-oriented, surplus-producing family farmers, but the overall "bimodal" pattern of polarization contrasts sharply with the "unimodal" pattern of, for example, the U.S. Midwest or post-land-reform Taiwan, Korea, and China (Johnston et al. 1987). In Mexico, sub-subsistence producers tend to be poorly organized beyond the community level, family farmers have recently become moderately well organized, and large growers are the most organized.

This polarized pattern is the inheritance of past state intervention. Government subsidies and irrigation investment induced the creation of much of today's modern agribusiness, while intermittent waves of agrarian reform settled large numbers of former farmworkers on rainfed and forest lands of uneven quality (Barkin and Suárez 1985; Esteva 1983; Grindle 1986; Sanderson 1981, 1986). This "two-track" policy, alternating between presidential administrations since the Mexican Revolution, has reflected competing policy currents within the state, one that saw the government's creation of the ejido, or agrarian reform community, as a temporary political expedient and a reserve migrant labor source, and another that saw the ejido sector as a key pillar of a political project of national development with social justice. Overall, rural policy emphasized investment and subsidies for the benefit of agribusiness, except during the mid-1930s and mid-1970s, when populists briefly dominated national agrarian policy making, and peasant movements were able to win significant concessions. Though largely forgotten in the course of Mexico's economic instability of the 1970s and 1980s, this two-track model of regulation in agriculture made a major economic and political contribution to what used to be called the "Mexican miracle" of import-substitution industrialization from the 1940s through the 1960s.

ECONOMIC CHANGE, RURAL SOCIAL IMPACT, AND POLITICAL BEHAVIOR

The recent changes in the state's role in the agricultural economy are not the only factors that shape rural politics. The panorama is crosscut by independent trends in civil society, political parties, and rural social organizations, which will be discussed further below. The state's economic intervention in peasant agriculture does set certain key parameters, however, and it is changing in three principal ways.

First, the state has withdrawn from its long-standing major regulatory role in most of the peasant economy. Multiple layers of government programs had long protected parts of the peasant economy from market forces. Since the early 1970s, state enterprises had provided most of the formal production credit, crop insurance, and fertilizer available to peasants, and had regulated most output markets for peasant products by protecting them from cheaper foreign imports while offering crop support prices to purchase significant minorities of national grains, oilseeds, and key industrial crops directly (coffee, sugar, cotton, tobacco, and forest products). Fruit and vegetable production for export was less regulated, though the state still played an important role via public investment in irrigation, heavily subsidized water, energy, and credit, and concessioned export licenses. Reformists attempted to reverse the antipeasant bias in agricultural policy with the 1980–1982 Mexican Food System (SAM), but political constraints led to a greater emphasis on production spending increases than on institutional change (Fox 1993). The 1982 economic crisis, provoked by a clash between ambitious state-led nationalist economic policies and international market forces, discredited the prevailing model of regulation. Agricultural subsidy and investment cuts followed, and by the end of the 1980s most agricultural agencies had been privatized or were cut back sharply.

One of the key levers of state intervention in smallholder production was its support prices for basic grains, but by the early 1990s only maize and beans still had "guaranteed" support prices.[3] The other major agricultural support policy, subsidized crop loans, was cut back to a small minority of relatively well-off peasants, leading to widespread defensive protests in 1993.[4] The generalized production supports were highly politically vulnerable, since they were widely considered corrupt and inefficient, but as of 1993 they had not been replaced by more targeted smallholder production policies. Most of the poorest producers had always lacked access to the generalized production supports, so those most affected were the surplus-producing peasants. Several key social safety net programs were maintained, however—most notably, the extensive networks of government-supplied village food stores and rural clinics, and the new National Solidarity Program's soft production loans and village-level public works programs. By the early 1990s, the

---

[3]See Appendini 1991, 1992; Hewitt de Alcántara 1994; Gordillo 1990; Salinas de Gortari 1990. In spite of government efforts to withdraw completely from the markets for wheat, sorghum, and soybeans, some ad hoc government purchases continued via negotiated prices (*precios de concertación*), depending on harvests, newly liberalized imports, and direct pressure from mobilized producers.

[4]Past official reports of smallholder credit access were probably highly exaggerated. According to a recent survey, during the 1985–1989 period, 22 percent of agrarian reform landholders received government crop loans, falling to 16 percent in 1990 (SARH-CEPAL 1992: 4).

dominant agricultural policy makers considered peasant producers to be an issue for social welfare rather than economic policy.

The second important change in economic policy was the reduction of agricultural trade protection, starting with oilseeds, sorghum, and wheat. By the early 1990s, only corn and beans still had more than ad hoc trade protection. Corn remained Mexico's most important crop in terms of land use and is the mainstay of the peasant economy (Appendini 1992; Hewitt de Alcántara 1994). Regulation of imports through licensing was a crucial backstop for the domestic white corn support price, which remained approximately 80 percent above international prices. Policy analysts debated the possible social effects of the likely opening of the corn sector under the proposed North American Free Trade Agreement (NAFTA). There was widespread agreement that since most peasant corn producers lacked irrigation and capital, they would never be competitive with U.S. producers.[5] Analysts disagreed, however, over whether significant numbers of new jobs would be created in export agriculture. In a worst case scenario of opening corn in the short run, one econometric model predicted that 850,000 heads of household would leave agriculture, representing 12 percent of the rural labor force.[6] Other studies of agricultural out-migration impact foresaw a more modest net increase, emphasizing the absorption of displaced farm labor in growing export agriculture (Cornelius 1992; Cornelius and Martin 1993; Levy and Wijnbergen 1991).[7] But diverse predictions of

---

[5]For example, 85 percent of *ejidatarios* grow corn but only 56 percent of them are able to purchase fertilizer. Average *ejidatario* corn yields are only 1.4 tons/hectare, and 40 percent less in rainfed areas (SARH-CEPAL 1992: 40). Irrigated growers of other crops, faced with increased international competition, switched to still-protected corn in the early 1990s, leading to national surpluses. Their yields could reach 8–10 tons/hectare.

[6]Six hundred thousand of those predicted to leave would go to the United States (Robinson et al. 1991; Solís 1991). Calva predicted even more dramatic disruption (Calva 1991; Calva et al. 1992). See also Encinas, de la Fuente, and MacKinlay 1992; González Pacheco 1992; Piña Armendáriz 1993; Salcedo, García, and Sagarnaga 1993.

[7]Levy and Wijnbergen (1991) stress the positive social impact of reducing corn prices for the rural poor who are net consumers. The landless poor do pay much higher prices for corn because of trade protection and support prices for corn producers. These authors' analysis overstates the benefits of trade opening because it assumes that if corn imports were completely liberalized, markets would automatically "clear" and consumers in remote rural areas would have access to significantly lower prices. Much of the countryside is characterized by fragmented, uncompetitive regional markets, however, which would not necessarily transfer price savings to rural consumers. Mexico's National Basic Foods Company (CONASUPO) already intervenes in many of these markets to some degree, supplying 18,000 village stores. In contrast to the millions of beneficiaries of Mexico's urban milk and tortilla subsidies, low-income rural consumers do not receive the benefits of low international prices in these stores, but the regulatory impact of the village store network does reduce consumer prices to levels significantly below what they would otherwise be. If corn imports were liberalized and this network made lower prices widely accessible, then the landless would be better off, surplus-producing smallholders would be worse off, and employment would fall. The impact on sub-subsistence producers would be ambiguous, since even though they produce less than needed to feed a family for a year, many now sell part of their crop at the high producer prices and buy corn for family consumption at the

Mexico's likely opportunities for growth in agroexports are quite mixed (Bardacke 1991; Monjarás et al. 1992; Zabin 1992). The key question may be one of sequencing: will new export-related jobs be created before, during, or long after the lowering of the corn price?

Though the North American Free Trade Agreement postponed the full opening of the corn sector for the maximum fifteen years, Mexican agricultural policy makers planned to lower domestic corn prices to international levels much more quickly, before the end of the Salinas administration (*Economist*, February 17, 1993). Salinas announced in January 1993 that the new policy, PROCAMPO, would be to support corn producers with direct compensatory payments, a system that would be more in line with NAFTA and GATT than with the existing program of high producer prices. The sequence of policy change, the institutional mechanisms for delivering the support, and its coverage and amount remained subjects of high-level policy debate throughout 1993. The key issues were whether the large corn growers would receive most of the proposed benefits, and whether all sub-subsistence producers would actually gain access as promised.[8]

The third important change in economic policy was the November 1991 reform of Article 27 of the Mexican Constitution. This measure permits the private sale and rental of land for the first time in the agrarian reform sector, which accounts for about half of Mexico's arable land. Prior to the 1991 constitutional reform, agrarian reform beneficiaries (*ejidatarios*) could not legally sell or rent their land-use rights, and many other forms of economic activity were sharply constrained by government regulations. The private sector had complained, meanwhile, that landholding ceilings and the threat of expropriation discouraged investment. In response, the reform formally ended the decades-long land redistribution process and legalized joint ventures with private investors and the direct ownership of land by agribusiness firms. The constitutional reform made major changes in the institutional structure of the ejido community, recognized its legitimacy as a form of tenancy (allowing intra-ejido land transfer and weakening the powers of the ejido "commissar" [*comisario*] while strengthening those of the membership assembly), and reduced government intervention in internal ejido affairs. The reform also creates an official "agrarian attorney general" and agrarian tribunals to deal with the backlog of adjudication

---

lower prices available in the government-supplied village stores. The general point here is that the conflict of interest between low-income producers and consumers of corn is real, but it can be and has been buffered by targeted public policies.

[8]See Gallegos 1993. The most extreme pro-market policy current reportedly supported using the private banking system to deliver the proposed support payments, while peasant organization advocates inside and outside the state proposed channeling them through the government crop procurement and storage agency (BORUCONSA), in conjunction with producer groups. The private banking system had no experience dealing with low-income producers, while BORUCONSA had an extensive network of infrastructure and relationships.

decisions and to encourage accountability in the process of land titling and boundary disputes.[9]

The impact of the land tenure reform is difficult to predict, but it will be far from uniform. Three simultaneous patterns of tenure change are most likely to emerge: (1) consolidation of medium- and large-scale irrigated agribusiness holdings through purchase, joint ventures, subcontracting, and long-term rental (especially in the northwestern states)[10] (2) transfer among smallholders, consolidating a capitalized small farmer class (especially in the central highlands); and (3) land concentration by local bosses, inside and outside ejidos, sometimes involving violence (especially in the south).[11] It is premature to predict the relative importance of each scenario, although the last one is likely to involve small amounts of land but high degrees of localized violence. Before changes in land tenure can be put into effect, however, the government must carry out the massive and complex task of individual titling of ejido members, so that decisions about property rights (ejido vs. private) are made based on documented holdings. This process is likely to be much slower than planned, in part because, according to the Ministry of Agriculture and Water Resources (SARH), only about 2,000 of the 28,000 ejidos have clearly defined internal boundaries between parcels, not to mention potential conflicts between communities over overlapping property rights.

It is difficult to predict the political impact of these three kinds of broad economic change for two main reasons. First, their eventual social impact is largely unknown, especially given the complex interactions between the three policy changes and newly invented land values for ejidos, fluctuating crop prices, the uncertainty of government support for economic conversion efforts, and labor market conditions that affect emigration decisions. For example, if corn prices fall to international levels and ejido land is sold before significant numbers of new jobs are created in other sectors of the economy, then rural wages are likely to be further depressed by an oversupply of migrant labor.

The second reason that the political impact of the state's economic withdrawal is difficult to predict is that even sharply negative social

---

[9]For the text of the reform and its enabling legislation, see SRA 1992.

[10]Among *ejidatarios*, 13.4 percent have irrigated lands, 11.2 percent are partially irrigated, and 75.4 percent are completely dependent on rainfall (SARH-CEPAL 1992: 4).

[11]On the implications of the tenure reform in Chiapas, for example, see García de León 1992. The lack of political space for democratic grassroots peasant organizing in Chiapas has fueled the growth of clandestine radical groups. In May 1993 the army carried out an unprecedented counterinsurgency sweep in the Ocosingo region of the state. In addition to independent journalistic accounts in *La Jornada*, See Minnesota Advocates 1993.

impact does not automatically translate into political behavior.[12] The withdrawal of many government agricultural programs has changed the context within which rural people decide whether and how to engage in collective action. As of 1993, electoral politics was still not sufficiently competitive in rural areas for voting to become a major channel for representation in national policy making. The main alternative channel for representation—peasant interest groups—has been in transition for a decade and a half. The traditional patterns of protest and petitioning no longer work, but newer forms of social bargaining (*concertación*) have yet to constitute a consolidated alternative, especially in the most authoritarian regions of rural Mexico, such as Chiapas. Perhaps most importantly, movements that represent the social and economic interests of the rural poor have yet to mesh fully with movements for *political* change either inside or outside the ruling party.[13]

CURRENT TRENDS IN PEASANT POLITICS

By the early 1990s the political situation in the newly liberalized peasant economy was a complex, diverse mosaic. The main trends can be organized in terms of the following themes: rural electoral politics, official rural development ideology, political conflict over public policies, and the ongoing transition from corporatist to more pluralistic forms of peasant interest representation.

ELECTORAL POLITICS AND THE COUNTRYSIDE

Rural votes still weigh heavily in contested national elections, even though Mexico's electorate is predominantly urban. Available evidence indicates that rural votes are still of national importance for three principal reasons. First, rural voters have little access to multiple sources of political information and viable alternative parties, greatly reducing effective electoral competition. Second, fraud is more widespread in rural areas, affecting both absolute and relative voting data.[14] Third, as

---

[12]Rural political behavior is hard to predict in part because very few opinion polls are carried out beyond large cities—with the exception of the government's own confidential polling, which it uses extensively to test out different policy options.

[13]On changes in the peasant movement in the 1980s, see, among others, Bartra 1989a, 1989b, 1990, 1991; Harvey 1990, 1992, 1993; Fernández Villegas 1991; A. García 1989; Fox and Gordillo 1989; Gordillo 1988a, 1988b; Hernández 1989a, 1989b, 1990, 1991, 1992a, 1992b; Martínez Borrego 1991; Mejía Piñeiros and Sarmiento 1987; Moguel, Botey, and Hernández 1992.

[14]According to Juan Molinar Horcasitas's comprehensive overview of party politics (1991: 9), "electoral fraud is a generalized practice in the Mexican electoral system, but it is not universal or homogeneous. It is more common and intense in rural and remote areas. . . . This is not only because the PRI gets better results using cacique-style clientelistic mechanisms of electoral mobilization rather than modern campaign techniques; it also has to do with the opposition, which, with few exceptions, only goes as far as the paved road."

far as congressional races are concerned, outdated district boundaries
lead to overrepresentation of rural zones.[15]

The most notable indicator of the continuing importance of the rural
vote was the geographic distribution of the returns from the 1988
presidential election. According to the hotly contested official tally,
Salinas's slim majority depended largely on rural votes. In "very urban"
areas Salinas won only 34 percent of the votes counted, but in "very
rural" areas he received 77 percent. While rural and semirural districts
accounted for 43 percent of the electorate, they produced 57 percent of
Salinas's official vote (López et al. 1989: 31–32).[16] Most of the questionable ballots were cast in rural precincts, where citizen oversight was
especially difficult and dangerous. The opposition's restricted access to
the broadcast media also had a disproportionately greater impact in
rural areas, and the threat of human rights violations limited freedom of
expression and assembly for the opposition.[17]

The ruling party claimed to have recovered its urban base with the
1991 midterm congressional elections. In its search for a more "modern"
image, its electoral dependence on the so-called green vote had come to
seem embarrassingly backward. The ruling party clearly did recover
urban support, but its rural share was still significantly higher according
to Gallup/Televisa's exit poll (74 percent vs. 51 percent) (Medina Peña
1991: 25). The continued controversy over the validity of the overall 1991
turnout figures makes it difficult to quantify the urban/rural breakdown. Officially, turnout was significantly higher than in the much more
important 1988 race, but sources involved in Gallup's extensive exit poll
estimate that overall voter turnout was *at least 10 percent less* than official
government claims. Moreover, the congressional races were much less
seriously contested than the 1988 elections; only the 1994 presidential
returns will allow a clear comparison. If one were to highlight an
indicator from 1991 for comparison with 1988, it would be the two
seriously contested governors' races in the states of Guanajuato and San
Luis Potosí, where the ruling party continued to produce overwhelming
victories in rural districts.[18]

In spite of continued rural electoral fraud, the Salinas government's
rural electoral strategy was much more sophisticated than its prede-

[15]District boundaries do not account for the effects of more than two decades of
urbanization. As one official in the Ministry of Agriculture put it, however, "it if isn't
broken, don't fix it."

[16]For a critical analysis of the 1988 election statistics, see Barberán et al. 1988.

[17]On the rural human rights situation, see Amnesty International 1986, 1991; Americas
Watch 1990, 1991; Minnesota Advocates 1993.

[18]The voting process in most of the rural districts in these states was not systematically
scrutinized by either independent observers or the media. With fraud so evident in the urban
areas, one might assume that it was at least as widespread in rural districts. Ironically, private
polls and some political insiders concur that, with so little effective competition in rural areas,
the ruling party might well have been able to win free elections in those states.

cessors. Traditionally the rural vote was seen as something to trade (for public works) in a context of clientelistic, machine politics that left little room for autonomous social or political organization.[19] But even in the absence in most rural areas of the broad programmatic debate generally associated with democratic party politics, the vote becomes more valuable to the rural poor when two new trends converge: more electoral competition, on the one hand, and the growth and spread of autonomous peasant organizations on the other. The ruling party continued to bargain for votes with patronage and projects, both before and after election day, but some campesino organizations gained greater leverage in the process. In regions where the "official" corporatist organizations have been eclipsed by new, more autonomous and representative organizations, voting patterns became harder to predict. Reformist state managers increasingly acknowledged that crude traditions of political imposition were counterproductive, but their influence over hard-liners was quite uneven.

These changes began to emerge in the mid-1980s in rural Sonora and Chihuahua, when federal and state authorities offered significant incentives in return for at least indirect support against the National Action Party (PAN).[20] Early in the 1988 presidential campaign, candidate Salinas's emissaries systematically met with leaders of a wide range of the more representative regional organizations, even though most had steered clear of electoral politics until then. Instead of the traditional process whereby government officials insisted on imposing their own preferred leaders along with offering some economic concessions, this new bargaining arrangement respected the new generation of peasant leadership. It offered to support their regional, self-managed economic development and to ally with them against their immediate enemies in local and state government, in exchange for at least indirect support in

---

[19]In his reflections on whether July 6, 1988, "truly awakened the deep Mexico," Guillermo Bonfil offers a well-informed discussion of voting patterns in indigenous areas. He supports Warman's suggestion that continued voting for the PRI in many regions indicates decisions made "'*en corto*,' that is, based on short-term considerations that have nothing to do with political programs offering alternative models of society for the future. The vote is seen there more as a resource for here and now, used to get promises to finish a road, build a school, put in drinking water, move along the bureaucratic titling of land, and other small contributions that help to resolve everyday problems, ancestral problems, those that overwhelm all moments of one's life. The other issues are still matters for 'the others,' the superimposed world created by the imaginary Mexico. The parties will have to dig very deep to get to the bottom and touch the levers capable of politically mobilizing the deep Mexico" (1990: ii–iii).

[20]In Sonora, for example, the famous Coalición de Ejidos Colectivos de los Valles del Yaqui y Mayo, a pioneer of autonomous peasant-managed economic development, reportedly made a deal to support the "official" candidate for governor in exchange for a government bailout after the group found itself overextended financially. In Chihuahua, the federal government made significantly more concessions to a mass movement for higher corn prices than it did for other similarly militant mass movements in states that did not face electoral competition (such as Nayarit and Chiapas) (Fox and Gordillo 1989).

the presidential race.[21] Remarkably, the principal national network of autonomous regional organizations, UNORCA (National Union of Autonomous Regional Peasant Organizations), maintained its pluralism under the strain when its members made their highly charged political choices, some opting for Salinas while others remained neutral or came out for Cárdenas.[22]

The balance of bargaining power for votes (whether through old-fashioned clientelism or new-style "concerted" deals) depended on perceived political alternatives. Most political parties were still absent from most of the countryside in the early 1990s. On the right, the PAN did not try to appeal to the rural poor, while significant organized rural support for the center-left opposition Party of the Democratic Revolution (PRD) was limited to a few states (Michoacán, Tabasco, Guerrero, and southern Veracruz). Rural support for Cárdenas's presidential race was quite uneven and diverse in the 1988 presidential race, including defections from traditional corporatist peasant organizations in La Laguna and Michoacán, diffuse civic anticorruption and antiauthoritarian sentiments, and a new electoral turn by some autonomous peasant organizations—perhaps not unlike the combination of diverse genres of support seen in urban Mexico, although the mix probably involved more independent social movements in the cities.

The best available poll of *ejidatarios*, sponsored by the Institute for Strategic Proposals, found that 20 percent sympathized with the PRD as of 1990, while the rest said they supported the Institutional Revolutionary Party (PRI). But more notable is that PRI support was quite thin; only 10 percent said their affiliation was based on "conviction." The rest reported that they supported the PRI because it was "convenient,"

---

[21] See Hernández 1989a, 1989b, 1990. In contrast to an official organizational endorsement, indirect support might involve a leader's declaration as an individual, or an at-least neutral-sounding public political statement. In these scenarios, bitter intra-organizational battles are avoided, while the group is removed from the potential opposition. The result was a series of newspaper spreads throughout the 1988 campaign season from many key regional nonofficial peasant groups. These declarations led to deep divisions within those groups that did not process the decision with the membership.

[22] UNORCA's key election campaign statement noted: "UNORCA is a *pluralistic* network of organizations, which means that some organizations are affiliated with various peasant federations (*centrales*) and others are not. We have been able to develop our convergence based on the most scrupulous respect for each organization's internal structures and decisions. . . . We understand . . . autonomy as the capacity of each organization to make its own decisions *internally*, and mutual respect for these decisions. Because of UNORCA's very nature, it cannot and will not take any partisan political position in the upcoming electoral process. Each regional organization is free to take, through its internal mechanisms, the position that it judges most convenient" (*La Jornada*, June 16, 1988, emphasis in original). UNORCA's August 1988 national meeting in the heart of Cardenista territory (Costa Grande, Guerrero) was another turning point, sustaining its commitment to political pluralism in spite of the sharply polarized political moment. For the report on the proceedings, see UNORCA 1988. Parenthetically, the frequency with which UNORCA's initials are spelled out in the press and other public forums without explaining that the "A" stands for "autonomous" is remarkable.

because of various kinds of imposition, or because they knew of no alternatives (Morett Sánchez 1991: 110–11).

Most analyses of democratic transitions focus on "high politics"— national-level elections and pact making. In Mexico, however, the institutionalization of free and fair elections evolved much more unevenly, moving more quickly at the municipal and state levels than at the national level (Fox and Hernández 1992).[23] Specifically rural democratization in Mexico remains rare, and so far it is led by local rather than national political actors. To encourage the sustained and sometimes risky mass civic action needed to promote the transition to electoral democracy in rural areas, locally attractive alternatives need to be combined with the perception that citizens' efforts could pay off. These two conditions are most likely to hold in local municipal elections, where the results of the actions of both electors and elected are most immediate and public.

The rural democratization process is most often led by regional civic and social movements, rather than by local branches of national political parties. As in much of Latin America, regional civic protest movements combine demands for the defense of the ballot box and accountable, representative government with economic demands for regional development investment (Fox 1992). As social organizations begin to play the role of local political parties, however, they risk subordinating long-term social and economic goals to short-term political exigencies. Their challenge is to participate in civic and political movements without losing their autonomous identity.[24]

Electoral conflicts force peasant organizations to make political choices. They can act as an interest group, pursuing their economic interests by playing parties off against one another. Or they can define a public political identity either through allying with an established party or by fielding candidates of their own. But under the current rules of the game in Mexico, the political trade-offs that peasant organizations face are rarely of their own choosing; defining a clear political or civic identity can endanger access to political elites and the discretionary resources

---

[23]This may fit the Indian Congress Party model, where the ruling party retains federal power while ceding state and local elections (suggested by Cornelius, Gentleman, and Smith [1989]).

[24]So far, however, in those cases where autonomous regional organizations have won local mayoral elections, the peasant organization has tended to lose force in the aftermath. This new process has yet to receive systematic study. Note, for example, the cases of the Unión de Ejidos "Lázaro Cárdenas" in Ahuacatlán, Nayarit, and the Cooperativa Agropecuaria Regional "Tosepan Titataniske," in Cueztalán, Puebla. In both cases key leaders won local office through the PRI, offsetting local elites with their federal contacts. One of the most successful experiences, from the point of view of the survival of peasant organization autonomy, was in Ignacio Zaragoza, Chihuahua, in the mid-1980s under the PSUM. Other notable cases of peasant-based municipal political victories—such as Juchitán, Oaxaca; Alcozauca, Guerrero; and rural Michoacán—were driven by political organizations rather than producer groups.

they control.[25] Even if they abstain from electoral opposition but defend the ballot box against fraud, as in Guerrero's Costa Grande region, they still put their limited access to government funding for self-managed economic development at risk.[26] Political conditionality was especially strict in the aftermath of the 1988 election, but it began to relax somewhat after the ruling party won the 1991 midterm elections.

One important trend in rural politics is the opposition's growing capacity to focus national political attention on long-forgotten small-town electoral conflicts. Pioneered by a local left-wing movement in Juchitán in the late 1970s, this process was led by the right-wing PAN in the mid- and late 1980s in medium-sized cities. National political attention did not focus on clearly rural municipalities, however, until the hotly contested 1989 local races in Michoacán and Guerrero. Conflicting views on how and whether to negotiate electoral outcomes complicated the opposition's response to fraud. Two kinds of patterns began to emerge, one more party-led, the other driven by local civic and social movements. The unprecedented popularity and success of the "Exodus for Democracy" antifraud mass protest march from rural Tabasco to Mexico City had a truly national impact on the PRD's fortunes in late 1991 as its first clear-cut success following the demoralization of the August 1991 elections. Where state and national opposition party elites mesh poorly with representative local social and political groups, however, this critical mass of pressure is unlikely to develop (for example, the Costa Grande region of Guerrero).

---

[25]See Bartra 1992. More generally, there are inherent tensions between social and political representation for the rural poor. First, depending on local political demography, electoral pressures may lead to a blurring of important class, ethnic, and gender conflicts, weakening the social organization's capacity to represent its original base. Second, electoral politics may permit social organization leaders to "take off" from their bases and, with the help of new national allies, pursue individual ambitions while leaving their original constituency underrepresented. Third, political party competition may introduce ideological divisions into organizations previously united by social and economic demands. Fourth, as social organizations get involved in electoral politics they may endanger their autonomy vis-à-vis political parties even if those parties are their allies.

[26]Note, for example, the case of the Coalición de Ejidos de la Costa Grande, based around Atoyac, Guerrero, one of Mexico's most consolidated, democratic, and autonomous regional organizations (A. García 1989). Most of the rank and file supported Cárdenas for president in 1988. The leadership was concerned about the long-term survival of their self-managed economic development project and chose to remain nonpartisan, knowing the government's unforgiving attitude toward open political opposition. Rank-and-file Cardenista sentiment expressed itself again in the 1989 municipal elections, which led to months of broad-based antifraud protests. After a long, drawn-out conflict, a compromise PRI candidate was named to lead a pluralistic municipal council, but the most authoritarian elements in the ruling party struck back again. The state police commander took over the town hall, proclaiming, "I've got a thousand men here to sit down and talk with you." Meanwhile, PRD leaders bypassed the Coalición in their own closed-door negotiations with the government. Both "official" and opposition party elites pushed the group to define its political allegiances, but the Coalición made the political choice to emphasize its democratic economic development project while defending electoral democracy from a nonpartisan stance. See Moguel 1991; Nava 1991. For background, see Bartra 1992.

NATIONAL IDEOLOGICAL CONTEXT

The constitutional reform brought together two debates that had long been kept separate—the agrarian issue, dealing with land tenure, and the agricultural issue, dealing with production and growth. Agrarian policy has long reflected a political stalemate. No significant land distribution has been carried out since 1976; land reform advocates were unable to revive it or to slow the widespread distribution of "untouchability certificates" for private landowners. At the same time, critics of the ejido were unable to challenge its legitimacy until recently. Because of this stalemate, since 1976 the rural policy debate had been largely framed in terms of agricultural rather than agrarian issues. The reform of Article 27 broke the stalemate and "re-agrarianized" the debate.[27]

The ideological importance of the constitutional reform resonated far beyond the agricultural sector, since it served as yet another sign that no hitherto sacred postrevolutionary legacy would remain untouched. This does not mean that the constitutional reform was a response to pressures from private capital, though one could get that impression from the business press. Rather, land tenure reform became an issue in the business media in response to lobbying by pro-deregulation advocates within the government who needed support to offset resistance by more traditional members of the political class.[28]

The rural ideological context has changed far beyond the land tenure issue. Official discourse recasts the entire relationship of the state to the rural poor. The new agrarian ideology keeps the state involved in rural society, but in a very different role. Postrevolutionary populism acknowledged the existence and legitimacy of class conflict; the state's role was to regulate this conflict and side, at least sometimes, with the oppressed. With the new discourse of Solidarity, the state reaffirmed that poverty is a problem, but it rejected its past position that class oppression was the cause and held that class struggle is certainly not the

---

[27]The previous round of the debate took place in 1980–1981, in the context of the Agrarian Development Law (LFA). Critics of the LFA misread the balance of forces within the state, equating the Mexican Food System (SAM) and the LFA in a contestatory discourse that fell into the trap of believing the state's own rhetoric, rather than looking closely at what state managers were actually doing with oil boom resources. In spite of the drastic predictions at the time that the LFA would roll back the agrarian reform, discreet critics within the government inserted provisions in the enabling legislation that made ejido joint ventures unattractive to business. The LFA served primarily as a pro-business ideological signal while the rest of the state's agricultural apparatus went about rapidly expanding interventionist operations in the name of the SAM (Fox 1993).

[28]The reform of Article 27 is a necessary but not sufficient condition for encouraging significant agribusiness investment, since many factors other than land tenure influence private agricultural investment decisions (such as trade barriers and, especially, exchange rates). The degree to which rural investment will increase and create significant numbers of jobs beyond a few irrigated enclaves is unknown. During the first year at least, most private investors maintained a wait-and-see attitude (Schwedel 1992). The first high-profile joint ventures between large firms and ejidos were highly subsidized by the government, so the prospects for a "spread effect" are uncertain.

solution. Rather than proposing to regulate markets and promote production, the state offered a practical problem-solving partnership with the poor to confront problems of public works and social welfare.[29]

Official rural development ideology occupies a remarkably broad ideological space. As with Solidarity's discourse, official rural development ideology synthesizes alternatives from both left and right, which divides potential opponents across the spectrum. There is something for almost everyone. As in other policy arenas, Salinas preempted the PAN's position with his focus on land tenure security, investor confidence, and the withdrawal of the state. The PRD, in contrast, rejected the reform in its entirety, defending the institutional legacy of agrarian state intervention inherited from Cárdenas and Echeverría. Initial PRD declarations insisted that the ejido as such did not have fundamental flaws. Instead, its main problem was lack of funding. This position was reportedly drawn up by former leaders of the PRI's dissident Democratic Current, with little consultation of national and regional peasant leaders, including many who sympathize with the PRD. In contrast to the PRD's defense of the institutional status quo, many peasant leaders across the political spectrum felt that the system did indeed need basic change (as well as increased funding). Although many differed with Salinas about the changes needed, they supported the official promises to reduce paternalistic government controls and to increase ejido autonomy.[30]

THE POLITICS OF RURAL POLICY MAKING

The two tracks of rural policy making—agricultural and agrarian—began to come together in the process of state withdrawal. In agricultural policy, state economic intervention shifted from sector-wide to organization-specific. In the past, declared policy toward the peasant economy focused on efforts to increase production on the smallest plots, though in practice it was tilted toward surplus-producing peasants and larger farmers (Fox 1993). State managers thought their capacity to regulate the economy was virtually unlimited, and sector-wide policies

[29]The ideology of Solidarity involves a sophisticated combination of diverse political strands, just like its Polish namesake. From the center, Solidarity draws on Christian Democratic notions of community participation. From the right, Solidarity resonates with the patterns of nonconfrontational, pro-management styles of labor organization that have long had influence from Costa Rica to Monterrey. Solidarity draws most directly, however, from Mexico's social left tradition, which has long played a key role in organizing autonomous social movements. Drawing its original ideological inspiration from the idealistic French interpretation of China's Cultural Revolution, these political currents focused on building mass organizations that would give poor people more control over their daily lives. The politics that is considered to really matter is local. Like the social left, however, Solidarity's idea of participation is limited to local participation, excluding debate over national alternatives.

[30]Not coincidentally, the authors of the new pro-autonomy official discourse included former critics Arturo Warman and Gustavo Gordillo (previously one of UNORCA's leading strategists). For his UNORCA-era works, see Gordillo 1988a, 1988b. For more recent analyses, see Gordillo 1990, 1992, and his remarks in CNC 1991b.

were the norm. As recently as the 1980–1982 Mexican Food System era, some policy makers considered rainfed peasant producers to be economic actors of national importance. Now they are treated as targets of welfare rather than production policy.

Since the withdrawal of the state in the late 1980s, peasant production policies have been targeted in terms of groups with bargaining power rather than the sector as a whole.[31] Targeting peasant production policy combines substantive concessions to the generally better endowed minority who already produce a surplus for the market, while assuming that most subsistence and sub-subsistence producers should change their occupations. This changing economic policy terrain inherently segments production politics in two ways. First, it reinforces the gap between the organized and the unorganized (the majority of ejidos, for example, do not function as economic units).[32] Second, it creates sharp political trade-offs for organizations, since those who challenge the national policies risk losing access to their targeted concessions. The outcome is much cheaper for the state than trying to increase the efficiency and accountability of past sector-wide policies. Moreover, as long as targeting is flexible, it can manage most protest.

For those producer movements that are trying to broaden and consolidate the organized smallholder enclaves that might have a chance of economic survival in the future, the path has been called the "appropriation of the production process." Advocates of peasant organization-managed production within the state turned this into official discourse, especially while Gustavo Gordillo was undersecretary of agriculture during 1989–1990. One of the most developed examples of state support for this process is in the coffee sector, but the results so far are mixed, highlighting the limits of group-specific supports in the absence of an overall hospitable policy environment for smallholder production. The

---

[31]The Ministry of Agriculture signed numerous "concertation" agreements to fund the development projects of producer organizations early in the Salinas administration. Both "official" and autonomous organizations were funded. Government-affiliated producer groups were funded in part to support the more "modern" wing of the "official" CNC vs. the entrenched agrarian political class (see discussion of CNC below), while many autonomous groups were funded in part because some had solid development management track records, and in part to dissuade them from joining the overt political opposition during the period of intense polarization in the aftermath of the contested 1988 elections. The traditional political class, threatened by both trends, counterattacked behind the scenes, claiming that this funding strategy was responsible for a perceived increase in producer protest in 1989–1990. Perhaps as a result, in 1990 a new coalition was named to run the Ministry of Agriculture, combining a strong secretary associated with the old political class with a pro-market deregulation economist in charge of policy reform. The concertation strategy funding was eliminated.

[32]See Morett Sánchez 1991: 9. There is little national public survey data regarding levels of peasant organization. As of 1981, 26 percent of *ejidatarios* were members of existing ejido unions (Fernández and Rello 1984). This finding seems to have been confirmed by Morett Sánchez, who also found that 21 percent of ejidos have some kind of internal organization (1991: 89). Varela's survey of rural individuals found that 18 percent participate in some form of organization (Varela et al. 1991: 8).

coffee sector is an especially important case because coffee is one of the few export crops grown by smallholders, and it supports two million people.[33] This process of extending self-management with capitalized group credit, processing, and marketing has clear limits as a policy alternative, since most peasants lack either the necessary organizational resources or viable productive alternatives (Bartra 1989a, 1990, 1991).

Much of the targeted supports for producer organizations, as well as the welfare supports for "nonproductive" producers, are channeled through the National Solidarity Program (PRONASOL; also referred to simply as "Solidarity"). PRONASOL combined elements of traditional clientelism with relatively "modern" pluralism (see Cornelius, Craig, and Fox 1994; Dresser 1991; Fox 1994). The principal traditional channel was through the municipal authority, including both public works and Solidarity's production credit line (on-your-word loans) for producers who fell below the government bank's threshold in terms of ability to pay. Mayors selected the recipients of these soft loans, who got the equivalent of U.S.$100 each—far less than enough to invest in production, and less than enough to support consumption until the harvest comes in. PRONASOL's spectrum of programs also included more innovative production-oriented programs, which built in more accountability mechanisms and strengthened representative producer organizations, especially in the case of the National Indigenous Institute's support for autonomous coffee-producer groups and its Regional Solidarity Funds for Indigenous Peoples' Development. The Regional Solidarity Funds aim to turn local socioeconomic investment decision making over to autonomous regional councils of representative indigenous social and economic organizations. In contrast to most PRONASOL programs, where the state created its own interlocutors, these new channels for pluralistic state-society interaction could bolster existing representative organizations.[34]

---

[33]On the politics of the coffee sector, see Ejea and Hernández 1991; Moguel and Aranda 1992; Hernández and Célis 1992.

[34]For details, see Fox 1994. More generally, one can frame the range of possible PRONASOL policy implementation scenarios along a continuum with three distinct categories. At one extreme are those social policies that are "captured" by traditional political elites. Their policy implementation style is generally associated with clientelism, corporatism, and corruption. At the other possible extreme are PRONASOL's most innovative elements, associated with the official discourse of equity, transparency, pluralism, and power sharing with civil society. In between are those PRONASOL activities whose targeting and policy style are most ambiguous. They are not traditional, in the sense that they do not condition access to benefits with crude partisan electoral manipulation. Nor are they completely pluralistic, in the sense of respecting the political diversity of civil society, since beneficiaries are obliged to organize through certain official channels, to petition within predetermined constraints, and to avoid public criticism of the government's broader policies. In this scenario, all politics is required to remain local. Citizens must sacrifice some of their political rights in exchange for "social rights." This subtle modernization of the state structuring of interest representation is sometimes called neocorporatism in Mexico, although the concept is usually poorly specified. This view of PRONASOL is widely held among Mexico's social movements. For example, in

Agricultural policy came firmly under the control of the pro-market de-regulation advocates by early 1991, and land tenure policy was next on their agenda. The debate followed a similar trend, with peasant organizations largely unable to influence national policy making but finding some room for maneuver in terms of their particular regional problems and projects. Policy was determined largely by the balance of forces within the executive branch. Peasant organizations had at most a partial, reactive impact, such as temporarily reversing some of the grain import policy decisions and encouraging the president to issue his "Ten Points of Freedom and Justice for the Countryside" as a follow-up to the Article 27 reform announcement.

The constitutional land tenure reform debate revealed a great deal about how decisions are made, although many crucial details remain secret. It was carried out in three phases. First, Salinas's cabinet and advisers debated options behind closed doors. The reform that was made public was a compromise, including pro-business and pro-ejido measures. The original proposals ranged from those that did not want a constitutional reform at all (promoted especially by individuals with strong ties to the old political class) to moderate pro-deregulation reforms, to more radical deregulation proposals. Some of the more business-oriented cabinet members reportedly supported immediate, obligatory parceling and privatization of all ejido land, although one policy maker suggested that this was a bargaining tactic to make the voluntary privatization position seem more moderate by comparison. In the end, the president's proposal left the privatization decision in the hands of *ejidatarios* rather than imposing wholesale privatization from above, consistent with official *autonomista* discourse.[35] Policy

the view of a leader of one of Mexico's more consolidated autonomous indigenous producers' organizations, "with PRONASOL the government tries to create the appearance that it recognizes us, but the reality is different; everything comes with strings attached" (author interview, October 1991).

[35]Dr. Gordillo, undersecretary of agrarian reform and former independent peasant movement strategist, framed the agrarian policy debate in a provocative way, arguing that it transcended past left-right dichotomies. In a September 1992 presentation at a meeting of the Latin American Studies Association in Los Angeles, he suggested that the agrarian debate over the last two decades can be cast along two axes, with more-vs.-less political freedom for peasants along one axis and more-vs.-less freedom for the market along the other.

	More state intervention ↔ More market freedom	
More state political control	Traditional corporatists	Neoliberal policy makers
↕		
More freedom of association for peasants	Most autonomous peasant groups	Article 27 reform?

In this view, the traditional corporatists in the old political class and the "official" peasant organizations defended both authoritarian politics and state intervention in the agricultural economy. The neoliberal policy makers promoted deregulation and free markets, but they did not encourage a rural political opening. The autonomous producer groups pushed for increased political pluralism and public-sector accountability to organized peasants, but they called for the state to play a major role in buffering the social impact of the market in the peasant economy. In this view, the constitutional reform represents a compromise, satisfying the pro-market forces with significant deregulation while recognizing the autonomy of the ejidos from government control and the legitimacy of independent peasant organizations.

makers who advocated the voluntary privatization approach emerged from the intense closed-door debates claiming that they won the first round, but many peasant movement leaders—not privy to the debate—disagreed, highlighting a major gap between ostensible allies in state and society.

The next phase of the debate began when the reform initiative became public. The proposal caught peasant leaders off guard across the spectrum, without coherent alternatives. This public phase of the debate split virtually all major peasant organizations along a whole series of fault lines (Hernández 1992a, 1992b; Moguel 1992, 1994). The initiative was seen as a threat by both traditional corporatist bosses and the traditional left, while the new generation of autonomous organizations was at least as angry about the closed-door, top-down process as it was about aspects of the initiative itself. While very few changes in the proposed constitutional amendment were forthcoming, the debate did oblige Salinas to meet with representative peasant leaders, leading him to elaborate on the ostensibly pro-peasant elements of the reform in his Ten Points, drawing directly from the words of independent leaders ("peasants should be the subjects, not the objects, of change").[36]

The Salinas administration managed to persuade almost all national and regional peasant leaders, whether "official" or independent, to either support or not oppose the reforms of Article 27.[37] The Permanent Agrarian Congress (CAP, the national umbrella group that included almost all major peasant organizations and originally promised more peasant representation in the policy process) turned out to have very little impact on the government's proposal. The government did address one of the group's important concerns—the distribution "backlog" for lands officially ceded to claimants by "presidential resolution" but de facto still in the possession of private owners. The government made payments to organizations for the value of the contested lands. Leaders who still opposed the Article 27 reform outright were threatened with loss of access to the few government support programs still available, as part of the overall policy of limiting support to peasant production to targeted programs.[38] Leaders who

---

[36]Even though concerned independent peasant leaders won relatively little in terms of substantive concessions with the Ten Points, they at least achieved recognized interlocutor status outside the "official" confines of the Permanent Agrarian Congress. The president began the Ten Points with: "This meeting with peasant representatives, with real leaders, is important." For the reform, the Ten Points, and the official positions of the main national organizations, see CAP 1992. For a range of critiques, see Bartra 1992; CIOAC 1991; Paré 1991. The most comprehensive forum for public debate, including peasant leaders, policy makers, and independent agrarian experts, was the Monday supplement of *Unomasuno*, edited by Julio Moguel beginning in November 1991 (which later became the monthly *La Jornada del Campo*).

[37]See the Manifesto of December 2, 1991, published in all major Mexican dailies.

[38]The leader of one traditional populist peasant organization, the Movement of the 400 Pueblos, accepted government payments in return for supporting the reform but then threatened to oppose it in an effort to extract further payments. Some government officials considered this blackmail, beyond the usual bounds of corruption, and jailed the leader.

signed on risked alienating major segments of their rank-and-file membership, which had very little information on which to base their own decisions and even less opportunity to express themselves in the narrow window of time nominally open for input. Nevertheless, open protest of the Article 27 reform was minimal.

The third phase of the debate focused on the enabling legislation, and here the pro-peasant organization policy makers lost ground. For the *autonomista* position, perhaps the single most important procedure in the reform is the privatization decision-making process, to be carried out in ejido assemblies. The fine print regulating the decision-making procedures is perhaps not so crucial in areas of consolidated peasant organization strength, but only a minority of the rural poor have such local advocates. Because of the lingering power of traditional caciques and the growing strength of agribusiness, it is possible that some minority of ejido assemblies will make major land-titling decisions that flout the will of the majority. The key question is how large a minority, which in turn depends on whether the decision-making procedures create "*candados*" (literally padlocks) that make manipulation more difficult. Some optimistic pro-ejido policy makers claimed that the enabling legislation would require a three-fourths majority to allow privatization of ejido lands. After some public debate, however, the legal threshold fell, quietly but significantly. The final enabling legislation indeed requires a two-thirds majority, but there is a loophole. If the first effort to call an assembly does not produce a quorum, the legal minimum for the quorum for the next assembly called is only one-half plus one of the membership (Articles 26 and 27). In this scenario—not difficult to arrange—one-third of the membership can therefore decide for the rest of the ejido, indicating an important shift in the mix of pro-ejido and pro-privatization elements of the reform.[39] More generally, the importance of the assembly in the legislation means that the political character of the privatization decision-making process will depend on the degree of internal democracy in each ejido.

The implementation of the Article 27 reform will test the limits of state capacity. Lessons from Salinas's earlier policy successes may not apply to the ejido reform. These initiatives involved surprise radical moves by using concentrated state power (for example, removing union bosses, privatizing the banks, and so forth), and they tended to work (see Córdoba 1991). Such was the process of legislative approval of the

---

[39] Another revealing indicator of the shift in the center of gravity of the pro-business/pro-ejido mix of provisions is the role of the "*áreas comunes*" (common lands) of the ejidos, which account for two-thirds of their area. The second of the Ten Points promised that: "To propose that the common lands be inalienable establishes at the constitutional level that social property in Mexico will be permanent" (in CAP 1992: 28). In the enabling legislation, however, the ejido "will be able to transfer control over common lands to corporations or joint ventures in which the ejido participates," under the oversight of the agrarian attorney general (Article 75). The implications are especially serious in the forestry sector.

Article 27 reform. But its implementation will be much more complex than past policy successes, requiring adjudication of hundreds of thousands of micro-decisions regarding land titles and boundaries, far from the purview of federal reformists. Providing written titles for ejido parcels is a prerequisite for most other land tenure changes, including sale, rental, and mortgaging of plots, but government plans to finish this difficult process within a year had to be revised (Nauman 1993).

As the ejido privatization trickles down through the system and confronts peasants directly, many will fully perceive the importance of the changes for the first time. Peasants may react defensively if the ejido privatization process is carried out with less democracy and accountability than promised, which is especially likely in the poorest rural areas of central and southern Mexico. Pro-ejido organization policy makers acknowledged that the process will be flawed in some cases, but they hoped that the importance of the decision would provoke a revitalization of grassroots participation within many ejidos (Warman 1992).

CHANGING CHANNELS OF RURAL SOCIAL REPRESENTATION

The economic-vs.-political cleavage continues to crosscut the whole spectrum of the peasant movement. Both independent and "official" peasant organizations can be divided into more political and more economic development-oriented wings. Among the nongovernmental groups, the militant movements (generally based in the poorest and most conflictive rural regions) tend to identify ideologically with the political opposition more generally. These include the Coordinating Committee of Agrarian Organizations (COA), the Independent Confederation of Agricultural Workers and Peasants (CIOAC), and the National "Plan de Ayala" Coordinating Committee (CNPA). Some are linked to political parties, but most are not. They were strongest in the early 1970s and grew again in the early 1980s, but by the late 1980s most had succumbed to internal divisions and pressures from the state.

Since the early 1980s, the main trend in the peasant movement was the change of terrain from agrarian to agricultural issues. Organized smallholders increasingly developed their own self-managed economic projects and learned how to bargain with both state and market. In contrast to past traditions of militant, all-or-nothing confrontation with the state, these organizations combined peaceful mass mobilization with practical negotiating styles and concrete policy alternatives. Many of these regional organizations formalized their convergence in the UNORCA in 1985. The UNORCA process later spun off a series of more sectorally focused national networks of peasant-managed credit unions, fertilizer distributors, and corn, coffee, and lumber producers. Many are struggling to survive in the new policy environment, encouraging a tendency to turn inward to defend their existing membership rather than broadening to include a larger fraction of small producers. Most are currently nonpartisan, but if the government does not follow through with its promises to buffer the impact of the economic changes, then some may decide to become active in rural electoral opposition. The long-term shift continues from the "central" or classic top-down pyramidal structure to the more horizontal network as the main form of national rural interest articulation.[40]

The government-affiliated groups, most within the CNC (National Peasants' Confederation), can also be divided into more political and producer-oriented wings. The political groups include the agrarian elements of the PRI left over from their heyday in the mid-1970s, and the old-fashioned rural electoral machines linked to authoritarian governors, some of whom quietly opposed Salinas on many issues. Some of these coalitions are behind continuing rural human rights problems, especially in Chiapas, Oaxaca, and Guerrero (Americas Watch 1990, 1991; Amnesty International 1986). The new, presidentially installed leader of the CNC, a former UN-ORCA strategist, emerged from a base in the "modern" commodity-producer branches and began to shake up the organization with what he called "CNCestroika." The power struggle within the CNC continued and its outcome is still unclear.[41] There was some common ground between the producer-group wings of both the independent and official organizations, and they began to meet at pluralistic conferences in 1991 and 1992 under the banner of the "New Peasant Movement." At the third such meeting, however, one speaker from an independent regional organization dared to criticize agricultural policy in Salinas's presence, embarrassing the reform leadership of the CNC and leading them to break off the convergence with the nongovernmental organizations (Hernández 1992a, 1992b).

---

[40]Many groups that stood to the left of UNORCA until the late 1980s, such as the General Worker-Peasant-Popular Union (UGOCP) (or the parts of the CNPA, have since moved quickly toward the center with their own *"cambio de terreno"* and signed a wide range of concertation agreements to get official funding and private-sector partners for their rural development projects. Some UGOCP leaders now lobby actively in favor of government policy and joint ventures. The CIOAC had in some ways pioneered this strategy when it received massive government funding for its national credit union in 1981. The Comisión Nacional Bancaria claimed that the credit union was a financial failure and withdrew official registry in 1991 after years of losses (perhaps not coincidentally, around the time of the ejido reform debate).

[41]See Araujo et al. 1992; CNC 1991a; Hernández 1992a, 1992b. Upon assuming the CNC national leadership, Araujo began "reorienting" most of the state and regional bodies (Pérez 1992). As of May 1992, seventeen state branches of the CNC had been shaken up to varying degrees, through ad hoc combinations of local elections and behind-the-scenes negotiated power sharing between the newly ascendent modernizers and the more traditional agrarian apparatus. Only Campeche and half of Coahuila changed leadership through direct base elections. Relatively few of the commodity associations (bean and ixtle producer groups were among them) were brought quickly under clear control of the new leadership, while the top leadership of some important ones (associations of corn and coffee producers) remained in the hands of the "dinosaurs" (author interview with member of the National Executive Committee of the CNC, May 1992). The CNC had little influence in the debate over the reform of Article 27.

The Article 27 debate greatly widened the existing gap between national and local peasant organizations. Most ended up internally divided, and the old-fashioned agrarian politics of both left and right were weakened. Even the CIOAC, the national group that most firmly opposed the reform, experienced a split as key elements of its Chiapas state leadership came out in favor of the reform, apparently under intense pressure from the governor. Even the CNC lacked influence. In fact, its old-guard leadership was one of the main targets of the reform.[42] National leaders were sandwiched between strong pressure from the government to at least frame their criticism in terms of nominal support, and a rank and file that was poorly informed and little engaged with the intricacies of proposed changes in agrarian law. Since the PRD declared that any peasant leader who did not share the party's position of total rejection was a sellout, it lost credibility with independent peasant leaders whose criticisms of the reform were more nuanced.

While the ejido reform and subsidy cuts encourage people to abandon family farming, farmworkers still lack social and political representation, in spite of their growing importance in the rural population.[43] Farmworkers are not unionized, nor are their interests represented by existing smallholder organizations. Farmworker unionization efforts peaked in the late 1970s and early 1980s, but the combination of repression with powerful labor market and migration pressures made sustained collective action very difficult (López Monjardín 1991; Zabin 1992). While independent farmworker unionization has long been de facto prohibited (except for a few official CTM contracts in Sinaloa), President Salinas promised to permit it as part of his Article 27 ejido reform package. Meanwhile, many of the organizations that in principle could have taken the president at his word and tried to organize farmworker unions were focused primarily on holding their own in the general atmosphere of economic uncertainty in the peasant economy.[44]

---

[42]During the early stages of the public debate, the CNC's Political Commission made a futile call for "unanimous rejection" of ejido privatization (Rojas 1991). After Article 27 was changed and the Salinista reformists had taken over the national CNC leadership, the new secretary general complained that government policy undermined his efforts to support the constitutional reform. Araujo declared: "the absence of policies in support of agriculture, together with a conservative and bureaucratic attitude in the government agencies, has generated feelings of irritation and deception among campesinos, who blame the situation on the reforms of Article 27" (Orduña 1993).

[43]According to a 1988 Ministry of Agriculture survey, farmworkers number over 4.6 million. Even with this low estimate, they account for 78 percent of the rural population. Almost one-third are women (Varela et al. 1991: 16).

[44]Some analysts of rural workers have noted trends toward the concentration of the farmworker population in the town centers of the agroexport regions, leading in turn to a "rurbanization" of their demands (De Grammont 1992). Rather than pursue the risky and often fruitless path of unionization, farmworkers have a much greater chance of winning improvements when they press "urban-popular" demands such as electricity or water. See López Monjardín 1991; Zabin 1992 on farmworker movements.

New forms of social organization are emerging in rural Mexico around issues of ethnic self-determination, natural resources, human rights, and gender, but the process is uneven. The most important new kind of rural organization is explicitly ethnically based.[45] The process began in the 1970s but accelerated significantly in light of the preparations for the five hundredth anniversary of the Conquest. Various initiatives to form national networks have yet to produce a unified national interlocutor.[46] The most notable indigenous protest—on October 12, 1992—was in San Cristóbal, Chiapas, where ten thousand people from at least seven ethnic groups marched, tearing down along the way a statue that was a hated symbol of colonial rule (Pérez and Henríquez 1992).

President Salinas actively tried to frame the national debates on indigenous issues, including a proposal to reform Article 4 of the Constitution to recognize officially Mexico as a multiethnic nation (though in the part of the Constitution dedicated to the protection of minors). The proposed reform was quite general and far from radical, but it provoked sharp opposition from both the PAN and the PRI. Even important elements of the PRD were unenthusiastic. The legislative lobbying coalition that eventually passed the amendment brought both independent and "official" indigenous rights activists together. As with the fine print of Article 27, however, the Article 4 reform's still-undefined enabling legislation will most clearly reveal the balance of forces and shape its actual impact in practice.[47] (At the end of 1993, this legislation was still tabled, and the reform was therefore frozen.)

Salinas also responded to increasing indigenous mobilization with an eighteenfold increase in the budget of the National Indigenous Institute (INI) and the nominal exemption of indigenous land reform communities from the privatization option under the new Article 27 (in the name of "respecting the territorial integrity" of ancestral lands). They can engage in long-term contracts with private enterprises, which is especially important in the forestry sector, and they also are permitted to vote to become ejidos and then decide to privatize their lands.

The increased national projection of ethnic movements for self-determination overlaps with two related movements with similarly long histories combined with recent growth: the movements for local control of natural resources and campaigns in defense of human rights. Indige-

---

[45] Mexico's fifty-six indigenous peoples are estimated to account for between 9 and 15 percent of the total population, adding up to the largest indigenous population in absolute terms in the hemisphere.

[46] For the most comprehensive overview of recent trends in ethnic politics, see Sarmiento 1991; see also Consejo Mexicano 1991. For background, see Mejía Piñeiros and Sarmiento 1987. For an important analysis of the social construction of ethnicity in Mexico, see Nagengast and Kearney 1990.

[47] For the best coverage of the Article 4 debate, see the journal *México Indígena* (now called *Ojarasca*).

nous peoples had been active in defense of their natural resources (especially in the cases of forestry and water rights) long before environmentalists became available as political allies (Bray 1991; Bray and Irvine 1993). The most notable indigenous-led environmental victory so far was the suspension of a planned hydroelectric dam in the Nahuatl region of the Alto Balsas, in alliance with Mexico City and international environmentalist and indigenous rights advocates—the first such victory in Mexico (Good 1992; M. García 1992).

Ethnic rights movements have also worked closely with human rights advocates, especially those based in the church, since statesanctioned violence and impunity are concentrated against the indigenous population (Pérez 1993). The 1992 Xi' Nich' grassroots protest march from Chiapas to Mexico City put the issue directly on the national agenda. Following the successful antifraud marches from San Luis Potosí and Tabasco, the Chiapas march focused specifically on violence and police abuse rather than electoral rights (Bellinghausen 1992).

Rural social movements for gender equality lag far behind ethnic, environmental, and human rights movements. Women's rights were left out of the Article 27 reform (Rojas 1992). Government programs have promoted group economic projects for women for two decades, but it is difficult to speak of a specific rural women's movement. These local development projects have yet to "scale up" to generate social subjects and encourage rural women to represent themselves politically, with the exception of several autonomous regional producer organizations that have promoted networks of women's economic projects.[48]

CONCLUSIONS

The broad trends that frame the diverse patterns in party politics, ideology, policy, and social organization in the peasant economy can be understood most generally in terms of the competing options of "exit" and "voice."[49] How will peasants decide whether to leave the countryside or to fight to remain peasants?

First, the economic viability of most of the peasantry—always precarious—is under qualitatively new levels of strain. Yet the response has not been, and probably will not be, overtly political. A few will be

---

[48]Pioneering women's networks have emerged within mixed-gender regional organizations in the Coalición de Ejidos de la Costa Grande (Guerrero), the Unión Campesina de Alamos (Sonora), and the Unión de Ejidos "Lázaro Cárdenas" (Ahuacatlán, Nayarit). See Aranda 1988; Arriaga et al. n.d.; Stephen 1991.

[49]Hirschman (1970: 76) observes that "the exit option can sharply reduce the probability that the voice option will be taken up." He also introduces the concept of loyalty, which makes exit less likely and may give voice more scope, depending on actor perceptions of their ability to exercise influence (p. 77). In this view, exit vs. voice decisions by Mexico's rural poor would depend on their estimation of their ability to influence the policy process. In some organizations, the threat of exit increases the power of voice and therefore loyalty, but this does not seem to hold for Mexico's agricultural policy makers.

able to capitalize themselves and become small farmers. This is not an option for most smallholders, but some may be able to ally with larger producers to lobby for particularistic benefits (such as trade-linked compensatory payments via PROCAMPO). Most of rural civil society will respond with family-based survival strategies most of the time, including out-migration and illicit crop cultivation, rather than engage in sometimes risky and often fruitless collective action. This could change if national political competition manages to make mass action seem more meaningful to more people at a future turning point, but this prospect will be decided in Mexico City. The first trend is exit.

The second trend, unfolding at the same time, is voice—the increasing capacity of peasant movements to speak for themselves, as a significant minority of rural civil society represents itself directly. This growing center of political gravity has shown a qualitatively new capacity to propose practical, pro-self-management policy alternatives. In spite of increased party competition in national politics, the peasant movement's autonomous political "gray area" between traditional "official" corporatism and militant independent opposition is growing rather than shrinking. Political parties are still not involved in the way most peasants are represented, most of the time, though municipal-level democratization has led to local breakthroughs in several regions.

This trend has contradictory elements. As peasant organizations move away from past efforts toward class-wide representation and demands, they find themselves pulled between interest group and civic identities. They mobilize for greater governmental accountability in the rural development process, but to what degree is there a spillover effect that benefits the vast majority who lack autonomous self-representation?

Is the withdrawal of the state from regulation of much of the peasant economy risky from the point of view of political stability? While growing numbers of agrarian brushfires may be in store as the ejido privatization process gradually unfolds, so far state managers have proven adept at putting them out before they can come together into a larger conflagration. Until the end of 1993, immediate production issues such as lack of credit had provoked more protest than had the constitutional changes in land tenure.

In this context, the state's economic withdrawal seems to be implicitly based on a twofold political calculation. First, policy makers seem to be gambling that most of those who are supposed to leave peasant agriculture for good will be too busy trying to find employment to engage in protest. Opposition movements are growing among immigrants in California, but since Mexicans lack the right to vote via absentee ballots, most parties have little incentive to appeal to their interests.

Second, policy makers seem to be betting that their urban strategy will be able to incorporate those rural out-migrants who go to Mexican cities. Recent rural reforms undermine one of the electoral pillars of the regime by greatly reducing the proportion of rural voters. In the medium run, however, it could well be easier for reformist state managers to incorporate displaced peasants into Solidarity's urban neighborhood organizations than it would be to create effective channels for rural participation. For those policy makers who want to keep antipoverty spending to a minimum, it is probably cheaper to encourage peasants to join the urban informal sector than it would be to sustain gainful employment in the countryside—as long as the peasants do not protest too much on their way to the city.

For those peasant movements that choose voice over exit, targeted production and welfare supports, combined with the threat of their withdrawal, will probably be sufficient to keep most dissent within the bounds of the political system (though authoritarian Chiapas may be an exception). The government's strategy depends on keeping peasant movements relatively small and segmented, because if they were to grow significantly, then they would be likely to propose broader policies to support the peasant economy as a whole, thereby challenging the government's low-cost targeted concession strategy. Political stability depends, then, on most of those whose livelihoods are being restructured choosing exit over voice. If voice becomes a more plausible political option for the rural poor, then the political outcome becomes increasingly unpredictable.

REFERENCES

Americas Watch. 1990. *Human Rights in Mexico: A Policy of Impunity.* New York: Human Rights Watch.
———. 1991. "Unceasing Abuses. Human Rights in Mexico One Year After the Introduction of Reform." New York, September.
Amnesty International. 1986. *Mexico. Human Rights in Rural Areas.* London: Amnesty International Publications.
———. 1991. *Mexico. Torture with Impunity.* New York: Amnesty International USA.
Appendini, Kirsten. 1991. "Los campesinos maiceros frente a la política de abasto: una contradicción permanente," *Comercio Exterior* 41:10 (October).
———. 1992. *De la milpa a los tortibonos: la reestructuración de la política alimentaria en México.* Mexico City: El Colegio de México/Instituto de Investigaciones de las Naciones Unidas para el Desarrollo Social.
Aranda, Josefina, ed. 1988. *Las mujeres en el campo.* Oaxaca: Universidad Autónoma "Benito Juárez" de Oaxaca.
Araujo, Hugo Andrés, et al. 1992. "¿Es o no es viable el campo mexicano?" *Nexos* 179 (November).
Arriaga, G., et al. n.d. *La participación de las mujeres en organizaciones campesinas.* Mexico City: Programa de Apoyo a la Mujer/Friedrich Ebert Stiftung.
Barberán, José, et al. 1988. *Radiografía del fraude: análisis de los datos oficiales del 6 de julio.* Mexico City: Nuestro Tiempo.

Bardacke, Ted. 1991. "Fresh Produce Exporters Look Beyond Barriers for Bountiful Harvest," *El Financiero International*, December 23.

Barkin, David, and Blanca Suárez. 1985. *El fin de la autosuficiencia alimentaria*. Mexico City: Océano/Centro de Ecodesarrollo.

Bartra, Armando. 1989a. "La apropiación del proceso productivo como forma de lucha," *Pueblo* 12:143 (April).

————. 1989b. "Prólogo al libro de Gustavo Gordillo: Estado, mercados y movimiento campesino," *Pueblo* 12 (May–June): 144–45.

————. 1990. "De modernidad, miseria extrema y productores organizados," *El Cotidiano* 7:36 (July–August).

————. 1991. *Pros, contras y asegunes de la 'apropiación del proceso productivo.'* Cuadernos Desarrollo de Base, no. 2.

————. 1992. "La ardua construcción del ciudadano. Notas sobre el movimiento cívico y la lucha gremial." In *Autonomía y nuevos sujetos del desarrollo rural*, edited by Julio Moguel, Carlota Botey, and Luis Hernández. Mexico City: Siglo Veintiuno/CEHAM.

Bellinghausen, Hermann. 1992. "Abril de Xi' Nich'," *Ojarasca* 8 (May).

Bonfil, Guillermo. 1990. *México profundo: una civilización negada*. Mexico City: Grijalbo/Consejo Nacional para la Cultura y las Artes.

Bray, David. 1991. "The Struggle for the Forest: Conservation and Development in the Sierra Juárez," *Grassroots Development* 15:3.

Bray, David, and Dominique Irvine, eds. 1993. "Resource and Sanctuary: Indigenous Peoples, Ancestral Rights and the Forests of the Americas," *Survival Quarterly* 17:1 (Spring).

Calva, José Luis. 1991. *Probables efectos de un tratado de libre comercio en el campo mexicano*. Mexico City: Fontamara/Friedrich Ebert Stiftung.

Calva, José Luis, et al. 1992. *La agricultura mexicana frente al Tratado de Libre Comercio*. Mexico City: Juan Pablos/Universidad Autónoma Chapingo.

CAP (Congreso Agrario Permanente). 1992. *Memoria sobre la discusión de la reforma al Art. 27 constitucional*. Vol. I. Mexico City: CAP.

CEPAL (Comisión Económica para América Latina). 1982. *Economía campesina y agricultura empresarial*. Mexico City: Siglo Veintiuno/CEPAL.

CIOAC (Central Independiente de Obreros Agrícolas y Campesinos). 1991. "Bajo las banderas de Zapata: una posición campesina unificada ante las reformas (propuesta)," *Cuadernos Agrarios* 3, nueva época (September–December).

CNC (Confederación Nacional Campesina). 1991a. "Congreso Nacional Extraordinario. Conclusiones de las mesas de trabajo."

————. 1991b. "Una vez más: acerca del ejido," *Cuadernillos de Análisis*.

Consejo Mexicano 500 Años de Resistencia India y Popular. 1991. "Declaración de principios y objetivos," *Cuadernos Agrarios* 2, nueva época.

Córdoba, José. 1991. "Diez lecciones de la reforma económica en México," *Nexos* 14:158 (February).

Cornelius, Wayne A. 1992. "Free Trade *Can* Reduce Mexican Migration," *Los Angeles Times*, February 28.

Cornelius, Wayne A., Ann L. Craig, and Jonathan Fox, eds. 1994. *Transforming State-Society Relations in Mexico: The National Solidarity Strategy*. U.S.-Mexico Contemporary Perspectives Series, no. 6. La Jolla: Center for U.S.-Mexican Studies, University of California, San Diego.

Cornelius, Wayne A., Judith Gentleman, and Peter H. Smith, 1989. "Overview: The Dynamics of Political Change in Mexico." In *Mexico's Alternative Political Futures*, edited by W. Cornelius, J. Gentleman, and P. Smith. Monograph Series, no. 30. La Jolla: Center for U.S.-Mexican Studies, University of California, San Diego.

Cornelius, Wayne A., and Philip L. Martin. 1993. *The Uncertain Connection: Free Trade and Mexico-U.S. Migration*. Current Issue Brief Series, no. 5. La Jolla: Center for U.S.-Mexican Studies, University of California, San Diego.

De Grammont, Humberto Carton. 1992. "El campo hacia el fin del milenio," *Nexos* 169 (January).

Dresser, Denise. 1991. *Neopopulist Solutions to Neoliberal Problems: Mexico's National Solidarity Program*. Current Issue Brief Series, no. 3. La Jolla: Center for U.S.-Mexican Studies, University of California, San Diego.

Ejea, Gabriela, and Luis Hernández, eds. 1991. *Cafetaleros, la construcción de la autonomía*. Cuadernos Desarrollo de Base, no. 3.

Encinas, Alejandro, Juan de la Fuente, and Horacio MacKinlay, eds. 1992. *La disputa por los mercados: TLC y sector agropecuario*. Mexico City: Editorial Diana/ Cámara de Diputados, LV Legislatura.

Esteva, Gustavo. 1983. *The Struggle for Rural Mexico*. South Hadley, Mass.: Bergin and Garvey.

Fernández, María Teresa, and Fernando Rello. 1984. *La organización de productores en México*. Mexico City: DICONSA.

Fernández Villegas, Manuel. 1991. *No queremos que nos den, no más que no nos quiten la autonomía campesina en México*. Cuadernos Desarrollo de Base, no. 2.

Fox, Jonathan. 1992. "New Terrain for Rural Politics," *Report on the Americas* 25:5 (May).

———. 1993. *The Politics of Food in Mexico: State Power and Social Mobilization*. Ithaca, N.Y.: Cornell University Press.

———. 1994. "The Difficult Transition from Clientelism to Citizenship: Lessons from Mexico," *World Politics* 46:2 (January).

Fox, Jonathan, and Gustavo Gordillo. 1989. "Between State and Market: The Campesinos' Quest for Autonomy." In *Mexico's Alternative Political Futures*, edited by Wayne A. Cornelius, Judith Gentleman, and Peter H. Smith. Monograph Series, no. 30. La Jolla: Center for U.S.-Mexican Studies, University of California, San Diego.

Fox, Jonathan, and Luis Hernández. 1992. "Mexico's Difficult Democracy: Grassroots Movements, NGOs and Local Government," *Alternatives* 17:2 (Spring).

Gallegos, Elena. 1993. "Promete Salinas apoyos directos a campesinos," *La Jornada*, January 7.

García, Arturo. 1989. "Organización autónoma de productores y lucha campesina en Guerrero," *Pueblo* 12:140 (January).

García, Martha. 1992. "Cancelada la presa en la zona nahua de Guerrero," *Ojarasca* 8 (May).

García de León, Antonio. 1992. "Los regresos de la historia, Chiapas y la reforma del artículo 27," *Ojarasca* 11 (August).

Golden, Tim. 1991. "The Dream of Land Dies Hard in Mexico," *New York Times*, November 27.

González Pacheco, Cuauhtémoc, ed. 1992. *El sector agropecuario mexicano frente al Tratado de Libre Comercio.* Mexico City: Juan Pablos/Universidad Nacional Autónoma de México/Universidad Autónoma Chapingo.

Good, Catherine. 1992. "'Making the Struggle, One Big One,': Nahuatl Resistance to the San Juan Dam, Mexico." Presented to the Yale University Agrarian Studies Colloquium, October 30.

Gordillo, Gustavo. 1988a. *Campesinos al asalto del cielo, de la expropiación estatal a la apropriación campesina.* Mexico City: Siglo Veintiuno.

———. 1988b. *Estado, mercados y movimiento campesino.* Mexico City: Plaza y Valdés/Universidad Autónoma de Zacatecas.

———. 1990. "La inserción de la comunidad rural en la sociedad global. Hacia un nuevo modelo de desarrollo para el campo," *Comercio Exterior* 40:9 (September).

———. 1992. "Dilemas de la nueva reforma agraria." Presented at the conference "The Transformations of Mexican Agriculture," University of California, Berkeley, December 3–4.

Grindle, Merilee. 1986. *State and Countryside.* Baltimore: Johns Hopkins University Press.

———. 1988. *Searching for Rural Development: Labor Migration and Employment in Mexico.* Ithaca, N.Y.: Cornell University Press.

Harvey, Neil. 1990. "The New Agrarian Movement in Mexico 1979–1990." Institute of Latin American Studies Research Paper, no. 23. London: University of London.

———. 1992. "Movimiento campesino y el estado en México: UNORCA entre el corporativismo y la concertación." Presented at the Seventeenth International Congress of the Latin American Studies Association, Los Angeles, September.

———. 1993. "The Limits of Concertation in Rural Mexico." In *Mexico: Dilemmas of Transition,* edited by N. Harvey. London: Institute of Latin American Studies, University of London.

Hernández, Luis. 1989a. "Autonomía y desarrollo," *Pueblo* 12:147 (September–October).

———. 1989b. "El fantasma del general: notas sobre la cuestión electoral y el movimiento campesino." In *Crónica del Nuevo México.* Mexico City: Equipo Pueblo.

———. 1990. "Las convulsiones rurales," *El Cotidiano* 7:34 (March–April).

———. 1991. "Doce tesis sobre el nuevo liderazgo campesino en México: notas sobre la UNORCA." Presented at the Sixteenth International Congress of the Latin American Studies Association, Washington, D.C., April.

———. 1992a. "Las telarañas de la nueva organicidad," *El Cotidiano* 8:50 (September–October).

———. 1992b. "Cambio y resistencia en el movimiento campesino." Presentation at the Universidad Nacional Autónoma de México, Mexico City, November.

Hernández, Luis, and Fernando Célis. 1992. "PRONASOL y la cafeticultura," *El Cotidiano* 8:49 (July–August).

Hewitt de Alcántara, Cynthia, ed. 1994. *Economic Restructuring and Rural Subsistence in Mexico: Corn and the Crisis of the 1980s.* Transformation of Rural Mexico Series, no. 2. La Jolla: Center for U.S.-Mexican Studies, University of California, San Diego/UNRISD.

Hirschman, Albert. 1970. *Exit, Voice and Loyalty, Responses to Decline in Firms, Organizations and States.* Cambridge, Mass.: Harvard University Press.

Johnston, Bruce F., et al., eds. 1987. *U.S.-Mexico Relations. Agriculture and Rural Development.* Stanford: Stanford University Press.

Levy, Santiago, and S. van Wijnbergen. 1991. "Agriculture in the Mexico-USA Free Trade Agreement." Unpublished document, April.

López, Arturo, et al. 1989. *Geografía de las elecciones presidenciales de México, 1988.* Mexico City: Fundación Arturo Rosenblueth.

López Monjardín, Adriana. 1991. "Organization and Struggle among Agricultural Workers in Mexico." In *Unions, Workers and the State in Mexico*, edited by Kevin J. Middlebrook. U.S.-Mexico Contemporary Perspectives Series, no. 2. La Jolla: Center for U.S.-Mexican Studies, University of California, San Diego.

Martínez Borrego, Estela. 1991. *Organización de productores y movimiento campesino.* Mexico City: Siglo Veintiuno.

Medina Peña, Luis. 1991. "Notas sobre una encuesta," *Examen*, December.

Mejía Piñeiros, María, and Sergio Sarmiento. 1987. *La lucha indígena: un reto a la ortodoxia.* Mexico City: Siglo Veintiuno.

Minnesota Advocates for Human Rights. 1993. "Civilians at Risk: Military and Police Abuses in the Mexican Countryside." A North America Project Special Report. New York: World Policy Institute/New School for Social Research, August.

Moguel, Julio. 1991. "Atoyac y los caminos del México moderno," *Unomasuno*, March 18.

———. 1992. "Reformas legislativas y luchas agrarias en el marco de la transición salinista," *El Cotidiano* 8:50 (September–October).

———. 1994. "The Mexican Left and the Social Program of Salinismo." In *Transforming State-Society Relations in Mexico: The National Solidarity Strategy*, edited by Wayne A. Cornelius, Ann L. Craig, and Jonathan Fox. U.S.-Mexico Contemporary Perspectives Series, no. 6. La Jolla: Center for U.S.-Mexican Studies, University of California, San Diego.

Moguel, Julio, and Josefina Aranda. 1992. "La coordinadora estatal de productores de café de Oaxaca." In *Autonomía y nuevos sujetos del desarrollo rural*, edited by Julio Moguel, Carlota Botey, and Luis Hernández. Mexico City: Siglo Veintiuno/CEHAM.

Moguel, Julio, Carlota Botey, and Luis Hernández, eds. 1992. *Autonomía y nuevos sujetos del desarrollo rural.* Mexico City: Siglo Veintiuno/CEHAM.

Molinar Horcasitas, Juan. 1991. *El tiempo de la legitimidad: elecciones, autoritarismo y democracia en México.* Mexico City: Cal y Arena.

Monjarás, Jorge, et al. 1992. "Tratado de Libre Comercio: las nuevas medidas de norteamérica," *Expansión* 24:605 (December 9).

Morett Sánchez, Jesús C. 1991. *Alternativas de modernización del ejido.* Mexico City: Instituto de Proposiciones Estratégicas, A.C.

Nagengast, Carole, and Michael Kearney. 1990. "Mixtec Ethnicity: Social Identity, Political Consciousness and Political Activism," *Latin American Research Review* 25:2.

Nauman, Talli. 1993. "This Land Is Our Land," *El Financiero International*, January 25.

Nava, Manuel. 1991. "Violento desalojo de la presidencia municipal de Atoyac, 18 Perredistas detenidos," *El Financiero*, June 19.

Orduña, Francisco. 1993. "CNC: decepciona a campesinos la reforma al 27," *La Jornada*, January 13.

Paré, Luisa. 1991. "¿Rezago agrario o rezagados del agro?" *Cuadernos Agrarios* 3 (September–December).

Pérez, Matilde. 1992. "Las dirigencias estatales y regionales de la CNC serán reorientadas, anuncia Hugo Andrés Araujo," *La Jornada*, February 13.

———. 1993. "Piden amnistía para más de 5 mil indígenas presos injustamente," *La Jornada*, January 6.

Pérez, Matilde, and Elio Henríquez. 1992. "Marcha de 10 mil indígenas en San Cristóbal contra la opresión," *La Jornada*, October 13.

Piña Armendáriz, Joaquín. 1993. "Efecto desastroso en el desarrollo agrícola," *Este País*, January.

Robinson, Sherman, et al. 1991. "Agricultural Policies and Migration in a U.S.-Mexican Free Trade Area: A Computable General Equilibrium Analysis." University of California Working Paper No. 617. Berkeley: California Agricultural Experiment Station, Giannini Foundation.

Rojas, Rosa. 1991. "Rechazo unánime cenecista a la privatización del ejido," *La Jornada*, October 31.

———. 1992. "CNC: debe ampliarse la posibilidad de sindicalización de los jornaleros," *La Jornada*, August 28.

Salcedo, Salomón, José Alberto García, and Myriam Sagarnaga. 1993. "Política agrícola y maíz en México: hacia el libre comercio norteamericano," *Comercio Exterior* 43:4 (April).

Salinas de Gortari, Raúl. 1990. "El campo mexicano ante el reto de la modernización," *Comercio Exterior* 40:9 (September).

Sanderson, Steven. 1981. *Agrarian Populism and the Mexican State*. Berkeley: University of California Press.

———. 1986. *The Transformation of Mexican Agriculture*. Princeton, N.J.: Princeton University Press.

SARH-CEPAL (Secretaría de Agricultura y Recursos Hidráulicos-Comisión Económica para América Latina). 1992. "Primer Informe Nacional sobre Tipología de Productores del Sector Social." Mexico City: Secretaría de Agricultura y Recursos Hidráulicos, Subsecretaría de Política Sectorial y Concertación, Proyecto SARH-CEPAL, June. Unpublished. (Available in published form as *Productores del sector social rural en México*, Transformation of Rural Mexico Series, no. 1 [La Jolla: Center for U.S.-Mexican Studies, University of California, San Diego, 1994].)

Sarmiento, Sergio. 1991. "Movimiento indio y modernización," *Cuadernos Agrarios* 2, nueva época.

Shwedel, Kenneth. 1992. "A Game of Wait and See, Agricultural Investment Slows in Aftermath of Ejido Reform," *Business Mexico*, December.

Solís, Dianna. 1991. "Corn May Be Snag in Trade Talks By Mexico, US," *Wall Street Journal*, December 27.

SRA (Secretaría de Reforma Agraria). 1992. *Ley Agraria 1992*. Mexico City: Instituto de Capacitación Agraria, SRA.

Stephen, Lynn. 1991. "The Gendered Dynamics of Democratization: Brazil, Chile and Mexico." Paper presented at the 47th International Congress of Americanists, New Orleans, July 7–10.

UNORCA (Unión Nacional de Organizaciones Regionales Campesinas Autónomas). 1988. "Memoria del tercer encuentro nacional campesino," *Cuadernos de UNORCA* 1.

Varela, Claudia, et al., eds. 1991. "Análisis socio político del campo mexicano." Mexico City: Consejo Coordinador Empresarial, August. Unpublished document.

Warman, Arturo. 1992. "El destino del campesinado mexicano." Presented at the conference "The Transformations of Mexican Agriculture," University of California, Berkeley, December 3–4.

Zabin, Carol. 1992. "Binational Labor Markets and Segmentation by Gender: The Case of Agriculture and the North American Free Trade Agreement." Presented at the Seventeenth International Congress of the Latin American Studies Association, Los Angeles, California, September.

11

The Art and Implications of Political Restructuring in Mexico: The Case of Urban Popular Movements

Paul Lawrence Haber

Economic restructuring in Mexico has compelled important changes in relationships among the state, political parties, and collective actors in civil society. The so-called popular sectors in Mexico—the urban poor, the peasantry, and the organized working class—are all incorporated through corporatist institutions. While the de la Madrid administration (1982–1988) was careful to guard against labor militancy that could have impinged upon the ability to implement far-reaching reforms, other sectors were not so carefully managed. Popular sectors increased their activities outside official corporatist channels in ways that weakened the regime's capacity to ensure that political activity remained supportive of the regime. This chapter begins by analyzing how social movements were able to form among the least incorporated of these sectors—the urban poor—and the extent to which these movements were able to influence political outcomes as relatively autonomous actors during the de la Madrid administration. The chapter then turns to its primary focus, analyzing how the administration of Salinas de Gortari (1988–1994) exercised the art of political restructuring so as to decrease the power of the tentative alliances that formed between social movements representative of the urban poor and the nationalist populist electoral effort headed by Cuauhtémoc Cárdenas.

The author thanks Vivienne Bennett, Maria Cook, Jonathan Fox, Judith Adler Hellman, Kevin Middlebrook, and Juan Molinar for insightful comments.

The 1988 election results demonstrated the costs of assuming that existing corporatist mechanisms were adequate for incorporating the expanded range of social actors that had either emerged or significantly augmented their memberships and political resources during the 1980s. The pace of neoliberal restructuring achieved during the first half of the Salinas administration would have been impossible without damage control to reinforce the Mexican presidency, an office whose image had been badly tarnished during the López Portillo (1976–1982) and de la Madrid administrations. Once in office, Salinas lost no time in establishing himself as an activist president willing and able to take bold actions. Motivated by a perceived need to establish a popular image and to underscore his demand for loyalty from elites willing and able to further his modernization scheme, he moved against unpopular business leaders and corporatist kingpins.[1] Salinas showed no hesitancy in removing from office, by whatever means necessary, political elites who questioned his authority and direction or who were unable to contribute to a "new PRI."[2]

Because it took office in the midst of political crisis, the Salinas administration—in sharp contrast to its predecessor—recognized the fundamental need to rebuild political relationships with the urban poor and with urban popular movements. Salinas worked diligently and effectively to establish a host of new relationships outside traditional corporatist mechanisms. These created new sources of regime support (or at least minimized antagonisms) while simultaneously undermining the coalition strength exercised by the National Democratic Front (FDN) during 1987 and 1988. Salinas's enthusiasm for establishing new relationships with popular movements helped ensure that the Party of the Democratic Revolution (PRD) would be unable to maintain the broad-based support Cárdenas elicited from civil society in 1988. It is important to remember that Cárdenas's main support in the 1988 presidential election was urban. It was no surprise, then, when Salinas directed substantial efforts to disrupt the kind of popular movement and FDN

---

[1] The most famous and influential case of Salinas moving against union leaders involved the Mexican Petroleum Workers' Union. In a dramatic show of strength that ended in a shoot-out between federal troops and oil worker militia, Salinas removed from power and jailed the union's secretary of social works and "moral leader," Joaquín Hernández Galicia (known as "La Quina"). This move against one of Mexico's most well-known and powerful caciques went far to establish Salinas's credentials as a strong and decisive president, thereby strengthening the presidency. The forced resignation of the long-time leader of the teachers' union, Carlos Jonguitud, after a period of sustained protest by the intra-union reformist movement (the National Coordinating Committee of Education Workers, CNTE) is another example of the way in which Salinas removed from power political strongmen unable or unwilling to act in ways that would bolster Salinas and his political objectives.

[2] Among his most important political "removals" of this type were the governors of Michoacán (Luis Martínez Villicaña), Baja California (Xicoténcatl Leyva), México (Mario Ramón Beteta), and Yucatán (Víctor Manzanilla Schaffer). These states were all centers of opposition strength where the standing governors apparently did not demonstrate the political efficiency demanded by Salinas.

alliance that had encouraged high levels of voter turnout in favor of opposition candidates.

The Salinas reforms affected many actors, representing the full range of Mexico's class diversity: peasants, the nonunionized urban poor, unionized workers, middle sectors, and owners of domestic and foreign capital. This chapter highlights the new relationships formed between Salinas and urban popular movements within the general context of *concertación social* (which the regime claimed decreases authoritarianism in favor of "partnership") and through the policy mechanism of the National Solidarity Program (PRONASOL), the Salinas administration's high-profile antipoverty program. This chapter presents information in support of the contention that *concertación* allowed Salinas to quicken the pace of neoliberal restructuring while creating serious divisions among popular movements and between popular movements and the PRD.

URBAN POPULAR MOVEMENTS, POLITICAL PARTIES, AND THE DE LA MADRID ADMINISTRATION

Mexico is still paying for the fiscal excesses of President López Portillo. He began 1981 with high expectations of establishing his place in Mexican history through a spending frenzy of long-term capital projects, one of the hallmarks of his administration. When revenues did not meet the administration's unrealistic expectations, deficit spending was financed with short-term loans. Mexico's balance-of-payments deficit grew from U.S.$6.7 billion in 1980 to U.S.$11.7 billion in 1981, a historical record (Banco de México 1982). By the end of 1982, the fiscal deficit was 17.6 percent of gross national product (GNP), a Mexican record; total foreign debt was U.S.$85 billion (89.9 percent of GNP); and interest payments alone absorbed 43.6 percent of the total value of exports (Heredia 1989: 9).

This left de la Madrid with the excruciating task of economic crisis management. Austerity measures and unpopular and divisive economic reforms encouraged popular participation in instances of collective dissent that mobilized millions of individuals, including large sectors of the middle class and the urban poor—along with smaller but still important subsectors of organized workers and the peasantry—that had previously been unwilling to participate as active members or supporters of the opposition. Popular organizations prospered on the local level, and national organizations capable of challenging political norms and procedures, as well as election and policy outcomes, were formed.

Mexico's extremely rapid transition from a rural- to an urban-based society is the key structural transition that made possible the scale of urban popular movement emergence in Mexico during the 1980s. Massive rates of rural-to-urban migration since the 1950s have transformed the urban poor into the single largest population group in Mexico today. Rapid demographic changes created a massive pool of potential recruits for urban popular movements during the de la Madrid administration, when cuts in state services combined with slow growth and inflation to undermine the urban poor's standard of living. Housing shortages began to emerge as a political liability for the regime in the 1970s. When continued high rates of rural-to-urban migration combined with economic crisis in the 1980s, the housing shortage became acute.

The emergence of urban popular movements that focused on this housing shortage and demanded government attention to it transformed housing issues into a serious political problem for the regime, particularly in Mexico City in the wake of the 1985 earthquakes. Self-help housing is certainly nothing new in Mexico. As is the case throughout Latin America, it is the most common form of construction. Beginning in the 1970s, however, and accelerating markedly during the 1980s, urban popular movements with radical political agendas directly opposed to the state assisted individuals who had previously acted alone or through links to PRI or state officials.

The popular-movement sector is highly dependent upon its ability to furnish housing to the urban poor, oftentimes acting as effective representatives in negotiation with the state and, to a much lesser extent, domestic nongovernmental organizations (NGOs) and international agencies. During the course of the de la Madrid administration, urban popular movements were responsible for turning attention to a "politics of consumption" that, at the very least, altered the left's traditional preoccupation with the "politics of production." They demonstrated a remarkable ability to assist both renters and shantytown dwellers with housing issues.[3] Success in this area was at the core of the movements' ability to garner political support and to transfer this political support to Cárdenas in 1988.

The rising tide of urban popular movements lobbying federal agencies on issues related to housing and other basic necessities—such as potable water, sanitation, electricity, roads, rent control, health, and education—during the 1982–1988 period further eroded the adequacy of existing corporatist arrangements formally charged with channeling the demands of the urban poor. The National Confederation of Popular Organizations (CNOP), the principal corporatist mechanism for controlling and channeling the demands of the urban poor, was clearly not up to the task during the 1982–1988 period. The de la Madrid administration did little to help shore up the CNOP's capacity to meet the twin challenges of increased migration flows into the cities and severe cuts in

---

[3]Details concerning the pathbreaking Mexico City renters' movement (the Assembly of Neighborhoods) and the Popular Defense Committee's role in the politics of housing in the northwestern city of Durango can be found in Haber 1992: chaps. 6 and 7.

federal spending. Urban popular movements prospered during this period in large part because they proved able to fill the vacuum left by inadequate corporatist bodies.

De la Madrid failed to initiate significant reforms in traditional corporatist arrangements, and he provided few auxiliary mechanisms to reinforce decaying and increasingly ineffective organizations. As a result, the regime lost legitimacy and support to urban popular movements that galvanized large numbers of the urban poor against the regime. In the Mexican political system, if corporatist relations prove inadequate and are replaced by opposition movements, then the inclusionary nature of Mexico's authoritarian regime is jeopardized. There are only three viable options: (1) the inclusionary system can be reformed by strengthening traditional institutions and creating new means for incorporating important social actors; (2) the regime can harden and be transformed into the kind of exclusionary regime that terrorized the Southern Cone during the 1960s and 1970s; or (3) the regime can democratize. The de la Madrid administration identified a fourth, nonviable option (that is, nonviable over the long term): ignoring political liabilities while concentrating on macroeconomic crisis management. The danger of this course of action was most visible in the electoral results of 1988, in which the Institutional Revolutionary Party's (PRI) presidential candidate did exceedingly poorly, particularly in urban areas.

De la Madrid came into office in 1982 seemingly unaware of, or uninterested in, the fact that urban popular movements had experienced rapid growth and organizational development between 1979 and 1982. Particularly relevant was the increasing severity of the housing crisis and the inability of PRIísta organizations and leaders to address the problem adequately. Shortages of housing available to low-income populations were the key appeal of urban movements, which demonstrated to the urban poor an ability to gain access to housing, an ability often outstripping the capacities of local PRI leaders.

De la Madrid increased spending for federal housing programs, particularly in response to the 1985 earthquakes. Unfortunately for the party/state, there was no parallel effort to incorporate the urban poor into these federal programs in ways that significantly improved the government's, let alone the PRI's, popularity. That is, new funding was made available for housing, but the regime did not create mechanisms to implement effectively the new housing programs, nor was it able to create a public relations victory. Moving to fill this vacuum, the urban popular movements established new cooperative forms, such as the National Coordinating Committee of the Urban Popular Movement (CONAMUP) and the Coordinating Committee for Earthquake Victims (CUD). These actions, along with increased levels of state repression, stimulated the formation of sectoral alliances and new horizontal relations among popular movements, thereby initiating forms of political action antithetical to state corporatism.

The 1979–1984 period was widely known as the "golden age" of the *coordinadoras*, those sectoral coordinating bodies made up of individual popular movement organizations.[4] The three most important were a peasant-based movement, the National "Plan de Ayala" Coordinating Committee (CNPA); a movement for union democracy within the larger PRI-affiliated teachers' union, the National Coordinating Committee of Education Workers (CNTE); and the National Coordinating Committee of the Urban Popular Movement (CONAMUP). The *coordinadoras*, and popular movements in general, challenged the de la Madrid administration on the grounds of being antinationalist. The president's refusal to incorporate these radical movements, thereby reducing their organizational power, further eroded his nationalist credentials as popular movements enlarged their membership and expanded their influence on public opinion.

Popular movements also enlarged their scope of activities during the early 1980s through the formation of three multisectoral fronts,[5] two national strikes in October 1983 and June 1984, and what have been referred to as "pre-party formations," known in Mexico as political currents. The most important new current to form during the early 1980s was the Maoist organization known as the Revolutionary Left Organization-Mass Line (OIR-LM). The importance during the early 1980s of the OIR-LM—along with other political currents such as the Revolutionary National Civic Association (ACNR) and the Socialist Current (CS)—derived precisely from a long history of deep antagonism and distrust between political parties and popular movements. The absence of strong working relationships between movements and parties had hindered the ability of leftist parties to make stronger electoral showings. These political currents provided important opportunities for individual popular movements to rethink their electoral strategies. Whereas in the 1970s most popular movements maintained an antielectoral strategy, over the course of the de la Madrid administration most came to favor active

---

[4]*Coordinadoras* act as confederations of popular movements, in which member organizations maintain institutional autonomy while also adhering to a set of basic principles and positions. The *coordinadoras* aimed at developing an essential program of action to which large numbers of individual movements could adhere. They also acted in defense of individual organizations threatened by repression.

[5]The National Committee in Defense of the Popular Economy (CNDEP) and the National Front for the Defense of Wages and Against Austerity and the High Cost of Living (FNDSCAC) began to form within days of each other in September 1982. The third front to form, the National Worker-Peasant-Popular Assembly (ANOCP), came together at the height of a strike wave in June 1983. The enthusiasm of the time propelled many organizations (some of which had previously been at odds within the FNDSCAC and CNDEP) to come together in what was projected to be an even more powerful alliance of urban movements, independent peasant movements, independent unions, and leftist political parties.

involvement in elections. The electoral reforms of the late 1970s provided the initial impetus. The electoral opportunities generated by de la Madrid's policies and his lack of attention to party reforms encouraged many popular movements to initiate their electoral participation prior to the emergence of Cárdenas as an independent political force.

How are we to explain this relative lack of attention to the widening gap between the regime's incorporative capabilities and popular sectors, the most significant being the urban poor? De la Madrid was necessarily focused on the macroeconomic dimensions of the economic crisis he inherited from his mentor, José López Portillo. While the president had to have, at a minimum, strained support from most of organized labor, this did not extend to the urban poor. The fact that influential members of his administration did not perceive or alert the president more effectively to the growing opposition emerging outside existing channels is in part explained by the simple fact that no multiclass coalition of forces had proved even remotely capable of challenging the regime on the national level since at least 1940. The most serious threats between 1940 and the 1980s had been largely sectoral in nature, the most important being the 1968 student movement. The system of alliances developing among independent labor and peasant sectors, urban popular movements, and from within the middle classes in support of a renegade political leader capable of coalescing these forces into a multiclass electoral force was a political development without precedent.

If the element of surprise in part explains de la Madrid's inattention to the deterioration of state power, the composition of his top aides reinforced the administration's inability to accurately perceive the growing trouble in civil and political society. Both the López Portillo and de la Madrid administrations were narrow; they were dominated by younger technocrats with weak links to the PRI and the provinces. This undermined the multiclass nature of the Mexican elite structure, previously characterized by broad regional representation by seasoned politicians who had risen through the party structure. The tendency for *técnicos* to dominate all aspects of federal decision making in Mexico reached its pinnacle under de la Madrid, to the extent that only one appointee in his initial cabinet had any prior electoral experience (Camp 1985). "The most remarkable feature of the new cabinet was the virtual monopolization of the financial specialists over the whole executive branch. Almost half of the new ministers came from the Ministry of Budget and Planning . . . and the rest came mostly from the Finance Ministry or from the Central Bank" (Heredia 1989: 11). The configuration of de la Madrid's inner circle in part explains the administration's concern with fiscal restructuring, inflation control, and the dismantling of the import-substitution industrialization (ISI) model, without parallel concern for the political fallout that resulted from the implied end of the traditional "social pact." Indeed, de la Madrid's policies signaled the end of a social pact that had acted as the foundation of the Mexican political economy for decades, with high degrees of elite cohesion and popular support.

The exclusion of *políticos* with regional ties and extensive networks of political loyalty known as camarillas not only translated into a shortsightedness regarding the implications of economic restructuring without political reforms, but it also encouraged *políticos* to support Cárdenas when he formed the Democratic Current (CD) in 1986. The austerity measures implemented by de la Madrid as part of the restructuring process weakened the corporatist system because it became less capable of maintaining patron-client relations through the provision of material rewards in exchange for political loyalty. This gave a significant advantage to popular movements, which found themselves in a much better position to compete with the PRI in the pursuit of state concessions and in opposition to the president, the PRI, and the regime in general. Popular movements competed with the PRI's corporatist sectors by mobilizing and organizing peasants and members of the nonunionized urban poor and by effectively presenting to the state their demands for material benefits. The PRI's National Peasants' Confederation (CNC) and the National Confederation of Popular Organizations (CNOP) found themselves competing against popular movements that were not only able to deliver services (oftentimes more effectively than these "official" organizations) but were also able to enlist enthusiastic rank-and-file support.

URBAN POPULAR MOVEMENTS, POLITICAL PARTIES, AND THE
SALINAS ADMINISTRATION

The costs of implementing economic reforms and austerity measures without paying equal attention to the need to reinforce, and in some cases rebuild, the system of state alliances became increasingly apparent in the summer of 1988 as the 1980s politics of opposition reached its zenith. Although there had been no shortage of elites and political observers warning the president and his closest associates that the form and content of the administration were undermining the regime's stability, these voices had gone largely unnoticed (or at least unheeded) by the commanding technocrats. This situation could not continue into the next administration without putting the entire regime in jeopardy, and it did not.

Even before the election results were in, Salinas was rebuilding the alliance system and devising ways to put a new, more popular face on economic reforms and austerity measures. Decision making remained highly concentrated, as it was during the de la Madrid administration, within the Office of the Presidency. What had changed was the governing style and the impression that more people were participating in *concertación* with the president. Rebuilding the system of international and domestic alliances—the most important actors being big business, the U.S. government, the National Action Party (PAN), and social movements—was a priority of the Salinas presidency. In combination with a partial economic recovery and internal splits within the opposition, the Salinas strategy succeeded in taking back from the opposition the momentum of increasing support and the "rightful" place of the president and his administration as primary implementors of the nationalist project and fulfillers of the revolutionary promise.

The new president's inner circle had impressive, diversified credentials and strengths designed specifically to deal effectively, as the previous administration had not, with the political implications of economic restructuring. Salinas created an "economic cabinet" out of his personal team, appointing individuals dedicated to the neoliberal project and educationally prepared to administer the economic side of his project. The notable aspect of the administration of Carlos Salinas, in contrast to that of de la Madrid, was that he did not stop there. Salinas also created a "political cabinet" loaded with *políticos* prepared to carry out the president's reforms. The *políticos* would be able to strengthen the authoritarian system by virtue of their own political networks, which contained the kind of connections likely to facilitate implementation of the reforms and also closely monitor the politics of implementation.[6]

Salinas began his programmatic reforms while still on the campaign trail. Multiple reforms were designed to instill new vigor into the traditional corporatist system, as well as to establish new linkages between the state and civil society. The following discussion will explore both types of reform. Attention will focus on "neocorporatist reforms," particularly the National Solidarity Program. PRONASOL will be analyzed primarily in terms of its ability to strengthen the regime and weaken the political opposition. The final section of the chapter examines how these initiatives have affected two of the most important urban popular movements in Mexico, the Popular Defense Committee (CDP) in Durango and the Assembly of Neighborhoods (Asamblea de Barrios) in Mexico City.

NEO-CARDENSIMO AND URBAN POPULAR MOVEMENTS, POST-JULY 1988

While Salinas was designing and implementing strategies for rebuilding the system of state alliances, Cárdenas was taking a number of positions

---

[6]Key members of the "political cabinet" included a number of seasoned politicians. The most important were Secretary of the Interior Fernando Gutiérrez Barrios, Secretary of Education Manuel Bartlett, Secretary of Labor Arsenio Farell, and Secretary of Agrarian Reform Víctor Cervera Pacheco. This list, when combined with the political reform wing led by Luis Donaldo Colosio (who began the administration as head of the PRI) and Manuel Camacho (then mayor of Mexico City), presented a wealth of political expertise and linkages that fanned out around the country. For excellent discussions of camarillas and the makeup of the Salinas cabinet, see Camp 1990; Ronfeldt 1988.

that badly damaged his credibility with popular movements.[7] Soon after the July elections, work began on the development of a new political party that would group some of those who had joined forces under the FDN banner. Internal cleavages had become apparent even during the campaign, for while all the parties within the FDN had supported Cárdenas for president, it had been impossible for them to agree on common candidate slates for the large number of federal, state, and local offices up for election. In most races the various parties ran competing candidates, thereby canceling out much of their force and allowing PRI candidates to win more offices than would have been possible had consensus been reached more often.

The FDN was a loose organizational coalition of parties, political currents, and social movements; it was destined to last only until the 1988 campaign and immediate efforts to mobilize against official electoral results had come to a close. Once it became clear that Cárdenas had lost his presidential bid, efforts to build a new political party became the focus. Throughout the first half of 1989 the basic characteristics of neo-Cardenismo remained unclear. The difficulty of building a single political party out of the FDN generated confusion and uncertainty, and this had a direct bearing on the fate and future political conduct of popular movements. Several key questions remained unanswered. First, would Cárdenas lead a social movement as well as a political party, or would his attentions, and those of the organization he headed, focus almost exclusively on electoral competition? Second, what would be the balance of power within the party among "ex-PRIístas" (or "neo-PRIístas," as they were sometimes called[8]), members of leftist political parties (particularly representatives of the Mexican Socialist Party [PMS]), and the leaders of political currents and popular movements? Related to this last point, what would be the party's position on acceptable standards for relations between popular movements and the Salinas administration? This last issue was at the top of the agenda, made more immediate by the fact that some movements such as the CDP in Durango had already begun the process of negotiating agreements with Salinas himself.

Over the protests of many popular movements, political currents, and intellectuals, the PRD and Cárdenas became concerned almost exclusively with running elections and protesting unfair and corrupt procedures alleged to have occurred during the multiple state elections held between 1989 and 1991, as well as the important federal elections in August 1991, in which the PRD was badly defeated. In the view of many, the PRD began its history with misplaced priorities, and this cost it dearly. Up until at least 1990, Cárdenas and the PRD spent inordinate

---

[7]Details of the Salinas reforms will be provided in the following section.

[8]This loose designation refers primarily to those people who came from the Democratic Current, but it also refers to members of "semi-state" parties such as the PARM, PPS, and PFCRN that joined forces with Cárdenas.

amounts of time, energy, and resources in continuing to promote Cárdenas as the lawful president of Mexico and refusing to accept the validity of the Salinas presidency. In addition, it seemed at times that Cárdenas's 1994 campaign for president began in 1989. Although the PRD controlled a number of municipal governments, these were concentrated in a small number of states, and most of the PRD municipalities were in politically unimportant areas. "By 1991, of the 176 municipalities in opposition hands, 116 were under PRD administration, and 40 were with the PAN. Most of the PRD victories were in villages and towns in a handful of states, however" (Hernández and Fox 1991: 17). Lack of funds (the Mexican federal government controls the overwhelming bulk of resources) further limited the influence of these victories on national politics, although some had important local implications.

While some rural and urban popular movements remained in the party (such as the Assembly of Neighborhoods), many others left or distanced themselves from party activities. It was not uncommon for even those popular movement leaders who stayed active in the party to suggest that intraparty tensions existed between popular movements and the PRD leadership, including Cárdenas himself. One representative example is an article by Leopoldo Enzástiga, who was affiliated with one of the PRD's strongest urban popular movement affiliates, the Union of Popular Neighborhoods (UCP). In the article, the "Popular Cardenista Movement" is defined as a mass movement that includes, but is not limited to, the PRD. Despite repeated but little-explored claims regarding successes of the Cardenista movement outside the electoral arena, toward the end of the article Enzástiga admits that Cárdenas's determining influence in the development of the PRD contributed to the fact that "the relation between the PRD and the popular movement appears as the weakest link" in the development of the movement (1990: 11).

Enzástiga's statement represents both the optimism and pragmatism of those movements that remained faithful to Cárdenas and the PRD, despite the short shrift given to popular movements in the party's agenda. Many movement leaders maintained their ties to the Cardenista movement in spite of the *caudillismo* (personalistic leadership) of Cárdenas and other top leaders from the Democratic Current, such as Porfirio Muñoz Ledo. They did so because they believed that Cárdenas and the PRD represented the best hope for a leftist front. Leaders' levels of optimism differed as to the prospects for increasing the influence of the popular movement agenda, an agenda that in most ways was considerably more radical (in terms of both political and economic orientation) than were the priorities and orientations of the CD leaders who retained firm control over the direction of the party through 1991.

The disenchantment of many popular movements with the PRD resulted in part from the judgment made by many movement leaders that they were underrepresented in key decision-making arenas of the party (for example, on the executive committee). Much more important, however, was PRD leaders' determination that the party was taking an overly rigid position concerning relations between popular movements and Salinas. The PRD position was that movements should undertake no actions that could serve to legitimize Salinas or his policies. Even before Salinas was inaugurated, he was promoting a policy of *concertación* in which he negotiated deals with diverse social actors in an effort to broaden support for his modernization policies. The PRD leadership responded by insinuating that public endorsement (such as the signing of public agreements known as *convenios de concertación*) violated basic PRD tenets.

Many movement leaders took strong exception to the moralistic and pedantic tone of PRD representatives who argued that gaining material and political favors from the state through high-profile programs that legitimated and reinforced the president's power and prestige was not only an inappropriate, but also an immoral, strategy. Because Salinas (judged by the PRD to be an "immoral president") was so closely identified with *concertación*'s most important policy instrument, PRONASOL, those who lent their support through participation in the program became immoral actors as well.

Strains developed as many popular movements refused to follow PRD guidelines concerning *concertación* and PRONASOL. By 1990, a deep split had opened between movements loyal to Cárdenas (such as the Assembly of Neighborhoods in Mexico City) and movements such as the CDP of Durango that were unwilling to give up the political and economic advantages of reaching tactical agreements with the Salinas administration. By late 1989, some commentators already spoke of popular movements as if the entire move toward unity during the 1980s had never happened.[9] In late 1990 this split was given important organizational acknowledgment in the formation and temporary recognition of the Labor Party (PT), which was made up in large part of popular movements participating (or wishing to participate) in *concertación* agreements with the Salinas administration. Although Cárdenas eventually changed his position in 1991 and acknowledged the fact that acceptance of PRONASOL funds by popular movements and PRD municipalities could not be avoided, the damage had already been done.

It was to be expected that Cárdenas would be unfavorably disposed to close collaboration between popular movements and Salinas. Because a key political motivation behind PRONASOL was precisely to under-

---

[9]For example, in an article in *La Jornada* (September 13, 1989), Rodríguez Araujo wrote, "The social movements . . . are disperse . . . and expressed in a somewhat individualized manner or, at most, at the level of the factory, union section, neighborhood, agricultural zone, educational institution. Each group has its own specific demands, and these do not necessarily translate into a collective demand that can encompass individuals outside the particular group" (in Street 1989: 5).

mine popular and popular-movement support for Cárdenas, this program was bound to be contentious. Two things became clear in 1989 concerning the relationship between Salinas and popular movements. First, PRONASOL proved to be an important element in Salinas's strategy for recapturing political ground and legitimacy lost during 1982–1988. Second, the Salinas administration sought to reduce criticism of the president and his policies from the levels that existed during the two previous administrations. As movements moderated their behavior in exchange for the political and economic resources associated with participation in PRONASOL, the program itself became the center of contention.

Although tension between PRONASOL beneficiaries and the PRD was probably inevitable, some schisms could in all likelihood have been avoided or at least mitigated had Cárdenas taken a more decisive and realistic position. Rather than simply arguing that participation in PRONASOL was wrong, Cárdenas should have forged a party position that recognized the inevitability of PRONASOL funding. Such a position might then have led to negotiations on a case-by-case basis between party and movement leaders regarding the politics of PRONASOL and to the design of movement strategies (and perhaps even the parameters of acceptable behavior) that would have lessened support for the president and the authoritarian political system in general. Clearly Cárdenas was at a disadvantage in competing with Salinas for movement support due to the immense resources available to the president and the relative lack of resources that Cárdenas could offer. It seems, however, that an opportunity for damage control was lost. Cárdenas appears to have forgotten, or discounted, the fact that the role of a popular movement leader is to secure material benefits for his or her constituents. Failing to deliver on this front almost always translates over time into a decline in the leader's appeal and, absent a change in leadership, a decline in the movement itself.

SOCIAL CONCERTATION

Salinas took office in December 1988 against the backdrop of a highly mobilized opposition with substantial multiclass support for the proposition that his presidency was illegitimate, the result of massive electoral fraud. Well before going public with his ambitious plan to increase the pace of North American economic integration via the North American Free Trade Agreement (NAFTA), it was clear that Salinas fully intended not only to continue but to speed up the pace of economic restructuring in which he had been so centrally involved during the previous administration. By 1990 it was also clear that Salinas had no intention of overseeing serious democratic reforms; rather, he fully intended to strengthen the authoritarian regime so as to make it more capable of overseeing "Salinastroika."

At the outset of the administration, many observers believed that Salinas was serious about political liberalization. He entered the presidency arguing the need for change in the political system. Along with a perhaps misplaced perception regarding Salinas's personal commitment to political liberalization, many observers reasoned that Salinas had little choice in light of the 1988 presidential vote. Those who thought liberalization possible reasoned that the costs of postponing it could prove disastrous or even fatal for the regime. It was, after all, 1989, a period in which the democratization of Eastern Europe created high expectations for the ability of democratic movements to force the liberalization of authoritarian regimes.

By 1991–1992, it became increasingly apparent that Salinas's political reforms were designed to strengthen the inclusionary authoritarian regime and that political liberalization had been definitively postponed. A process of democratic opening in Mexico requires above all a radical change in the existing relationship between the "official" party and the state. Salinas was quite explicit that such a reform would cause disruptions capable of threatening his economic liberalization program. He was decidedly, and unwaveringly, unwilling to risk what was clearly the hallmark of the administration. Mexico under Salinas reinforced the view that political and economic liberalization are not necessarily mutually interdependent.

It also became apparent that political liberalization was unnecessary for maintaining or reinforcing political stability, at least in the short run. Salinas moved aggressively to improve relations with those social strata with the most potential to disrupt. Relations between Salinas and business, while not without conflict, continued to improve because the neoliberal project was in net terms conducive to the interests of big capital. Small businesses, which were potentially more adversely affected, did not have the political clout to cause substantial political damage. The middle class had been quelled with the strong peso and the lifting of import restrictions. The urban poor had been courted with the promises of PRONASOL.

An aggressive policy of neoliberal economic reforms meant continuing the policies of fiscal austerity and inflation control via wage and price controls. That is, Salinas faced the challenge of dividing the opposition and incorporating important social actors "into the system." And he had to accomplish this without the kind of fiscal expansion available to President Luis Echeverría (1970–1976). Both Salinas and Echeverría were dedicated to quelling opposition voices and incorporating (sometimes "reincorporating") important social actors into the fold. While Salinas followed the Echeverrista policy of bringing members of the opposition directly into his administration (particularly within PRONASOL), he also created the political ideology and associated programs of *concertación social* and channeled a substantial proportion of social spending (probably at least 50 percent) through the neocorporatist mechanisms of PRONASOL. Fiscal constraint required that Salinas direct PRONASOL funds to those social actors with the political resources to disrupt the neoliberal project and threaten the overall legitimacy of the regime.

Concertación social and PRONASOL became vital means for reestablishing the state's nationalist credentials, particularly in relation to the poor and the working class. *Concertación* also provided the rubric for reconciling competing interests so as to gain support for Salinas's new and evolving definition of the "national interest." Under this rubric were programs that addressed the interests of important social actors (business sectors, the urban poor, middle classes, the peasantry, and labor) by promoting economic development and distributing wealth in ways that promoted the national interest.[10] The implementation of *concertación*, particularly through PRONASOL, was also designed to ensure that the coalition of forces gathered together into the FDN would not emerge intact in the PRD. Salinas needed a program capable of offsetting the political negatives of wage and price controls and continued austerity policies, both within and outside traditional corporatist relationships. In this sense, *concertación* was extremely successful.

PRONASOL: FOCUS ON URBAN POPULAR MOVEMENTS

PRONASOL provides a particularly illustrative case for analyzing the way in which Salinas attempted to legitimize his development model and modernization course within the confines of Mexico's "new nationalism" (which allowed for closer U.S.-Mexican relations, a more market- and export-oriented economy, and a reduced role for the state in economic production and the provision of subsidies). It was also one—perhaps the most—important expression of Salinas's intention to modernize corporatist relations through reform of existing relationships and the creation of new, "neocorporatist" relationships with powerful social actors heretofore operating outside the inclusionary system's boundaries. The way in which PRONASOL was implemented demonstrates well the degree to which *concertación social* was politicized under Salinas. It was the single most important element of

---

[10]The idea of *concertación social* has gained ground in other Latin American countries as well. Although it may be too early to tell, this new ideology may legitimate the current stage of capitalist development in many of Latin America's most important countries in much the same way that "developmentalist populism" was used to reconcile contradictory goals and social interests during the industrialization phase of the 1950s (see Cardoso and Faletto 1979). There currently is a widely held conviction in Latin America regarding the need to build a new consensus and legitimate the new power system associated with the "neoliberal," market-oriented policies being pursued in Mexico, Argentina, Brazil, Chile, and elsewhere. Social concertation is one possible ideological construct in the service of this important state function.

the Salinas strategy for establishing new forms of political relations with important urban popular movements. Salinas demonstrated a willingness to provide not only the economic, but also the political, resources associated with PRONASOL to "cooperative" urban popular movements when they engaged in regional conflicts, such as disputes with governors.[11]

Salinas introduced PRONASOL as an arm of *concertación social* soon after taking office. Purportedly funded by proceeds from the sale of state-owned enterprises and other savings associated with increases in government efficiency, PRONASOL's official budget remained relatively small, although it grew from less than U.S.$1 billion in 1989 to almost U.S.$2 billion in 1991. Many observers noted, however, that actual outlays were well beyond official figures, pointing to the use of discretionary funds in the budget of the Office of the Presidency and other public funds that went unmonitored (Dresser 1991).

Although the program undoubtedly addressed issues of concern to the "poorest of the poor," it was certainly inadequate to meet their needs, whatever the actual outlays may have been. Furthermore, it became increasingly obvious that the program's central intent and implications were not to be found in mitigating poverty. The intent of the program was clearly political, and in this sense it succeeded. PRONASOL did not keep up with overall cuts and hardships suffered by the poor during the first years of the Salinas administration, let alone redress the decline in living standards for the poor between 1982 and 1988. The reason that PRONASOL was so successful politically was that it was targeted at important actors in order to mitigate their opposition to the president and to the regime, introduce competition to moribund corporatist mechanisms (by subsidizing popular movement competitors), and draw the movements out of the neo-Cardenista fold.[12]

The partial success of the PRI and the state in persuading the public that PRONASOL supported the administration's claim that "modernization is for everyone" combined well with the effort to entice important FDN supporters to participate in the program. PRONASOL divided the left by creating tensions between those who participated and those who chose not to, between those who participated and those who were not able to receive funds or felt they had not received a just share, and within individual movements, between those who wanted to participate and those who did not.

---

[11]A case in point is the Popular Defense Committee (CDP) in Durango, one of the main movements behind the formation of the Labor Party (PT). Salinas repeatedly intervened on the side of the CDP in its disputes with the governor (see Haber 1992: chap. 6).

[12]For example, PRONASOL funds directed to the CDP in Durango in 1989 caused considerable discomfort and increased activity in the CNOP as the PRI's "popular sector" struggled to fulfill the program's rigorous criteria for receipt of funds, a discomfort that was encouraged by increased media attention to CNOP activities.

As many observers of individual movements have pointed out, and as new social movement theorists in particular have been at pains to emphasize, social movements are not monolithic entities but rather comprise a host of identities constantly in creative and destructive flux. It follows, then, that a decision as important as whether or not to participate in PRONASOL would generate divisions within many movements. This is precisely what happened. Splits occurred within sections of the peasant movement, the independent labor movement, the urban popular movement, and others. Many observers have argued that PRONASOL's strategy of dividing organizations one from the other succeeded because each organization signed its own agreement, and thus the state was able to pit movements against each other in the competition for scarce resources. Some critics designed and advocated strategies that would have encouraged movements to form a solid bargaining bloc, at least at the sectoral level (urban poor, peasants, and so forth), as a way of building cohesiveness between movements and pressuring Salinas to make more funds available. Such blocs, however, failed to materialize.

PRONASOL funds were targeted on areas and groups that caused problems in the July 1988 elections.[13] "PRONASOL claimed in early 1991 to be operating in 171 out of 173 municipalities controlled by the opposition" (Dresser 1991: 9). It emphasized urban areas over rural areas because that was where the PRI experienced its worst electoral losses in 1988. Although PRONASOL was not officially a PRI program—and in principle PRI organizations had to compete with non-PRIísta organizations for PRONASOL funds—it was obvious that one of the program's principal goals was to restore the PRI's electoral competitiveness, particularly in the most troublesome urban areas.

The fact that PRONASOL was presented as a state program that was explicitly tied to the Office of the Presidency and had no official ties to the PRI was fundamental to its success in luring popular movements away from the Cárdenas camp. Despite the fact that many popular movements participating in PRONASOL were criticized, it was possible for these participants to develop persuasive rationales for accepting public funds in the name of the poor they represented. The participating movements' main argument was that granting PRONASOL funds was a concessionary act on the part of the government which recognized the power and influence of those popular movements that truly represented the interests of the poor. One, perhaps the only, key measure of "representation" among urban popular movements was the demonstrated ability to secure funding and successfully implement community development projects. The state was obligated to disburse funds to the poor, and popular movements should be sophisticated enough to carry out the complexities of economic develop-

---

[13]Funds were also channeled to areas that presented no significant electoral threat to the PRI. The motivations for funding were diverse, and opposition electoral strength was only one indicator, albeit an important one.

ment. Developing such a defense would have been difficult, if not impossible, had the program borne a closer relationship with the PRI.[14]

While *caudillismo* no doubt persisted in the de la Madrid administration, efforts were made to increase the degree of bureaucratic rationality in the disbursement of public funds and the implementation of high-profile programs, even when this approach carried with it certain political liabilities, such as the estrangement of local political elites. The culture surrounding PRONASOL was evidence that this tendency was at least somewhat reversed during the Salinas administration.[15] Disbursement of PRONASOL funds under the leadership of Carlos Rojas, with noticeable involvement by Salinas, was characterized by a very personalistic leadership style. Leaders of popular movements that enjoyed long personal relationships with Rojas— such as the CDP in Durango and Land and Liberty (Tierra y Libertad) in Monterrey—fared particularly well under PRONASOL.[16] The PRD maintained that municipalities under its political control were

---

[14]The list of popular movement organizations that chose to participate in PRONASOL programs is long. Many of these organizations strived to develop rationales for doing so, arguing above all else that participation sacrificed neither their autonomy nor their credentials as members of the revolutionary opposition. Furthermore, while movement participation in PRONASOL was in 1989 and 1990 the most important issue within the social-movement sector, during 1991 and 1992 it became somewhat less divisive as more and more movements were forced to participate because of the paucity of alternative sources of funding. CONAMUP members were initially quite divided on the issue of PRONASOL participation, but increasing numbers eventually followed the early lead of the CDP in Durango and Land and Liberty in Monterrey, two highly influential urban popular movements that supported *concertación* early on and later founded the PT.

[15]Salinas's populist style, combined with the need to regain the political control lost during the 1982–1988 period, transformed a number of federal programs that at one time disbursed funds according to strict technical criteria into political rearmament tools for the party/state. For example, compare FONHAPO—the federal housing authority responsible for stimulating housing construction among the Mexican poor— as it operated under the directorship of Roberto Eibenschutz before the 1985 earthquakes with its functioning during the period of reconstruction after the earthquakes and particularly after 1988. The earthquakes politicized the disbursement of funds in favor of popular movements formed immediately following the earthquakes, thereby reversing much of what Eibenschutz had put in place during the previous period. After 1988, FONHAPO's political criteria moved against popular movements. Eibenschutz argued that adherence to technical criteria worked to the advantage of popular movements over the long term, for while political criteria might be used to the advantage of popular movements during those rare periods when the political opportunity structure shifts in their favor (as it did during 1985–1987 in Mexico City earthquake reconstruction), these periods are short lived. He also argued that, even during periods of increased funding, the rational disbursement of funds according to strict technical qualifications works to the advantage of the poor, although he conceded that such criteria would have undermined the growth of some influential urban popular movements formed during the period, such as the Assembly of Neighborhoods (author interview, February 1991).

[16]Alberto Anaya, leader of Land and Liberty, also enjoyed a long relationship with President Salinas, dating back to when they were both economics students at the National Autonomous University. This relationship contributed to the high levels of funding enjoyed by Land and Liberty and other movements closely associated with Anaya, such as the CDP.

plagued by delays and other "red tape strategies" and marshalled evidence that they claimed substantiated the charge that the disbursement of PRONASOL funds was highly politicized (PRD 1990). Independent analysts documented a number of cases that suggested the politicized nature of PRONASOL funding, which involved helping allies and attempting to undermine the credibility and effectiveness of political enemies (see, for example, Dresser 1991; Moguel 1990a, 1990b).

Although there is ample room to dispute who within the original FDN coalition was to blame for the political success of PRONASOL, or whether or not a different PRD position on PRONASOL would have preserved better relations between the PRD and social movements, the program's success (measured in terms of how many popular movements participated in it or wished to do so) is not in question. For relatively little money, Salinas designed and implemented a program that was decisive in splitting off movements from the Cárdenas camp and in encouraging them to relegate national considerations to a lower priority in favor of concentrating on their own organizational development.[17] In this way the state, through Salinas's *concertación* programs, decisively diminished the national coalition of opposition forces assembled behind Cárdenas in 1988. Protest in Mexico reached its zenith in 1988 as local organizations became increasingly willing to combine their own regional concerns and actions in support of a national opposition movement agenda. It declined in the post-1988 period as this tendency toward combined action was reversed, thanks in great measure to PRONASOL.

Popular movements can act in ways that encourage elite conflict, or they can act in ways that diminish the importance of such conflict. One way to deflate conflict is for protest movements to split among themselves and/or decrease their support for leaders attempting to form a national front. This is what happened in Mexico after 1988. Social movements, once virtually united in their support for Cárdenas and the National Democratic Front, split apart. Some continued to support Cárdenas and the PRD. Others adopted a neutral stance. And still others became active critics of the PRD. For Cárdenas to survive as a national force in Mexico he had to maintain his ability to disrupt "normal procedures." This is because Mexico's political norms, laws, and procedures are authoritarian and biased against power contenders operating outside the party/state system. His ability after 1988 to effectively challenge most official election results was at least partially undermined

---

[17]The Salinas administration was particularly keen on dissuading popular movements from concentrating on two "national considerations": the reconstruction of a national multiclass electoral front led by Cárdenas, and a critique of the political economy that blamed Salinas for decreases in the standard of living and that failed to support the idea that the economic recovery begun in 1989–1991 would continue into the future and expand its benefits to the poor.

by his waning support among popular movements capable of mobilizing their members behind this agenda.

CONTRASTING EXPERIENCES OF TWO URBAN POPULAR MOVEMENTS

The experiences of the Popular Defense Committee in Durango and the Assembly of Neighborhoods in Mexico City provide an interesting contrast of how popular movements fared under the Salinas presidency. The CDP was a leading organization in *concertación*, while the Assembly maintained close ties with the PRD and became a leading critic of *concertación*.

The CDP grew directly out of the Mexican student movement of the late 1960s–early 1970s and the failure of the 1970s armed insurgency. Beginning in the 1970s, what is now called the CDP worked to establish *colonias populares*, mostly in the area surrounding the capital city of Durango, Durango, with a population of about half a million. During the 1970s and into the early 1980s, the CDP maintained a militant stance that was highly critical of the Mexican political economy of authoritarian capitalism and advocated its revolutionary overthrow and a new socialist order. Relations with the government at the local, state, and federal levels were often highly conflictual and occasionally violent. Between 1980 and 1986, the CDP increased its efforts at territorial expansion through the creation of ten new *colonias*. In the 1980s, the CDP combined its militant mobilizations and land invasions with an increasing ability to negotiate with federal and state government authorities. This not only decreased violence against the movement during land invasions, but it also very often brought housing credits and services to movement supporters. By 1990, twenty CDP *colonias* existed in and around the state capital, with a population of approximately sixty thousand, and CDP committees were established in twenty-seven other *colonias*, with over one thousand active members. Although the CDP's core of strength had always been in the capital, it branched out to include several other municipalities in the state.

In 1986 the CDP changed its long-held position against electoral participation and began to field candidates, first under the banner of the PRT, then changing to the PMS and to Cárdenas in 1988. In 1989 it formed its own state-level party, had a serious conflict with the PMS/PRD over its involvement in *concertación*, and in late 1990 began the effort to construct a new Labor Party (PT). The percentage of the vote and total votes received increased with every election after 1986. In 1989, the first year that the CDP ran on its own party ticket, it received 7 percent of the vote. In the 1991 elections for federal deputies, it received 35,779 votes, or 11 percent of the total in the state of Durango. In the August 1992 elections, the CDP candidate for municipal president in the capital city won the election with 43,000 votes, against 35,000 for the PRI and 33,000 for the PAN.

In February 1989 the CDP became the first popular movement to sign a *convenio de concertación*, the initial step for participating in PRO-NASOL. After that time, the CDP continued to grow closer to the Salinas administration, receiving large amounts of both official and unofficial support. The economic support was used to build up the CDP's organizational capacity to implement public works projects and garner votes. The CDP also benefited from political interventions by the president himself in the CDP's disputes with the governor (Haber 1992: chap. 6).

The 1992 election was illustrative of the type of political risks and benefits associated with an urban movement strategy that embraced PRONASOL. The CDP/PT was clearly in the process of transforming its place in Durango's politics. During the 1992 Durango campaign there was a dramatic increase in the CDP's material resources. A major topic among virtually all political observers in Durango was the amount of money that Alejandro González Yáñez ("Gonzalo," as he was referred to throughout Durango[18]), candidate for the municipal presidency of Durango, had at his disposal. Although the CDP denied that it received any unofficial campaign support, the amounts spent were impossible to explain without allowing for federal donations.

The campaign was reminiscent of images of Lázaro Cárdenas and the "official" party in the 1930s. It was classic populism, responding to (or appearing to respond to) citizen demands for basic necessities. Gone were references to socialist transformation. In their place were promises of more, and more efficient delivery of, state services (roads, medical clinics, potable water, and so forth). Candidates running on the CDP ticket sought to differentiate themselves and their party from the PRI by pointing to the CDP's demonstrated ability to respond to citizen demands and the PRI's loss of that ability. For the most part, the CDP used the same terms to contrast itself to other parties: in the area of public works, neither the PAN nor the PRD nor any of the other smaller parties was any match for the CDP.

Gonzalo moved from campaign stop to campaign stop, handing out millions of pesos to initiate specific public projects. Given the history of conflictual relations between Durango's conservative middle class and the radical socialist CDP, his ability to draw large crowds in middle-class neighborhoods was particularly impressive. One noticed a slight change in rhetoric and style, but the message remained essentially the same: elect me and you will receive more effective responses to your demands for public services. The CDP moved aggressively into *colonias* previously controlled by the PRI or sympathetic to the PAN, launching

---

[18]Alejandro González Yáñez continues to use the name Gonzalo, which was first given to him as a *nom de guerre* during the 1970s.

new public works projects in an effort to erode the PRI's or the PAN's control and gain new support for itself. Gonzalo left the impression that the campaign money was only a beginning; if the *colonia* stuck with the CDP, win or lose, it was sure to get public works it would not receive from any other party—including the PRI. There was reason to believe this. The CDP/PT campaign for municipal president clearly rivaled that of the PRI in terms of money spent, and Gonzalo was an excellent candidate, much more politically skilled than the PRI's candidate.

REAL AND POTENTIAL COSTS OF THE CDP'S STRATEGY

The benefits of running a populist campaign in the style of the old PRI are clear. More power to the CDP meant more public works more effectively carried out than was the case under the PRI. But there were both real and potential costs as well.

• Efforts to form an alliance among the PAN, PRD, and CDP failed. The CDP claimed that negotiations for a PAN/PRD/PT electoral alliance broke down because the PAN was unwilling to give the PT the government positions it wanted. Obviously, the most important position was the municipal presidency in Durango for Gonzalo. CDP leaders argued that the PAN was unwilling to support Gonzalo's candidacy in exchange for CDP support for the PAN's candidate for the governorship.

Many observers found this hard to believe. What seemed much more likely was that entering into such an alliance would have endangered the CDP's ties with Salinas and the official and "unofficial" funds provided by PRONASOL. If this was indeed the case, there was a real cost involved—the potential victory of the opposition over the PRI for key offices, including the governorship. A PAN/PRD/PT alliance held the real possibility of gaining state power in Durango. Without such an alliance, electoral victory was very unlikely. The case of Durango thus raises an important question: in how many other instances did PRONASOL undermine potential electoral alliances capable of winning key offices?

• The CDP claimed that the strategy of close collaboration with the Salinas administration promoted democracy in Durango, for it put in power an organization that was much more responsive to popular demands than either the PRI or the PAN.[19] Although this was true, the strategy also appeared to help Salinas strengthen Mexican authoritarianism by establishing new and reformed corporatist mechanisms.

The damage here was to electoral democracy. The democracy promoted by the CDP is the kind of democracy envisioned by Lázaro Cárdenas, a certain degree of pluralism within an authoritarian regime.

---

[19]The PRD was extremely weak in Durango, with the notable exception of the La Laguna area and the city of Gómez Palacio in the eastern part of the state.

This approach does not guarantee the right to gain state power through running clean elections in which all parties compete on a level playing field, with none more advantaged than the others in terms of state resources. The CDP elected to pursue a strategy of accepting state funding for its campaign rather than continue the struggle to force the government to run clean elections. The PRD strategy continued to concentrate on breaking the existing relationship between the PRI and the state, thereby forcing the PRI to function as "just another party" in the Mexican party system, without the "unfair" advantages it currently receives from the state. The CDP continued to refer to the need for further democratic reforms, but this was clearly not the major thrust of its strategy.

The CDP responded to such charges of "aiding and abetting" Mexican authoritarianism by arguing that the struggle for electoral democracy is naive and wrongheaded, for two reasons. First, they argued that it was not feasible at that historical moment. Thus, pursuing electoral democracy was an ineffective strategy not worth the costs and lost privileges of pursuing a more "cooperative" relationship with the Salinas administration, especially given the likelihood that Rojas would continue to play a key role in the next administration. Second, they asserted that electoral democracy was overrated anyway. It was promoted by bourgeois intellectuals and others relatively uninvolved in the more important work of improving material conditions.

• Durango very clearly is a state rich in natural resources (primarily minerals and timber). Nevertheless, it remains poor because it cannot efficiently exploit these resources. The main impediment to a development boom in Durango has long been its lack of ground transportation. Its only access to the Pacific Coast is the road to Mazatlán, which is unpassable for large trucks. Studies by the federal government regarding potential improvements to this road suggested that it would be much more efficient to construct a new road from Durango to Culiacán. This option has several additional advantages. It would fit well into the national effort to improve the highway system by establishing a quicker route from Mexico City to Tijuana. It would also cut down on traffic between Mazatlán and Culiacán, which is already a problem. Because many national interests would benefit from such a road, including Monterrey business interests, it was a high priority for the Salinas administration and would in all likelihood continue to be so for the next administration as well.

The construction of a new highway would not end Durango's transportation problems, but it would certainly stimulate secondary road construction and new investments in timber and mining from both domestic and foreign sources. It seems reasonable to expect that in ten years Durango will be in a very different economic position than it is today. The generation of new wealth, particularly in the extractive industries, will create a new politics of distribution in Durango. A potential cost of the CDP's strategy of cooperation with the state is that it might compromise its medium- and long-term ability to act as a powerful voice in defense of a more generous distribution of new riches. The CDP leadership has dismissed this concern by saying that the CDP always practices situational politics and will adjust its strategy to this new reality if necessary. That is, today's politics do not require large doses of autonomy from the state. If it is needed tomorrow, it will be "taken back."

It may be, however, that autonomy may prove to be something that movements such as the CDP cannot buy and sell at will. An argument can certainly be made that the strategy of building up the CDP was undertaken by Salinas and supported by other powers with an eye toward the longer term. It is possible, of course, that the CDP's organizational and political power gains in the next few years will actually enhance its ability to lobby on behalf of workers, small land owners, and other interests involved in any significant surge in Durango's extractive industries. If this is the case, concern over this potential cost is unfounded. If, on the other hand, today's politics of cooperation work to compromise tomorrow's ability to act with militant independence, then the decision to pursue short-term advantage may prove to be very costly over the long run.

The history and practices of the Assembly of Neighborhoods in Mexico City stand in sharp contrast to those of the CDP. Established in 1987, the Assembly grew out of the mobilizations and reconstruction that followed the 1985 earthquakes. The Assembly's base is made up largely of renters, and it is of a somewhat higher income level and more class diverse than is the CDP's membership.[20] At its membership peak in 1987, the Assembly could claim over fifty thousand members. That number dropped to about ten thousand by 1993, although, like the CDP, Assembly candidates for office receive support that transcends movement membership.

In stark contrast to the CDP, the Assembly of Neighborhoods developed a harsh public critique of PRONASOL. Unlike the CDP, it refused offers from government representatives (in the Assembly of Neighborhoods' case, it was Manuel Camacho, then mayor of Mexico City) to develop their own party separate from the PRD. They remained loyal PRD supporters. In fact, all four members of the Assembly's top leadership council have held top offices within the party.

---

[20]The CDP would argue, with reference to its growing peasant-sector and middle-class electoral support, that it had become much more multiclass over time. Although its electoral support certainly extended beyond the *colonias*, the rank and file continued to be drawn predominantly from among the urban poor.

The Assembly consistently argued that the kind of public support for Salinas that CDP-style participation in PRONASOL entails undermines efforts to promote democratization, efforts that are best pursued by continuing to build a unified opposition under the PRD umbrella. Although far from happy with all of Cárdenas's policy positions and long aggravated by the continued dominance of neo-PRIístas in the party hierarchy, Assembly members have continued to insist that the CDP and other movements that followed the traditional strategy of under-the-table bargaining served to strengthen Mexican authoritarianism.

The short-term advantages of the Assembly's position are difficult to identify. Interviews with the leadership in summer 1992 revealed a movement that had lost active membership and experienced the onset of anomie. Although the movement continued to struggle for housing rights—always its main material concern—it encountered mounting institutional obstacles, in sharp contrast to the CDP, which gained increased access to elites and state programs. The Assembly gained access to political offices. However, according to movement founder and PRD federal deputy Francisco Saucedo, the route to reform via legislation was stymied repeatedly by the PRI majority (author interview, summer 1992).

Although the Assembly's analysis may prove to be correct—that participation in PRONASOL helped undermine the electoral movement for democracy—the CDP demonstrated the considerable short-term benefits of pursuing *concertación*. The fact that the survival—let alone prosperity—of most urban popular movements (as well as peasant movements) is highly dependent upon their continued ability to extract state concessions helps to explain why so many were forced into PRONASOL, despite its costs.

CONCLUSION

Evaluations of the consequences of PRONASOL for the popular-movement sector are perhaps inevitably biased by the theoretical and political predispositions of the analyst. If the political potential of movements is equated with their ability to disrupt and produce crisis (Piven and Cloward 1977), then participation in PRONASOL should be perceived largely in terms of its eroding effects on movement potential. If, on the other hand, the analyst allows for the possibility of favorable outcomes resulting from alliances (some of which are very uneasy and temporary) between popular movements and state reformers, then the *concertación* potential for change appears in a brighter light (Fox 1993).

There are several important considerations to be kept in mind when thinking about PRONASOL. First, formal outlays for the program did not represent a major increase in antipoverty funding. More than new money, PRONASOL represented a reorganization of previously existing programs. One important caveat here is that there were significant amounts of under-the-table monies targeted to important actors as further compensation for participating in Salinas's program. A key example is money funneled to the PT, formally called the Labor Party but composed mostly of social movements active in PRONASOL. Second, the informal economy of PRONASOL extended beyond economic development funds to political resources as well, including interventions by the president on the side of PRONASOL-supporting popular movements in local disputes, including those with governors. Movements that did not participate in PRONASOL, particularly those that made a point of engaging in public critiques of the program and the president, often encountered severe costs in terms of access to state resources. Third, whatever its costs, participating in PRONASOL strengthened the capacity of many individual social movements to act as agents of economic development. And in some cases, PRONASOL expanded these movements' horizons as political actors. The case of the CDP illustrates the empowerment potential of PRONASOL. It is hard to imagine the CDP's electoral victory in the state capital without PRONASOL funds. Many Mexican popular movements have long been clamoring for the state to reform its antipoverty approach so as to give a more active role to popular movements in the design, implementation, and evaluation processes. Movement activists who celebrate PRONASOL argue that it is the type of program they have been calling on the federal government to initiate for years.

REFERENCES

Banco de México. 1982. *Informe anual*. Mexico City: Banco de México.

Camp, Roderic A. 1985. "The Political Technocrat in Mexico and the Survival of the Political System," *Latin American Research Review* 20:1:97–118.

———. 1990. "Camarillas in Mexican Politics: The Case of the Salinas Cabinet," *Mexican Studies/Estudios Mexicanos* 6:1 (Winter): 85–107.

Cardoso, Fernando Henrique, and Enzo Faletto. 1979. *Dependency and Development in Latin America*. Berkeley: University of California Press.

Dresser, Denise. 1991. *Neopopulist Solutions to Neoliberal Problems: Mexico's National Solidarity Program*. Current Issue Brief Series, no. 3. La Jolla: Center for U.S.-Mexican Studies, University of California, San Diego.

Enzástiga, Leopoldo. 1990. "El Movimiento Popular Cardenista a dos años de julio," *Barrio Nuevo* 1:5 (July).

Fox, Jonathan. 1993. *The Politics of Food in Mexico: State Power and Social Mobilization*. Ithaca, N.Y.: Cornell University Press.

Haber, Paul Lawrence. 1992. "Collective Dissent in Mexico: The Politics of Contemporary Urban Popular Movements." Ph.D. dissertation, Columbia University.

Heredia, Blanca. 1989. "The Political Economy of the Mexican Crisis, 1982–1988." Presented at the conference "Economic Crisis and Third World Countries: Impact and Responses," Kingston, Jamaica, April 3–7.

Hernández, Luis, and Jonathan Fox. 1991. "Mexico's Difficult Democracy: Grass-roots Movements, NGOs and Local Government." Mimeo.

Moguel, Julio. 1990a. "National Solidarity Program Fails to Help the Very Poor," *Voices of Mexico* (UNAM) 15 (October–December).

———. 1990b. "El Programa Nacional de Solidaridad. ¿Para quién?" Mimeo.

Piven, Frances Fox, and Richard A. Cloward. 1977. *Poor People's Movements: Why They Succeed, How They Fail*. New York: Pantheon.

PRD (Partido de la Revolución Democrática). 1990. *Crítica y alternativa a la política económica*. Mexico City: Grupo Parlamentario del PRD, July.

Ronfeldt, David. 1988. "Whither Elite Cohesion in Mexico?: A Comment." Document P-7509. Santa Monica, Calif.: Rand Corporation, November.

Street, Susan. 1989. "The Role of Social Movements in the Analysis of Sociopolitical Change in Mexico." Presented at the Fifteenth International Congress of the Latin American Studies Association, Miami, Florida, December 4–6.

PART V

REGIME CHANGE IN MEXICO: CONTEMPORARY PERSPECTIVES

12

Mexico's Political Formula, Past and Present

Marcelo Cavarozzi

INTRODUCTION

In the aftermath of Mexico's 1988 presidential elections, a group of prominent Mexicanists gathered to assess the alternative political futures facing Mexican society.[1] One alternative scenario was a worsening economic situation and intensified delegitimation and political upheaval—in other words, a process of chaotic adjustment.[2] Cornelius, Gentleman, and Smith (1989), as well as Laurence Whitehead (1989), correctly underlined the fundamental features that an adjustment of this nature might assume. The former authors did so by pointing to the possibility that the initial accomplishments of the 1987 Economic Solidarity Pact (PSE) might fade away if, "Under pressure from the leftist opposition, the government might slow down the implementation of its economic liberalization policies and increase spending on programs to attack social problems, until fiscal realities forced it to retrench. The inevitable austerity measures would raise social tensions and further delegitimate the political system" (p. 38).

Whitehead (1989) largely concurred with Cornelius, Gentleman, and Smith and formulated a similar warning: "[One of] the prospect[s] is

---

Translated by Aníbal Yáñez.

[1] The occasion was the conference "Mexico's Alternative Political Futures," held at the Center for U.S.-Mexican Studies, University of California, San Diego, in March 1988. The specialists' conclusions are summarized in the introduction to the volume resulting from the conference. See Cornelius, Gentleman, and Smith 1989.

[2] A recent article analyzed the basic features of the chaotic adjustments that predominated in many Latin American countries during the 1980s. See Cavarozzi 1992.

for a succession of further ad hoc emergency stabilization packages, adopted within a broader setting of continued economic stagnation, social insecurity, and therefore, eventually, also of political breakdown" (p. 212). It is clear that this alternative scenario did not materialize. Under President Salinas (1988–1994) Mexico moved away from the path that might have led to chaotic adjustment, in contrast to developments in Brazil, Argentina, and Peru during the 1980s.

The success of Mexico's adjustment and restructuring program, and the way in which an anticipated collapse of the political regime was averted, did not lead Mexican society to a political democracy, either with or without a dominant party. Instead, a situation emerged that is similar to the controlled liberalization posited by Cornelius, Gentleman, and Smith as another possible alternative outcome. Mexico's political regime was transformed based on the partial redefinition of the president's role, a decline in the importance of corporatist mechanisms, and, finally, political liberalization[3]—whose most significant features included the opening of some democratic niches at the state and local levels and the relative veto power gained by one of the opposition parties, the National Action Party (PAN).[4]

The changes that occurred in Mexico after 1988 do not fit into the linear frameworks of analysis inspired by the experiences of other contemporary Latin American societies. Unlike Mexico, all of the South American countries that faced similar crises in the 1980s eventually succumbed to a sharp change of political regime.[5] Mexico, in contrast, despite having navigated through a crisis equal in intensity to that experienced by several South American nations, seems to have overcome that crisis without radical political change.

How, then, can we approach the analysis of Mexico's current situation? The high inflation and fiscal imbalances of the 1980s have been significantly reduced. In fact, fiscal accounts registered surpluses in recent years. However, the very success of the adjustment programs generated new problems, and these problems have prevented the Mexican economy from addressing weaknesses that have plagued it since the early 1980s.

---

[3] The corporatist mechanisms for the political control of workers and peasants have not been completely dismantled. What has occurred is that popular sectors are subjected to other types of restrictions and, in the final analysis, controls that are more closely related to market pressures.

[4] The three remaining alternatives that Cornelius, Gentleman, and Smith discuss are: (1) authoritarian modernization, (2) partial democratization (that is, with the PRI still the hegemonic party), and (3) full democratization from below (1989: 40–45).

[5] The only countries whose regimes survived the 1980s were Colombia and Venezuela. Due to the prudence with which its governments handled economic policy, Colombia did not experience major upheavals and maintained a reasonable rate of growth during that period. Venezuela, on the other hand, did not resolve the problems typical of the 1980s and, with a certain "delay," appeared to enter an acute political crisis in the 1990s.

At the same time, Mexican politics has been significantly transformed at certain institutional levels and in the practices of political
society more generally. Nevertheless, analysts who approach this issue
seeking only to measure how much Mexican politics has been democra-
tized may overlook some key features of the changes under way.

This chapter does not attempt to predict the future. Rather, it
analyzes the principal elements that may aid our comparative understanding of the trajectory followed by Mexican politics in recent years.[6]
It first considers whether the Mexican political formula is unique. In this
sense, the Mexican case is characterized as an experience of permanent
accumulation of political capital, in contrast with South American
societies, where this capacity for accumulation has been weaker or even
nonexistent. This explains why the countries of South America repeatedly found their political regimes—whether democratic or authoritarian—to be weak. This is a situation that Mexico has avoided.

The chapter then reviews the political processes that unfolded in
Mexico during the first five years of the Salinas government, a period
that ended with the nomination of Luis Donaldo Colosio as the candidate
for the Institutional Revolutionary Party (PRI) to succeed Salinas, the
insurrection of the Zapatista Army of National Liberation on January 1,
1994, in Chiapas, and Colosio's assassination in March 1994.

THE MEXICAN POLITICAL FORMULA: CONSTRUCTIVENESS AND PLASTICITY

The concept of a state-centered matrix (SCM) is useful when comparing the
course of Mexico with that of early-modernizing South American countries
over the last decade (see Cavarozzi 1992). The principal characteristic of the
state-centered matrix was not (as some have erroneously concluded) an
elevated degree of *dirigismo*, especially if by this we mean state intervention
in the economy. Rather, the key feature was that politics revolved primarily
around the actions of the state. The presidency, executive agencies, and
some decentralized administrative institutions played a quite exclusionary
role, often filtering or eliminating strongly democratizing societal forces.
The executive employed a variety of strategies to achieve this end, ranging
from restrictions on electoral participation to the kinds of direct relations
established between political leaders and the masses.

This concept helps highlight three fundamental features of the political
formulas and processes that unfolded in Latin America beginning in the
period between World War I and World War II. First, the space for civil
society became more expansive and more complex within the SCM. The
span of this process extended from the emergence and strengthening of

---

[6]The comparisons will be in reference to the other early-modernizing countries in Latin
America—that is, Brazil and the countries of the Southern Cone—and, to a lesser extent,
Venezuela, Colombia, and Peru.

popular-sector organizations (especially organizations of workers and the urban poor) to the modernization and secularization of private spaces, such as the family, school, and workplace. Furthermore, specifically political arenas tended to expand and become more plural and inclusive by incorporating sectors excluded during the oligarchic stage. This process included significant segments of the middle and popular classes. However, their inclusion was balanced, and at times counterbalanced, by the articulation of various mechanisms of political and sociocultural control that were implemented or redefined by the state.

Second, within the SCM the legitimacy of political regimes tended to be of a *substantive* character (that is, it depended on their ability to distribute benefits) or a *foundational* character (that is, it varied with the relative strength of foundational myths, such as the nationalist and anti-oligarchical Mexican Revolution, the consensual legacy of Uruguayan Batllism,[7] or Peronism's inclusionary impulse in Argentina). In contrast, the *procedural* legitimacy of state-centered regimes was extremely limited. When these regimes were unable to offer tangible benefits, or when their foundational myths weakened, neither decision-making procedures nor the social rules and bonds upon which they were based reinforced regime legitimacy "from the bottom up."

Finally, in the pattern of statist politicization that defined the SCM, the way that conflicts were resolved made it very difficult to renegotiate decisions once they were made. Therefore, what were at one moment benefits were transformed into congealed privileges and prerogatives, which in turn became constituent elements of the regime itself. This led to the formation of a complex pattern of accumulating conflicts and oppositions with a multidimensional character, which may be characterized as the *sedimentation of conflicts*. Political institutions became overloaded since the rules by which they were governed proved ineffective for resolving the conflicts that arose. One consequence of the emerging pattern of political action was institutional instability. Therefore, a track developed in Latin America that differed from that of the countries that Barrington Moore included in the classic parliamentary route: England, France, and the Scandinavian countries. In contrast to these classic cases, when oligarchic systems in Latin America were transformed or collapsed, broader participation did not reinforce political regimes. The weakness of Latin American regimes stemmed from the fact that political exchange took place almost exclusively through the channels of the executive-state.

With one significant exception (related to the tendency toward the sedimentation of conflicts, discussed below), the state-centered formula also applied to Mexico. One can say with little risk of error that postrevolutionary Mexico was characterized by: (1) an abrupt transition from an elitist

---

[7]This is a reference to José Batlle y Ordóñez, president of Uruguay (1903–1907 and 1911–1915) and a democrat who carried out political, economic, cultural, and social reforms. — *Translator's note.*

society to mass politics, including a profound institutional break; (2) the creation of ironclad mechanisms of state control over political and social participation; (3) the centrality of the president-executive; (4) weak internalization of juridical norms; and (5) a "dense" political regime in which formal rules, while often having considerable symbolic importance, had little operational effectiveness. In the case of the last three of these attributes, the degree of discretional power in public decision making was considerable.

Thus, Mexico shared the fundamental features of the state-centered formula. However, after the 1930s its political regime—in contrast to those in South America—strictly fulfilled the rules of constitutional succession, and it demonstrated an ability to adapt to changes in prevailing political-ideological alternatives and in the dynamics of the international market (and the economic models in vogue). These features guaranteed regime survival.

To a large extent regime longevity depended on the Mexican formula's ability to surmount a series of critical junctures and successively resolve the challenges each presented. Thus, in contrast to the South American cases, where similar junctures and unresolved conflicts eroded regimes and eventually led to their overthrow, the Mexican regime was progressively better able to accumulate the resources of political capital that were generated as a result of the effectiveness of its practices.

An early watershed separating Mexico's political course from that of the early-modernizing South American countries was the issue of military intervention in politics—how it was perceived and how it was resolved. The 1928–1929 juncture in Mexico (when the assassination of Alvaro Obregón and the definitive defeat of the Cristero rebellion framed Plutarco Elías Calles's decision to create an "official" party) marked the end of a period of acute political instability.[8] The contradictory and multidimensional nature of the Mexican Revolution had contributed to the resurgence of phenom-

---

[8]Instability, of course, was scarcely new in Mexican history. The nineteenth century was a turbulent period, especially from 1810 to 1875. The colonial order collapsed through a process that had many of the characteristics of a civil war. The result was the militarization of politics, the breakdown of central authority, and a resulting relocation of political power to the regional and local levels. This, as Tulio Halperín Donghi (1969) noted, was a fairly common phenomenon in Spanish and Portuguese America; Chile, Brazil, and Paraguay (in this last case, until the War of the Triple Alliance) were the exceptions to the rule. In the other cases, including Mexico, caudillo militarism and regional powers (frequently tied to the ascent or transformation of emerging landowning oligarchies) to a greater or lesser extent undermined attempts to build national states until the last third of the nineteenth century. Perhaps the only exceptional fact about nineteenth-century Mexico was the country's considerable loss of territory as a result of its unfortunate proximity to the United States, which was possessed by its vision of Manifest Destiny.

The Porfiriato placed Mexican society on the track of authoritarian order, which spurred the modernization of important segments of Mexico's economy and culture. This push was interrupted by the revolutionary process unleashed in 1911, a process that not only brought conflicts contained within Porfirian society into the open but also generated new confrontations. The memory of the tumultuous period that had preceded Porfirio Díaz returned during the 1910s and 1920s, especially because of such phenomena as the severe devaluation of printed money and conflicts of a political-religious character.

ena that apparently had been left behind: the militarization of politics, the regional fragmentation of power, and religious rebellions with fundamentalist overtones. Furthermore, once the most acute phase of military conflict ended around 1916, Mexican society was also "disordered" by the processes of modernization, secularization, and urbanization that came with renewed economic dynamism.

As occurred in the South American cases alluded to earlier, in Mexico the transition from oligarchic regime to state-centered politicization was also decisively marked by a reinsertion of the military in politics. However, there was a fundamental difference between the pattern in South America and that in Mexico. The South American military deployed different forms of political intervention beginning in the 1920s. In cases such as Argentina, Brazil, and Peru, the armed forces intermittently interrupted the "normalcy" of civilian politics between the 1920s and the 1960s. In Chile, on the other hand, for forty years the military remained an option of last resort for keeping the left from power.

However, in all the South American countries mentioned, in the three or four decades following the demise of oligarchical rule, the military continued to hold the civilian government as the point of reference for its actions. In other words, civilian governments were regularly watched, threatened, disciplined, redefined, or replaced by military caudillos or by the armed forces themselves. This is why until the 1960s—after institutional military coups in Brazil, Argentina, and Peru, when the military set out to erect permanent nondemocratic regimes—the axis of politics continued to pass through political parties, political movements, and other forms of competition linked to voting.[9]

In contrast, in Mexico during the 1910s and 1920s political competition was largely limited to confrontations that were resolved, in the end, by force of arms. This does not mean that the symbolic and institutional dimensions were totally absent from political conflicts. Furthermore, under the tutelage of the ascendant Sonoran dynasty, new structures of regional power were interwoven with a clientelist and corporatist base. However, politics was indeed remilitarized to the beat of competition among caudillos heading various revolutionary clans and subclans.

In the South American countries, the genesis of contemporary authoritarianism was rooted in *the military's remaining in politics* once the collapse of oligarchic constitutional normalcy had brought them back in. But in Mexico, *the military left politics* as formal and informal mechanisms were stabilized that gave the presidency—and hence civilian governments—authority over the armed forces.

---

[9]Nevertheless, this competition was often subject to restrictions derived from procedures for registering voters, electoral legislation itself, or the exclusion of leftist and populist parties that were perceived to be a threat.

As noted earlier, the demilitarization of politics began in 1929 with the creation of the Revolutionary National Party (PNR). It culminated with the defeat of the last armed rebellion in 1938 and the dissolution of the ruling party's military branch in 1940. Thus, in less than two decades the Mexican political system fully resolved the problem of subjecting the military to civilian authority. It achieved this end, however, through the creation of an authoritarian civil power.

During the two decades following the creation of the ruling party, then, the Mexican regime left behind the uncertainty associated with the militarization of politics. It achieved this, however, at the cost of also eliminating the uncertainty entailed in voting. And, in reality, during the regime's foundational stage—which extended through the administration of Miguel Alemán (1946–1952), the first civilian president—the manipulation of elections was in part a response to the persistent conception of politics as war. Mexico's governing class did not lose the conditioned responses it developed during the years of what has been defined as the destructive stage of the revolution; any electoral adversary perceived to represent a challenge to "national unity" and was therefore treated as an enemy to whom no space should be ceded.

Nevertheless, the regime gradually accumulated political capital of an institutional character. First, postrevolutionary leaders reestablished the constitutional prohibition against presidential reelection. Second, President Lázaro Cárdenas (1934–1940) institutionalized the mechanisms of consensus and subordination of popular sectors and created channels for negotiation within the political class. Finally, the Manuel Avila Camacho (1940–1946) and Alemán (1946–1952) presidencies articulated a new type of agreement with the capitalist classes. The principal consequence of this agreement was the withdrawal of those classes from forms of direct political action in exchange for the implementation of "pro-business" policies.[10]

The new order rested on two supports of its own making. One was the enforcement of strict limitations on electoral competition. This did not mean, however, that the mechanisms allowing the political class to compete for economic and political resources were eliminated; rather, they simply were unrelated to the vote. The other support was the subordinate consensus of popular sectors and the alliance with capitalists. Numerous conflicts arose in these two spheres—internal conflicts within the political class, and a variety of social and sectoral conflicts— but they were metabolized in an institutional way, with scrupulous respect for their parallel but separate identities. In subsequent decades, the Mexican economy was stabilized on these two supports and the

---

[10]Nora Lustig (1992: 14–16) analyzes how the golden years of "stabilizing development" during the 1950s and 1960s were associated with policies favoring businessmen.

particular way in which they were articulated, while the process of constituting the political regime continued to advance.

A second critical juncture developed in the late 1940s and early 1950s, a moment at which Mexico followed a course different from that of Latin America's other industrialized societies with more autarchic economies. Carlos Díaz Alejandro noted some time ago that the more complex Latin American economies faced a dual problem on the external front in the postwar years (Díaz Alejandro 1980, 1981, 1983). On the one hand, the automatic protection that World War II had provided against imports from the industrialized countries gradually evaporated. On the other hand, with the exception of the brief boom associated with the Korean War, both the demand for and prices of most Latin American exports tended to drop. The way out of the inevitable balance-of-payments crisis was currency devaluation.

In the Southern Cone and Brazil, initial devaluations triggered or reinstated inflationary processes, leading to new devaluations. However, inflation was not merely an economic phenomenon. Postwar inflation was a mechanism for political negotiation typical of the SCM (Cavarozzi 1994). Within the matrix, inflation was the outcome of the implicit negotiating style established between various socioeconomic actors and the state. On the one hand, different actors tried not to be left behind in the race of relative prices, although their respective abilities to defend themselves were unequal. On the other hand, the public sector was able to resort to printing money as an effective means of improving its share of available resources. The semi-closed character of these economies retarded the learning process through which private actors' experiences in the 1970s would school them to protect themselves from the inflationary effects of public policies.

Escalating inflation did not necessarily lead to economic stagnation. It is true that the Chilean and Uruguayan economies were virtually idle beginning in the 1950s, and that the Argentine economy experienced only mediocre growth. But on the other hand, the most dynamic Latin American economy in the postwar period was the Brazilian economy, where development and monetary instability did not prove to be incompatible. In all cases, the main impact of rising inflation was the intensification of strains on the formulation and implementation of economic policies. The politicization of distributive conflicts and the "lubricating" effects of inflation ended by destabilizing SCM regimes in which political participation significantly broadened.

During the 1950s there was a breakdown of the political formulas that had arisen or been refined during the rise of fascism and through World War II—that is, the national-popular regimes in Argentina and Brazil and the party-based reformist regimes in Chile and Uruguay. In the mid-1950s both the first Perón regime in Argentina and the Getulio Vargas regime in Brazil collapsed in dramatic fashion, while the central features of the political systems in Chile and Uruguay underwent major redefinitions. In the latter two cases, the regimes whose respective axes had been the Radical Party and neo-Batllism[11] were dismantled. The Chilean and Uruguayan party systems continued functioning until the early 1970s. However, the volatility of their political formulas became more marked because no stable pattern emerged in the correlation of forces among the various parties.

Mexico, in contrast, navigated the 1950s juncture in a way that differed from the rest of Latin America. As noted earlier, the other early-industrializing Latin American societies experienced a crisis in their more openly participatory regimes. Although this would only be understood in retrospect, that crisis set the Southern Cone and Brazil on the track that would lead to the imposition of military dictatorships with foundational intentions.[12] In Mexico, on the contrary, the regime continued to construct mechanisms that reinforced its political solidity. Adolfo Ruiz Cortines (president of Mexico from 1952 to 1958) and a small group of technocrats (the most visible of whom was Antonio Ortiz Mena) launched Mexico's period of "stabilizing development." In this way they were able to combine two terms that in other countries had been irreconcilable: growth and monetary stability.[13]

The "technical" success of Mexico's anti-inflationary policies was based, of course, on the political pillars that supported them. Unlike its South American counterparts, the Mexican state developed the power to insulate (at least in relative terms) the process of economic policy formulation from sectoral pressures aimed at improving groups' respective positions in the distributive tug-of-war. Of course, sectoral pressures existed, but in comparative terms they did not much hinder the state's capacity to act preventively. In other words, redistributive policies either anticipated demands or were implemented once the demands were silenced.

Similarly, presidential rotation and the renovation of the political class every six years reinforced the regime's institutionality. Each transmission of power from a president to his successor gradually reduced

---

[11] This is a reference to Luis Batlle Berres, president of Uruguay from 1947 to 1951 and president of the second National Government Council from 1955 to 1959. Regarding the "original" Batllism, see note 7 above. — *Translator's note.*

[12] Until the 1950s, military interventions in countries like Argentina, Brazil, and Peru were aimed at preventing "inconvenient" movements or parties such as Peronism or the APRA from coming to power. In this pattern of tutelary or corrective intervention, the armed forces did not aim to install long-lasting nondemocratic regimes. Only beginning in the 1960s did the military set out to establish foundational dictatorships that would radically reform the existing political order. These dictatorships tried to eradicate once and for all the forms of popular participation that had developed in previous decades.

[13] Díaz Alejandro would remind us that Colombia, beginning in the late 1950s, also grew with comparatively low rates of inflation (Díaz Alejandro 1981). However, the erosion of oligarchic patterns of political domination came later than in the other countries mentioned here.

(although it did not eliminate) the losers' temptation to challenge the hegemony exercised by the heirs of Calles and Cárdenas.[14] Each incoming president created opportunities for new (and old) aspirants to occupy public posts at all levels. Given the hierarchical character of the regime, this mechanism served periodically to decompress tensions within the political class while simultaneously reinforcing presidential discretionality.[15]

In a way, the Ruiz Cortines presidency ended the foundational stage of the Mexican regime. During the quarter century that began with the Maximato in 1928,[16] the accumulation of political capital proceeded at an accelerated rate, allowing the ruling elite to lay the bases for a stage of "normalcy" that would extend until the early 1970s. The Echeverría administration (1970–1976), in turn, marked a new cleavage: the end of normalcy in the Mexican formula. Beginning with Echeverría, the formula proved less efficient in handling conflicts generated both in society and in politics. Because of this, during the 1970s and 1980s there was an intensification of political turbulence and social tensions. Under Echeverría and his successor, José López Portillo (1976–1982), there were attempts to solve problems within the traditional parameters of the SCM: the government increased public investment as part of expanded state intervention in the economy, and it sought to relieve tensions by boosting material and symbolic payoffs to various social sectors.

The failure of these attempts to resolve Mexico's growing crisis through state-centered mechanisms had a dual effect: the worsening of economic imbalances and the further deterioration of political authority. In the two six-year presidential terms that followed (those of Miguel de la Madrid, 1982–1988, and Carlos Salinas de Gortari, 1988–1994), efforts to resolve the crisis underwent a radical change of sign. On the one hand, based on the diagnosis that the SCM was irreversibly exhausted, state elites concluded that existing imbalances required a radical economic reformulation—even the elimination of many of the mechanisms of state economic management that had existed since the 1930s. On the other hand, when the delegitimation of the political regime reached its highest level following the 1988 presidential elections, state elites embarked on a course to reverse the deterioration of political authority. This process of reconstituting authority (which had important successes) was based on

---

[14] As Juan Molinar Horcasitas (1991: 48) has pointed out, postrevolutionary Mexico faced the problem of what to do with the "political cadres who were thrown to the periphery of the regime by the construction of the hegemony of one sector of the postrevolutionary elite."

[15] Blanca Heredia pointed this phenomenon out to the author. She should not, of course, be held responsible for the way in which the author presents her idea.

[16] This refers to the presidencies of Emilio Portes Gil (1928–1930), Pascual Ortiz Rubio (1930–1932), and Abelardo Rodríguez (1932–1934), during which Calles dominated politics from behind the scenes and was called the *jefe máximo de la revolución* (hence Maximato). — *Translator's note.*

preserving some basic features of the political formula that had been forged over the previous half century. In particular, its aim was to preserve the ruling elite's prerogative to decide when to give way and on what terms. Although this attempt has been successful so far, Mexico's elite has been forced to broaden the space of what is negotiable, especially regarding how electoral contests are decided.

All this seems to confirm the uniqueness of the Mexican political formula within the Latin American—perhaps even the world—context. The reflections in the preceding pages suggest that the continuity of Mexico's postrevolutionary regime is closely associated with its capacity to accumulate political capital. This circumstance allowed it to face the critical junctures outlined above with a greater degree of success than its South American counterparts. Our assessment of how the Mexican regime will overcome the third critical juncture—the one that began in the 1980s—will be significantly enriched if we do not concentrate exclusively on the question of a transition to democracy. Without disputing the normative and practical relevance of this issue, whether Mexico will join the wave of democratizations that began in the previous decade, or whether the regime will dig in behind its authoritarian fortifications, is only one of several issues that enter into an analysis of political change in Mexico. Given this fact, the next section explores the links between the problems of democratization and other relevant dimensions of Mexican politics.

THE SALINAS *SEXENIO*

It was noted in the previous section that Salinas's assumption of the presidency in 1988 marked the beginning of the governing elite's effort to recover the political initiative. This took place despite the fact that the context surrounding the inauguration was extremely unfavorable. Economic policy under de la Madrid clearly leaned toward restructuring the exhausted state-centered economic model. However, the economic crisis that began in 1982 had evolved into a lingering recession, whose most dramatic (though not only) effects had been a drastic drop in real wages, cutbacks in subsidies to low-income sectors of the population, and a marked deterioration in the social services provided by the public sector.[17]

One key political impact of the economic crisis was the deep erosion of the presidential figure of Miguel de la Madrid. However, unlike events in the 1976 and 1982 transitions (when only the outgoing presidents suffered a serious loss of prestige), in 1988 the deterioration of the

---

[17]The strongly recessionary impact of the first six years of the restructuring process has been noted by Nora Lustig (1992). Lustig also underlines a point taken up below: Mexico's delay in overcoming stagnation was basically due to negative trends in the international capital market.

presidency also hurt the PRI candidate and his electoral appeal. The precarious situation in which Salinas assumed the presidency, as well as the delegitimation of the regime that resulted from the 1988 electoral outcome, would stimulate the governing elite to make strategic changes. Despite Salinas's promises of democratization, his administration's strategy was based in part on more of the same—including the selective manipulation of electoral results and the subordination of state governors and the legislative and judicial powers to the federal executive. However, the strategic reorientation also included a new element linked to the political utilization of economic reforms and their impact. The policies that the governing elite implemented after 1988 can be envisioned as a two-front strategy.

THE NEW ELECTORAL SCENARIO AND THE PRI'S TWO-FRONT STRATEGY

The 1988 presidential elections were undoubtedly the most complicated ever experienced by a PRI candidate since the party's creation. This was expressed, first, in the calculated way in which the election results were announced. Despite government maneuvers, the recently created Federal Electoral Commission (CFE) was forced to admit that Salinas had won with the lowest margin of victory in the entire history of the "official" party.

The most important new element in 1988, however, was the new configuration of the electoral arena, which included three credible presidential candidates. PRI candidate Carlos Salinas was flanked on the right by Manuel Clouthier of the PAN and on the left by Cuauhtémoc Cárdenas of the National Democratic Front (FDN). In reality, the surprising electoral architecture of 1988 was not the outcome of a party system in consolidation. Rather, it was a mosaic in which processes with different logics overlapped, and whose timing had little to do with one another. The fact that the 1988 oppositions coincided in time exacerbated the political crisis of the PRI-controlled regime. Yet this coincidence tended to mask the contradictory dimensions of the 1988 juncture. The governing elite would later take advantage of this circumstance to turn around the unfavorable situation in which it found itself.

What does it mean to say that the oppositions represented by the PAN and by the leftist front that would later create the Party of the Democratic Revolution (PRD) obeyed different logics? Expressed schematically, the strengthening of the PAN was rooted in the crisis of the Mexican SCM, especially the crisis of its political formula. In contrast, the dizzying rise of the FDN-PRD opposition resulted from the very responses that the governing regime put together beginning in 1982 to address the exhaustion of the SCM. This difference in logics inspired the governing elite's differential responses to its two principal adversaries.

Moreover, these lines of action sought to maximize the advantages that the PRI could gain from an electoral terrain split into two spaces: one in which it struggled against, but often reached agreements with, the PAN; the other in which it cornered the PRD and employed drastic measures to reverse the latter's July 1988 electoral success. Let us see why and how this peculiar electoral terrain took shape.

The PAN, established in 1939, had been built around values opposed to the ideology and practices of the regime that was heir to the Mexican Revolution. This extra-revolutionary party questioned the exclusion of the opposition, which the governing elite promoted beginning in 1929. It championed suffrage and political democracy, in association with conservative, pro-Catholic, and antisocialistic views, especially regarding official agrarian policy. This orientation limited the PAN's ability to make headway among popular sectors for several decades. But the real Achilles' heel of the conservative opposition was its inability to attract capitalists.[18]

Beginning with the Echeverría administration in 1970, however, Mexican presidents increasingly elicited resistance and mistrust from the business sector. This trend, which became more acute in the final years of the López Portillo administration, enabled the PAN to gain a foothold among Mexican capitalists. Since the mid-1980s, the PAN has been able to challenge the PRI's one-party rule in some northern and north-central states, a phenomenon not unrelated to the PAN's newfound ability to attract support from some of the country's principal business groups.

In addition to addressing strictly economic matters, the changes made in Mexico's economic strategy after 1982 also aimed to close the political gap that had opened in the government's relations with big business. Segments of the governing elite represented by Miguel de la Madrid (and by Salinas as well) recognized that continuing the state-centered policies in effect since the Great Depression (the last implementation of such policies was López Portillo's nationalization of the banks in 1982) would deepen the crisis of the state. In turn, they calculated that this crisis would alienate big business and, over the long term, constrain the state's initiative in its relations with the business sector.

Beginning in 1988, a change in traditional PRI electoral behavior complemented this aspect of the governing elite's "political-economic" strategy. Whereas previously the PRI had corralled its electoral adversaries and refused to recognize their occasional triumphs, Salinas was disposed to recognize state- and local-level PAN victories. This signified a partial opening of electoral space to the conservative opposition, and it gradually gave the PAN a certain veto power with regard to the most

---

[18]This idea was first suggested to the author by Blanca Heredia, who in this case also must not be held responsible for the distortions it may have undergone.

antidemocratic affronts perpetrated by regional and local PRI leaders. There was, however, a concurrent attempt to undercut the PAN's potential bases of social support among regional bourgeoisies. This was the first expression of the governing elite's two-pronged strategy. It is important to note that the full significance of this new approach toward the opposition cannot be adequately captured by a characterization of the governing elite's strategy toward the PAN as simple co-optation.

The leftist coalition's challenge to PRI hegemony in 1988 was more serious than that posed by the PAN. Two factors made it so. The first (and perhaps the most important) was that the Cardenista challenge attacked the governing regime's basic working principle—the separation of internal conflicts within the political class from sectoral and social conflicts. Although the coalition that formed around Cárdenas's candidacy included several leftist groupings and three small parties (which Molinar Horcasitas [1991] refers to as "parastatal" parties), its main component was the Democratic Current (CD). This dissident sector had been pushed to the margins of the PRI when its leaders challenged both the shift in economic policy initiated in 1982 and the antidemocratic methods that the PRI promoted inside and outside the party.

The second factor complemented the first and accentuated its effects: while it is true that the leftist front had the support of middle sectors and university students, it also significantly eroded the PRI's electoral support among popular sectors.[19] After six years of severe economic crisis and an economic adjustment process that had not produced visible fruits, the PRI government was vulnerable to a "left-wing popular" challenge. Added to the PRI's reduced capacity to offer rewards was the ideological gap that opened when the PRI abandoned some of the basic precepts of postrevolutionary mythology, especially state tutelage over the unprotected and the promotion of economic nationalism. The regime's legitimacy developed cracks along the two basic dimensions of the SCM referred to at the beginning of this chapter: the substantive and the foundational.

Predictably, the governing elite's response to the electoral success of Cuauhtémoc Cárdenas and the FDN was much stronger than the PRI's response to PAN advances. On the strictly institutional front, the government aimed to annihilate the PRD politically and electorally, seeking in this way to keep it from gaining new spaces of public power at the regional or local level, especially in the states it carried in the 1988 presidential elections. Beginning with the 1989 local elections in Michoacán, the PRI brought into service its entire arsenal of electoral tactics, legal and otherwise, to block a PRD victory.

---

[19] As Molinar Horcasitas (1991: 197) notes, the Cardenista candidacy "bit into" the PRI's own electoral turf.

However, the regime's strategy against this new and dangerous adversary went beyond resorting to the old medicines it had been administering to opponents since 1940. The government also tried to close the second political gap that had opened during the most acute period of crisis, a gap through which the Cardenista challenge had slipped quite effectively. This was the regime's diminished ability to offer substantive rewards to popular sectors.

Beginning in 1988–1989, changes in the international economy and the discipline with which Mexico's adjustment program was carried out made it possible for the policies implemented by de la Madrid to bear fruit. This circumstance gave Salinas greater room for maneuver, especially in the area of social policy. But the decisive change took place at the end of the 1980s: the transformation of society's expectations with regard to the state and state policies. Mexican society had endured several years of high inflation, giving many social actors a new appreciation of stabilization policy and its achievements. Salinas and his team successfully turned stability into one of the fundamental values of a "desirable society."

In 1987 and 1988 significant segments of Mexican society had added their open discontent with sharply deteriorating economic circumstances to their embryonic disenchantment with the government's lack of respect for democratic principles and practices. Faced with this dangerous combination, Salinas reacted as Ruiz Cortines had done nearly four decades earlier: first he would try to ensure stability and restore growth in the understanding that, with stability and growth assured, democracy could follow. Until the end of 1993, at least with regard to the Cárdenas challenge, Salinas's strategy succeeded at the electoral level; the PRI regained votes, and PRD support diminished. However, Cardenismo has not ceased to challenge the legitimacy of the political system and its electoral rules.

SUCCESSES AND FRAGILITIES

From the perspective of Mexico's governing elite, the processes that unfolded beginning in 1988 produced two successes. First, the consolidation of the new forms of economic intervention allowed the state to recover some of the strength it had lost during the previous decade and a half. Second, the resolution of the acute phase of the crisis and the initial transition toward an alternative political-economic matrix took place, as noted earlier, without destroying the political regime that dated from the 1920s. This regime seemed to demonstrate anew its plasticity and its capacity to survive critical junctures. In contrast, as noted before, authoritarian regimes in South America collapsed during the 1980s.

The preceding statement is contradicted, however, by the obvious predicament that pervades the contemporary Mexican scene. What are its manifestations? One relates to Mexico's pattern of economic recovery since 1989. In an analysis of recent growth trends in the six largest Latin American economies, Damill et al. (1993) suggest that Mexico (like Argentina) has overcome the imbalances characteristic of the 1980s, but at the cost of creating new problems.[20] These economists stress that the region as a whole has benefited from two interrelated trends: a significant reduction in prevailing interests rates in international financial markets and the restoration of capital flows toward Latin America.[21]

These phenomena, in turn, have produced important transformations. Five years ago most Latin American countries were compelled to generate large trade surpluses in order to service their foreign debts. In 1992, in contrast, the renewed inflow of capital meant that for the first time in ten years the region's trade balance was negative. Mexico has been the main recipient of capital in Latin America, and it has also had the largest trade deficit. Notwithstanding the mounting deficits in its trade and current accounts, in the early 1990s Mexico still held an excess supply of foreign currency. The country was forced to devalue the peso, and this helped to correct fiscal imbalances and to reduce inflation significantly.

Despite these advances, the Mexican economy has two points of weakness. The first has to do with the unlikelihood that capital flows into Mexico will remain high and interest rates will remain low. In order to sustain increased levels of imports, Mexico must significantly expand its exports. However, overvaluation of the peso works against this objective. Second, the crisis of the 1980s seems to have gravely damaged the ability of countries like Mexico to regain rates of sustained economic growth. Domestic investment and savings levels are still very low. Decreased public investment as a result of fiscal adjustment is a major cause of this situation. As public investment fell, it produced a negative impact on private investment.

However, the precariousness of the refounding of the Mexican state has to do with more than the weakness of the economic recovery. The political regime surmounted serious obstacles, but at the cost of generating new imbalances. The successive reforms of electoral practices that were implemented beginning in 1977 helped generate a proto-system of parties and introduced a greater degree of competition for some elected

[20] An English-language version of this article was included in the *Trade and Development Report, 1993* (New York: United Nations). The article focuses on six cases—Venezuela, Brazil, Mexico, Argentina, Chile, and Colombia—and identifies three types of current situations. In Venezuela and Brazil, according to the authors, inflation and fiscal crisis—the typical problems of the 1980s—have not been overcome. In contrast, in Mexico and Argentina the favorable resolution of adjustment problems has gone hand in hand with the appearance of new obstacles that recreate economic weaknesses and hamper the renewal of acceptable rates of growth. Finally, Chile and Colombia would be two examples of adjustment that were consolidated before interest rates fell and capital became more available. As a result, their bases of growth are relatively more solid.

[21] In 1988–1989 the average annual flow of capital to Latin America was U.S.$7.7 billion (Damill et al. 1993: 238). This figure rose to U.S.$48 billion in 1991–1992.

positions. Although these reforms have not yet led to the establishment of full democracy, they have created a new dynamic—accelerating the pace of political demands and irreversibly upsetting the equilibrium maintained by the postrevolutionary order until the end of the 1960s.

Until the waning moments of the Díaz Ordaz presidency (1964–1970), the political regime had both neutralized social conflicts and absorbed internal tensions within the political class. It had also maintained the ability to generate rules (generally of an informal nature) and discourses (combining revolutionary mythology with the ability to maintain order), which together had largely organized political action. During the following three administrations, the state's ability to generate rules and discourses was substantially weakened. In other words, the regime lost part of its political capital.

The recovery of presidential power under Salinas decisively prevented Mexico from slipping down the slope of chaotic adjustment and political disorganization. But Salinas accomplished this at the cost of exacerbating the effects of corrosive processes begun during preceding administrations. First, Salinas accentuated the presidency's central role in the political system. Both as a guarantor of the new rules for the operation of the economy and as the country's leading political figure, the president's interventions became more frequent and his discretionary powers more formidable. Second, the ruling PRI became even further removed from public decision making. Paradoxically, this did not contribute to the democratization of the political system; rather, it further weakened PRI members' support for the formal and informal rules upon which the Mexican political order had been based.

Similarly, the mechanisms of corporatist, cultural, and economic control that defined the state-centered formula were dismantled, in part deliberately and in part not. This made it possible to redefine important aspects of the state's relationship with the business sector. In this way, tendencies toward the disorganization of the economic system were reversed. However, in this process the state also disarticulated many of the traditional mechanisms that integrate Mexican society. These mechanisms depended to a large extent on the promise—partly kept, partly unfulfilled—of increasing social and cultural equality and expanding popular access to public spaces. These processes depended, of course, on the initiatives of a state that was able to manage material and symbolic resources and to distribute payoffs.

In synthesis, the partial "de-statization" of politics increased the complexity of Mexican society, but it also contributed to its growing disintegration. The retreat of the state was not accompanied by a simultaneous strengthening of the institutions of political or civil society. That is, there have not yet emerged alternative mechanisms capable of reknitting the meaning of social behavior formerly organized around the state, its policies, and its symbols.

The disorganization of the Mexican SCM may justify the expectation that society will be gradually rearticulated around an emerging and consolidating democratic political society. However, a note of caution is in order. Two of the political class's main segments—those grouped in the PRI and those in the PRD—still hold antiquated (related but dissimilar) visions of political democracy. The ruling party has not yet let go of its conception of democracy as a threat to order and governability. This perspective is, no doubt, associated with Mexico's state-centered legacy—that is, with a negative perception of the tensions that democratic demands introduce into a formula emphasizing control over and limits on participation. For its part, the PRD nourished the PRI's fears to some extent. The main leftist opposition has used demands for democratization of the electoral system as a basis for political blackmail in its struggles with the ruling elite.[22] This instrumental use of electoral democracy is not far removed from a nostalgic stance regarding the state-centered past. The PRD has yet to advance beyond its criticism of "market society," and it lacks a proposal that responds to the exhaustion of the old matrix.

In sum, the Mexican political formula in the early 1990s is subject to tensions and imbalances that may be impossible to overcome. It is not clear how Mexico's democratization, if indeed it ever fully materializes, will contribute to their resolution.

REFERENCES

Cavarozzi, Marcelo. 1992. "Beyond Transitions to Democracy in Latin America," *Journal of Latin American Studies* 24 (October): 665–84.
———. 1994. "Politics: A Key for the Long Term in South America." In *Democracy, Markets, and Structural Reform in Latin America,* edited by William C. Smith, Carlos H. Acuña, and Eduardo A. Gamarra. New Brunswick, N.J.: Transaction Books.
Cornelius, Wayne A., Judith Gentleman, and Peter H. Smith. 1989. "Overview: The Dynamics of Political Change in Mexico." In *Mexico's Alternative Political Futures,* edited by W. Cornelius, J. Gentleman, and P. Smith. Monograph

---

[22]Cavarozzi, in characterizing the SCM in Latin America, defines some of the features of this type of blackmail:

> Within this formula, the effectiveness of electoral participation by the masses was fundamentally related to its disruptive potential, not to the desire to contribute to the legitimation of decision-making mechanisms or to the will to promote a higher degree of accountability by public officials. Electoral participation, or even the mere threat that it would materialize, frequently became a tool of political blackmail used by almost everyone to undermine the authority of both civilian and military regimes. Political representatives of the middle and lower classes, as well as of antidemocratic elites, at one time or another resorted to this tactic. As a result, the systematic expansion of participation did not contribute to the consolidation of governability within the model (Cavarozzi 1994).

Series, no. 30. La Jolla: Center for U.S.-Mexican Studies, University of California, San Diego.

Damill, Mario, et al. 1993. "Crecimiento económico en América Latina: experiencia reciente y perspectivas," *Desarrollo Económico* 33 (July–September).

Díaz Alejandro, Carlos. 1980. "Latin America in Depression, 1929–1939." Discussion Paper No. 344. New Haven, Conn.: Economic Growth Center, Yale University.

————. 1981. "Stories of the 1930s for the 1980s." Discussion Paper No. 376. New Haven, Conn.: Economic Growth Center, Yale University.

————. 1983. "¿Economía abierta y política cerrada?" *El Trimestre Económico* 50 (January–March).

Halperín Donghi, Tulio. 1969. *Historia contemporánea de América Latina*. Madrid: Alianza.

Lustig, Nora. 1992. *Mexico: The Remaking of an Economy*. Washington, D.C.: Brookings Institution.

Molinar Horcasitas, Juan. 1991. *El tiempo de la legitimidad: elecciones, autoritarismo y democracia en México*. Mexico City: Cal y Arena.

Whitehead, Laurence. 1989. "Political Change and Economic Stabilization: The 'Economic Solidarity Pact'." In *Mexico's Alternative Political Futures*, edited by Wayne A. Cornelius, Judith Gentleman, and Peter H. Smith. Monograph Series, no. 30. La Jolla: Center for U.S.-Mexican Studies, University of California, San Diego.

13

Prospects for a "Transition" from Authoritarian Rule in Mexico

Laurence Whitehead

Because "democracy" and "authoritarian rule" are not just descriptive but also evaluative categories that are charged with strong positive and negative connotations, respectively, it is not surprising that in Mexico (as elsewhere) they have become contested concepts. This chapter follows the dominant current of political interpretation that classifies the party-state regime that has ruled Mexico continuously since 1929 as an authoritarian regime. However, there is room for debate about how well, and in precisely what ways, this terminology fits the Mexican case. The object in the first section of this chapter is not to condemn the Institutional Revolutionary Party (PRI) regime, or to impose language that prejudges its scope for reform from within. Rather, the aim is to identify the strategic singularities of the Mexican variant of authoritarian rule in order to establish how far it differs from other authoritarian regimes, and then to deduce the implications of these distinctive characteristics for any prospective regime transition or transformation. Subsequent sections of this chapter take up these questions.

THE MEXICAN VARIANT OF AUTHORITARIAN RULE

The term "political regime" denotes a defined set of institutions and "rules of the game" that regulate access to, and the uses of, positions of public authority in a given society. A regime can be said to persist, or to reproduce itself, so long as the inevitable changes in institutions and rulers that occur over time come about incrementally, without changing the basic principles of the system. A "transition" from one regime to another concerns the set of interacting changes arising when basic operating principles are altered. What in any concrete case constitutes incremental development *within* a regime, as opposed to basic changes *between* regimes, is not always self-evident. Nevertheless, at least in the abstract, the basic operating principles of authoritarian rule are clearly distinct from those of democracy.

Mexico's formal political institutions can be largely traced back to the 1917 federal Constitution, but the informal rules of the game crystalized quite a bit later. This informal system is closely associated with the creation of a unified, disciplined governing party, which derived its resources and discipline from its exclusive control over the state apparatus. But whether we date the current Mexican regime back to 1917 or only to 1929 (or even, in its finished form, to the 1940s), one crucial distinguishing feature is its remarkable and unbroken longevity. A second key characteristic is its unusually strong institutionalization. These features have powerful implications for any prospective transition to a regime based on alternative principles because this long-standing, well-institutionalized regime has also secured effective legitimation.

The basic principle underlying the PRI regime was that it derived its right to rule from military and political victories secured in the Mexican Revolution. Thus it enjoyed revolutionary legitimacy, it identified itself with the state and the nation, and it secured a mass popular base by administering social reforms traceable to the insurgency. Over time, other principles of legitimation (national conciliation, socioeconomic modernization) were increasingly invoked to reinforce or even displace these initial justifications, but without openly repudiating the regime's foundational principles. However, since the mid-1980s the switch from earlier to later forms of justification has proceeded at an accelerating pace, a disjuncture which for many is symbolized by the North American Free Trade Agreement (NAFTA). Following the liberal provisions of the 1917 Constitution, the regime has also always claimed an electoral mandate, but this has long been a contested arena. Until recently, it was a secondary consideration in the regime's armory of legitimizing self-justification.

Popular sovereignty in essence provides an entirely distinct set of principles for the foundation of a political regime. Elsewhere in Latin America, both Bolivia and Nicaragua have shifted from regimes founded on the principle of revolutionary legitimacy to regimes founded on the principle of popular sovereignty. Something similar has occurred in a number of ex-communist countries in eastern Europe, as well as in certain countries that experienced counterrevolutionary legitimation following the defeat of Communists in civil wars (Spain, Taiwan, South Korea). Thus comparative experience suggests that regimes with origins comparable to those of Mexico can shift to full electoral democracy, and that it is not unusual for the individuals and parties that held power during the period of revolutionary legitimation to do well under conditions of popular sovereignty.

Yet comparative experience also indicates that such shifts do require an explicit transition from one set of operating principles to another. Nowhere else has such a shift occurred without a considerable degree of rupture and, except at intervening periods, of uncertainty and renegotiation of foundational principles. Moreover, in every case the transition had a severe impact on major interests that had grown up under the shelter of the pre-democratic regime. It also produced considerable turbulence and realignment of personnel within the political elite.

The fundamental reason why regime transition and its attendant risks and uncertainties proved unavoidable in all these cases is that popular sovereignty had to be demonstrated and asserted as prevailing over earlier principles of legitimacy. The shift could not simply be taken on trust. Nor could the rival principles blur imperceptibly into one another, because in that event the electorate would continue to feel itself disempowered. Only by means of some high-profile act of political theater could the voters be convinced that henceforth (in contrast to earlier periods) their autonomous choices would be heeded. Only through some open process of political confrontation could the losing sectors associated with the pre-democratic regime be forced to relinquish their claims to authority.

In Mexican conditions, the shift from *dedazo* to *sufragio efectivo* would necessarily involve a major discontinuity in attitudes and practices both within the ruling elite and across the electorate. Judgments about just how destabilizing such a shift would be raise the question of institutionalization. From one perspective, a regime with a very strong institutional base should be better placed to manage the transition from one set of governing principles to another without undue dislocation. However, this assumes that the institutions in question provide a relatively neutral framework for containing political change. In the Mexican case, government institutions are not only long established and well developed, but they are also profoundly penetrated by the PRI system of authoritarian rule. Thus a major shift in the principles of legitimation could not simply be contained within the existing neutral institutions of the state. It would require a far-reaching restructuring of those institutions, perhaps to recuperate their original functions but certainly to recast durably their current modes of operation. One has only to reflect on the rubber stamp attributes of the Congress, or the submissiveness of the judiciary, to appreciate the scale of the transformations that would be required.

This long-standing, strong interpenetration between the informal rules underpinning the dominant party system and the formal processes that characterize constitutionally established institutions has ambivalent implications for Mexico's transition prospects. On the one hand, it means that in effect there are no institutions with a credible claim to full impartiality (that is, autonomous enough to stand above the influence of the incumbent president). Neither the Federal Electoral Commission nor the Supreme Court, the minister of defense, or the papal nuncio is an untainted authority capable of serving as a trustworthy "bridge" between the present authoritarian regime and any prospective successor.[1] Yet at the same time, it also means that the Mexican variant of authoritarian rule involves far more acceptance of the discipline arising from formal rules and procedures than is typically the case in less institutionalized (or more arbitrary) authoritarian regimes.

In important respects Mexican politics functions under an effective rule of law, rather than just the rule of men. This may seem a surprising claim, given the enormous discretionary power concentrated in the person of the president, the prevalence of impunity for those in the inner circle, and the notorious deficiencies of the Mexican legal system. But in contrast to many other authoritarian regimes, there are some essential ways in which even the most powerful political figures in Mexico are subject to the discipline of impersonal rules they can do nothing to alter. Neither the president of the republic, state governors, nor members of Congress can stand for reelection at the end of their terms. In fact, ex-presidents (who are typically only about fifty years old when they leave office) are expected to spend the rest of their lives in near political purdah. After commanding so much authority for six years, they know they will not be entrusted with anything but the most token public responsibilities thereafter. In a similar way on the electoral front, the *calendario fijo* of polling dates for public offices can hardly be varied; it is almost as rhythmic and predictable as the U.S. electoral calendar, whereas politicians in most other Latin American countries (both authoritarian and democratic) constantly tamper with their political timetables in pursuit of short-term partisan advantage.

The strong institutionalization of the Mexican political system provides a significant potential barrier against some of the manifestations of "plebiscitarian" instability encountered elsewhere. In principle, it might also provide a promising basis for the subsequent strengthening of more democratic institutionality, as such impersonal rules are extended to control a wider range of undemocratic practices. Since Mexico has long secured its regime against the insubordination of the military, against *autogolpes* like that engineered by Fujimori in Peru, and against prorogation, why not simply establish equally effective politico-institutional

---

[1] Nor, of course, is there a hereditary ruling family, an eminent cohort of political exiles awaiting the opportunity to return, or an external association of democratic nations such as the European Community available to broker and facilitate a transition in Mexico, as they were in some other countries. Indeed, the Mexican system has been systematically organized to resist any such intrusion from outside on the grounds that it might be appropriated by counterrevolutionary forces. However, under NAFTA the U.S. Congress has acquired some incipient institutional leverage in this area.

barriers against electoral fraud, judicial subservience, and congressional abdication of responsibility?

The answer to these questions is that, although the Mexican regime *is* strongly institutional and sui generis, it is also—in its own distinctive way—deeply authoritarian. The strong, impersonal rules that have been enforced were those that best served to stabilize and perpetuate the regime. In particular, they were rules that guaranteed elite circulation on a regular and frequent basis, thus providing strong incentives for the pursuit of political ambitions *within* the established structure. The necessary counterpart of this was, however, the maintenance of equally strong disincentives to challenges from without. This is the authoritarian counterpart to institutionalization, and the two elements are united in a single system. Any attempt to operate as though only the incentives to cooperation were required, and to disengage from the harsher aspects of the disincentives to defiance, would tend to destabilize the authoritarian system. Specifically, if electoral transparency and judicial and congressional authority were to be made as impersonal and reliable as the "no reelection" rule, the entire system would be transformed. It would then need to function according to a different logic (which *might* be that of liberal democracy, although one should not assume that this is the only possible alternative available to Mexico).

For over sixty years, virtually every state governor and federal senator, and almost every directly elected member of the federal Chamber of Deputies, has been a candidate of the ruling party. This required a phenomenal suspension of disbelief. Not only was the ruling party able to produce the most popular candidate for the presidency, but it also invariably fielded the most popular local executives in all thirty-one states of the republic. Not only did it achieve permanent congressional majorities (Japan's Liberal Democratic Party could also claim that), but it reduced all rival parties to such a marginal role that they could only scrape into Congress thanks to special concessionary provisions designed to bolster the legal opposition. Not only that, voters—contrary to all the fundamental tenets of electoral sociology in competitive party systems—never tired of turning out to underline their positive endorsement of the victors. It seemed that there were few "free riders" in the Mexican electorate, and few government supporters ever felt so complacent (or disillusioned) that they were inclined to stay home when another triumph seemed assured.

Not only that, but the very party that operated this system with such confidence and reliability could also present itself to the media (both domestic and foreign) as the one reliable vehicle of domestic improvement and reform. Whenever an electoral vice was uncovered, the PRI regime was always there to correct it and to reassure everyone that no such blemish on Mexico's civic reputation would be allowed to recur. It was never those currently in power who were responsible for electoral fraud or imposition; it was always their predecessors, or their subordinates, or forces of reaction they were in the process of overcoming. Even when it proved possible to organize honest elections in the Philippines, Bolivia, Namibia, and Outer Siberia, the rulers of Mexico somehow found themselves unable to overcome mysterious obstacles to electoral transparency at the local level. However, on grounds of national sovereignty, it was always unthinkable to countenance the assistance of foreign electoral observers.

Even the most fearless of Mexican intellectuals, authors of bestsellers denouncing corrupt union bosses or praising "democracy without adjectives," could be relied on to rally the regime against the dangers of uncontrolled electoral sovereignty. Small wonder that Mario Vargas Llosa found the Mexico of Carlos Salinas de Gortari *"una dictadura perfecta"* ("a perfect dictatorship").

In a sense, then, the Mexican regime's authority has rested on a spectacular suspension of disbelief about its electoral legitimacy. But this is a very sweeping statement that requires careful restatement. The public record clearly shows that government officials, radio and television broadcasters, many journalists, and not a few academics and intellectuals did indeed continuously transmit or endorse the impressive list of impossibilities just mentioned. What they believed privately is more difficult to determine, but it generally seems that the closer they came to the centers of power, the more they tried to convince themselves that the Mexican regime was electorally legitimate. Far more important, but also more difficult to assess, is what the population at large believed about the electoral rituals in which it was immersed at regular intervals. All judgments about this are bound to be highly speculative, not least because Mexican society is so heterogeneous and compartmentalized.

Nevertheless, analysts of the Mexican variant of democratization must consider this issue because, unless we take a position on how much of the official discourse was internalized, we cannot assess either the stability of the authoritarian regime or the scope for democratic transition. If more than half of those taking the trouble to participate in a Mexican presidential election vote against the ruling party, and their suffrages are then denied effective expression (which seems to have occurred at least in 1940 and 1988), what they thought about official discourse designed to cover up the fraud against them becomes a crucial issue. In reality, even those who voted *for* the regime would be likely to distinguish between an authentic and an artificial electoral majority. So the question becomes what the bulk of the electorate can have believed when the outcome of the voting process was falsified. Many voters must have observed from their personal experience that the opposition had strong support and that the governing party was in trouble.

Yet to generalize from personal observation to the balance of popularity in the country as a whole requires a series of intermediate steps that are difficult for ordinary voters to take. The logical consequence of concluding that the entire structure of administration and public authority has conspired to falsify the national vote is that one must resist—but it is understandable that most individual Mexican citizens would recoil from the implications of this conclusion. Many of those willing to vote for an opposition candidate did so with anxiety, and they lacked the commitment to follow through. To assist them, the authoritarian regime and its acolytes would provide a barrage of threats, rationalizations, and distractions. Only the most politicized of individuals would hold to their certainty of national fraud. Most would experience some doubt, some uncertainty, some reluctance to conclude that all their most established sources of authority were engaged in coordinated deception. In short, so long as the authoritarian regime could effectively co-opt or neutralize most opinion formers, the mass of the electorate could be demoralized or reduced to apathetic resignation.

Thus one major reason why the "no reelection" rule is so rigidly upheld is that the counterpart of "effective suffrage" is known to be a pretence. Once genuine confidence in the honesty of the electoral process is established, it will become possible (and, indeed, logical) to relax the proscription against reelection. If voters were sovereign they could choose a legislature that might serve as a real counterweight to decisions taken by the executive. But to play this role, the Congress would need a cadre of experienced parliamentarians, which is impossible under the present no immediate reelection rule because every *diputado* leaves office after three years. Moreover, with no possibility of running for reelection, incumbent representatives have no incentive to cultivate the support of their constituents. This is just one example of the way in which the different components of Mexico's system of institutional authoritarian rule are interconnected. Other examples include the roles played by state governors and the judicial system. Major changes in any one of these areas would trigger a chain reaction affecting the logic (and stability) of the system as a whole. In short, this is not a system that can make the transition from authoritarian to democratic rule "by stealth" or without visible discontinuities.

It is important to underline the distinctively institutionalized character of Mexico's authoritarian regime, even though stressing this dimension may seem to ignore the widespread objection that many transition studies overemphasize elite interaction and formal rule making in the process of regime change, while neglecting "bottom-up," civil society-based, and participatory aspects of democratization. In general, however, this is a false distinction. Alan Knight, for example, has persuasively argued that evaluations of Mexican strategies of elite interaction must give appropriate emphasis to the broader processes of social incorporation that arose from the Mexican Revolution and that stabilized the postrevolutionary order.[2]

In any event, a characterization of the sui generis nature of Mexico's authoritarian regime would be radically incomplete if it is confined to formal institutional structures and processes of political recruitment. The regime has had not one but multiple bases of mass support, built through land reform and labor incorporation, the promotion of a national business class sheltered from foreign competition, and a multifaceted, long-sustained cultural policy. If it is an institutionalized, civilian authoritarian regime, it is equally an inclusionary authoritarian regime. In all these respects it has differed fundamentally from other authoritarian regimes in Latin America.

Just as it is possible to unite institutional and authoritarian characteristics in a tight, self-replicating political system, so it is equally possible to unite inclusionary strategies of mobilization with authoritarian structures of decision making. This was the central concern of a large body of literature on Mexican-style corporatism and Mexican strategies of "co-optation and control." It was also a weak point of the system that was exposed in Mexico City at the time of the 1985 earthquakes. Its continuing centrality to the authoritarian nature of state-society interactions in Mexico is evident in the record and practices of the National Solidarity Program (PRONASOL) under Salinas.

The whole system of inclusionary authoritarianism is so tightly integrated that the reform or democratization of a single component would produce a chain reaction of readjustments. Imagine, for example, that Mexico's "official" labor bosses lost their near monopoly over worker representation and were therefore compelled to compete for the support of union members in the same way that private firms are now supposed to compete for customers. In such circumstances, the entire system of popular representation (in Congress, in political parties, in the media, and even in the countryside) would come into question. The result *might* be a stable, inclusionary democratic regime. But this is not the assured outcome, and at best it could only be attained after considerable intervening turbulence.

THE MEXICAN VARIANT OF "REGIME TRANSITION"

The extreme longevity of the Mexican regime and its inclusionary character mean that in this case it is not possible to "restore" an earlier model of democratic politics. There can be no redemocratization as occurred in the Southern Cone, southern European, and Baltic transitions.

---

[2]See Knight 1992. Similarly, I argued some time ago that Mexican elite unity was cemented by fear of uncontrollable pressures from below; see Whitehead 1980.

The highly institutionalized system of political recruitment and rapid elite circulation mean that any potential division in the ruling coalition between "hard-liners" and "soft-liners" will be more effectively contained in Mexico than elsewhere. The Mexican formula of government routinely balances these two components, hardly ever allowing one element or the other complete control over policy. The pattern of rapid elite circulation means that when a particular policy stance has outlived its usefulness and become an object of criticism and division, a new cohort of politicians can be drafted to vary the mix and recreate a belief in the possibilities of reform from within. Incoming "reformists" clearly understand that their mandate is to revive the system, not to dismantle it.

This same pattern creates distinctive and characteristic problems for the democratic opposition. Although opposing a repressive military regime may be dangerous, it has some advantages. The democratic opposition is likely to feel that it has an unquestioned moral advantage that compensates for its physical vulnerability. Indeed, democrats' unity and morale are often reinforced by the way their opponents respond under challenge. An important factor fueling democratic resistance is the conviction that, however strong the authoritarian regime looks, it is really quite brittle and has little capacity to reform itself.

The Mexican regime, however, concedes none of these advantages to its opponents. It strenuously avoids presenting an unambiguously repressive facade to the population at large (however intimidating it may choose to be in relation to targeted opposition groups). It is a past master in the use of "safety valves" and diversionary tactics to blunt the force of an opposition attack. Divide-and-rule has been perfected as the technique for system maintenance, as the whole history of legal opposition parties in Mexico demonstrates and as the current division between the National Action Party (PAN) and the Party of the Democratic Revolution (PRD) confirms. Given this heritage and the regime's unparalleled record in co-opting key elements of the opposition (especially popular organizations with relatively urgent social demands that only the state can satisfy), it is very difficult for opposition leaders to maintain the confidence of their followers that, with one or two more pushes, the whole edifice will tumble down. The fixed electoral calendar offers very occasional opportunities (such as 1994) when such a claim may gain in credibility. But the rest of the time it defends the regime from destabilization, and it stifles opposition energies.

At this point one might conclude that no transition from authoritarian rule can be achieved in contemporary Mexico. Is it possible that the system is so well defended, so capable of reproducing or reequilibrating itself, that one should only consider its capacity for gradual, internally driven reform, but nothing else? In fact, since the mid-1980s there have been growing indications that the regime is encountering ever greater difficulties in preserving itself. It is not necessary to argue this point at length because the events triggered by the Chiapas insurrection on New Year's Day 1994 have rendered commonplace what was previously a controversial view. The tragic assassination of Luis Donaldo Colosio, the PRI's presidential candidate, on March 23, 1994, only underscored the vulnerability of the old system of electoral imposition. Thus the remainder of this chapter will take it as given that some kind of transition is now possible in Mexico. However, we must proceed with care in specifying the prospective dynamics of a political transition given the sui generis features of the Mexican system outlined above.

THE DISTINCTIVE WEAKNESSES OF THE MEXICAN REGIME

The literature on regime transition is often criticized for its lack of well-specified "theory." Its account of regime breakdown tends to operate within an ad hoc range of contributory factors; it does not specify how these factors might combine or interact; and it avoids predictive statements. Those analysts offering such criticisms are, of course, welcome to develop more rigorous alternatives and to use them predictively. But at least when considering the prospects for transition in contemporary Mexico, it is difficult at present to see how one can assay anything more than a highly tentative, underdetermined sketch of a possible regime breakdown. It is easier to draw attention to certain long-term processes that erode the foundations of authoritarian rule in Mexico than to specify the relatively precise mechanisms by which an eventual breakdown and transition might be triggered.

Given its distinctive structure, the Mexican regime has long been secure against certain sources of breakdown that have been important elsewhere. It was never going to embark on a military adventure that could expose it to external defeat. Nor was it ever going to become so identified with the personality of an individual ruler that its fate would become entangled with his biography. (The closest such identification was with Díaz Ordaz in 1968, which was quickly unscrambled.) The Mexican regime would never allow itself to become a showcase for U.S.-sponsored democratization from without. Nor would it ever abdicate domestic political space to a coalition of democratic challengers, whatever their composition. Such terrain would always be fiercely contested by the ruling party and/or its affiliated mass organizations.

While all these points of potential vulnerability have been well covered, the Mexican regime also has its characteristic weaknesses. Presidential succession is the principal point of weakness because every six years all the authority and leadership capacity concentrated in the presidency must be transmitted—by an undisguisedly authoritarian mechanism—from one incumbent to the next. At the same time, the losing aspirants must be induced to acquiesce. This has been a source of danger to the system from its inception, as political crises in 1935, 1940, and 1952 all testify. However, the problem became much more acute in the 1980s and early 1990s, as first Cuauhtémoc Cárdenas in 1987–1988 and then Manuel Camacho Solís in 1993–1994 questioned the long-established tradition of presidential *dedazo* (by which the incumbent imposes his successor as the PRI's presidential candidate).

In major respects the Mexican regime's fixed political calendar averts or diffuses potential instabilities by channeling opposition into very narrow and predictable paths. Yet it also means that at the appointed moment in the political cycle there is no escape from an effectively constituted challenge. At that point, the regime can no longer rely on all the defensive mechanisms that otherwise protect it so well. During presidential elections the opposition's appointed role is, of course, to put up enough of a fight to make the ruling party's victory look credible, but without ever shattering the illusion of its invulnerability. In the 1970s, when the opposition was too weak to perform this function adequately, PRI-sponsored reforms strengthened opposition parties. Beginning in the mid-1980s, first the PAN and then the PRD began to do too well, so the regime adopted corrective measures to check the opposition's new electoral strength. But government efforts to fine-tune the opposition is another point of regime weakness, not a source of strength. Such efforts expose the regime's authoritarian core to public view, and they are inherently both unstable and potentially counterproductive.

There is a third vulnerability linked to these two characteristic weaknesses in the PRI system: the isolating and self-deceiving consequences of the regime's constant monologue with itself. Very occasionally, as at the moment of the Mexico City earthquakes or in the weeks following the Chiapas rebellion, it is clear to all that the official discourse is entirely hollow. The government quickly covers this gap with a new legitimizing discourse, but the discovery that every so often the regime's monopoly of self-approval cannot be sustained has a powerful impact on underlying popular attitudes.

Different analysts may have different views concerning the nature of the longer-term social processes that have eroded the bases of the Mexican system. One might emphasize the long-term impacts of the 1968 crisis and the emergence of a much better educated, more self-confident urban elite with illusions about the scope for easy democratic transformation through the empowerment of the next generation.[3] Similarly, one might view the statism and economic interventionism of the 1970s either as failed attempts to breathe new life into the old authoritarian model, or as necessary learning experiences through which a more autonomous and assertive market society gained

---

[3]It would be useful in this regard to compare systematically the political consequences of Tlatelolco and Tiananmen.

strength. In any event, the Mexican state's capacity for relegitimation through economic growth was drastically curtailed by the debt crisis, and in due course an alternative, market-oriented formula of economic management has come to the fore. Whatever the justification for this change, it has in important ways weakened the social basis of authoritarian rule. While the private sector and foreign investors have been empowered, it has undermined the regime's old corporatist structures by depriving them of essential resources. The shift also produced new difficulties for the established system of elite circulation because maintaining market confidence requires continuity in both policies and personnel.

In addition to these material impediments to the continued good functioning of the authoritarian system, the shift to a neoliberal philosophy has also created a series of ideological problems for the regime. The governing coalition is no longer composed of groups more or less united in agreement that their right to rule emanates from an agreed revolutionary nationalist project. Indeed, their commitment to necessary ruling myths has faded as the basis of their governing project has shifted. But that leaves members of the ruling elite more isolated than before from prevailing attitudes in society at large (their embarrassment in early 1994 over the persisting attraction of the Zapatista myth was palpable). It also complicates the task of reconciling conflicting tendencies within the ruling group. Self-interest was never sufficient on its own to produce the high degree of discipline and elite unity that served the Mexican regime so well; it was always reinforced by broader claims to legitimacy that are now open to dispute.

There are also conflicting interpretations concerning the political impact of NAFTA and North American integration more generally. Is NAFTA a stimulus to the eventual democratization of Mexico, or is it perhaps another economic project designed as a substitute for overdue political reform? Part of this debate concerns the nature of the democratic outcome eventually envisaged, and part of it is linked to arguments about the sequencing of economic and political reforms (that is, whether it is best to undertake economic reform first, in the belief that the conditions for democratic progress will be strengthened thereafter). Those debates should be left open at this point, partly because the evidence is still coming in and partly because, at the theoretical level, the alternatives are posed in too mechanistic (or too ideological) a manner. North American integration undoubtedly is part of a series of international developments (the discrediting of Marxism, the worldwide resurgence of liberal democracies, and so forth) that all operate on the Mexican regime from without, reinforcing pressures on it either to democratize or at least to reequilibrate itself. But these international pressures and influences are somewhat ambivalent in sign, and it will take additional time for their consequences to be fully felt.

In concluding this brief discussion of the potential sources of breakdown in the Mexican authoritarian regime, it is more useful to revert to domestic considerations. Most of the discussion so far has concerned processes that potentially erode the long-term stability of the regime. However, this does not rule out the possibility that the governing elite—having time to see what is beginning, and retaining the initiative—might produce responses that rescue the situation some way or another. Yet when the underlying supports of a regime are being eroded, it becomes vulnerable to certain "trigger" events or processes that may accelerate its recomposition. Transition theorists have, on the whole, been reluctant to acknowledge the major role that political violence can play in this trigger stage. Events in Chiapas and Tijuana confirm that this is not an element that can be safely omitted from the analysis.

HOW SHARP A DISCONTINUITY

It is not possible to predict with any degree of confidence either how long it will take for Mexico to undergo a transition from authoritarian rule, or what type of transition to expect. Nevertheless, we can draw some conclusions from the foregoing analysis about the main issues in contention and the major ways in which a Mexican transition would be likely to differ from most others.

Let us begin by reviewing the arguments for and against the idea that the Mexican regime might achieve a gradual, incremental transition—democratization "by stealth," without the high levels of uncertainty and instability that have characterized processes of democratic "rupture." The key argument is that in such circumstances the transition would take place over an extended period of time, with unresolved conflicts over when it started, when it ended, and what it amounted to. Although this is admittedly a possible scenario, and although a wide range of dominant interests both within and outside Mexico will be very anxious to ensure that any change of regime is muffled and slowed down, one must be skeptical about whether such delaying tactics can permanently avert the momentum building up for a more discontinuous regime change. The final (more speculative) section of this essay therefore rehearses the arguments for expecting that in due course Mexico will undergo a relatively sharp period of "rupture," a destabilizing interregnum as the political system shifts from one underlying basis to another.

One major argument for "stealth" is that the ruling coalition in Mexico shows few signs of the catastrophic loss of cohesion that has characterized most democratic ruptures. External defeat à la Greece, Portugal, or Argentina can be disregarded, not least because this is not a military regime. The collapse of self-confidence that shattered the

Communist Party's will to rule in East Central Europe has yet to affect the PRI. Moreover, even many opponents of the regime fear its abrupt disappearance. The PAN's strategy is to seek a gradual regime transformation without risking a rupture of its institutional framework. Even the PRD at times indicates that, although its demands for political change are nonnegotiable, it may recognize the need to offer relatively strong reassurances of continuity in such areas as business confidence, institutional stability, and foreign policy.

One frequently observed method for limiting uncertainty during a regime transition is to establish a democratizing "pact," in which the contending forces agree on certain basic rules of the game. However, the preceding discussion of the sui generis nature of the Mexican regime highlights various impediments to such a solution in this case. The extreme longevity of the regime means that there are no bridging institutions capable of guaranteeing such a pact. All existing institutions are deeply implicated with the authoritarian system of rule. Moreover, opposition forces are divided, and they lack the autonomy and moral authority needed to force a trustworthy and neutral agreement out of a slippery and devious government.

The Mexican regime has a long record of negotiating pacts—with opposition parties, with labor and business, and with a wide range of other social actors. But these have all been semi-imposed or officially orchestrated pacts whereby those in power have exercised dominance, offering relatively secondary concessions to weaker partners without ever putting the basic authority of the regime at risk. This pattern of semi-corporatist pact making is so well established and so successful that it has created a set of attitudes and expectations that might well block participants from engaging in genuine, pluralist-style pact making. Mutual trust and recognition would be absent. It is probably much harder to dismantle and reshape strong institutions (including electoral commissions, courts, and so forth) that are geared to partisanship than simply to create new, neutral institutions in areas where previous regimes of exception operated arbitrarily.

The case for transition by stealth is that the Mexican authoritarian regime does not recognize itself to have been defeated, nor does it acknowledge the existence of a democratic alternative with either the strength or the capacity to displace it.[4] It does, however, recognize the need for electoral credibility, and it may be willing to make a continuing sequence of concessions to carefully chosen critics in order to generate confidence that eventually political reforms will transform the system. Thus *some* opposition governors may be allowed to take office, minority representation in the federal Chamber of Deputies can be extended to

---

[4]If democratic transition is explained as a second-best outcome that is selected when contending hegemonic forces find they have reached a deadlock, then the Mexican regime is not yet resigned to a democratic stalemate.

the federal Senate, domestic and foreign observers may be allowed to monitor elections, and so forth. Concessions of this kind have been dribbling out since the mid-1970s, and the "transition by stealth" perspective would forecast a further continuation of this process over a protracted period until (it is assumed) the authoritarian legacies of the past have all been gradually smoothed or negotiated away. Throughout any such process we must expect government authorities to announce that the Mexican transition has already effectively been accomplished, while the political opposition struggles to keep alive the pressure for further reforms. According to one influential school of interpretation, the Mexican regime can more or less retain the initiative by launching one controlled "liberalization" measure after another, without ever being forced to the fatal further step presupposed by the democratization literature—that is, the point at which the consequences of liberalization escape official control and "institutionalized uncertainty" comes to prevail regarding the election of the next government.

Opinions will differ about the viability of this option over the long run, but it must be conceded that this scenario emerges quite plausibly from the way the Mexican regime is characterized in the analysis presented here. If this is the way Mexican politics evolves, the "transition" would be very extended over time. (Once past the hurdle of the 1994 presidential elections, there would be no further major opportunity for democratic rupture before the year 2000.) Government authorities, still in control, could use all their formidable resources of persuasion to convince doubters that in essence the transition had already been completed, and that therefore no further risks of uncertainty should be countenanced. The democratic opposition would have to engage in a protracted, frustrating "war of positions," attempting to demonstrate that, on the contrary, the old authoritarian order had merely found new ways to disguise itself and perpetuate its ascendancy. Thus the political debate would continue to revolve around these unresolved questions: What in Mexican conditions does a regime transition really amount to? When does it start and end? How can we tell?

THE REVOLUTIONARY PRINCIPLE OF *SUFRAGIO EFECTIVO*

There is at least one alternative scenario. This would involve the Mexican regime shifting to a clear alternative basis of operation, in which effective suffrage is accepted as the *ultima ratio* of popular sovereignty. This is not the same as suggesting that Cuauhtémoc Cárdenas must be elected president of Mexico. In some respects it could involve much less than that, and in other respects much more. Whoever the president might be, his (or her) conduct would be shaped by a radically new set of incentives and constraints. For example, under multiparty electoral democracy it is possible that, after the first three years of a six-year presidential term, legislative elections could produce an opposition majority in the Congress. The manner in which the executive would have to coordinate with party supporters (and opponents) in Congress would, accordingly, be transformed. Similarly, state governors would be chosen solely according to the preferences of their respective electorates, rather than vetted for approval by the *gran elector* in the presidential palace. Again, such a change would transform state-federal political relationships. In a competitive democratic system, elected politicians would become much more answerable to their respective constituents, and they would have far less incentive to show deference to centrally constituted authority. Far more coordination would arise through negotiations between autonomous actors, and there would be far less political imposition from above. Public opinion would be less readily corralled into endorsing whatever the current batch of *científicos* or state intellectuals judged to be in its best interest.

These are all commonplaces of democratic politics that would have to acquire a Mexican content and reality for there to be a full, conventional "democratic transition" south of the Rio Grande. Such changes would have to occur whether or not the candidates of the currently ruling party were chosen by the electorate. In a full transition to democracy, opposition parties would acknowledge the PRI contender's right to govern (assuming that was who the electorate had chosen), and the PRI would equally acknowledge victory by the opposition (where the electorate made such a choice).

The scenario sketched out here is certainly banal, but anyone familiar with the texture of Mexican political life will also recognize that it sounds extremely far-fetched. It could hardly come about through "stealth" because it would require a drastic revision of deeply entrenched practices and operating assumptions—not only on the part of ruling political forces, but also on the part of opposition strategists and in the perceptions and expectations of the public at large.

The essence of any such democratic rupture is that the still dominant principle of revolutionary (or at least inherited) legitimacy would be replaced by the quite distinct principle of popular electoral sovereignty. In order to confirm the switch to this alternative principle of government (and to overcome the cynicism about the electoral process that is rooted in over seventy years of systematic manipulation), the electorate will have to be seen to prevail in the course of some visible conflict over its authority. This requirement for visible rupture contrasts with the regime's hopes of achieving a democracy by stealth, a process in which the illusion is maintained that these alternative principles of representation need never clash. To maintain this illusion, the regime seeks to deny all possibility of *future* incompatibility between the two principles, while evading or denying the fact that they were ever at variance in the past. Thus the regime requires both historical oblivion and a suspension of disbelief about the future. Unless these requirements can be sustained, democratization inevitably involves a "rupture" of consciousness.

It is hard to envisage how a visible display of the sanctity of the electorate's will can be mounted in Mexico without courting a considerable degree of at least short-term political instability. Mexicans of many different backgrounds have all been strongly socialized into authoritarian convictions about the nature of the electoral process in their country. If confronted by a visible demonstration that henceforth popular sovereignty and "institutionalized uncertainty" about election outcomes were to prevail, even the most farsighted and democratically inclined political actors would take some time to absorb the full implications. A series of experiments and episodes of political theater would, therefore, be needed in order to create the new mental pictures required in order for actors to operate in a democratic manner. This might also require rather complex and extensive processes of historical revisionism, as suppressed questions (for example, about the 1940 election, the 1952 election, and so on) came up for reconsideration. It is hard to judge how much of the consensual past would have to be unraveled and reknitted in order to accommodate the supremacy of popular sovereignty as a governing principle.

In addition to this somewhat subjective ("psychological" or "political culture") impediment to accepting a democratic rupture in Mexico, there are also other, more tangible obstacles. The system of presidential dominance means that in essence there is only one (indivisible) electoral prize up for democratic contention, with almost nothing in the way of real compensation prizes for the losers. Perhaps the starkness of this reality could eventually be softened by some system of increased power sharing between the federal executive and a revitalized Congress, but that remains at best a distant and elusive prospect. In the meantime, democrats will have to contend with the Mexican presidency as it has long operated, with its huge and embedded subculture of patronage, placemanship, political imposition, and impunity. A democratic rupture would necessarily subject this inherited structure to far-reaching criticism and calls for its restructuring. The political interests at stake would be unlikely to accept without resistance such a frontal assault on their privileges, so here, too, a degree of political theater would be required to convince doubters that past undemocratic practices really were open to correction.

Moreover, it is not just the privileges of the state bureaucracy or the political class narrowly conceived that would have to be reconsidered. The regime has lasted so long, and functioned so effectively, that a whole battery of *fuerzas vivas* has grown up in the economy and in society, enjoying the privileges nurtured under the shelter of authoritarian rule. The private television monopoly, the Labor Congress, the newly minted generation of Mexican billionaires—all these, and many others, will view the possibility of a shift to *sufragio efectivo* as involving a degree of risk and uncertainty that could place their vital interests in jeopardy. Thus strong resistance to a democratic rupture can be anticipated not just as a product of psychological inertia or the legacy of an authoritarian political culture, but also as a rational strategy of self-protection by dominant interests.

The point here is not that the possibility of a clear democratic rupture in Mexico can be discarded for the foreseeable future; rather, the point is that if it occurs, it will involve a strongly destabilizing interregnum. Reviewing the prospects as they are outlined here, one might well conclude that prudent democrats should draw back from the very evident risks involved and settle instead for whatever incremental reform might be attainable through "stealth." This is the logic of both the PAN and the soft-liners within the regime who always draw back from outright defection when breakdown seems to loom.

However, underlying processes of regime delegitimation make it progressively harder for the ruling elite to preserve the existing order without assuming the risks of a shift to the principle of *sufragio efectivo*. The various expedients that have been tried in recent years to fend off the necessity for a full transition to democracy (including NAFTA, ever more frantic cycles of political reform legislation, and improvised devices to split or buy off disaffected elements) all seem to be less and less efficacious. The hope that "just once more" the system can buy itself another six years of continuity disguised as liberalization could well prove a triumph of authoritarian self-deception in the face of an awakening of civil society that can no longer be postponed. The idea that liberalization need never escape the control of its authors is contrary to all we have learned from studying transition processes in country after country outside Mexico. Consequently, despite all the risks it could involve, one must conclude that a realistic observer of Mexico should pay due attention to the possibility of an imminent democratic rupture.

UNSETTLING PROSPECTS

Certainly in 1994 Mexico is scheduled to hold not a *normal* election, but a watershed event. For good or ill, Mexican voters will assume that there is really only one political prize for their adjudication, and that is the presidency. Because Salinas cannot run again but Cárdenas can, it is impossible to guess how the bandwagon might run. (It is also difficult to judge how the ruling party might respond if it seems as though the electorate might be allowed to vote the matter out.) This "all or nothing" quality of the 1994 election contest makes it difficult to see how Mexico could achieve conventional electoral democracy "by stealth." The election of another PRI president would be unlikely to inaugurate an era of genuine pluralism, and the election of an opposition candidate would be extremely traumatic and destabilizing—whether or not the eventual result was a political democracy.

Neither the historical record nor the all-or-nothing character of the 1994 presidential contest offers much encouragement for the view that this time the popular mandate will be sacrosanct, whatever the people's verdict may be. However, the stigma of the 1988 fiasco, the political requirements for smooth North American economic integration, and the *prise de conscience* resulting from the Zapatista challenge in Chiapas all make it more urgent than before for government authorities to persuade a skeptical domestic and foreign public that what is expected to be Mexico's last big popular consultation of the twentieth century is clean and aboveboard. It will probably no longer be possible for the government to reject the presence of official foreign observers (from Latin American countries rather than the United States) on supposedly nationalist grounds. Jorge Carpizo, appointed minister of the interior in January 1994, has more of a reputation for integrity than his predecessor, and he is less certainly committed to the preservation of the dominant party system regardless of cost. Yet in the last analysis, it is President Salinas who has final responsibility for whatever system of election management prevails.

Salinas's indecision on this issue is evident in the succession of "political reform" laws he enacted (three in six years) and from the contrasting positions of his closest advisers. No sooner had the Congress rubber-stamped his second package of electoral reforms in September 1993 than the president began to fear it would be insufficient to legitimize the 1994 elections. His November 1993 State of the Nation address more or less conceded as much, and so opened the way to the negotiation of a further "Pact for Peace, Democracy, and Justice" (signed by eight of Mexico's nine registered political parties, including all three leading presidential contenders) on January 27, 1994. Its provisions included an external audit of voter registration lists, the creation of a special prosecutor for electoral crimes, a better balance of party representation on the Federal Electoral Commission, a lower ceiling on party campaign financing, and fairer political party access to the mass media. Provided the Institutional Revolutionary Party can win without artificial reinforcements, the president's gamble could pay off. But no one can be sure how either voters or candidates will react if it appears that on this occasion, for the first time since the 1910–1920 revolution, the regime has really agreed to the "institutionalized uncertainty" of an open, competitive election.

There is a fashion among U.S. political scientists to argue that the best way for Latin Americans to consolidate their democracies is to establish parliamentary systems of government. These analysts view presidentialism as a form of elected authoritarianism that fails to generate accountability, political openness, or stable coexistence among political contenders. Although there are good reasons to dissent from strong versions of this thesis, it must be said that in the Mexican case there is a compelling argument to answer. How can Mexico achieve multiparty democracy, or even the checks and balances required for accountable constitutional rule, so long as the rewards of office are so exclusively concentrated in one executive post? A party that has ruled on its own authority continuously for over sixty years just *might* be persuaded to go into opposition for a period, provided that restraints on the incoming government were extremely robust and that the prospects for an eventual return to power with a democratic electoral mandate looked sufficiently appealing.[5] But neither the PRI nor the PAN is inclined to countenance six years of a Cárdenas presidency in which all the current privileges of office would be monopolized by such a powerful rival.

Thus, if real democracy *were* to come to Mexico by stealth (not just the facade of democracy dreamed of by the perpetuators of PRI supremacy), it would have to be accompanied by a far-reaching political reform and a redistribution of governmental functions. Such a deal could possibly be in the interests of opposition parties, and under some circumstances it might even find supporters among the more farsighted and liberal elements in the Salinas entourage—especially if they thought they were in danger of losing control over the governing apparatus. But it would certainly encounter strong resistance from the PRI as a whole and from large segments of the state bureaucracy, and it is likely to be viewed with alarm by the business community and its foreign backers.

Indeed, these sectors would probably only contemplate a dilution of executive power if they were convinced that Cárdenas, or someone like him, was sure to win the presidency. Most important of all, the Mexican electorate would need to be persuaded that in order to achieve popular sovereignty, and to have its choices respected in the normal democratic way, the attributes of the presidency must be redefined and shared. Only thus can electoral choices be offered that are noncatastrophic in their consequences (and therefore genuine in their content). Only thus can real electoral democracy be constructed in Mexico. Such changes are too dramatic to be achieved by stealth!

REFERENCES

Knight, Alan. 1992. "Mexico's Elite Settlement: Conjuncture and Consequences." In *Elites and Democratic Consolidation in Latin America and Southern Europe*, edited by John Higley and Richard Gunther. New York: Cambridge University Press.

Whitehead, Laurence. 1980. "Por qué México es casi ingobernable," *Revista Mexicana de Sociología* 42:2 (January–March).

---

[5]This consideration may have tipped the balance for the Sandinistas in Nicaragua following their electoral defeat in February 1990. The example of communist parties in East European countries is not relevant here because they came to power through imposition.

Acronyms

ABM	Asociación de Banqueros de México/Mexican Bankers' Association
AC	Alianza Cívica/Civic Alliance
ACNR	Asociación Cívica Nacional Revolucionaria/Revolutionary National Civic Association
AMCB	Asociación Mexicana de Casas de Bolsa/Mexican Association of Brokerage Houses
AMERI	Asociación Metropolitana de Ejecutivos de Relaciones Industriales/Metropolitan Association of Industrial Relations Executives
AMIS	Asociación Mexicana de Instituciones de Seguros/Mexican Association of Insurance Institutions
ANOCP	Asamblea Nacional Obrero Campesino Popular/National Worker-Peasant-Popular Assembly
CAMCO	Cámara Americana de Comercio/American Chamber of Commerce
CANACINTRA	Cámara Nacional de la Industria de Transformación/National Chamber of Manufacturers
CANACO-MEX	Cámara Nacional de Comercio de la Ciudad de México/National Chamber of Commerce of Mexico City
CAP	Congreso Agrario Permanente/Permanent Agrarian Congress
CCE	Consejo Coordinador Empresarial/Private-Sector Coordinating Council
CD	Corriente Democrática/Democratic Current

CDP	Comité de Defensa Popular/Popular Defense Committee
CFE	Comisión Federal Electoral/Federal Electoral Commission
CIOAC	Central Independiente de Obreros Agrícolas y Campesinos/Independent Confederation of Agricultural Workers and Peasants
CISLE	Centro de Investigación sobre la Libre Empresa/Free Enterprise Research Center
CMHN	Consejo Mexicano de Hombres de Negocio/Mexican Council of Businessmen
CNA	Consejo Nacional Agropecuario/National Agricultural and Livestock Council
CNC	Confederación Nacional Campesina/National Peasants' Confederation
CNCPC	Confederación Nacional de Cámaras de Pequeño Comercio/National Confederation of Small Business Chambers
CNDEP	Comité Nacional para la Defensa de la Economía Popular/National Committee for the Defense of the Popular Economy
CNG	Confederación Nacional Ganadera/National Cattlemen's Confederation
CNOP	Confederación Nacional de Organizaciones Populares/National Confederation of Popular Organizations
CNPA	Coordinadora Nacional Plan de Ayala/National "Plan de Ayala" Coordinating Committee
CNPP	Confederación Nacional de la Pequeña Propiedad/ National Confederation of Smallholders
CNTE	Coordinadora Nacional de Trabajadores de la Educación/National Coordinating Committee of Education Workers
COA	Coordinadora de Organizaciones Agrarias/Coordinating Committee of Agrarian Organizations
COFIPE	Código Federal de Instituciones y Procedimientos Electorales/Federal Code of Electoral Institutions and Procedures

CONAMUP	Coordinadora Nacional del Movimiento Urbano Popular/National Coordinating Committee of the Urban Popular Movement
CONASUPO	Compañía Nacional de Subsistencias Populares/National Basic Foods Company
CONCAMIN	Confederación Nacional de Cámaras Industriales/National Confederation of Chambers of Industry
CONCANACO	Confederación de Cámaras Nacionales de Comercio/Confederation of National Chambers of Commerce
COPARMEX	Confederación Patronal de la República Mexicana/Mexican Employers' Confederation
CS	Corriente Socialista/Socialist Current
CTM	Confederación de Trabajadores de México/Confederation of Mexican Workers
CUD	Coordinadora Unica de Damnificados/Coordinating Committee for Earthquake Victims
EZLN	Ejército Zapatista de Liberación Nacional/Zapatista Army of National Liberation
FDN	Frente Democrático Nacional/National Democratic Front
FESEBES	Federación de Sindicatos de Bienes y Servicios/Federation of Goods and Services Unions
FNDSCAC	Frente Nacional en Defensa del Salario y Contra la Austeridad y la Carestía/National Front in Defense of Wages and against Austerity and the High Cost of Living
FONHAPO	Fondo Nacional de Habitaciones Populares/National Popular Housing Fund
FSTSE	Federación de Sindicatos de los Trabajadores al Servicio del Estado/Federation of Public Service Workers' Unions
GATT	General Agreement on Tariffs and Trade
GDP	Gross domestic product
IFE	Instituto Federal Electoral/Federal Electoral Institute
IMSS	Instituto Mexicano del Seguro Social/Mexican Social Security Institute
INEGI	Instituto Nacional de Estadística, Geografía e Informática/National Institute of Statistics, Geography, and Informatics

INI	Instituto Nacional Indigenista/National Indigenous Institute
LFA	Ley de Fomento Agropecuario/Agrarian Development Law
LOPPE	Ley Federal de Organizaciones Políticas y Procesos Electorales/Law on Political Organizations and Electoral Processes
NAFTA	North American Free Trade Agreement
OIR-LM	Organización de Izquierda Revolucionaria-Línea de Masas/Revolutionary Left Organization-Mass Line
PAN	Partido Acción Nacional/National Action Party
PARM	Partido Auténtico de la Revolución Mexicana/Authentic Party of the Mexican Revolution
PCM	Partido Comunista Mexicano/Mexican Communist Party
PDM	Partido Demócrata Mexicano/Mexican Democratic Party
PECE	Pacto para la Estabilidad y Crecimiento Económico/ Pact for Stability and Economic Growth (after October 1992, Pacto para la Estabilidad, Competitividad y Empleo/Pact for Stability, Competitiveness, and Employment)
PFCRN	Partido del Frente Cardenista de Reconstrucción Nacional/Party of the Cardenista Front for National Reconstruction
PMS	Partido Mexicano Socialista/Mexican Socialist Party
PMT	Partido Mexicano de los Trabajadores/Mexican Workers' Party
PNR	Partido Nacional Revolucionario/Revolutionary National Party
PPS	Partido Popular Socialista/Socialist Popular Party
PRD	Partido de la Revolución Democrática/Party of the Democratic Revolution
PRI	Partido Revolucionario Institucional/Institutional Revolutionary Party
PRM	Partido de la Revolución Mexicana/Party of the Mexican Revolution
PROCAMPO	Programa de Apoyos Directos al Campo/Direct-Support Program for the Farm Sector

PRONASOL	Programa Nacional de Solidaridad/National Solidarity Program
PRT	Partido Revolucionario de los Trabajadores/Revolutionary Workers' Party
PSE	Pacto de Solidaridad Económica/Economic Solidarity Pact
PST	Partido Socialista de los Trabajadores/Socialist Workers' Party
PSUM	Partido Socialista Unificado de México/Mexican Unified Socialist Party
PT	Partido del Trabajo/Labor Party
PVEM	Partido Verde Ecologista de México/Mexican Green Party
SAM	Sistema Alimentario Mexicano/Mexican Food System
SARH	Secretaría de Agricultura y Recursos Hidráulicos/Ministry of Agriculture and Water Resources
SIDERMEX	Siderúrgica Mexicana/Mexican Steel Company
SIPCSCRM	Sindicato de la Industria Petroquímica, Carboquímica, Similares y Conexos de la República Mexicana/Mexican Union of Petrochemical Industry Workers
STRM	Sindicato de Telefonistas de la República Mexicana/Mexican Telephone Workers' Union
TELMEX	Teléfonos de México/Mexican Telephone Company
UCP	Unión de Colonias Populares/Union of Popular Neighborhoods
UGOCP	Unión General Obrero Campesino Popular/General Worker-Peasant-Popular Union
UNE	Unión Nacional de Enlace/National Union for Citizen Linkage
UNORCA	Unión Nacional de Organizaciones Regionales Campesinas Autónomas/National Union of Autonomous Regional Peasant Organizations

Contributors

Jorge Alcocer V. is General Coordinator of the Centro de Estudios para un Proyecto Nacional, S.C., in Mexico City and an essayist for the weekly magazine *Proceso*. He received a master's degree in economics from the Universidad Nacional Autónoma de México. Between 1978 and 1990 he was a member of the Mexican Communist Party (PCM), the Mexican Unified Socialist Party (PSUM), the Mexican Socialist Party (PMS), and the Party of the Democratic Revolution (PRD).

Marcelo Cavarozzi is Professor and Chair of the doctoral program at the Facultad Latinoamericana de Ciencias Sociales in Mexico City (FLACSO-Sede México), as well as a research associate of the Centro de Estudios de Estado y Sociedad (CEDES) in Buenos Aires and Visiting Professor of Government at Georgetown University. His recent publications include: "Politics: A Key for the Long Term in South America," in *Democracy, Markets, and Structural Reform in Latin America*, edited by William Smith, Carlos Acuña, and Eduardo Gamarra (1994); (coauthor) "Economic and Political Transitions in Latin America: The Interplay between Democratization and Market Reforms," in *A Precarious Balance*, edited by Joan Nelson (1994); "Beyond Transitions to Democracy in Latin America," *Journal of Latin American Studies* (1992); (coeditor) *Muerte y resurrección: los partidos políticos en el autoritarismo y las transiciones en el Cono Sur* (1989).

Maria Lorena Cook is Assistant Professor at the New York State School of Industrial and Labor Relations, Cornell University. She received her Ph.D. in political science from the University of California, Berkeley. Professor Cook was a Visiting Research Fellow at the Center for U.S.-Mexican Studies in 1988–1989 and a Chancellor's Postdoctoral Fellow in political science at the University of California, San Diego in 1990–1991. She has written extensively on Mexican labor politics, social movements, and regional integration. Professor Cook is coeditor of *Regional Integra-*

tion and Industrial Relations in North America (1994) and author of a recently completed book manuscript titled "Organizing Dissent: Unions, the State, and the Democratic Teachers' Movement in Mexico."

Wayne A. Cornelius is the Gildred Professor of U.S.-Mexican Relations and the founding director of the Center for U.S.-Mexican Studies at the University of California, San Diego, where he is also Professor of Political Science. Professor Cornelius has conducted field research in Mexico since 1962, and he has published extensively on Mexican politics and rural-to-urban migration in Mexico. He is author of *Politics and the Migrant Poor in Mexico City* (1975), and he is coauthor of *The Mexican Political System in Transition* (1991). He is also editor or coeditor of *Mexico's Alternative Political Futures* (1989), *Mexican Migration to the United States: Process, Consequences, and Policy Options* (1990), and *Transforming State-Society Relations in Mexico: The National Solidarity Strategy* (1994). Professor Cornelius is a former president of the Latin American Studies Association.

Enrique de la Garza Toledo is Director of the Labor Sociology Program at the Universidad Autónoma Metropolitana-Iztapalapa in Mexico City. He has written extensively on labor politics, workplace relations, and industrial restructuring in Mexico. Professor de la Garza is the author of *Ascenso y crisis del estado social-autoritario* (1988); *Crisis y sujetos sociales en México* (1992); *Reestructuración productiva y respuesta sindical en México* (1993, winner of the Premio Jesús Silva Herzog); and *Democratización y política económica alternativa* (1994). He is also coauthor of *Crisis y reestructuración productiva en México* (1988). In 1982 he received Mexico's prestigious Premio Nacional de Economía. Dr. de la Garza is also Director of the *Revista Latinoamericana de Estudios del Trabajo*.

Denise Dresser is Professor of Political Science at the Instituto Tecnológico Autónomo de México. She received her Ph.D. in political science from Princeton University. Professor Dresser is the author of *Neopopulist Solutions to Neoliberal Problems: Mexico's National Solidarity Program* (1991), as well as numerous articles on contemporary Mexican politics. She has been a Visiting Research Fellow at the Center for U.S.-Mexican Studies at the University of California, San Diego and a postdoctoral fellow at the Center for International Studies at the University of Southern California. Professor Dresser has also been a consultant to the United Nations Development Programme and the United Nations Economic Commission for Latin America and the Caribbean, and she serves on the advisory board of *Este País*. She has recently completed a book manuscript on the politics of economic adjustment in Mexico.

Jonathan Fox is Associate Professor of Political Science at the Massachusetts Institute of Technology. He is author of *The Politics of Food in Mexico: State Power and Social Mobilization* (1993), editor of *The Challenge of*

Rural Democratisation: Perspectives from Latin America and the Philippines (1990), and coeditor of *Transforming State-Society Relations in Mexico: The National Solidarity Strategy* (1994). He has also published numerous journal articles on social movements, rural development policy, and local politics and democratization in Mexico and other Latin American countries. Professor Fox is currently completing a study of community participation in rural Mexico, and he is at work on a project examining the impact of transnational social movement/nongovernmental organization coalitions on World Bank programs.

Paul Lawrence Haber is Assistant Professor of Political Science at the University of Montana. He received his Ph.D. in political science from Columbia University. Professor Haber is the author of "Cárdenas, Salinas, and the Urban Popular Movement," in *Mexico: Dilemmas of Transition*, edited by Neil Harvey (1993); "Political Change in Durango: The Role of National Solidarity," in *Transforming State-Society Relations in Mexico: The National Solidarity Strategy*, edited by Wayne A. Cornelius, Ann L. Craig, and Jonathan Fox (1994); and "Salinastroika, Neocardenismo, and the Urban Poor," in *Mexico and the United States: Economic Growth and Security in a Changing World Order*, edited by Bruce M. Bagley et al. (1994). His current research interests include U.S.-Mexican relations, urban popular movements and the politics of poverty in Mexico, social movement theory, and third party politics in the United States.

Joseph L. Klesner is Associate Professor of Political Science and Director of the International Studies Program at Kenyon College in Gambier, Ohio. He received his Ph.D. in political science from the Massachusetts Institute of Technology. Professor Klesner has written extensively on electoral politics in Mexico, and he has received Fulbright grants for research in Mexico and South America. He is completing a book manuscript titled "Political Liberalization in Mexico: Electoral Reform and Opposition Party Development."

Julio Labastida Martín del Campo is General Secretary of the Facultad Latinoamericana de Ciencias Sociales and Vice President of the International Council of Philosophy and Human Sciences at the United Nations Educational, Scientific, and Cultural Organization (UNESCO). He holds a postgraduate degree in sociology from the Sorbonne. Professor Labastida has held a number of distinguished positions at Mexican universities and international educational organizations, including Coordinator of the Humanities at the Universidad Nacional Autónoma de México (UNAM, 1983–1985, 1990–1993), Associate Director of the Social Sciences and Humanities at UNESCO (1985–1989), President of the Asociación Latinoamericana de Sociología (1979–1983), and Director of the Instituto de Investigaciones Sociales at UNAM (1976–1983). He is the author of many articles on Mexican politics and state-society relations and on democratization, public education, and political economy issues in Latin America.

Soledad Loaeza is Professor of Political Science at the Centro de Estudios Internacionales at El Colegio de México. She received her Ph.D. in political science from the Institut des Etudes Politiques in Paris. Professor Loaeza has written extensively on Mexican politics, with a particular emphasis on political parties, elections, the conservative opposition, church-state relations, and the political role of the middle class. Her publications include *Clases medias y política en México: la querella escolar, 1959–1963* (1988), *El llamado de las urnas* (1989), and (coeditor) *La vida política mexicana en la crisis* (1987). Professor Loaeza is a member of the editorial board for the journal *Nexos* and a columnist for the daily newspaper *Reforma*. She is currently at work on a book-length study of the National Action Party (PAN).

Kevin J. Middlebrook is Director of Research at the Center for U.S.-Mexican Studies, University of California, San Diego. His research on state-labor relations and political change in Mexico has been published in major political science and interdisciplinary journals, as well as in numerous edited books. He is the author of *The Paradox of Revolution: Labor, the State, and Authoritarianism in Mexico* (forthcoming 1995). Dr. Middlebrook is also editor of *Unions, Workers, and the State in Mexico* (1991), and he is coeditor of *The United States and Latin America in the 1980s: Contending Perspectives on a Decade of Crisis* (1986). He is currently at work on a book-length comparative study of political cleavages, conservative political parties, and democratization in Latin America.

Juan Molinar Horcasitas is Professor of Political Science at the Centro de Estudios Sociológicos at El Colegio de México. He is author of *El tiempo de la legitimidad: elecciones, autoritarismo y democracia en México* (1991) and numerous journal articles on elections, political parties, and democratization in Mexico. His recent publications include (coauthor) "Electoral Determinants and Consequences of National Solidarity," in *Transforming State-Society Relations in Mexico: The National Solidarity Strategy*, edited by Wayne A. Cornelius, Ann L. Craig, and Jonathan Fox (1994). Professor Molinar's research interests include the impact of institutions on political change in hegemonic party systems.

Jaime Ros is Associate Professor of Economics at the University of Notre Dame and Faculty Fellow at the Kellogg Institute for International Studies, University of Notre Dame. He holds a master's degree in economics from the Universidad Nacional Autónoma de México and a Diploma in Economics from the University of Cambridge. Professor Ros's research interests focus on development, trade, and the macroeconomic problems of developing countries. He has published widely in economics journals, and he is coauthor of *La organización industrial en*

México and editor of *MODEM: un modelo macroeconómico para México*. He has been a Visiting Scholar at the Department of Applied Economics at the University of Cambridge, St. Antony's College (University of Oxford), and the World Institute for Development Economics Research (Helsinki). Professor Ros has also done research for the United Nations Economic Commission for Latin America and the Caribbean, the South Commission (Geneva), the International Labour Organisation, and the United Nations University. He has been director and editor of *Economía Mexicana*, associate editor of *El Trimestre Económico*, and an editorial board member for several other economics journals. He is a member of the Mexican Academy of Political Economy.

Víctor L. Urquidi is Professor Emeritus at El Colegio de México. He is a graduate of the School of Economics and Political Science at the University of London. Professor Urquidi is the author of many books and articles on economic and social development in Latin America, including *Free Trade and Economic Integration in Latin America* (1962), *The Challenge of Development in Latin America* (1964), (coeditor) *América Latina en la economía internacional* (1976), (coeditor) *Población y desarrollo en América Latina* (1979), and (editor) *Science and Technology in Development Planning* (1979). He has conducted economic research for the Banco de México, other public-sector agencies in Mexico, and the United Nations Economic Commission for Latin America. From 1966 to 1985 Dr. Urquidi was President of El Colegio de México. He has attended numerous international conferences, including the United Nations conference on the human environment in Stockholm in 1972. Between 1980 and 1983 he was President of the International Economics Association.

Francisco Valdés Ugalde is Faculty Researcher at the Instituto de Investigaciones Sociales at the Universidad Nacional Autónoma de México, where he is also Coordinator of the Political Sociology Program. Dr. Valdés is the author of several articles on the private sector and state reform in Mexico. These include (coauthor) "Businessmen and Politics in Mexico, 1982–1986," in *Government and Private Sector in Contemporary Mexico*, edited by Sylvia Maxfield and Ricardo Anzaldúa Montoya (1987) and "Concepto y estrategia de la reforma del Estado" in a special issue of the *Revista Mexicana de Sociología* (1993) on "Las instituciones de la política en México," which Dr. Valdés edited. He is currently organizing a research project on the institutional rationality of recent economic, political, and social reforms in Mexico.

Laurence Whitehead is an Official Fellow in Politics at Nuffield College, Oxford, and coeditor of the *Journal of Latin American Studies*. Jointly with Guillermo O'Donnell and Philippe C. Schmitter, he edited *Transitions from Authoritarian Rule* (1986). Professor Whitehead has written a number of articles on Mexican politics, and in 1985–1986 he served as Acting

Director of the Center for U.S.-Mexican Studies at the University of California, San Diego. His major research interest is in the comparative politics of democratization, and he is currently coordinating a collaborative research project (sponsored by the Joint Committee of Latin American Studies of the Social Science Research Council) on the interactions between economic and political liberalization.